The
SEDUCTION
of
HILLARY RODHAM

DAVID BROCK

**FREE PRESS
PAPERBACKS**

THE FREE PRESS
New York   London   Toronto   Sydney   Singapore

To William and Ian

FREE PRESS PAPERBACKS
A Division of Simon & Schuster Inc.
1230 Avenue of the Americas
New York, NY 10020

Copyright © 1996 by David Brock
All rights reserved,
including the right of reproduction
in whole or in part in any form.

First Free Press Paperbacks Edition 1997

FREE PRESS PAPERBACKS and colophon are trademarks
of Simon & Schuster Inc.

Photo Research by Natalie Goldstein

Manufactured in the United States of America

10   9   8   7   6   5   4   3   2   1

Library of Congress Cataloging-in-Publication Data

Brock, David
      The seduction of Hillary Rodham / David Brock.
          p.   cm.
      Includes bibliographical references and index.
      ISBN 0-684-83451-0   ISBN 0-684-83770-6 (Pbk)
      1. Clinton, Hillary Rodham.   2. Presidents' spouses—United
States—Biography.   3. Clinton, Bill, 1946–   . I. Title.
E887.C55B76   1996
973.929′092—dc20
      [B]   96-36030
                                                          CIP

CONTENTS

PREFACE

In mid-January 1996, Hillary Rodham Clinton published her first book, *It Takes a Village*, in which she outlines her prescription for "how we can make our society into the kind of village that enables children to grow into able, caring, resilient adults." The book became a Number One bestseller, and seemed to herald her triumphant return to the public stage after the humiliating defeat of her health care reform initiative and the subsequent Republican takeover of congress in the 1994 mid-term elections.

Within days of her book's publication, however, Hillary was hauled before a federal grand jury in Washington where she was grilled by the Whitewater independent counsel on her legal work for a corrupt Arkansas savings and loan association. Thus was her long anticipated moment of triumph, like so many others in her life, irretrievably spoiled.

This rapid-fire sequence of positive and negative events was a dramatic reminder of the contradictions in Hillary's own life as well as the growing cognitive dissonance about the first lady in the minds of the public and the press. Hillary's shining reputation for personal integrity and selfless dedication to her causes, reflecting her life's work on behalf of children and families, didn't square with the witchlike image of Hillary clad in a long black cape leaving a Washington courthouse under cover of nightfall, at the center of a criminal investigation.

Yet that contrast also embodies what is so fascinating and, to many, so infuriating about Hillary Rodham Clinton. Long before she faced legal troubles, Hillary had set off a mad scramble to divine her true identity. Who is the real Hillary Clinton? Is she the articulate lawyer and political activist who first emerged in the "two-for-one" Clinton candidacy of the 1992 presidential campaign? The cookie-baking Super Mom who soon replaced her? The Lady Macbeth of Little Rock? A latter-day Joan of Arc, bringing health coverage to all? A foul-mouthed lamp-throwing harridan? Saint Hillary, exponent of "the politics of meaning"? The Ivan Boesky of cattle-futures trading? Or, finally, a virtual recluse in the White House, comically "channeling" the spirit of Eleanor Roosevelt?

More than almost any figure in recent history, Hillary has elicited strongly polarized reactions from Americans across the social spectrum—impassioned paeans from her supporters and vitriolic attacks from her foes. Newsweek posed the question on its cover in February 1996: "Saint or Sinner?" Oddly, there seems nothing in between.

Recently, however, a cultural consensus has produced a composite portrait—not to say caricature—that is uniformly negative. Toward the end of the first Clinton term, even Hillary's allies had turned on her, and she has been left with few, if any, defenders. Two New York Times columnists on opposite ends of the ideological spectrum, William Safire and Maureen Dowd, seem to agree on one thing: Hillary's deeply flawed character. Safire famously called her a "congenital liar," and Dowd described her as "Mommie Dearest." Others have compared Hillary to Leona Helmsley, Ma Barker, Eva Braun, and Minister Louis Farrakhan. Newt Gingrich's mother revealed on national television that her son had referred to Hillary as a "bitch." U.S. News quoted a Clinton aide referring to Hillary as a "dragon lady" and "the house SOB." And Sally Quinn, the reigning doyenne of Georgetown society, was quoted in the New Yorker as saying, "There's just something about her that pisses people off."

The prospect of Hillary going to jail has become a stock punchline of talk-show host David Letterman's Top Ten list. Shock-jock Don Imus airs a derisive adaptation of "The Lady Is a Tramp," a double parody in which a Rush Limbaugh character sings: "She goes to State dinners with her lesbian friends/makes big investments with high dividends/Forgets to pay taxes but then makes amends/That's why the first lady is a tramp."

Tapping into an almost archetypal demonization of female power, three recently published bestselling books on the Clintons by authors of widely divergent backgrounds and political views have reached roughly the same judgment on Hillary, providing a stereotype to appall all constituencies. From the right, FBI agent Gary Aldrich, author of Unlimited Access, writes of "Queen Hillary," a deranged, power-mad emasculator.

From the left, historian Roger Morris portrays a deeply cynical, ruthless shrew at the service of Arkansas' corporate oligarchy in *Partners in Power.* Perhaps most surprising is *Blood Sport,* by Pulitzer-Prize winner (and professed Clinton supporter) James B. Stewart, which depicts Hillary as a selfish, money-grubbing cheat. Stewart is a trusted financial journalist and his book, which appeared to give more credence to the word of two now-convicted Whitewater felons than to Hillary, was perhaps the final sign of a decisive turn against her on the part of mainstream liberals.

More ink has been spilled writing about Hillary Rodham Clinton—from her policy pronouncements to her latest hairstyle—than on the activities of any prior presidential spouse. Yet the beliefs, motives, and character of this most divisive and unpopular first lady remain shrouded in confusion, secrecy, and outright misrepresentation. Because she touches so many nerves—as a professional spouse and working mother with an office in the West Wing of the White House; as the bearer of the historical consciousness of the post-Watergate generation; and as the informal head of the liberal wing of the Democratic party—few seem able to view Hillary from a sober analytical stance. Indeed, she now seems to exist almost completely in the realm of cultural mythology as a figure upon whom allies and enemies alike can project their hopes and their fears, their expectations and their disappointments.

In some respects, Hillary has been treated no differently from previous first ladies who became lightning rods for criticism when they appeared to exert too much influence. Yet while she has frequently been compared to former first ladies from Eleanor Roosevelt to Nancy Reagan, Hillary Rodham Clinton, as the first presidential spouse in history to assume a formal government post, exercises her considerable influence not just to help her husband but also to advance the many social and political causes in which she deeply believes and which she has spent a lifetime pursuing. Little is known about these activities, and her precise ideological cast and mode of operation therefore remains obscure. But it is important to understand the breadth of Hillary's significance: despite the impression that she is a spent force in the Clinton administration, as she made plain in her speech to the 1996 Democratic convention, she will undoubtedly return in a second term—to be reckoned with.

Hillary's power derives from her partnership in a unique political marriage, the like of which has never been seen before. This surprisingly durable pairing has carried the Clintons through more than twenty years of tough political tests and trying personal challenges in Arkansas, all the way to the White House. To be sure, the political landscape is littered with power couples—Republican presidential nominee Bob Dole and his wife Elizabeth are perhaps the most prominent current example. But the Clintons are different: in the vigor of Hillary's independent activist commitments; in the unapologetic exertion of leadership in her own right; and most of all in the extraordinary extent to which Bill relies on her to balance his shortcomings and to guide his political career.

Through this marriage Hillary has seen not only the heights of political triumph but also the depths of personal defeat. It was Bill Clinton who brought her into contact with the gritty money-politics system of Arkansas, entangling her in a web of unsavory associations from which she attempted to distance herself—first in Little Rock, then in Washington—but which followed her to the White House and ultimately wreaked havoc on her life and reputation. Because she has been forced to make hard compromises to protect both her marriage and Bill's political future, Hillary's struggle to preserve her dignity and integrity has become the central drama of her life.

While Hillary's credibility is in tatters and her reputation and political effectiveness are all but ruined, Bill, strangely, has gone virtually unscathed by the scandalous revelations and is generally favored to win re-election. According to poll data, as Hillary's negatives soared to new heights in 1996, with almost half the public saying it believes she is a liar, Bill's positives have risen in almost direct proportion. While Bob Dole and former president George Bush attacked Hillary from the podium at the 1996 Republican convention, a *New York Times* story on the eve of the Democratic convention suggested that White House officials have cynically sought to spin the attacks on Hillary to Bill's political advantage.

Hillary's story is that of an intelligent, talented, ambitious, and very determined woman who nevertheless succumbed to powerfully seductive forces—philosophical, political, and personal. These include the easy moral certitudes of the Christian left; the fashionable instrumentalist legal doctrines disseminated at Yale Law School; the situational ethics and power-based political philosophies of a certain strain of 1960s radicalism; the dangerously tempting belief, instilled by influential mentors, in the beneficent potential of government as a force for social progress; the frictionless ease of manipulating the levers of a power in a corrupt one-party state; and the idealized vision of a new kind of political partnership with her husband that proved impossible to realize. Above all, she has repeatedly succumbed to the seductive attraction of Bill Clinton himself, perhaps the most articulate, beguiling, and empathetic figure ever to emerge on the American political scene. Given Hillary's apparent strength and confidence—and her position as a virtual paradigm of the modern feminist movement—the question is, what made her vulnerable to these seductive forces in the first place?

One bitter cold evening in February 1996, in the midst of a snowstorm, I stood in line for several hours at a bookstore in McLean, Virginia where the first lady was signing copies of *It Takes a Village*. When I finally reached the head of the line, I introduced myself and asked her when I could have an interview for this biography. "Probably never," she answered with a wry edge.

Considering my prior reporting on the Clintons, of course, I could hardly blame the First Lady for turning me down. Given my record, I had fully expected to write the book not as a Clinton insider but as a knowledgeable outsider, and Hillary did not disappoint me. My first professional encounter with the Clintons had come during Christmas week in 1993, when I published in the *American Spectator* the infamous "Troopergate" story, which exposed Bill Clinton's improper use of his Arkansas security detail in his pursuit of sexual partners. The story provoked enormous controversy, setting off a debate about both the relevance of the charges and the credibility of the sources.

As I ventured into the netherworld of petty corruption and intrigue in Arkansas, I had also considered the troopers' credibility and the newsworthiness of their allegations. Indeed, though I had spoken with them several times over the course of three months, corroborating their stories and testing their consistency, I was still on the fence about publication. Then I learned that Clinton had allegedly called one of the troopers and offered him a federal job, apparently in an effort to contain the story. At that point, I decided the story needed to be told. (The *Los Angeles Times* reached the same judgment, publishing a similar story two days after mine appeared.)

One can only imagine what Hillary Rodham Clinton must have

thought of me. Not only had I published the outré trooper story but I had also been the first journalist, in the spring of 1994, to place her at the center of the travel-office firings and of the subsequent White House effort to whitewash her role. The piece was even accompanied by a facetious caricature of Hillary as a witch! Hillary's role in that affair eventually placed her squarely in the sights of the Whitewater independent counsel and congressional investigators.

No doubt Hillary would have been surprised to know that, by the time I sought her out in that Virginia bookstore in early 1996, I had come to believe that the Republican effort to make her the arch villain of the Whitewater saga was wrong. While one cannot easily dismiss the allegations swirling around her, efforts to disentangle them and learn the truth should never have become a witch hunt. My suspicions about Republican motives were heightened when one of the Senate Whitewater committee's GOP lawyers told me he intended to "kick Hillary's ass." Later, I was told that Republican Senator Lauch Faircloth of North Carolina had turned to an aide and said of Hillary's confidantes Susan Thomases and Maggie Williams: "You want me to call them lying bitches, I'll call them lying bitches." There was something wrong here, and it wasn't with Hillary.

The danger of such *ad hominem* attacks is that they pave the way for a succession of fallacious charges, from secret trysts at the Marriott Hotel to conspiracy theories promoted by Reverend Jerry Falwell and others about the "murder" of White House deputy counsel Vincent Foster. (The Arkansas troopers, too, had gotten caught up in the hate-mongering, opening up their credibility to question once again this spring with their improbable claim, aired by the Senate Whitewater Committee, that Foster died not in Fort Marcy Park, where his body was found, but in the parking lot of the White House.)

At this late date, the constellation of scandals surrounding the Clintons has been so thoroughly investigated, producing such a voluminous public record, that what is needed now is neither name-calling nor "gotcha" journalism but an effort to understand the partnership at its crux. Therefore, this is not a book about another loan application allegedly filled out fraudulently or supposed secret seances in the White House residence, but rather an effort to interpret the dynamics of this unlikely pair and to reach a considered judgment especially about Hillary's character and actions.

Hillary has gotten a bad rap from all sides. Ultimately, one must take a much more mixed and nuanced view of her than the opinion polls suggest. As Hillary herself remarked in response to the *Newsweek* cover story "Saint or Sinner?": "[I'm] not as good as some people say . . . [or] as bad as other people claim . . ." Hillary should be approached as neither an icon nor a demon but as a real person who has had a remarkable life and, it could be argued, has been more important to America than her husband.

1

Hillary for President

In Hillary Rodham, the qualities of a firstborn high-achieving straight-A student, world-class organizer, determined operator, and gifted proselytizer were evident from the beginning. As a student at Maine South High School in Park Ridge, Illinois, she took part in the speech and debate club, the student newspaper, the National Honor Society, and the annual music variety show. She was voted vice president of the class council, most likely to succeed, and chairman of the prom committee. Hillary had "a sense of her own importance. She was very ambitious," recalled Arthur Curtis, a former classmate at Hillary's high school in the Chicago suburbs. "I was an overachiever and it was impossible to upstage her."[1]

Curtis did upstage Hillary in one respect—Hillary graduated in the top 5 percent of her class, but he made valedictorian, not she. "She didn't take very many honors classes back then. So she really couldn't be first or second in the class, because you got more points for [honors classes]," he said. Hillary excelled in both academics and extracurricular activities, but in a clinch she put organizing, and later activism, first. Like many a budding politician, Hillary was a classic student leader type, "outgoing, civic-minded, and ambitious," as her classmate Penny Pullen, a future Republican state legislator in Illinois, recalled.

Though in awe of her talents and determination, some of Hillary's fellow students were put off by her palpable ambition. Penny Pullen pointed to Hillary's campaign to win the school's first Daughters of the American Revolution Good Citizens Award for exhibiting the qualities of "dependability, service, leadership and patriotism." Hillary sought it because "she said it would look good on her résumé. Nobody went after it. I mean, that was not appropriate to go after it," Pullen said. "You got the award because of your citizenship activities, because of your concern for your country, not so you could get the award."

Hillary often cited her father Hugh Rodham as the source of her drive to succeed. Hugh was the child of hardworking immigrants from England; his father had gone to work at age eleven in the lace mills of Scranton, Pennsylvania; his strong-willed mother was known as Hannah Jones Rodham. Hugh grew up in Scranton, played football for Penn State, served in the navy in World War II, and took a job selling curtains in Chicago. He met Dorothy, his future wife, when she applied for a secretarial job at the same company.

Dorothy Howell had had a troubled upbringing. Born in Chicago to a fifteen-year-old Scottish-French mother and a seventeen-year-old Welsh father, her parents soon divorced and Dorothy and her younger sister were sent by train to live with their grandparents in Pasadena, California. According to an account given by Hillary, the grandparents raised the girls in hardscrabble environs, mistreating them with harsh and arbitrary discipline. At age fourteen, Dorothy—who had learned to rely on the kindness of teachers for milk money—moved out of her grandparents' house and went to work in another woman's home, taking care of her children.[2]

Hillary Diane was born in Chicago, and the family soon moved to Park Ridge, a new bedroom community outside Chicago where many G.I.s settled after the war to raise their families. In the provincial, overwhelmingly Republican, township, Hugh started his own small business (printing and making curtains). Dorothy, Hillary, and her two younger brothers, Hugh and Tony, helped out in the store, which also had one part-time employee. By local standards, the family was prosperous: Hugh drove a Cadillac and the family vacationed at a Pennsylvania cottage. But Hugh was not a professional, as were many of his neighbors. And he was famously frugal, possessed of a Depression-era mentality. Even in the dead of winter, Hillary recounted, he shut off the heat in the house every night, causing the children to wake up freezing in the morning.

Hillary's direct and sometimes chilly demeanor—her high school classmates named her "Sister Frigidaire," predicting a future as a nun—may have reflected that of her father. "I think he ran a rather austere home. I don't think he was a bully in any respect, but I think I would describe him as fairly authoritarian," said the Reverend Don Jones, a close friend of Hillary's and youth minister at the Methodist church she attended in high school. Hugh, something of a social misfit in Park Ridge, struck the family friend and neighbor Rawls Williams as "kind of a recluse, kind of a moody guy. When [we] would go to watch baseball games, he sat by himself in a little lawn chair way down the third base line. Way out in left field by himself. And that was Mr. Rodham. He rarely socialized with anybody."

Hugh taught his daughter to read the stock tables in the newspaper and to play touch football with the boys. He was extremely demanding of all three children. As Hillary has told the story, no matter how hard she tried to please her father with good grades and extracurricular achievements, it never seemed to be enough. On being shown one of Hillary's straight-A report cards, Hugh once remarked, "You must have gone to an easy school." While a lesser spirit might have been crushed by this pattern of rejection, Hugh's attitude seemed only to spur Hillary on.

She also appeared to adopt her father's rather sharp-edged attitude toward others. "It's funny, since most Anglo-Saxon Protestants were taught this great emphasis on politeness and never hurting anybody's feelings, telling little white lies to make people not feel bad," Arthur Curtis said. "Hillary didn't have that. She didn't have that compulsion always to be polite." This characteristic bluntness of speech and occasional abrasiveness would elicit strong and contrasting reactions to Hillary throughout her public life.

Though not mentioned by Hillary as often, her mother, Dorothy, seems to have been at least as important an influence as Hugh. "Mr. Rodham had his own business, would go to work early, worked hard, and Mrs. Rodham was more of a homebody," said Rawls Williams. "And I always felt that Mrs. Rodham was the driving force behind Hillary—Hillary says her dad was . . . in the stuff I have read. But I always felt that Mrs. Rodham was the driving force there."

Hillary pointed to her mother, not to Hugh, when recounting the most important lesson of her childhood. As the new kid on the block when her family moved to Park Ridge from Chicago, the four-year-old Hillary was teased and roughed up by an older girl, and returned home in tears every afternoon for weeks. One day, Dorothy met Hillary at the door, told her that there was no room in the house for cowards, and sent her back out to defend herself and confront the girl.

Not only the firstborn but also the only girl, Hillary seemed to garner the lion's share of Dorothy's attention. In prodding her daughter to distinguish herself in life, Dorothy may have been venting some of her own frustrations. Growing up in the Depression in the 1930s, she had barely been able to finish high school, much less consider a career. After her three children were grown, however, she managed to go back to school and earn a degree, the first mother in the neighborhood to do so.

Dorothy pushed Hillary "to be her own person and to do things and accomplish things," said one of Hillary's childhood friends, Judy Osgood. Dorothy herself told the *Washington Post* in 1992: "I was determined that no daughter of mine was going to have to go through the agony of being afraid to say what she had on her mind." Dorothy had hoped that Hillary would be the first woman on the Supreme Court, "but Sandra Day O'Connor beat her to it," she told the *Post* interviewer.

Dorothy Rodham was grooming a future chief justice, not a prom queen; she inspired her daughter to succeed as a competent professional rather than get by on her looks. Dorothy taught Hillary not to fuss over her appearance or worry about how to catch a man. "[Some] male classmates say Hillary's plain looks discouraged romance," a 1994 profile of Hillary's high school graduating class in *Chicago* magazine reported. "She had an average figure and thick legs; she wore unflattering purple glasses and unfashionable sack dresses. 'Hillary wasn't considered a great catch,' a friend admits. . . . 'Guys didn't think she was attractive.' " Leon Osgood, who taught the Sunday School class Hillary attended at First United Methodist Church in Park Ridge, remembered Hillary as "too intelligent for the average boy." When it came time for the senior prom, Dorothy's neglect and Hugh's parsimony converged to put a damper on the occasion. "In a letter [Hillary] wrote to me while she was in high school," the Reverend Jones recalled, "she talked to me about going to the prom and getting her father to buy her a new dress, but she wrote, 'All of my girlfriends will look very well dressed next to me because it is so plain.' And then she wrote that she was surprised she got the dress at all and it probably was because her parents were going to be chaperones."

Though Hugh's staunch Republican politics—he had worked on behalf of Senator Robert Taft over Dwight D. Eisenhower in 1952—are well known, Dorothy's political views have been obscured in published accounts of Hillary's upbringing. Dorothy was probably a closet Democrat and would-be feminist in the right-wing Republican stronghold of Park Ridge, a center of John Birch Society activism. In an interview with the *Toronto Star* shortly after President Clinton's inauguration, Dorothy seemed to take issue with the popular portrait of Hillary as a "Goldwater girl," a born-and-bred conservative Republican, saying, "I don't think Hillary was ever really conservative except in a fiscal sense." According to *Chicago* magazine, Rick Ricketts, a close childhood friend of Hillary's, asked Dorothy at the presidential inaugural, "How in the world did Hillary get to be a Democrat?" Dorothy replied, "I was a Democrat." In a 1996 interview, even Hillary acknowledged a "sneaking suspicion" that Dorothy, though she had never said so, went against her husband and the local tide and voted for John F. Kennedy over Richard Nixon in 1960. Hillary has also credited Dorothy as the source of her concern about social injustice.

Hillary led her high school's political club, heading the membership committee of Students for Goldwater. Given the views of the community and particularly of her father, Hillary's early support of Goldwater was expected. As Susan Pearson, a classmate of Hillary's, put it, in Park Ridge, "everybody thought Republican." For decades, the congressional district in which Hillary was raised has uniformly elected hard-core conservatives.

The most telling part of her experience as a Goldwater girl came just before the school voted, when Hillary participated in a mock debate. As a Goldwater supporter, she was selected to represent President Lyndon Johnson's position. One of the few vocal supporters of LBJ at the school was asked to speak on behalf of Goldwater. Hillary later pointed to this as a crucial event in which she "had to study all these positions and I had to learn things from a different point of view, not just what my father had said or what my community believed . . . that opened me up to looking at things from a different point of view."

More than anyone, the Reverend Don Jones encouraged Hillary to question the traditions and prejudices of her Park Ridge upbringing. The antithesis of Hugh Rodham and perhaps a surrogate father figure for Hillary, Jones was an intellectual, a committed liberal, and a free spirit. Hillary's experience with him marked the beginning of a shift from what her classmate John Peavoy called the "pretend politics" of high school to the social gospel activism that would come into view years later in her "politics of meaning" speeches as first lady. Jones was the first of several influential mentors who led Hillary down a path of political activism, and her relationship with him may be considered the first stage in her political seduction. His injunction to regard the Bible as a basis for political action rooted her politics in the tradition of the Christian left. It also seems to have inspired in Hillary a crusading zeal that led her to view traditional authority as sometimes a hindrance to good works, as well as a tendency to cast opposition as arbitrary or even immoral. Jones gave her a "sense of social mission" and "a personal commitment to faith that I found very unifying," Hillary told the *Washington Post* in 1993. On the presidential campaign trail the year before, she had announced: "So, from an early age, my church said to me, 'Yes, your personal salvation is more important, but you have a scripturally ordained responsibility to reach out and help others as well.' "

The Rodham family traces its Methodism back to John Wesley's movement in England and Wales in the eighteenth century. "Do all the good you can, in all the ways you can, in all the places you can, at all the times you can, to all the people you can, as long as ever you can," Wesley said in one of his better-known exhortations. The historian Paul Johnson, discussing the wealthy English families within the Methodist movement, writes in his *History of Christianity,* "When it [the Methodist movement] split from the Anglicans they remained within the Establishment and sought to evangelize it from within. They were primarily concerned with moral reform, but also to some extent social reform, since they believed that poverty, squalor and cruelty were enemies of the Ten Commandments. They wanted to make society more moral by making it more livable; but of course they did not want to change its structure." Much of the Rodham family's work involved helping children and the economically deprived. "My father traced his family back to the early Methodist preaching . . . reaching out to the people in the coal mines and all that. So it was like my personal history," Hillary told the *Washington Post* in 1993.

Paul Johnson also described a more political branch of Methodism in England. "Methodist radicals were more likely to become political reformers—the beginning of a tradition which made Methodism and other nonconformist sects the allies of the liberals, then of the Labour Party." Significantly, the Methodist radicals were advised by Wesley not to employ radical means. Wesley "urged his converts to strive actively to prevent economic or political discontent, breaking out into violence, and to obey the law in all its rigour," Johnson points out.[3]

Brought to America by British missionaries, Methodism quickly attracted one of the largest followings among the mainline Protestant churches. In the nineteenth century, the Methodists opposed slavery and were strongly associated with the Christian temperance movement. "[The Methodists] were lobbying Lincoln and Stanton at Sunday evening prayer meetings, recruiting troops for the North. And they were fierce abolitionists," observed Reverend Jones, who is now a theology professor at Drew University in New Jersey and an expert on the political ideas and role of Methodism during the Civil War. "John Wesley stood with [William] Wilberforce, the great parliamentarian, and called for the abolition of slavery in the early eighteenth century," Jones said. "He thought politics could be used for the good of people and there was a Christian duty to engage in political activity to promote human flourishing. And Hillary clearly believes that. That's why I think she had a more positive view of government and what government can do—partly because of that heritage."

Jones, then around thirty, was often seen tooling around the staid Chicago suburb in a fire-engine-red '59 Chevrolet Impala convertible. He called his ministry "The University of Life" and he recommended Bob Dylan's music and François Truffaut's films as an adjunct to spiritual insight. "I didn't want to seem like an ordinary minister because my own view was that religion becomes a barrier to God. . . . And so part of my ministerial style was to intentionally not talk like all the Methodist ministers that I ever had. That didn't mean that I was using profanity or anything like that. But I used kind of a secular approach that I thought was biblically based. Not many people when I grew up used T. S. Eliot or [E. E.] Cummings or Wallace Stevens in order to discern a spiritual dimension of culture."

Jones introduced the young Hillary to philosophers and theologians like Kierkegaard, Niebuhr, and Barth, with a special emphasis on Paul

Tillich, the theologian who led his followers to question the authority of religious creeds which, he said, could not be accepted at face value. Highlighting the tension between faith and intellect, Tillich sought to relate Christian belief to secular thought (comparing theology to philosophy, religion to culture, Lutheranism to socialism). Jones also drew parallels between Marxist-Leninist Utopianism and Christianity. "I did a little program on the parallels between the Communist faith and Christianity, pointing out that they have a doctrine of paradise, which was a precapitalist society, and then a doctrine of redemption, the bloody revolution, and then an eschatology of the Kingdom of God on earth, the classless society," Jones said.

Jones's ministry exemplified many of the changes and tensions within the mainline Protestant churches in the late 1950s and 1960s at the time of the civil rights movement, which many conservative Protestant clergymen resisted. Chicago was then one of the most racially segregated cities in the North. Jones took Hillary and her class to hear Martin Luther King, Jr., speak, and the class took field trips to tutor inner-city Hispanic and black children whose parents worked in nearby fruit orchards and vegetable fields. Along with the stories of Dorothy Rodham's troubled childhood, these outings were an early inspiration for Hillary's lifelong commitment to children.

Jones observed a practical side to Hillary, and has pointed out that her spiritual foundation "gives her some distance from all the good causes she's for. She is both idealistic and pragmatic. Really, she embodies that dialectic." Paul Johnson discerned a similar strain in Wilberforce's thinking: "There was, too, an element of high-minded deviousness underneath the Evangelical disclaimers of worldly ambitions. Wilberforce had a doctrine of 'usefulness' which led him to concentrate on those who were influential or important in some way."

In addition to Jones, two young teachers at Hillary's high school helped set her on her political trajectory. One was Smith College graduate Karin Fahlstrom. "Fahlstrom had Hillary in a class called 'Problems with Democracy.' . . . She [Fahlstrom] was much more liberal than the average person in Park Ridge. And she was heavily criticized by staff members for that," said Otto Kohler, chairman of the history department, who also taught Hillary in her senior year. "But I think she probably influenced Hillary. I think she would have because she was very pretty, very sharp, [an] eastern school type. Hillary was recommended by Karin for the [history] department award."

The second and perhaps more influential young woman was Janet Altman Spragens, a student teacher from Northwestern University who grew up in Washington, D.C., and had graduated from Wellesley the previous spring. Though most of the students from Maine South went on to midwestern colleges and universities, Hillary had approached Spragens seeking information about colleges in the East. "I was talking to her about a new horizon, something that she just hadn't considered before," Spragens recalled. "I really credit her with the fact that she was adventuresome enough not to follow the traditional path that most of her contemporaries were following and chose instead to go east for education. . . . If you were a woman who was graduating from high school at that time the absolute best you could do, the top of the ladder, was to go to one of the Seven Sister schools."

Founded in 1870 in the pre-suffrage era, Hillary's alma mater, Wellesley College, presents a prism through which to view the changing roles of women in this period. The school's mission is "to educate women who will make a difference in the world," and its motto is "Not to be served, but to serve." Wellesley's original function was to train young women to be volunteer social workers.

Hillary fit easily into the mold of the Wellesley woman, which classmate Ann Sherwood Sentilles described in a 1994 PBS documentary on Hillary's class of 1969: "We'd all worked hard. We'd all achieved across the board. We'd all done basically the same things. We were all editors of the yearbook or heads of government or whatever it was. We were all— we were all pretty much the same and we were all pretty much white Anglo-Saxon Protestants." In 1994, *U.S. News & World Report* commissioned a survey of Wellesley women spanning five classes over forty years—from 1939 to 1979—which showed that, overall, 85 percent of the respondents were married, 81 percent were mothers, and 63 percent held advanced degrees. Eighty percent were working in academia, law, and medicine, or comparable fields.

Hillary's class matriculated during the birth of the women's movement, which was reflected in the class members' financial independence and outlook on women's rights. In 1994 her class was the first to report a significant number of married women—42 percent—providing half or more of their total household income. More than half held bank accounts in their own names. Seventy-three percent of Hillary's classmates were Democrats, and a majority, according to the survey, supported "such feminist goals as equal pay, women candidates, paid family leave, government-sponsored child care, and government-funded abortions for the poor. All but a few dozen are pro-choice."

Hillary Rodham's early sense of intellectual self-confidence could only have been confirmed on that first day of class at Wellesley in September 1965, when the assembled students were told they were "the cream of the cream." As her classmate Johanna Branson told PBS, "that sounds really bratty and elitist now to me when I say it. But at the time it was a wonderful thing to hear if you were a girl. It was wonderful to be told that you didn't have to take a second seat to anybody and that you were one smart cookie."

The period between Hillary's enrollment at Wellesley in 1965 and her graduation four years later was one of enormous change in America, encompassing Lyndon Johnson's Great Society, the civil rights movement, the Vietnam War protests, and the assassinations of Robert F. Kennedy and Martin Luther King, Jr. The leading New Left organization, Students for a Democratic Society (SDS), had adopted its Port Huron Statement in 1962, introducing the concepts of participatory democracy and student power, later echoed in the Free Speech movement at the University of California at Berkeley in 1964, and elsewhere throughout the country. On elite campuses like Wellesley, the student movement demanded changes in the academic curriculum and in the way schools were governed. "Impersonal and unresponsive" university administrations were pegged by student revolutionaries as the enemy, tools of an allegedly repressive bureaucratic capitalist establishment.[4]

For Hillary, as for so many others, it was a time of political and personal tumult. Hillary told the PBS interviewer, "My world exploded when I got to Wellesley." Alan Schecter, a political scientist at Wellesley who was Hillary's senior thesis adviser, said that when Hillary got to college, "she met people of all kinds of different backgrounds and she had already begun to be exposed to a liberal message through her minister [Don Jones]. And the political events of that era were so dramatic that they either radicalized people and turned them off; or radicalized them and made them strong anti-war radicals; or with a student like Hillary, turned them into an activist trying to reform the society. And I would argue that everything that Hillary has done in her adult life afterwards—from the decision to go to Yale Law School and the jobs she chose after law school—strikes me as a classic Wellesley kind of graduate concern: families and children and social reform."

At Wellesley, Hillary continued on the student leader path. A political science major, she was elected president of the college government and chosen to give the first commencement speech ever by a student in the history of the institution. Achieving national acclaim at a very young age, Hillary struck many classmates as someone who would certainly seek public office someday. "I expected her to hold some kind of political office. I wouldn't be foolish enough to say president, but I remember we clearly thought she'd probably be at least a senator," Kris Olson, a Wellesley classmate, has been quoted as saying. "She was an effective communicator, she was articulate, she was willing to stand up and speak out and not just shrink to the sidelines. And she had a political astuteness in terms of building bases of support. It's fair to say we did expect something political from her."

To student activists in the 1960s, changes in the old rules and standards and administrative procedures on campuses were seen as victories against a wider pattern of social oppression. One important tenet of the SDS philosophy was that students had to gain control over their own lives. Grades were to be eliminated in favor of a pass-fail system; all campus decisions were to be made communally; the academic program had to be made "relevant"; and such things as curfews and parietals, seen as a bow to middle-class morality, had to be ended so that students could "express themselves" without fear of reprisal.

Hillary's class is considered to have done more to change campus life than any in Wellesley's history—and Hillary herself led the movement. Along with such friends as Eleanor Dean Acheson, the granddaughter of former secretary of state Dean Acheson, and her roommate Jan Piercy, Hillary worked for changes in the curriculum, in university governance, and in student life. When Hillary arrived at Wellesley, men couldn't visit dormitory rooms, cars weren't allowed on campus, and skirts were required in the dining room and for trips to town. By the time the class graduated, a pass-fail system was instituted, parietals and the skirt rule were ended, and interdisciplinary majors and a black studies class had been added. Yet in contrast to the student strikes being called on many other campuses, Hillary was able to co-opt the campus administration by calibrating student demands and winning change through the system.

"Wellesley was a very traditional college at that point and I think she helped remake this place," recalled Edward Stettner, a political scientist at Wellesley at the time. "She was a very forceful presence on the campus. She was an articulate student. She thought that changes needed to be made in the way Wellesley had done things, but she was always someone who very much worked within the system here. And she was a very effective student leader in that sense."

"Hillary was someone who knew how to get things done," classmate Janet Whitman added. "She wasn't encouraging people to strike on the campus or throw firebombs. . . . She appealed to people's sense of logic and people's common sense. She was definitely the lawyer from day one."

Hillary's ability to work the political process and maneuver bureaucratically had been joined to her principled moralism to maximum effect. Hillary took a strong position on behalf of racial equality in protesting the Wellesley housing director's policy of pairing students according to race, ethnicity, and religion. "I remember that [Hillary] took a stand on things, that she befriended the very few black students in our class when other people didn't," one classmate remarked. "She was out there. She told everybody what her opinions were." Student protests and pressure tactics eventually forced the housing director to resign.

When she arrived at Wellesley, Hillary still considered herself a Republican. But her views on race were the basis for a broader shift toward a more liberal Rockefeller Republicanism, according to Geoff Shields, a Harvard student who had grown up in Lake Forest, an affluent Chicago suburb not far from Park Ridge. Shields and Hillary dated for three years while she was at Wellesley. "My recollection of Hillary's shift to an active liberal philosophy had to do with her concern about civil rights," he said. "She became more convinced that she wanted to actively pursue influencing the government [on] issues relating to lack of fairness in treatment of minorities and discriminated-against groups, including women."

Hillary became president of the Young Republicans group, and supported the elections of liberal Republican John Lindsay as mayor of New

York City in 1965 and liberal Republican Senator Edward Brooke of Massachusetts in 1966. Opposition to the Vietnam War, however, soon prompted Hillary to join the Democratic Party. "She was doing a lot of self-educating about the war," said one friend. "She learned the history of the people and the geography of the place. She was very disciplined about it."

According to Shields, Hillary's opinions on Vietnam were shaped during the summer of 1966, when she lived in Michigan and worked for Wellesley political scientist Anthony D'Amato, who was editing part of a book called *The Realities of Vietnam: A Ripon Society Appraisal.* "I drove over there a couple of times and stayed with them overnight, with the professor and his family," Shields said, "and had some walks on the beach with Hillary, talking about what she was doing, and I remember her becoming very convinced that the Vietnam War was a mistake and being quite passionate about the discussions."

By 1968, Hillary had withdrawn as president of the Young Republicans group and was working on behalf of Eugene McCarthy's anti-war candidacy for president, canvassing for votes door to door in the Boston suburbs. She went home to Chicago that summer and was a spectator at the violent and controversial Democratic National Convention, where anti-war protesters, chanting the name of the North Vietnamese leader, "Ho Ho Ho Chi Minh," clashed with police. "We saw kids our age getting their heads beaten in. And the police were doing the beating," Hillary's high school friend Betsy Johnson Ebeling, who had accompanied Hillary to the convention, told the *Washington Post.* "Hillary and I just looked at each other. We had had a wonderful childhood in Park Ridge but we obviously hadn't gotten the whole story."

That summer Hillary appeared to get caught in a confusion of loyalties: between the Republicanism of Hugh Rodham and the Democratic sympathies of her mother Dorothy. She had been accepted into Wellesley's Washington internship program the previous fall and planned to spend the summer of 1968 in the nation's capital. Hillary initially had requested that she be assigned to the House Republican Conference. Though by the spring of that year she was organizing a student strike on Vietnam and supporting Eugene McCarthy, she decided to go to Washington anyway. Once there, she was able to find a niche among liberal Republicans who opposed the ascendancy of Richard Nixon in the party. That summer, she also went to the Republican National Convention as a supporter of the effort to draft Nelson Rockefeller—who had pledged to end the Vietnam War—and thereby stop Nixon, whom her father staunchly backed.

In the fall of 1968, when Hillary returned to Wellesley for her senior year, student strikes and teach-ins swept campuses from coast to coast. Though Hillary's responsibilities as president of the college government led her to support calls for student strikes during the Tet Offensive, she did not embrace the more extreme tactics of some campus activists, such as the so-called "die-ins." Hillary Rodham's position "wasn't radical at the time. . . . Compared to the classes four years prior to that, sure it was radical. But compared to what was happening then and compared to her classmates, she was not radical at all," said Marshall Goldman, who was a professor of economics at Wellesley in the 1960s. "I mean, I had students who were attacking me personally. There was an underground newspaper that singled me out for criticism. She was not part of that at all."

"She was very anti-war but she was a little more conservative than the others," commented one student. Like the Methodist evangelicals, "Hillary was unsure about how much campus life should be disrupted. . . . She didn't want to tear down the structure."

That fall Hillary met with adviser Alan Schecter to decide on a project for her senior thesis. She told Schecter she wanted to analyze one of the poverty programs of the Great Society—an idea she had gotten after visiting with the legendary political organizer Saul Alinsky in Chicago that summer. According to Schecter, "[W]e discussed Hillary taking advantage of the fact that she knew Alinsky. So she read all of Alinsky, and she was able to go and see him."

Thirty years before, in the late 1930s, Saul Alinsky had become known for building the Back of the Yards Council, an effective political pressure group that advocated better working conditions and social services in the notorious slum neighborhood surrounding Chicago's stockyards. According to his biographer, Sanford D. Horwitt, Alinsky considered himself to be not an abstract theoretician but a political realist, the advocate of a concrete philosophy "aimed at real people." He also believed in the Puritan values of "hard, tedious work." Horwitt described Alinsky as an energetic, charismatic figure, an "organizer-magician" and a "great seducer," intellectually, of his young disciples.

Alinsky's philosophy and strategies were set forth in the 1947 best-seller, *Reveille for Radicals,* which became a classic on the left, mirroring the reception on the right for Friedrich von Hayek's best-seller, *The Road to Serfdom,* published in 1944. In his book Alinsky contrasted radicalism with liberalism: while liberals favor reform of the capitalist system, radicals "want to advance from the jungle of laissez faire capitalism to a world worthy of the name of human civilization. They hope for a future where the means of economic production will be owned by all of the people instead of just a comparative handful." Alinsky also believed that liberals "fail to recognize that only through the achievement and constructive use of power can people better themselves. They talk glibly of a people lifting themselves by their own bootstraps but fail to realize that nothing can be lifted or moved except through power."

Alinsky criticized the labor union movement for trying to reform "monopolistic capitalism" from inside the system. Echoing Lenin's call for "professional revolutionaries," Alinsky argued that to be truly effective, the organizer had to be a neutral outside agitator with no stake in the economic system: "In order to be part of all, you must be part of none." He advanced no-holds-barred tactics, encapsulated in the motto, "whatever works to get power to the people, use it." Such tactics included gross intimidation of opponents and civil disruption—such as dumping mass quantities of garbage on politicians' doorsteps to protest inadequate sanitation services and organizing rent strikes and public protests in the neighborhoods of landlords. One of his organizational tactics was the purposeful incitement of political opposition, which he called "mass jujitsu."[5]

Reveille for Radicals was criticized by leading liberals in the mid-1940s. In 1946, the *New Republic* called Alinsky's philosophy "a move in the direction of a corporate state . . . it expresses a point of view which runs the risk of developing away from the democracy that the author speaks of with such fervor." Others were disturbed by Alinsky's antinomian emphasis on attaining power through any and all means. A 1947 article in the liberal Protestant magazine *Christian Century* depicted Alinsky as "Machiavelli in Modern Dress."

By the mid-1960s, when Hillary first became aware of him, Alinsky's radical goals and rogue tactics had remained unchanged since the founding of the Back of the Yards Council in the '30s—he still bragged of being jailed for civil disobedience, and his followers disrupted corporate board meetings in pressing demands for job training and higher wages. But as mainstream liberalism was overtaken by the ascendancy of the New Left, Alinsky had become respectable, even venerated. In 1965, *Harper's* magazine ran a laudatory two-part series called "The Professional Radical: A Conversation with Saul Alinsky." *The Nation,* which had once found *Reveille for Radicals* too extreme, now hailed Alinsky as "this country's leading hellraiser."

Originally, the Back of the Yards movement had been built with the cooperation of the Catholic Church in a white, ethnic, working-class ghetto. With the federal civil rights laws of 1964 and 1965 ensuring equal access to public accommodations and voting rights as a backdrop, Alinksky's challenge was to expand his organizing activity into the burgeoning black communities and to overcome the frankly racist sentiments of many of his Back of the Yards followers. "It is indisputable that Saul Alinsky brought the first large-scale modern civil rights effort to Chicago," wrote Sanford Horwitt, noting that the moral crusade of civil rights helped soften Alinsky's Machiavellian image. Alinsky's organization was instrumental in bringing civil rights leaders Ralph Abernathy and Martin Luther King, Jr., to Chicago to speak in the Woodlawn section south of Hyde Park, the site of Alinsky's first political project in a black community. The Reverend Jones had taken young Hillary and her classmates to hear King.

Alinsky's power-based political philosophy was very influential in New Left circles. In 1971, he published *Rules for Radicals,* which was addressed to the new generation of student activists. In this book Alinsky set forth what he called a "science of revolution," a set of rules that laid out his philosophy of ends and means. "Power," he wrote, "is the very essence, the dynamo of life. . . . It is a world not of angels but of angles, where men speak of moral principles but act on power principles; a world where we are always moral and our enemies are always immoral; a world where 'reconciliation' means that when one side gets the power and the other side gets reconciled to it, then we have reconciliation. . . ." In fighting for "revolution," Alinsky wrote, the man of action "asks of ends only whether they are achievable and worth the cost; of means only whether they will work." By the late 1960s, Alinsky was bringing this message to many college campuses, where he was popular with students who were "pro-civil rights, opposed to the war, and often involved in student power or campus reform movements," according to Horwitt.

Hillary was involved in inviting Alinsky to speak at Wellesley. She also interviewed Alinsky for her senior thesis, an analysis of the Community Action Program, one of the centerpieces of LBJ's Great Society. The CAP channeled federal money to states and localities and created new community agencies to help organize the poor politically. Though his ideas had actually inspired the program, Alinsky denounced the CAP as a "prize piece of political pornography." He argued that the money should be diverted to neighborhood councils in the poor communities, where the poor would decide for themselves how to spend it, rather than going to white-dominated municipal governments and social service bureaucracies, which the poor did not control. "An anti-poverty program must recognize that its progress has to do something with not only economic poverty but also political poverty," he wrote.

Today, Hillary's thesis is under lock and key on the campus of Wellesley, whose administration unilaterally cut off public access to the senior theses of "all presidents and first ladies" in early 1993, soon after Clinton was inaugurated. Alan Schecter, however, recalled that in her thesis Hillary criticized the CAP's notion of participation of the poor as inadequate and said that fundamental change was needed along the lines suggested by Alinsky. "She pretty much concluded that increased participation of the poor would help them out but would have short-term impact . . . it would never solve their major problems," Schecter said. In a 1993 interview with the *Washington Post*, Hillary said, "I basically argued that [Alinsky] was right. . . . You know, I've been on this kick for 25 years."

Alinsky wasn't the only radical influence from which Hillary was taking her political cues. At Wellesley, she avidly read *motive*, a now defunct radical magazine for young Methodists published by the church's university Christian movement. Hillary's attraction to *motive* and specifically to the Marxist theoretician Carl Oglesby, who became the head of Students for a Democratic Society, underscored the political tone of her Methodism. In a November 1994 article in *Newsweek*, Hillary cited a 1966 piece in *motive*, "World Revolution and American Containment," by Oglesby, as having made an indelible mark on her. "I still have every issue they sent me," she said.

At the time Hillary was reading the magazine, articles appeared on such topics as life in a commune; how drug-induced hallucinations are similar to religious experiences; problems within the New Left movement; university protests against war and racism; and society's responsibility to the poor. The United Methodist Church, which had underwritten the monthly publication for thirty years, began slashing its funding with the March–April 1969 issue, published during Hillary's senior year at Wellesley. The offending issue, devoted to the women's liberation movement, featured such articles as "The Subversion of Betty Crocker," "The Realities of Lesbianism," and "WITCH Power." In 1971, the church ceased funding the magazine altogether.

In the *motive* article cited by Hillary, Carl Oglesby asked: "What would be so obviously wrong about a VietNam run by Ho Chi Minh [or] a Cuba by Castro. . . ?" The author maintained that the United States wanted only a certain kind of peace, in which the "world will be safe for the American businessman to do his doings everywhere, on terms always advantageous, in environments always protected by friendly or puppet oligarchies, by the old foreign grads of Fort Benning—or if push comes to shove, by the Marines themselves. We want a world integrated in terms of the stability of labor, resources, production, and markets; and we want that integrated world to be managed by our own business people. The United States, that is, is an imperialist power."

Oglesby also defended political violence. "I am no advocate of violence: but as an American, as one therefore who need only choose the rich life in order to have it, I cannot presume to judge those whose condition forces violence upon them. I do not find it hard to understand that certain cultural settings create violence as surely as the master's whip creates outcries of pain and rage," he wrote. "I can no more condemn the Andean tribesmen who assassinate tax collectors than I can condemn the rioters in Watts or Harlem or the Deacons for Defense and Justice. Their violence is reactive and provoked, and it remains culturally beyond guilt at the very same moment that its victim's personal innocence is most appallingly present in our imaginations."

Of the Vietnam conflict, Oglesby commented: "What does this national capacity for computerized slaughter make of us? . . . How many of us have wondered what the decent Germans were doing when the Stukas raked Madrid and when the punctilious Eichmanns carried out their orders at Auschwitz? . . . Nothing that could possibly result from our departure could exceed the horror of our continued stay."

Like Alinsky, Oglesby was an avid student of power. "Carl Oglesby was only one of the well-known Maoist or Marxist theoreticians who was interested in and had a theory about splitting and manipulating the ruling class," explained Stephen Schwartz, a leading historian of the American Communist Party and himself a former Communist. "Oglesby had what he called the Yankees versus Cowboys theory. The theory was that the American capitalist class was deeply factionalized between eastern old money and western new money—the Yankees versus the Cowboys. And Oglesby's theory was that the Vietnam War and the Kennedy assassination reflected a conflict at the top between the Yankees and the Cowboys. Oglesby wanted to set the Yankees against the Cowboys; get the two of them fighting; use them against each other.

"In 1966, for a sensitive, intellectual, gawky woman seeing the whole world begin to take fire with the sixties, at that moment, to read an essay like Carl Oglesby's on world revolution, would have the effect of an atomic bomb on her," Schwartz added. "A person like this could simply not walk away from it."

In the spring of 1969, Hillary had to decide what she would do after graduation. One option she considered, according to her thesis adviser Alan Schecter, was to go to India to do volunteer social work. Another was to enroll in law school. A third possibility was to take a job as an organizer with Saul Alinsky, who had opened a new training institute in Chicago under the auspices of the Industrial Areas Foundation (founded back in 1940). "The reason for the training institute is because of the appalling dearth of persons who know how to organize in and for a free society," Alinsky wrote. Potential recruits were interviewed and asked, "Why do you want to organize?" They were to answer with one word: "Power."

Alinsky offered Hillary a paid position as a trainee, a sign that he recognized in her a valuable combination of true believer and tough pragmatist—the "dialectic" that Don Jones had seen in her as well. At the time he sought to recruit Hillary, one of Alinsky's key disciples was Cesar Chavez, the radical labor organizer, who had helped Alinsky expand his movement into California. Another was the socialist agitator Staughton Lynd, who had gone to Hanoi with Tom Hayden in 1965 to meet with North Vietnamese leaders. Though Alinsky died in 1972, his training institute spawned nationwide community political movements around the issues of the environment, consumer protection, jobs, and inner-city renewal, and produced such political leaders as San Antonio Mayor Henry Cisneros.

When Alinsky offered her the post in his organization, Hillary told him that she had decided to go to law school instead. In *Reveille for Radicals,* Alinsky had taken liberal lawyers to task specifically for what he saw as a hopeless effort to change the system from within. "I remember him saying, 'Well, that's no way to change anything.' And I said, 'Well, I see a different way than you. And I think there is a real opportunity,' " Hillary told the *Chicago Daily News* in an interview in the summer of 1969 about her Wellesley commencement address.

It was a testament to Hillary's self-confidence and strength of character that at age twenty-one she voiced her open disagreement with a powerful male mentor whom she deeply admired. Her thesis showed that she agreed with Alinsky's emphasis on attaining political power to push through more radical change than the Great Society envisioned. But in the *Chicago Daily News* interview, Hillary suggested that she did not think Alinsky's strategy of fighting for power from outside the system as a professional revolutionary would work. She believed that power could be seized by working within the system, rather than being independent of it, as Alinsky argued. Alinsky's radicalism, Hillary said, would not go over well with "the kind of people I grew up with in Park Ridge."

Hillary was not alone in reaching these conclusions. Other members of her generation also felt that the best way to advance their radical ends was not to destroy "the system" but to co-opt and reform government from within. "She rejected that [community organizing] in favor of going to law school because she felt that what she would get out of [law school] she could use more effectively," Schecter said. "The decision to go to law school was based on her assessment that, given her talents, her skills, she could be most effective in improving society in that fashion as an advocate. That's a very classical upper-middle-class, primarily liberal reformist approach, of a pragmatic sort, not a radical sort. . . . If you think of what Hillary has done with her life, she was a forerunner in that group of women who basically had the same sorts of values of helping the underprivileged, but who now wanted to do it through having a career. And so the legal career was her method of accomplishing an old American social uplift purpose."

As graduation approached, several Wellesley students, including Hillary, Eleanor Acheson, and Jan Piercy, raised the idea of having a student speaker at the commencement—a speaker who would mark the changes that their class had wrought in the previous four years. Although most of the elite schools asked the valedictorian or another representative of the class to speak, Wellesley had never had a student speaker. After a discussion in a constitutional law seminar taught by Alan Schecter, Hillary, Acheson, and several other students went to see Wellesley president Ruth Adams to propose the idea. When Adams rejected it out of hand, Hillary, hoping to be chosen as speaker, faded into the background, leaving it to Acheson and the others to mount a campaign to press the issue. Adams soon bowed to the pressure. Though the selection was not unchallenged, as president of the college government Hillary soon emerged as the choice of her fellow students. A committee was hastily formed under Jan Piercy's direction to draft the speech.

Senator Edward Brooke, the Republican senator from Massachusetts whom Hillary had supported for election in 1966, was the invited commencement speaker. On graduation day, with such dignitaries as former secretary of state Dean Acheson and diplomat Paul Nitze in attendance, Senator Brooke began by paying tribute to the student movement: ". . . the protest movements reflect and stimulate the healthy self-criticism taking place throughout the nation. It is a very significant fact that America has identified more precisely than ever before the nature and magnitude of its acute social problems. Racial and social injustice is being seen in concrete terms, as a root cause of human misery and as a principal obstacle to the further development of this nation. Poverty, hunger, unemployment, inferior education, inadequate health care— these grave inequities are now being recognized for what they are—the responsibility of society as a whole as well as the individual involved."

Though Brooke was evidently conscious of his left-leaning student audience, he singled out the Students for a Democratic Society for criticism and called on Wellesley students to reject violent protest. "Whatever the romantics may say about violence in our national life, the use of force is repugnant to the spirit of American politics. . . . In short, it behooves the disciples of politics as protest to reconsider the alleged merits of coercive tactics. By now, they should be able to see that, apart from being morally insupportable, such methods are politically ineffective."

Most Wellesley students apparently felt that Brooke's address was a pro forma commencement speech, which failed to recognize the enormous changes that had taken place both on the campus and in the nation during their four years of school. Hillary later described Brooke's speech as a "defense of Richard Nixon [who had been elected president the previous November] . . . 'the world awaits you, we've got great leadership. America is strong abroad.' "

When it was time for her to take the podium, looking upon an audience of hundreds that included her father (but not her mother,) Hillary ad-libbed a retort to Brooke, delivered without notes. Read today, both Hillary's extemporaneous remarks and the prepared text seem confused and self-indulgent, a jumble of themes that include everything from the liberal theology of Don Jones to the culture of resistance and the rejection of middle-class values preached by Saul Alinsky and the SDS. Addressing Brooke by name, Hillary said, "Part of the problem with empathy with professed goals is that empathy doesn't do anything [for us]. We've had lots of empathy; we've had lots of sympathy, but we feel that for too long our leaders have used politics as the art of the possible. And the challenge now is to practice politics as the art of making what appears to be impossible, possible. What does it mean to hear that 13.3 percent of the people in this country are below the poverty line? That's a percentage. We're not interested in social reconstruction; it's human reconstruction."

The rebuttal to Brooke was a mark of how much Hillary Rodham's perspective had changed in her four years at Wellesley. Classmate Catherine Kennett recalled that earlier in her academic career Hillary had spoken of the kind of conventional goals a girl from Park Ridge might have had. "I recollect, specifically, that her ideal car in life was a yellow Jaguar XKE convertible. [She] wanted to be class president—and so obviously she was politically ambitious—and she wanted that car." Now, Hillary sounded a note that could be read as a reproach to her parents and the materialism of her suburban Park Ridge upbringing. "We are, all of us, exploring a world that none of us understands and attempting to create within that uncertainty. But there are some things we feel, feelings that our prevailing, acquisitive, and competitive corporate life, including tragically the universities, is not the way of life for us. We're searching for more immediate, ecstatic and penetrating modes of living. And so our questions about institutions, about our colleges, about our churches, and about our government, continue. . . ."

The overwhelming majority of her fellow students as well as many faculty members rewarded Hillary for speaking her mind with a thunderous, seven-minute standing ovation. Those who knew Hillary personally were struck by the way her passions seemed to overcome her typical lawyerly caution. "I was stunned," said one friend. "I remember thinking, 'Oh my God, I can't believe this.' She had always struck me as someone who, no matter what she is thinking or feeling, would think things through before saying anything." Added Professor Marshall Goldman, "It's a pretty gutsy thing to do to stand up and challenge an American senator, especially one who is black."

Another way of describing the speech was that it exemplified perfectly the morally self-righteous temper of the times. But even as they were swept up in the drama of the moment, some students were discomfited by Hillary's overheated rhetoric. "It was brash. It was brilliant . . . And I can remember squirming in my seat. At the same time, you know the inner me was saying, 'All right!' " classmate Jan Dustman Mercer told *Frontline*.

To all appearances, Hillary was already poised at an early age to become one of the leaders of her generation. She was marked for distinction by her peers and showed a clear sense of her own purpose and also of her symbolic significance to the young activists who would come after her. "I think she embodied the feeling that a lot of people in our class had—I don't think that I ended up leaving this way—but the core of people who were most active in the class I think left Wellesley with this feeling that they really could do anything," said another classmate, Kathy Ruckman. "They were smart enough and understood it and knew what they were after. And were going to go after it; they weren't going to let anybody stop them. And Hillary definitely was one of those people."

While Dean Acheson sent Hillary a complimentary note asking for a copy of the speech, many of the assembled parents expressed shock and dismay. "I would have thought someone could have stopped her. I would have liked to stop her. But her class absolutely encouraged her and when she finished they rose in a body and applauded her," Marge Wanderer, the mother of student Nancy Wanderer, told *Frontline*. "And I will never forget it because Nancy said to me at the end of graduation, 'Take a good look at her. She will probably be the president of the United States someday.' "

2

A Seminar for Radicals

In choosing a law school, Hillary faced another important crossroads. "She chose Yale because of its reputation as a more socially oriented, committed law school as opposed to a corporate-type law school like Harvard or Chicago," according to Alan Schecter, who helped her select Yale. Unlike many other top schools, Yale Law School advanced a legal philosophy explicitly dedicated to achieving social and political aims. It was precisely the approach that Hillary would need to prove Alinsky wrong about the role of lawyers in achieving radical social change.

Harvard Law School, the other leading contender, and Yale were both highly regarded for academic excellence and drew the very top tier of applicants, but Harvard was more traditional than Yale. Hillary described a visit to Harvard's Cambridge campus in a later interview with the *Arkansas Democrat-Gazette:* "This tall, rather imposing professor, sort of like a character from the 'Paper Chase,' looked down at me and said, 'Well, first of all, we don't have close competitors. Secondly, we don't need any more women.' That's what made my decision . . . that fellow's comments iced the cake."

The choice of Yale meant a world of difference in approach to legal education. One-third the size of Harvard, Yale had a more flexible curriculum and a pass-fail grading system. While Harvard emphasized the intimidating Socratic method of "case study," as dramatized by John Houseman's portrayal of Professor Kingsfield in *The Paper Chase,* Yale was steeped in the theory of legal realism, which first emerged in the 1930s and considered the impact of politics, economics, psychology, and the social sciences on the law. Legal rules must be examined in context, said a well-known proponent of the theory, Yale Professor Thurman Arnold, an anti-trust advocate and appellate judge.[1]

By the time Hillary arrived on campus, legal realism had already made an important contribution to American intellectual life, informing Franklin Delano Roosevelt's New Deal brain trust (which included Arnold), and emerging in the late 1950s and 1960s as the animating intellectual force behind the Supreme Court activism of Chief Justice Earl Warren and the Court's reigning liberal conscience, Justice William O. Douglas, an FDR appointee who had served on the Yale faculty. Douglas was known for his expansive view of rights under the Constitution. The historian Arthur M. Schlesinger, Jr., once described the influential "Douglas wing" at Yale: "The Yale thesis, crudely put, is that any judge chooses his results and reasons backwards . . . marshaling judicial power to social results." The Warren Court's decisions to desegregate the schools, expand the rights of defendants, and vigorously enforce the anti-trust laws against business were hailed as important steps toward achieving social justice. But the Court's legacy proved ambiguous and divisive: conservatives criticized the judges for making public policy by fiat, usurping and undermining the role of legislatures rather than hewing to a strict interpretation of the law as written.

The Yale curriculum was more freewheeling and experimental than Harvard's, and there was as much talk in the classroom about public policy and advocacy as about law. A few traditionalists like future Supreme Court nominee Robert Bork held forth on dry common law legal principles and precedents, but more typical courses featured Burke Marshall on civil rights and Thomas (or "Tommie the Commie," as students called him) Emerson on the First Amendment. One could even take courses with radicals like Charles Reich, author of *The Greening of America,* the best-selling expression of the late sixties idealism that recommended dropping out of conventional society and extolled the virtues of marijuana ("using marijuana is . . . like what happens when a person with fuzzy vision puts on glasses").

Yale Professor Harold Koh has described the school's guiding spirit as "the simple idealistic notion that talented and passionate women and men trained in the law can make our unjust and imperfect world so much the better." By all accounts, this idea of law as a branch of politics and social work was one that Hillary absorbed at Yale, where she would meet not only her future husband, Bill Clinton, but also several significant early mentors: Burke Marshall, the Yale faculty member and civil rights giant who was considered an attorney general-in-waiting for a future Democratic administration; Professor Kenneth Keniston, a politically active legal scholar whom Hillary assisted in his path-breaking research on children's rights; and, foremost among the group, Marian Wright Edelman, an influential advocate for liberal social policy as founder of the Children's Defense Fund.

At Yale, Hillary's left-leaning inclinations flowered into full-blown activism. Not only did her political seduction continue and intensify, she also met and formed long-lasting associations with the like-minded liberal activists of her generation—whose figurehead and unofficial leader she would eventually become. "She was one of the leaders of the group both in terms of intellect and personality," said Robert Weller, a member of the Yale class of '72 who participated in a small seminar with Hillary. "That was a very political time at Yale, and Yale was very much an activist law school, and to be somebody who would stand out in one of those groups would certainly take a real activist."

David Masselli, a member of the Yale class of '73, likened Hillary to the serious, intense, long-haired girl who appears as Woody Allen's first girlfriend in all of his 1970s movies. Hillary's uniform consisted of white socks and sandals, and the loose-fitting, flowing pants favored by the Viet Cong, for which she was teased by classmates. Ever present were obtrusive glasses needed to correct poor eyesight. "She wouldn't have won any beauty contests," one Wellesley classmate recalled. "She wore those thick glasses and her hair was kind of piled up on top of her head. She just obviously didn't bother." Dorothy Rodham, of course, had taught her not to care about such ephemera, and by the early 1970s, rejecting traditionally "feminine" concerns such as one's physical appearance was seen as a political statement as well. Fellow Yale Law student Richard Grande remarked that Hillary belonged to the "look-like-shit school of feminism."

Notwithstanding her anti-establishment posture and stylistic affectations, Hillary's choice of law as a profession showed she was not willing to give up her place in the system to join the revolution. "The profession depends upon the functioning of the capitalist system. Everybody wanted to be an anti-poverty lawyer or an environmental lawyer, working for a cause, but still that is working as part of the system. It was kind of tough to be a law school Marxist," said Michael Medved, who was a close friend of Hillary's at Yale and (though now a conservative film critic) a major figure in the anti-war protests on campus.

The Yale curriculum encouraged students to connect legal theory to actual practice for course credit. Through her courses at Yale's child study center, run by Kenneth Keniston, Hillary worked with the staff of the Yale New Haven Hospital to draft guidelines for the treatment of abused children. In his book *All Our Children* Keniston argued that minors should be recognized as competent under the law, and he advocated a federally guaranteed wage for every family with a child. The effort to discern and define rights for children in the law, which had traditionally presumed that parents were best suited to represent a child's interests, was squarely in the tradition of the rights-based liberalism of the Douglas wing at Yale. It was also an incipient legal adjunct of the women's movement.

"[Hillary] was going to be a public interest lawyer," said Guido Calabresi, a member of the Yale faculty in the early 1970s, later dean of the law school and a Clinton-appointed federal appeals court judge. "She was in the mold of a person who goes into public interest. She was going to do that with children, which is why she was spending time at the child study center and doing things that would lead to work with the Children's Defense Fund. It was the beginning of a very strong feminist movement. But that was, you see, very much part of the tradition of using law for social change rather than rebelling against law."

Hillary's decision to affiliate with a fledgling left-wing alternative journal called the *Yale Review of Law and Social Action,* rather than with the more mainstream but still very liberal *Yale Law Journal,* clearly reveals her orientation at this stage of young adulthood. The *Journal* would have been the choice of a student planning a career in law as it has been traditionally practiced: in a law firm, corporation, or academia. The *Review* attracted more politically inclined students. Stephen Wizener, who worked with Hillary in a clinical program at Yale as an instructor and supervising attorney, described the *Yale Review*'s origin: "It was started by students who thought that what was being taught at the Yale Law School was not sufficiently related to the legal needs of the poor and the oppressed and the downtrodden, and thought there should be a law review at the Yale Law School that tried to think about law in a reflective way—that also focused on the actual legal needs of poor people. There was a feeling among students—and I think there still is among some students—that academic law reviews don't have anything to do with the world, and that we have an obligation as law students and law teachers to try to think about ways of using law to benefit the poor and disadvantaged. Her interests were not in the legal academy. They were in the legal profession and the use of law in the service of people."

Hillary was a member of the board of editors of the *Yale Review*'s inaugural issue in the spring of 1970. Her membership amounts to a clear endorsement of the *Review*'s strategy of pushing the system as far as possible while still remaining nominally within it. A general note of introduction written by the editors explained their purpose: "This, the first issue of *Law and Social Action*, begins our exploration of areas beyond the limits of traditional legal concerns. For too long, legal issues have been defined and discussed in terms of academic doctrine rather than strategies for social change. *Law and Social Action* is an attempt to go beyond the narrowness of such an approach, to present forms of legal scholarship and journalism which focus on programmatic solutions to social problems."

Her work on the journal brought Hillary into an influential circle. Robert Borosage, a leading student radical and another of the journal's founders, would become an important operative behind the Institute for Policy Studies, the Washington think tank founded in 1963 to help craft programs for the Great Society. In the 1970s, the Institute promoted pro-Soviet movements in the Third World at the height of the renewed Cold War. Another notable figure writing for the *Yale Review* during Hillary's tenure on the board of editors was Duncan Kennedy, one of the founders of the Critical Legal Studies (or "Crits") movement, which applied deconstructionist philosophy to the law. Critical Legal Studies was a 1970s descendant of the legal realists' view that the law could be used as an instrument of political power.[2]

Though traditional liberals like William O. Douglas wanted the law to reflect and even affect social and political change, they still believed that more or less neutral legal principles could be massaged to produce a just result for society. Unlike lawyers and judges of Douglas's bent, the Crits rejected the liberal reformist agenda in favor of a neo-Marxist philosophy whose application would subvert existing democratic institutions. In an effort to "subvert the dominant paradigm" of legal reasoning, the Crits experimented with abandoning common law rules, traditions, and lines of precedent, and even rules of logic and rhetoric. They believed that legal concepts were themselves meaningless, created only as a way to enforce the capitalist order, and that judges weren't so much social engineers as unwitting pawns of "the system." Other branches of this movement, such as the Fem Crits, soon followed, arguing that law was simply a tool used by the patriarchy to oppress women. From this position, it followed that lawyers had no ethical obligations to the law itself.

The seeds of what would blossom into a full-fledged academic movement under Duncan Kennedy's leadership as a tenured professor of law at Harvard University could be seen in a 1971 article he wrote for the *Yale Review* called "How the Law School Fails: A Polemic." In his essay, Kennedy referred to law school as a "social construction" and assailed the majority of the courses for their "mediocrity or intellectual shallowness." And in a sentiment that echoed Alinsky's dictum that "Justice, morality, law, and order, are mere words when used by the Haves, which justify and secure their status quo," Kennedy advocated "legal hippieism," writing, "It is often true that the 'rules' must be changed, but the rules are just 'things' like money or status."

Two other people associated with the *Yale Review* would later become prominent figures in the Clintons' political circle: Mickey Kantor and Robert Reich. Mickey Kantor was a legal services lawyer in South Florida in the 1960s. By the early 1970s, he had left a legal services job at the federal Office of Economic Opportunity and was lobbying to take the program out of the executive branch and form an independent Legal Services Corporation. The alternative magazine's staff interviewed Kantor about his efforts in the fall of 1972, Hillary's third year at Yale. Law student Robert Reich wrote a heavily footnoted article in the same issue of the *Yale Review* entitled "Solving Social Crises by Commissions," that attacked the use of federal commissions—like the Johnson-appointed National Advisory Commission on Civil Disorders (Kerner Commission), which studied the causes of urban violence—as "ideal vehicles for keeping the public occupied and content that the social crisis is being 'handled.' "

The *Yale Review* took up all the important radical causes of the day. These included the anti-Vietnam War movement and the violent protests of the Black Panthers, a black power group that allied itself with Communist movements in the Third World, and condoned violence as a means of fomenting revolution. At the time, some Black Panther members, including chairman Bobby Seale, were on trial for murdering one of their number who had allegedly informed on the Panthers to the police. The trial was held in New Haven, the grim Connecticut port city that housed the Yale campus, a bastion of white middle-class guilt surrounded by a black ghetto. Hillary was "pretty taken up with the protest orientation of the school," said Walter McMonies, Yale Law class of '72. "Political issues interested her more than academics, more than being a superstar student." He added that Hillary's friends "were the ones who wore the ragged jeans. They were the ones into the Bobby Seale trial."

Yale Law grad Peter Harvey remembered Hillary taking a prominent role at rallies on campus concerning both the Bobby Seale trial and the Vietnam War in the spring of 1970. "Hillary was very outspoken and in your face. . . . She was very strong. I had a certain grudging admiration for her." Fellow student Richard Grande said, "I remember her raising her voice. She could be abrasive. I remember her in the Quad going at it hammer and tongs. . . . She liked the give-and-take. She gave as good as she got."

A huge regionwide protest and student strike was scheduled for May Day, 1970, demanding that the Black Panther trial be stopped on the grounds that black defendants could not receive a fair trial in a white-dominated justice system. The argument reflected the view of law, promoted by the *Yale Review*, as an oppressive racial and class construct.[3]

In an indication of that view's wide currency on campus, Yale president Kingman Brewster issued a controversial statement endorsing the sentiments of the protesters: "I personally want to say that I am appalled and ashamed that things should have come to such a pass that I am skeptical of the ability of black revolutionaries to achieve a fair trial anywhere in the U.S." Brewster opened the residential college dorms to May Day demonstrators and allowed radical lawyer Charles Garry, the leading Black Panther attorney, to live on campus during the trial. Hillary's connection with Garry, formed at this time, would lead her to still deeper involvement in left-wing legal circles.

Law enforcement authorities feared that the May Day rally would incite a race riot in which protesters would attempt to free the Panthers by force or simply burn down the city. In rallies leading up to the big demonstration, Black Panther members had announced "all power to the good shooters" who would "create peace by destroying people who don't want peace"—a thinly veiled threat to assassinate the police. It was expected that the National Committee to Stop Fascism would pass out rifles on the New Haven Green. Leaflets on campuses throughout the Northeast exhorted students: "Come to New Haven for a burning on May Day." On the eve of the demonstration, the National Guard was called in. Businesses closed up shop and nailed plywood over their windows. Blasting caps were stolen from a campus chemistry lab and a building on the nearby Connecticut Wesleyan campus was fire-bombed. The *New York Times* reported that on two occasions the National Guard fired tear gas at protesters who were throwing rocks and bottles at the troops.

When May 1 dawned, "Burn Yale" signs could be seen in the crowd of fifteen thousand, but the worst fears of the authorities were not realized: the demonstration was largely peaceful. Some students watched from their dormitory-room windows as throngs of scruffy protesters ate handfuls of granola distributed by the Yale administration. Others went to law school teach-ins which addressed such topics as "Immunity and Contempt," "Arrest and Search," and "Colonization and Race in Plantation Society." Kenneth Keniston, the children's rights advocate and author of a book called *Young Radicals,* spoke at the rally as well.

The main target of the denunciations from the podium appeared to be Richard Nixon, who was pilloried for his prosecution of the Vietnam War, his domestic "police state," and his allegedly racist, anti-intellectual "hard-hat" movement in the South. Chicago Seven defendant Jerry Rubin famously screamed into the microphone: "Fuck Nixon! Fuck Nixon! Fuck Nixon!"

Hillary was not just one of the faceless thousands who appeared on the Green to show symbolic support. Rather than fire-bombing buildings, she was busy using the legal system to further the Panther case. "Hillary and fellow students in First Amendment scholar Thomas Emerson's class attended court proceedings of the Panthers' cases, some as independent studies, others wholly extracurricular as part of Emerson's efforts to assist the American Civil Liberties Union," *Washington Post* reporter Donnie Radcliffe wrote in *Hillary Rodham Clinton: A First Lady for Our Time.* "Hillary's job was to organize shifts for her classmates and make certain no proceeding went unmonitored. 'We were supposed to be monitoring civil rights abuses as they occurred throughout the trial, then we would write papers on them, discuss them in the class and do reports for the ACLU,' Kris Olson [a Wellesley and Yale classmate of Hillary's] said. It meant going in and out of the Black Panther headquarters to obtain documentation and other information. 'It was pretty obvious that we were being surveilled by the FBI. I remember people parked in cars across the street. And I remember Emerson filing Freedom of Information Act requests to find out what photographs were being taken of students.' "[4]

The inaugural issue of the *Yale Review,* coinciding with the May Day rally, had a cover photo of armed police officers wearing gas masks to illustrate the article "Universities and the Police: Force and Freedom on Campus." Kas Kalba and Jay Beste's article on "Lawyers and Revolutionaries: Notes from the National Conference on Political Justice" featured remarks by Chicago Seven lawyer William Kunstler, Charles Garry, and Jerry Rubin, the yippie who opined, "Freedom in America is the right to grow up and oppress your children, dig it. . . . We're gonna get stoned with our kids. . . . Seven year olds know where it's at . . . before they get into the schools."

By the winter of 1970, Hillary had been named an associate editor of the *Review.* Most of that issue was devoted to the Black Panther trial. The main article, "The Black Panthers in Court: The Lonnie McLucas Trial," maintained that McLucas, one of the Panthers charged with murder, had not received a fair trial. Pictures and drawings accompanying the article depicted policemen as pigs. One drawing, of a black woman with a child, was accompanied by the statement: "If I should return, I shall kiss you. If I should fall on the way, I shall ask you to do as I have in the name of the revolution." Another depicted rifle-toting pigs, representing the police, thinking: "Niggers, niggers, niggers." On one pig's uniform was the word "fascist." A drawing of a wounded pig posed the question, "What is a pig?" The definition read: "A low . . . beast that has no regard for law, justice, or the rights of the people; a creature that bites the hand that feeds it; a foul, depraved traducer, usually found masquerading as the victim of an unprovoked attack." Finally, there was a picture of a decap-

itated, dismembered, and wailing pig over the phrase, "Seize the Time!,"
the title of a book by Bobby Seale.

Through her association with the *Yale Review* and her work in the Black
Panthers' cause, Hillary met two former Communist Party members, Jessica Mitford, the British author and political journalist, and her husband
Robert Treuhaft, a lawyer in the San Francisco Bay Area. The Treuhafts
were visiting New Haven in 1970 to assist Treuhaft's associate Charles
Garry in the trial, and Jessica Mitford threw a house party to raise money
for the Panthers' defense.

Until 1958, Robert Treuhaft had worked as a lawyer for the Communist Party. In her book *A Fine Old Conflict,* Jessica Mitford reported that
Treuhaft had fought to allow Communist Party members to hold office
in labor unions and mounted a defense of the leadership of the California Communist Party in a 1951 subversion trial. A pamphlet produced
by the House Un-American Affairs Committee, *Communist Legal Subversion: The Role of the Communist Lawyer,* listed Treuhaft as among the thirty-
nine most "dangerously subversive" lawyers in the country, according to
the Mitford book. In sharp contrast to most of the New Left, Treuhaft
and Mitford were die-hard supporters of Stalinism. By the early 1970s,
the sector of the American left that Treuhaft occupied was a scorned, almost underground minority. "This was not a group of socialists," said historian Stephen Schwartz. "This was a group of hard Communists who
had been running the Communist Party of Northern California. . . . It
was a political organization whose loyalty to the Soviet Union was explicit,
whose discipline was Stalinist, and whose intellectual attitudes were
mainly Stalinist. . . . Treuhaft is not like the Black Panthers. Treuhaft is
a man who dedicated his entire legal career to advancing the agenda of
the Soviet Communist Party and the KGB."

In 1971, Hillary accepted a summer internship in Treuhaft's Berkeley law office. The opportunity to work for Treuhaft likely arose from her
activities on behalf of the Black Panthers with Charles Garry, a Treuhaft
associate, and almost certainly did not signify a pro-Stalinist orientation
on her part. Treuhaft said he believed that Thomas Emerson, who was a
friend of his, may have told Hillary of the position. "My law firm was
called a left-wing firm, a 'movement' law firm," Treuhaft commented.
"All I can say is some people would have been bothered by being associated with my law firm, and she wasn't." (Hillary's involvement with the
firm wasn't made public until *San Francisco Chronicle* columnist Herb

Caen mentioned it in a column shortly after Clinton was elected president in 1992.)

If there were three kinds of activists at Yale, the mainstream liberal, the radical, and the yippie (a politically committed hippie), Hillary was somewhere on the continuum between mainstream liberal and radical. As her willingness to work for Treuhaft showed, Hillary took her moral bearings from the radicals, while favoring establishment tactics—precisely the formulation she had told Saul Alinsky would be most effective. This enabled her to work within the mainstream and to retain the respect and admiration of those in power. She was always "careful not to stray," said Robert Borosage. "For example, the yippies erected an air balloon tent on campus and lived in it. She wasn't a part of that. She probably had a sense that that was a politics that wouldn't work."

Though the staff of the *Review* usually marched in ideological solidarity, there was a major controversy over an article written by James Blumstein, one of the cofounders of the journal. Blumstein proposed that "large numbers of people [migrate] to a single state for the express purpose of affecting the peaceful political takeover of that state through the elective process. . . . Experimentation with drugs, sex, individual lifestyles or radical rhetoric and action within the larger society is an insufficient alternative. Total experimentation is necessary. New ideas and values must be taken out of heads and transformed into reality." In a reprise of her disagreement with Alinsky, Hillary opposed running the piece on the grounds that its radical stance might alienate potential converts to the student movement, according to a former editor of the *Yale Review*. She may also have been put off by the countercultural references to experimentation with drugs and sex: the hippie drug culture and the sexual permissiveness of the time were never part of Hillary Rodham's political commitment—another reason why her brand of "establishment" radicalism has consistently eluded definition.

Professor Guido Calabresi remembered Hillary taking the lead in protecting a campus library after it had been targeted by demonstrators and partially destroyed by fire. Some believed that the fire was set by radicals in retaliation for law school dean Louis Pollak's failure to support the Black Panther cause. But in another case, Hillary revealed her radical sympathies. Though she would probably not have employed the tactics herself, Hillary seemed willing to forgive an assault on the academic freedom of Eugene Rostow, a former Yale Law School dean known as a Democrat who supported a strong defense policy. Rostow returned to Yale in 1970 after a stint as Undersecretary of State for Political Affairs in the Johnson administration at the height of the Vietnam War. His campus office was broken into and vandalized soon after his return.

"A number of us identified with the anti-war movement, including Hillary, were considering going to Rostow and saying even though we disagree with you on the war, this is unforgivable. Hillary took a different approach, one of our few disagreements," said one student who was very involved in campus politics with her. "She said, 'You know, I wouldn't put down those people so easily. You've got to understand the rage they feel. You know, because they are disenfranchised; they are not empowered.' She was sort of taking the position that 'Well, our real enemies are society and the establishment.' "

By the end of her first year at Yale, it was clear that Hillary abjured the in-your-face political tactics of Jerry Rubin as well as the exhibitionistic and hedonistic side of the 1960s. She was practical, pragmatic, and mainstream in her strategies, tactics, and presentation. In terms of her core convictions, however, her attraction to the free-style religiosity of Don Jones was now infused with New Left politics of a particularly radical variety. Drawn as she was to the theories bandied about by Saul Alinsky, Carl Oglesby, the Treuhafts, the Black Panthers, the Crits, and her colleagues at the *Yale Review*, in retrospect it was possible to see that Hillary drew from these experiences a belief in situational ethics and in legal rules and procedures as a function of power. Though her profile would remain that of a moderate liberal and traditionalist, only years later, and under great pressure, did this instrumentalist approach emerge to her detriment.

Owing to her commencement speech at Wellesley, Hillary Rodham had been a celebrity even before she arrived at Yale. The speech was excerpted in a *Life* magazine roundup of the notable commencement addresses of 1969, and it earned her a spot on the nationally televised Irv Kupcinet talk show. Back in Park Ridge, Paul Carlson, one of Hillary's high school history teachers, remembered tuning in to the show: "I was quite shocked when I read about her vociferous demands [at the Wellesley graduation]. . . . [T]here she was with her granny glasses, with her hair tied back in a bun, her granny outfit on, no makeup, and I turned to my mother and I said, 'My gosh, Hillary has gone radical.' "

"Hillary Rodham was a star," Michael Medved wrote in the *Sunday Times* of London during the 1992 presidential campaign. "Everyone knew about her speech [at Wellesley] and talked in reverential tones about the extraordinary wisdom and eloquence that her address had displayed."

After her first year at Yale, Hillary had established herself as a leading light in activist circles on the campus. As the academic year closed, a huge meeting of the entire law school student body convened to plan a student strike to support the Panthers at the May Day rally. Young Hillary, then only a freshman, took control of the sometimes unruly crowd and deftly moderated the discussion.

Hillary's networking beyond the confines of the Yale campus also began that spring of 1970 when civil rights lawyer Marian Wright Edelman gave a speech on the campus. Edelman had grown up in segregated South Carolina and was the first black woman admitted to the bar in Mississippi. After graduating from Yale Law School, she had married Peter Edelman, an aide to Robert F. Kennedy, who had read about Hillary in *Life* the previous summer and invited her to a national conference of young leaders sponsored by the League of Women Voters. At the conference, Hillary met a number of young political leaders, congressional staffers, and Democratic activists. She so impressed the organizers that she was invited to speak to the league's national convention the following spring. Speaking in 1970 of the political movement of the 1960s, Hillary delivered a rather remarkable call-to-arms: "Our social indictment has broadened. Where we once advocated civil rights, now we advocate a realignment of political and economic power. Where once we exposed the quality of life in the world of the South and of the ghettos, now we condemn the quality of work in factories and corporations. Where once we assaulted the exploitation of man, now we decry the destruction of nature as well."

Marian Edelman's speech at Yale in 1970 moved Hillary so much that she approached Edelman immediately afterward and asked if she could work with her that summer at the Washington Research Project (a public interest group later renamed the Children's Defense Fund). When Edelman told Hillary that she couldn't afford to hire her, Hillary applied for and obtained some grant money from Yale. In the summer of 1970, Edelman assigned Hillary to work with a Senate subcommittee, chaired by Senator Walter Mondale of Minnesota, which was studying the plight of migrant workers in labor camps. Hillary conducted field interviews for the project with migrant workers and their children, and later told friends that the experience had made an indelible impression on her.

"She knew people in Washington," Medved said. "That was one of the standards of clout in the law school. Who did you know? And how were you connected?" By the time Bill Clinton arrived on campus one year behind Hillary, "she was a standout," echoed Douglas Eakeley, a roommate of Bill's at Yale who had also been a Rhodes Scholar with him. "Bill Clinton was a relatively unknown quantity compared to Hillary Rodham upon entry to Yale Law School."

Like Hillary, Bill Clinton of Arkansas was an instantly recognizable student leader type and an apparent political soulmate. In high school, he had been president of his junior class and as a senator in Boy's Nation had shaken JFK's hand. The allure of politics drew Clinton to Georgetown University, where he was president of the freshman class. One summer he worked in the gubernatorial campaign of Democrat Frank Holt back home. The next year, he interned on Capitol Hill with Arkansas senator and chairman of the Senate Foreign Relations Committee J. William Fulbright. Fulbright had entered the Senate as a traditional southern conservative and segregationist. But by the time Clinton worked for him, he had become a liberal icon for turning against LBJ and the war in Vietnam. After his internship, Clinton, encouraged by Fulbright to seek a Rhodes Scholarship, spent two years at Oxford, a prestigious hiatus that allowed him to put on hold a notice from his draft board to serve in Vietnam. Rather than finishing his course work, he decided to return to the States to dive into politics and get a law degree. In the summer of 1970, Bill also worked in Washington, this time with Project Pursestrings, a drive to force Congress to cut off funding for the war.

In his biography *First in His Class*, David Maraniss suggests that, like Hillary, Clinton chose Yale because of its reputation for encouraging political engagement. Though he registered for classes, Bill devoted little attention to his studies and signed up with the Connecticut Senate campaign of Joseph D. Duffey, a New Politics candidate labeled a "revisionist Marxist" by Vice President Spiro Agnew. Duffey was running in one of the most closely watched races that year, which pitted him against incumbent and independent candidate Thomas J. Dodd and Republican Lowell P. Weicker, Jr. Though Duffey lost the race, he and his future wife Anne Wexler would become part of the Clintons' political network.

Bill was chiefly known on campus because of his involvement with the Duffey campaign, and for being one of the few white students who broke the racial barrier in the school cafeteria. He eagerly joined the tables of black students who had segregated themselves from their white counterparts. Given Hillary's history of tutoring in black ghettos in Chicago and Boston and militating against the segregated housing policies at Wellesley, she must have recognized in him a kindred spirit.

No one can say precisely what draws two people together. The Clintons' own public statements and those of their friends are perhaps the best evidence in attempting to discern their original attraction and intentions. In an interview with *People* magazine after he became president, Bill said he had been "genuinely afraid" of involvement with Hillary because "she was a star." Since Bill went on to a spectacular rise in elective politics, this seems hard to fathom in retrospect, but it becomes quite understandable when one appreciates the fact that he was regarded by his classmates not as a future president but as a glad-handing hillbilly in floodwater pants. "There were forty or fifty guys" at Yale who seemed better presidential material than Bill Clinton, according to classmate Richard Grande.

Though Clinton had a certain raw political talent that everyone recognized, he seemed overeager and unrefined. "He talked to anybody who would listen about his plans to run for office, and there was a certain amount of humor in that," Michael Medved commented. "Because everybody knew that if you go to Yale Law School that you knew a certain number of your classmates are going to be senators, governors, and congressmen. That's just the way it is. That's why you go to a law school like that. But it was considered rather bad form to talk about it. Bill was unabashed. You really only had to know the guy for a very brief amount of time before the conversation turned to his political future."

For anyone with Bill Clinton's driving ambition, Yale Law School would be a critical springboard. But it was especially important for Clinton because Arkansas was neither fertile ground for building a cadre of progressive policy intellectuals, nor could it have generated the funds necessary to back a successful presidential drive. Thus Yale served as a second home base. An October 1993 article in the *Los Angeles Times* reported that one committee alone of Yale Law alumni raised $2.5 million for the Clinton campaign in 1992.

Yet this progressive Yale milieu was much more to Hillary's taste than

Bill's. "She was much more into the anti-war causes than Bill," Robert Borosage recalled. "You have to remember that at the time the protest movement was where the action was," said another friend of the couple. "If you were politically ambitious, the peace marches were the place to be. And she was more committed than he was, through her involvement with the Panthers and the anti-war movement. He was a networker and she was part of his networking, and vice versa."

Among those on the Yale scene were Rhodes Scholar Robert Reich; Strobe Talbott, another Rhodes alum and future *Time* writer; and Lani Guinier, the future civil rights scholar. Among these politically committed Ivy Leaguers, Hillary was the authentic item, but Bill was a pretender from the Arkansas backwoods. She was thus the means by which he could gain entree to campus activist circles, and he surely recognized the status, respect, and gravitas that involvement with Hillary Rodham would confer. "Going back to high school, she was probably considered to be marked for success," said Jerome Hafter, an associate editor of the *Yale Law Journal* and director of Yale's moot court. "He could have ended up selling insurance in Hot Springs."

Bill may have also been drawn to Hillary's genuineness and reliability. "Hillary, unlike some students, was able to rise above the competitive nature of the law school and be supportive of people around her. Law school is a difficult time for most people. . . . She was a very supportive person," said her classmate Robert Pozen. Another student, Gilbert Rotkin, who was from an adjoining town in the Chicago area, described how Hillary helped him at a very difficult time: "My mother had cancer, which she ultimately died of, and I didn't have any money. My father was out of work and I had the largest ever scholarship given at Yale Law School. I wasn't able to go back to Chicago and see my mother. Anyway, Hillary was able to go back a couple of times and she called my mother just as a nice gesture to see how she was and tell her how I was doing, because as I say I didn't have the money even to make phone calls from New Haven. She was kind enough to call my mother and my father and just tell them I was doing okay."

For her part, Hillary has been quoted as saying that she was attracted to Bill Clinton because he was the only fellow in law school who "was not threatened by me." This suggests what Hillary may have found most seductive about Bill: he seemed to be a prototypical "new man" of the early 1970s. The impression of Clinton's sensitivity, which stemmed from his personal insecurities, dated back at least to high school, where rather than play on the football team—a rite of passage for males, especially in the South—Bill had been an overweight band boy. Warm, gregarious, appreciative, and ingratiating, with his long hair and scraggly beard, Bill was the opposite in every way of Hillary's father Hugh, who was a cold, demanding man's man with a military record and an austere demeanor. In marked contrast to her father, Bill also had a disarming and no doubt powerfully seductive habit of lavishing sincere public praise on Hillary. He also may have represented to her the fulfillment of a new ideal of marriage envisaged by the members of their liberal activist cohort. As Hillary likely saw it, Bill was someone who would listen to a woman's views, treat her as an equal, and share her political ideals on issues ranging from Vietnam to civil rights to women's liberation. Theirs could be a new kind of relationship—a truly equal partnership combining personal and political commitments. She evidently didn't see the ersatz quality of his appeal that many other classmates, especially men, picked up on.

Allowing for the sort of embellishment couples sometimes employ to romanticize their first meeting, the official account by the Clintons supports the "new man" theory as it shows Hillary to be in an equal, if not dominant, position. As the story goes, Bill and Hillary eyed one another for several awkward minutes at the Law School library before Hillary came over, introduced herself, and asked his name. With Hillary cast as direct and focused, and Bill appearing passive and unsure, the scene presents an intriguing reversal of traditional sex roles.

If Bill needed Hillary, she had her own insecurities. By the time of this first meeting, Bill had broken not a few hearts in Arkansas, Washington, D.C., and London, and he was casually dating during his early months at Yale. Much less experienced in the world of dating, Hillary was not the type to get invited to the campus "Drink Until the Keg Runs Dry" parties or skinny-dipping outings. "She was like a den mother to all the guys," Michael Medved said. "She was not somebody who was considered date bait, because of her weight and her presentation. She was not a glamorous figure by any stretch of the imagination. She was everybody's best friend." This being so, Hillary must have found the attention from Bill intoxicating. One might also say that Bill's gregarious, extroverted nature served not just to complement her socially—taking the edge off

Hillary's sometimes cool and abrasive demeanor—but to "complete" her in a political sense, forging a new and remarkably effective symbiosis.

Medved remembered seeing Bill and Hillary together soon after they began dating that spring of 1970. He attributed their attraction not only to physical desire but to a mutual desire to change the world. He described his first impression of their romance:

"I was walking back from a movie when I ran into Hillary on the street. She was walking with Bill. It startled me to see the two of them together and so obviously in love, since Hillary had been so solid, sweet and substantive and Bill had generally struck me, despite his eating achievements, as such a lightweight. Nevertheless, there they were, basking in each other's admiration, taking pride in their mutual possession.

She called me aside and it was like she was so proud to be with Bill Clinton. She was so proud of him. . . . It struck me that these two had real physical chemistry. These two people unequivocally had the hots for each other. She was so in love. It was so painfully obvious and he looked like he had just swallowed the canary. He was so pleased with himself. And I remember him leaning back and Hillary taking me aside and talking to me and the whole point of the conversation was, "Look at this. I'm in love. I am happy and I have got this great guy who is going to change the whole world."[5]

In Bill's second and Hillary's third year at school, the couple moved into an apartment near campus. "One image I have of Hillary is she invited me and my friend over to her apartment for dinner to meet her new boyfriend at the beginning of the third year of law school," a female Yale Law School colleague remembered. "They seemed to be very happy together. It was very much 'I met this fantastic guy and I'm moving in with him.' It was a very immediate thing. I don't remember her sappy, sweet, or gushy, but I do remember her as kind of having instantly fallen in love with him." Soon after Hillary began living with Bill, she made a professional and financial sacrifice for his sake—the first of many. She chose not to graduate with her class in the spring of 1972 and begin her own career, but rather stayed at Yale for another year so they could continue to live together and graduate in 1973.

Not one to let grass grow under her feet, Hillary used the extra time to take additional courses at Yale's child study center and to work with the child psychologist Joseph Goldstein, Hillary's family law professor, who was collaborating with Anna Freud and Albert Solnit on their book *Beyond the Best Interests of the Child.* The book described the inadequacies of the court system in dealing with child abuse cases and argued that the legal presumption that a "child's parents are generally best suited to represent and safeguard his interests" should be reversed in favor of status for the child "as a person in his own right." Marian Wright Edelman also helped arrange a part-time job at the Carnegie Council on Children where Hillary assisted Kenneth Keniston on another book, *All Our Children,* in which he recommended giving children the right to make decisions about health care, schooling, and employment even over parental opposition.

Bill and Hillary were soon recognized as a power couple, playing off one another's strengths. Hillary was the better student and sometimes tutored Bill, who managed to do well enough in the final exams even for the classes he skipped, due to a virtually photographic memory. Although the school graded on a pass-fail basis, according to David Maraniss, Professor Thomas Emerson kept a private list of grades for his course. Hillary got one of the highest grades in the class, a 78, while Bill got an average 70. "Hillary was very, very bright," said Guido Calabresi, then a professor at Yale. "But in a totally different way. She is much more of a traditional kind of lawyer's mind—quick, you know, a little brittle. One can describe it [the difference between them] a little bit like the difference between taking a cold shower and a hot bath. Bill is much more a kind of all-encompassing intelligence, with a great deal of originality, and I associate it with a hot bath. And Hillary is more of a cold shower, just directly to the point, stimulating, and so on. So that in a way, while he is very smart, hers is the kind of intelligence that one sees more in a law school."

In teaming up for the Thomas Swan Barrister's Union Prize Trial, Bill and Hillary displayed the dynamics of their future political partnership. Pairs of students worked in tandem, arguing in mock trials before a visiting celebrity judge and a jury drawn from students and the New Haven community. One could clearly see what made the couple an unusually effective team: Hillary studiously did the pre-trial preparation, while Bill did the talking in the courtroom.

They also networked with fellow students and especially with faculty members like Burke Marshall, who had connections beyond the campus.

Marshall had been a Washington lawyer and assistant attorney general for civil rights in the Kennedy administration before joining the Yale faculty, where he wrote a book on civil rights and was one of the editors of a book on the Vietnam War entitled *The My Lai Massacre and Its Cover-up.* A Kennedy family intimate, he had been one of the first people summoned after the Chappaquiddick incident. Marshall would soon recommend both Bill and Hillary to his protégés in Washington for jobs as lawyers on the House Watergate Committee.

In *The Clintons of Arkansas,* a collection of personal reminiscences about the Clintons, Yale classmate William T. Coleman III wrote of how the ambitious pair cultivated their connections. The son of the Washington lawyer and Ford administration cabinet secretary William T. Coleman II, the younger Coleman recalled that while Bill had many more acquaintances than Hillary, she directed her energy like a laser beam on people who could help her achieve her goals. "Hillary's list of close associations was less expansive than Bill's but by far better placed, and they tended to have a more direct and profound influence on her," Coleman wrote.

In May 1972, Hillary took her concerns for the rights of children to a regional meeting in Boston which had been called by the platform committee of the Democratic National Committee. A little-noticed account in the *New York Times,* under the headline "Minority Planks Urged in Boston," told of a procession of activists—black, female, and gay—seeking revisions to the Democratic platform, which they criticized as being too conservative. Marian Wright Edelman and Senator Birch Bayh of Indiana, McGovern delegates to the convention to be held that summer in Miami Beach, presided over the session.

The Boston hearing centered on "rights, opportunities and political power," and about fifty witnesses gave testimony, including Hillary. According to the *Times* account, the Reverend Walter Fauntroy, the delegate to the U.S. House of Representatives from the District of Columbia, "served notice that blacks were expecting the massive assistance that civil rights leaders have said was drained away by the Vietnam War." Ernest O. Reaugh, leader of a national coalition of gay activists, "said homosexuals were demanding drastic changes in criminal laws and institutional procedures regarding homosexual behavior." And "Mrs. [sic] Hillary Rodham of the Yale Law School said the party must respond to a growing movement to extend civil and political rights to children."

At the age of twenty-five, Hillary had maneuvered herself into a position where she was able to share a stage at Faneuil Hall with several rising figures in the Democratic Party, including the mayors of Providence and Boston. Thus it should be no surprise that it was Hillary's political potential, as much as Bill's, that attracted notice when the two worked together in George McGovern's campaign that summer and fall. Bill helped manage the Texas operation—not an especially good assignment in a campaign that had virtually no hopes of carrying the state. While Hillary organized a voter registration drive in San Antonio.

In Texas, the pair met Betsey Wright, who had been active in the liberal wing of the state's Democratic Party. Wright believed that women would restore a sense of ethics to American politics, and she thought Hillary would lead the movement. "I was less interested in Bill's political future than Hillary's," Wright told Clinton biographer David Maraniss. "I was obsessed with how far Hillary might go, with her mixture of brilliance, ambition, and self-assuredness. There was an assumption about all the incredible things she could do in the world."

At the point when Wright met them, Bill and Hillary were on an equal footing and following a similar path. Had Hillary not followed Bill to Arkansas, Wright believed, it was possible to imagine her having had a career in elective politics as a governor, senator, even president. "I was disappointed when they married," Wright later told *Vanity Fair*. "I had images in my mind that she could be the first woman president." After the McGovern campaign, Wright went to work for the National Women's Political Caucus, a "point from which she dreamed of helping Rodham begin a long march to the White House," Maraniss wrote. Hillary and Betsey Wright would end up working together again in politics a decade later, though not quite in the trail-blazing way Wright had once envisaged.

3

Love and Squalor

In spring of 1973, a few months before graduation, Bill brought Hillary home to Arkansas for the first time, and they both took the bar exam. Though was a clear sign that the couple was considering settling down together in Bill's home state, Hillary's first reaction to Arkansas was not promising. Clinton took her to see his friends Paul and Mary Lee Fray, at whose wedding Bill had been best man. When the two drove up to the dilapidated apartment house north of Little Rock where the Frays were living, Hillary wouldn't leave the car until Bill talked her into it. At least, that was how the Frays themselves interpreted the scene. Of course, Hillary's reluctance to meet Bill's friends may have been more the result of strains between the couple after their long drive. But the Frays' reaction was indicative of the view that most Arkansans would adopt of Hillary as standoffish and insultingly fastidious.

Their next stop, to see Clinton's mother in Hot Springs, was even less auspicious. By most measures, Virginia Kelley and Hillary Rodham were opposites. Virginia spent hours every morning plying her face with heavy makeup; Hillary wore none. Virginia smoked, drank, gambled, and slept around; Hillary didn't. Virginia geared her life toward pleasing her men and making a home; Hillary was, in the jargon of the day, liberated. "Hillary stopped by our house first after a long trip and she didn't even wash up before going over to Virginia's," Mary Lee Fray recalled. "The reception wasn't very good."

When they graduated a few months later, Hillary decided to stay in New England and pursue her commitment to public interest law by taking a job at the Children's Defense Fund office in Cambridge. Bill headed home to Arkansas to teach at the University of Arkansas Law School in Fayetteville, a college town nestled in the Ozark Mountains. Bill's friend Paul Fray, five years his senior, was already advising him on a future in politics. A wily operative who called Bill "the boy," Fray had met Bill during the 1966 gubernatorial campaign of Frank Holt, the candidate of segregationist governor Orval Faubus's Democratic machine. Fray had been president of the Young Democrats at Ouachita Baptist University in Arkadelphia, where he met Bob Riley, who was then the head of the political science department. Fray managed Riley's 1971 run for lieutenant governor and then served as his chief of staff. Riley was also a mentor of the Clintons' future Whitewater partner Jim McDougal, whom he had hired to teach at Ouachita in the mid-1960s. McDougal, in turn, hired Mary Lee Fray to work in the Little Rock office of Senator Fulbright when he later managed it in the late 1960s.

Knowing the ropes of Arkansas politics, Fray advised Clinton that the state's premier law school, the main training ground for the political establishment, was the perfect launching pad for a young politician. Fray foresaw that the offspring of the state's elite would be a readymade source of campaign volunteers, and their parents, in turn, might open their checkbooks and come forward with endorsements if they received favorable word from their children.

Since Bill's uncle Raymond Clinton, the brother of his deceased stepfather Roger, was a political wheelhorse in Hot Springs, Bill might have easily won a seat in the state senate from that area. But Clinton aimed for the U.S. congressional seat in the third district, which encompassed his hometown of Hot Springs; the university town of Fayetteville; the conservative enclave of Fort Smith, which housed a military installation at Fort Chaffee; and Springdale, the bustling industrial center where Tyson Foods and Wal-Mart were based. Though the district was 85 percent Democrat, it was very conservative. George Wallace carried it in 1968 (as he did the whole state), and Richard Nixon took 70 percent of the vote there against George McGovern in 1972. Since 1966, the district had been represented by John Paul Hammerschmidt, the first Arkansas Republican elected to Congress in one hundred years. The popular, constituent-oriented Hammerschmidt, who had won reelection in 1972 with a commanding majority, was thought to be entrenched in office.[1]

In early 1974, Bill Clinton was convinced that if he could just win the Democratic primary, Hammerschmidt would be fatally wounded by his association with President Nixon, who was under public pressure to resign his office because of the Watergate scandal. Influencing Bill's political analysis from behind the scenes had to be Hillary, who had left the Children's Defense Fund after only a few months in January 1974 to join the Washington staff of the House committee preparing Nixon's impeachment.

For Hillary, landing a plum position on the Watergate Committee meant vaulting over her peers onto a very fast track through the ranks of the political establishment and winning a front-row seat at the defining event of her time. For Bill and Hillary's generation, Watergate was not just an unprecedented legal and political battle but a moral crusade. At age twenty-six, Hillary had been given the power to collect and weigh the evidence of crimes potentially committed by a sitting president who was routinely likened to Adolf Hitler by her friends, mentors, the national Democratic Party, and partisans in the press. Joining this elite corps of lawyers was the premier credential of the era for an aspiring Democratic lawyer and political activist.[2]

John Doar, the committee's top lawyer, first met Hillary when she invited him to Yale to judge the Barrister's Union prize trials. She was recommended to him for the Watergate job by Professor Burke Marshall, whom Hillary had courted through Peter Edelman. Marshall recommended Bill for a position on the committee as well, but he was preparing for his congressional race in Fayetteville.

Doar, a liberal Republican with political roots in Wisconsin, was another morally self-assured mentor of Hillary's. A civil rights lawyer under Burke Marshall in the Kennedy Justice Department, Doar was described in a May 1974 *Newsweek* profile as "a Gary Cooper-like figure who walked on countless marches through the South, shared a room with James Meredith at Ole Miss and helped shoulder George Wallace out of a University of Alabama schoolhouse door in 1963. When Medgar Evers, the black civil rights activist, was murdered that year, Doar walked into the no man's land between a group of white cops and an angry black mob in Jackson, Mississippi and talked a riot out of happening. 'My name is John Doar, D-O-A-R. I'm from the Justice Department, and anybody around here knows I stand for what is right.' " Doar left the Johnson administration in 1967 to work on Robert F. Kennedy's urban renewal project in the Bedford-Stuyvesant section of Brooklyn, where he remained until being named head of the impeachment committee staff.

While Watergate special prosecutor Leon Jaworski carefully assembled his grand jury case against the president's men, the congressional special committee staff—hired by the Democrats in the House of Representatives—was criticized by some as a partisan operation flying under neutral colors. Since the Kennedys were viewed by the public as enemies of Nixon, their connection to the inquiry, through Marshall and Doar, seemed to place in question Doar's assurances of political independence. To allay these concerns, Doar informed Congress that each prospective staffer was asked whether he or she had taken a position on whether Nixon should be impeached before being hired. If the lawyer had a preconceived opinion, Doar said, he or she was eliminated from consideration.

Throughout the spring of 1974, Doar repeatedly and defensively claimed that he and his staff were neutral with respect to Nixon's guilt or innocence. Only later was it revealed that Doar had begun the inquiry with the specific goal of impeaching Nixon. In a little-noticed article published in 1976 in the *Atlantic Monthly*, Renata Adler, a member of an informal group of Doar advisers, revealed that months before Doar was named to head the inquiry, he and his "ad hoc irregulars"—five to seven friends who did "the real work" of the Watergate Committee, according to Adler—had already reached a verdict. While Doar was special counsel, Adler reported, he referred to the inquiry as "war" and "the cause."

On its face, Doar's stated intention of hiring independent lawyers was hard to square with Hillary's bona fides as an ex-McGovern campaign worker and anti-war activist. But given Doar's own political predisposition, the appointment of Hillary Rodham at Burke Marshall's recommendation made perfect sense. Doar "got these highly political people," but expected them to put ideology aside, said Jeff Banchero, a committee colleague of Hillary's. Though the staff was under orders not to discuss politics in the office while the committee's work progressed, the lawyers at the center of the political action naturally couldn't help themselves. Richard Gill, a lawyer on the committee, recalled, "I was more conservative than [Hillary] was. We used to laugh about it. You know, she would call me a right-wing kook and I'd call her a pinko because . . . she certainly had a more liberal view."

Hillary, exercising real power for the first time, soon emerged as one of the most radical of the forty-three warriors on Doar's legal staff. In Hillary, the activist view of law as a function of power seemed to have translated into a willingness to manipulate the bureaucratic setting and legal process of the Watergate Committee in the service of her strong moral biases.

According to Tom Bell, who shared an office with her during the inquiry, Hillary thought Nixon was "evil," an opinion that Bell, who had voted for McGovern in 1972, shared. According to Bell, Hillary believed that Nixon should be prosecuted or impeached not just over Watergate but over his conduct during the Vietnam War, specifically his order for the secret bombing in Cambodia.

"I think that she saw it from the perspective of the McGovern campaign and the war in Vietnam," said Bell. "She felt that he had done things that were illegal in Vietnam. And the reason I remember that is because . . . she couldn't sell that to me, and by that I mean it didn't make any difference. He wasn't going to be impeached or not impeached because of what he did in Vietnam." When one of Nixon's men was acquitted on a perjury charge, Hillary revealed her emotion and partisanship in cursing the legal process that had produced the verdict. Bell recalled that she became "upset . . . that they were all going to get off." To her it may have been more of a mission. In a figurative sense, Hillary was taking Jerry Rubin's injunction to "Fuck Nixon" to its logical extreme.

By the time the Doar staff was appointed, White House aides H. R. Haldeman and John Ehrlichman had resigned; White House counsel John Dean had accused Nixon of participating in a cover-up in sensational Senate testimony; special prosecutor Archibald Cox had been fired in the Saturday Night Massacre (only to be replaced by Jaworski); and Nixon, citing executive privilege, was refusing to comply with a court order to turn over the subpoenaed Watergate tapes containing evidence of the White House cover-up.

While working for the Watergate committee, Hillary rented a room in the house of her friend Sara Ehrman, whom Hillary had met when they both worked on the McGovern campaign. Every morning that winter and spring, Hillary left Ehrman's Dupont Circle town house at dawn to begin her eighteen-hour days in the Watergate Committee's makeshift offices in the old Congressional Hotel on Capitol Hill. Security at the hotel was tight—prison bars covered the windows of the old building, thick steel locks were put on the doors, and motion detectors kept watch over the document rooms. The staff was analyzing the tapes, documents, and diaries the Judiciary Committee received from Sam Ervin's Senate committee, after they dribbled out of the White House.

Hillary's work involved her in two important projects. Under the direction of Bernard W. Nussbaum, another Kennedy Justice Department lawyer, she was responsible for drawing up highly restrictive rules of procedure that were to govern the impeachment process. The rules were a source of bitter contention within the House Judiciary Committee (also known as the Watergate Committee), of which the Doar staff was an adjunct. The committee's general counsel, Jerry Zeifman, believed that Doar and his lieutenants were drafting the rules to enhance their power at the expense of the Judiciary Committee. As Zeifman wrote in his recently published book *Without Honor,* "Nussbaum and Rodham espoused such arcane procedures as obtaining gag orders from the courts to restrict members of the Judiciary Committee from disclosing the contents of documentary evidence; denying the president representation by counsel; prohibiting committee members from hearing any testimony from live witnesses or participating in any form of cross-examination; and denying committee members the power to draft or amend articles of impeachment—leaving such power solely to Doar and the impeachment inquiry staff." Zeifman also charged that the Doar staff had lied to him about the procedures as they were being drawn up. The staff was "unworthy of either public or private trust," he concluded.[3]

Zeifman was fighting for more than bureaucratic control of the investigation. He believed that keeping Judiciary Committee members and staff in the dark about the progress of the investigation was a deliberate scheme to transfer to the impeachment inquiry staff impeachment power, which the Constitution gives to the House. Rigging the rules purely for strategic advantage, moreover, made the process fundamentally unfair to the accused. Zeifman's concerns about the aggressive tactics, obsessive secrecy, and bitter partisanship of the Doar staff were reflected in contemporaneous diary entries, portions of which he later published in his book. "I am incensed with Doar and some of his top assistants, such as Joe Woods and Hillary Rodham. It seems to me that Haldeman and Ehrlichman are crude amateurs at arrogance in comparison to the more polished and sophisticated arrogance and deceit of some of Doar's assistants," Zeifman wrote at the time.

Hillary's second project was to oversee the preparation of a confidential history of presidential abuse of power—drafted under the direction of the Yale historian C. Vann Woodward, a colleague of Burke Marshall's—that was kept from the committee members and staff. It was expected that Nixon would mount a defense to the effect that actions in the Watergate affair were not inconsistent with those of many previous administrations. So Vann Woodward, Hillary, and twelve legal scholars went to work on a brief that, while presented as objective legal scholarship evenly weighing the precedents on both sides, was attacked by Nixon supporters for calculatedly omitting many well-established presidential abuses of authority, which might have refuted their conclusion that Nixon had committed the most outrageous abuse of power in American history. "Professor Woodward's study survives . . . as a sad example of academic expertise marshaled for political purposes," wrote former Nixon White House counsel Leonard Garment in a 1986 article in *Commentary* on the political effects of Watergate. "It is a compendium of presidential wrongdoing that manages to pass over a large number of established abuses of power, including Attorney General Robert Kennedy's authorization of the FBI's wiretapping of Martin Luther King's hotel rooms. It omits altogether Lyndon Johnson's use of odious King materials, his taping of the Mississippi Freedom Democratic party during the 1964 Democratic convention, and his spying on Richard Nixon's 1968 presidential campaign for alleged national security purposes."[4] To omit discussion of evidence that would contradict one's own hypothesis is a breach of the scholarly integrity lawyers are expected to bring to their briefs. Though commonplace for editorial writers, partisan polemics, or low-level adversarial lawyering, the tactic is usually disdained at this high level of legal practice.

When the Nixon tapes began to be made available in the spring of 1974, the committee staff concluded that impeachment was inevitable. The tapes were removed from under lock and key in a safe in Doar's office, and transcribed by committee lawyers, who listened with headphones in a special soundproof room. Sometimes John Dean came by to help with the transcriptions. Hillary listened intently, particularly to the so-called tape of tapes, in which Nixon taped himself as he listened to conversations with Haldeman and Ehrlichman, which he had recorded in secret, and tried to explain away what they had discussed. "You would hear him say, 'What I meant when I said that was . . .' I mean it was surreal, unbelievable," as Hillary described it in an interview years later. "[Nixon] is a person who is flawed. You can't place yourself above the law even if you think it is for moral or historical reasons."[5] Hillary's stern judgment here is notable in that it seems to contradict the view of law as an instrument of political power advanced by Saul Alinsky and some Yale legal theorists. The contradiction is only apparent, however. For in the view of these activists, and (as will shortly become clear) of Hillary as well, the procedural constraints of liberal democracy need only apply to those who are not to be trusted with power.

One of three women on the staff, Hillary quickly established herself as a Doar favorite. As a result, she had access to the confidential executive sessions of the full Judiciary Committee as one of the very few staffers who accompanied Doar to the confidential executive sessions in May and June where he argued that Nixon should be impeached on grounds of obstruction of justice, abuse of power, and contempt of Congress. She worked with another committee lawyer on an analysis of the decision-making process within the White House, basing her findings on the tapes, which enabled her to trace the cover-up to the Oval Office before Nixon's fate was sealed.

That spring Hillary raised more than a few eyebrows when she arranged for Bill to tour the secure committee offices. "[W]e had a fairly secure work space and I recall only . . . that one evening he was in town and she brought him in and he was actually allowed in, which was kind of a rarity," said John Labovitz, a staff lawyer. "[H]e was kind of going around meeting and greeting in an almost political way, which was in that context, given the security concerns we had . . . rather unusual." Hillary had already spoken to her colleagues about Bill's race for Congress and his ultimate designs on the presidency. "You know, Bernie Nussbaum tells a story . . . about how he used to give her a ride home," Labovitz said. "She would talk about her boyfriend Bill and Bernie would say things like, 'What's going to happen? What is he going to do?' And she said, 'He's going to be president.' And Bernie thought, 'What kind of horseshit is this?'" Tom Bell did not read too much into Hillary's comments, either: "I just remember that she said that on one or two occasions [that Bill would become president some day] and I just kind of rolled my eyes. . . . Well, she was in love with the guy, you know."

Information from Hillary seems to have been the source of Bill's conviction that it would be possible to defeat Republican Hammerschmidt, a die-hard Nixon loyalist. It also helped him gauge how to play the sensitive issue in the district. The Frays, who by this time had moved to Fayetteville at Bill's behest to manage his campaign and were temporarily living with him, remembered hearing news from Bill about the Watergate inquiry that went well beyond what they knew from the press.

Clinton was careful to soft-pedal the issue in the more conservative areas of the district. "The people of this country do not perceive Watergate as completely a party problem. One man could not have created all the trouble we have in the country today," Clinton said in one typical speech. But he took the opposite tack on the Fayetteville campus. Describing a campus panel discussion in which Clinton participated, law student David Matthews wrote in the Arkansas Law School's alumni magazine: "Those attending that panel discussion were immediately impressed with the fierceness of Clinton's belief that the presidency and America's constitutional system of laws was at peril during this unique time. Clinton later took those same concerns and his perspective on the constitutional threat facing our nation to many civic clubs and organizations throughout the Northwest Arkansas area. Students would hear him refer to the concerns of 'friends' of his who were staffing the House Judiciary Committee. Only after the constitutional crisis had passed did the students learn that his 'friend' was Hillary Rodham."

While Hillary was in Washington waging war against political corruption, Bill was learning to master the politics of his home state, where the corrupt mixing of public and private interests was the coin of the realm. Public office was routinely used for private gain, and private interests routinely bought favors from public officials. Elections themselves were compromised: In the northwest Arkansas district where Clinton was running, paper ballot boxes could be stuffed or dumped in the river for $250. Since many people didn't have checking accounts, contributions were made in cash and often disappeared. In the Fort Smith area of the district Clinton was running in, there were more than 10,000 black votes, all of them essentially for sale.

The power broker in the third congressional district was Don Tyson, who was well on his way to owning the biggest family chicken farm in the world. Clinton was introduced to Tyson by Billie Schneider, a gap-toothed, chain-smoking, three-hundred-pound woman who ran the Gas Lite, a local bar in town, as well as a roadside steakhouse on the way to Springdale where Tyson's headquarters was based. Local eccentric though she was, Schneider was an important member of the third district's old guard, and her bar was the major political listening post in the region. Any night of the week, one might find Tyson, accompanied by two of his hangers-on, at the Gas Lite eating two-inch steaks, drinking beer, and making ridiculously large cash bets.

Tyson appears to have first met Clinton that spring at a private fund-raiser thrown for him by Schneider at her steakhouse. "Tyson didn't come for Clinton, he came because Billie asked him to," recalled Neal McDonald, who was Fayetteville campus coordinator for the campaign. Tyson's support meant not only the assurance of personal contributions from him and his family but also contributions funneled through Tyson employees and use of the Tyson plane. "He [Bill] would arrange for the plane through Billie," McDonald said. Don's brother Randal spent time at Clinton's Fayetteville headquarters and underwrote the campaign's phone bank. Bill appears to have amply returned these favors. In 1974, when Tyson failed to turn a profit and blamed U.S. sales of subsidized grain to the Soviet Union, which were driving up the price of chicken feed, Clinton campaigned against the U.S.-Soviet grain deal.

Clinton's main opponent in the Democratic primary was a state senator from Fort Smith named Gene Rainwater, who enjoyed the support of organized labor, the key to raising money in the primary. Clinton surprised political observers by winning labor's endorsement after a personal interview in which the bushy-haired law professor convinced labor leaders that Hammerschmidt could be beaten by tying him to Nixon.

After winning a runoff in June with Rainwater, Clinton ran on a general election platform designed by Paul Fray to appeal to the varied constituents who comprised the vote in the third district—from chicken farmers to retired military people to college students. In contrast to Hammerschmidt, who was heir to a timber fortune, Fray positioned Clinton within the state's populist tradition: He called for ending deficit spending, cutting foreign aid, and imposing a new income tax on big corporations.

Hammerschmidt, a war veteran, served on the House Veterans Affairs Committee, where he tended to the needs of the military retirees near Fort Smith. Despite his history of anti-war protest at Yale and Oxford, Bill said virtually nothing about the military or the Vietnam War (which Hammerschmidt supported). "The strategy was to wall off Fort Smith. He did not want to get into the posture of having to answer about his military record," said Paul Fray, to whom Clinton had confided his efforts to evade the draft in 1969.

The big break in the Watergate case came in July, when the Supreme Court handed down its decision in the Nixon tapes case. Clinton quickly called for Nixon's resignation, though Hammerschmidt refused to do so. The House Judiciary Committee began debate on five articles of impeachment. Three articles were accepted and two were rejected, including one on the Cambodia bombing. On August 9, 1974, Nixon resigned. "I remember Bill getting a call from Hillary before Nixon resigned [telling him of Nixon's decision]," Paul Fray said. "He'd been talking about Hillary for months, about how she had the finest mind he'd ever been exposed to, in a woman, because [Senator J. William] Fulbright was the exception. She could be a U.S. senator, stuff like that. Anyway, I told him he better bring her down here. And he said, 'I don't want her down here.' He had three girls down here at the time."

As a young lawyer fresh out of the Watergate Committee, Hillary could have written her own ticket. She had already interviewed with Washington super-lawyer Edward Bennett Williams of the prestigious Williams & Connolly law firm and had received every indication that a position was hers for the asking. Many of her Watergate colleagues went this route, including Richard Ben-Veniste, an associate prosecutor on the Jaworski staff, and James Hamilton, deputy counsel to the Senate Watergate Committee. Others, like William Weld, the future governor of Massachusetts, returned to their home states and pursued careers in elective politics.

Hillary, however, was committed to public interest law. She had never wanted to work in a major corporate law firm, nor did she have the desire to return home to Illinois to begin building a political base for elective office, as Bill had done. In fact, months before Nixon's resignation, Hillary had begun making plans to join Bill in Fayetteville, where she could teach at the university and help out in his campaign. On a trip to Arkansas earlier in the year, she interviewed for a teaching job at the law school and was given an offer for the 1974 fall term that she was now ready to accept. Sara Ehrman told friends that she had come home one August evening to find Hillary packing her bags. When Ehrman asked where she was going, Hillary had said "I'm going to Arkansas to marry Bill Clinton." Ehrman asked if Bill knew this. "Not yet," came the reply. Ehrman tried to talk her out of moving to Arkansas, but Hillary had made up her mind.

By choosing to live in Fayetteville, Hillary knew she was stepping off the fast track—but only for a moment. Though she told friends of her reservations about Arkansas, both she and Bill firmly believed that he would win the congressional race, which meant that they might marry and she could be heading back to Washington for a high-profile career in law and political activism in as little as six months. Perhaps she would join Williams & Connolly after all, or more likely, return to public interest law with the Children's Defense Fund while Bill served in Congress.

Immediately upon her arrival in Fayetteville, Hillary turned her attention to the race, helping Bill find his political voice and encouraging him to condemn the Republicans in moral terms. Hillary's influence was critical in shaping Bill's profile as a young, idealistic candidate representing the forces of political change.

As Bill and his staff planned his attendance at the Democratic state convention in Hot Springs, it became evident that Hillary Rodham had imported her sense of political mission to Arkansas. When Hillary arrived, "Clinton intensified his denunciation of corruption, arrogance and abuse of power at the hands of Republicans," according to *Arkansas Democrat* reporter Meredith Oakley. At the state convention, Clinton denounced Hammerschmidt as "one of the strongest supporters of, and apologists for, the abuse of presidential power and policies that have wrecked the economy," as Oakley quoted him. He praised Democrats for "protecting the American people from virtual dictatorship."

President Gerald Ford's pardon of Nixon that fall added more fuel to the fire. "I recall overhearing both of them cursing the 'Nazis' in Fort

Smith," said Erwin Davis, a lawyer and longtime observer of state politics, whose help Clinton requested for his 1974 congressional campaign and several subsequent campaigns. "Fort Smith is a conservative factory town. Lots of Republicans, which is unusual in northwest Arkansas. And very large. The largest county in the third district. They would cuss the 'Nazis' because they knew they were big Hammerschmidt voters." Davis also recalled Hillary privately coaching Clinton. "She was instrumental in coming up with such things as 'perception is all there is,' " Davis said. "I can recall her, and I can recall Bill [repeating] on a number of occasions, 'perception is all there is.' "

Bill Morse, a local politician in Washington County, of which Fayetteville is the county seat, often traveled with Bill that spring and was flabbergasted when Hillary entered the picture. "I heard, not from him, that he had a fiancée that had just showed up in Fayetteville and I almost dropped dead, considering how he'd been behaving out in the county. She started going around with us. Whenever we got back in the car, she would tell him what he did wrong at the last event. She'd say, 'You need to say it like this.' I said to myself, 'That's what that girl is doing here.' "

Had Hillary known what awaited her, her decision to follow Bill to Arkansas might have been different. Seeing Bill in his own milieu, she must have gradually become aware that the pristine idealist working to change the world whom she had known at Yale also had a dark side.

The Fayetteville campus was one of the leading party schools in the South and in the desk drawers at the Clinton campaign headquarters one could find brown bottles filled with unidentified prescription pills sitting next to bottles of Jack Daniel's whiskey, according to Clinton campus coordinator Neal McDonald. The Frays recall that parties at the home of a campaign official featured illicit drugs, with syringes strewn about on tabletops and pills and marijuana in sight. Bill's younger half-brother Roger, who would later be arrested on drug charges, occasionally came to town and was observed toking away. The situation was so bad that Governor Dale Bumpers called Paul Fray seeking assurances that Clinton himself wasn't using drugs along with his campaign workers. The reformist Bumpers had just upset Senator Fulbright in the Senate race of the century, and Clinton, who was linked to the defeated senator, badly needed Bumpers' endorsement. As far as the Frays knew, Clinton wasn't personally using drugs, but they were still troubled by his apparent indifference to the rather obvious problem with his campaign workers. At a staff meeting just before Hillary's arrival, Paul Fray had voiced loud concerns about open drug use in the headquarters.

The Frays found a receptive ear for these concerns when Hillary arrived in August 1974, and Paul Fray made use of her mature presence to bring discipline to the unruly Clinton headquarters. "I used to tell the volunteers that Hillary was coming in any minute. I knew she wouldn't be there until the end of the day. It was the best way to get them to clean things up and get to work," he said.

Hillary became fast friends with Mary Lee, a native Virginian and ex-Goldwater girl. Fray's two-year-old son Robbie also took to "Miss Hillary," seeking out her company over all the other women in the headquarters. He sat on Hillary's lap for hours as she praised his artwork and read to him from the children's book, *When I Grow Up*.

Hillary, meanwhile, sought advice from Mary Lee on how to adjust to life in Arkansas. "I had to tell her that the dirt farmer who comes into the headquarters in coveralls might be a millionaire. Sam Walton [Wal-Mart's founder] drove around in an old beat-up pickup." Mary Lee also admonished Hillary that the opinions she expressed on the campaign trail had to be Bill's. Although Hillary didn't accept much of that advice at first, she must have been getting an idea of how hard it was going to be to establish the kind of equal partnership with Bill here in Arkansas that she had envisioned at Yale. Hillary was also concerned about her image. "She asked me how a wife should dress, never a girlfriend. I told her she needed to look like a southern belle. She needed to wear dresses, hose, delicate, sexy sandals, fix her hair, and wear brightly colored nail polish. She wouldn't do it. All she did was get these thick, ugly sandals with a low heel."

Hillary also looked to Mary Lee for help as she began to realize that she was competing for Bill's affections with his young female volunteers, who were totally devoted to him. Though it was no secret that Clinton had slept with many of the female volunteers in the headquarters, the women worked contentedly side by side, hanging on his every word. "My sister worked in the 'seventy-four campaign. All the college girls were in love with him. They all thought they had a shot at him," said Julia Hughes Jones, who served as state auditor during most of Clinton's governorship. In *The Grapevine*, an alternative campus newspaper, Michael Gaspeny described Clinton's troop of campus groupies: "These are the kind of people who stand in the rain at high school football games to distribute campaign leaflets. The workers are influenced by the Dexedrine-like effects of campaigning white-line fever, an inversion that naturally seizes members of a cult. The volunteers are extremely reluctant to talk about themselves. They constantly mutter the aspirant's name in hushed tones: 'Bill thinks . . . ,' 'Bill feels . . . ,' 'Bill does . . .' "

In addition to Clinton's girlfriends in the campaign, women who had met Clinton while he was on the road were calling the headquarters from all twenty-one counties in the district. "Finally I went to Paul and asked, 'What in the hell is going on?' He [Bill] had a girlfriend in every county," said Neal McDonald.

Earlier in the campaign, Hillary had dispatched her father and brother to Arkansas from Illinois, and they were put to work posting "Clinton for Congress" signs throughout the district. Hugh Rodham, who spent much of his time fly-fishing in the lakes outside Fayetteville, cut quite a figure in Bermuda shorts and a golf cap as he drove his huge Cadillac, with its Illinois plates, through the back roads of the Ozarks. McDonald, who roomed with Hugh Rodham, Jr., suspected the Rodhams were on a reconnaissance mission for Hillary. Once in town, Hillary pushed her brother to take out one of the women Bill was dating, but the ploy didn't work. While Bill was out on the campaign trail, Hillary rifled through his desk and tore up girlfriends' telephone numbers.

When Hillary sought her counsel, Mary Lee didn't know quite what to say. Unbeknownst to Hillary, one of Mary Lee's jobs in the campaign was to hide Bill's other girlfriends from Hillary. Sometimes, the women would be literally rushed out the back door of the headquarters as Hillary came in the front way. "In order to avoid complications in the office," the Frays began to keep a list of the women, whom they called Bill's "special friends."

"Hillary knew something was going on from the beginning, but she was too much of a lady to ask about it," Mary Lee said. Hillary picked up the signs that she wasn't welcome: The campaign office manager, for example, failed to reserve her a room at the state convention in Hot Springs, and Virginia Kelley wouldn't let Hillary stay at her home with Bill.

By the oblique references Hillary made to Clinton's womanizing at this time, she revealed the manner in which she was beginning to rationalize his behavior. Hillary told Mary Lee she viewed Bill's girlfriends as air-headed beauty queens who wouldn't hold a candle to her intellectually. "She thought they were all Miss Rednecks," Mary Lee said. "And she blamed us for bringing him girls, which wasn't true. I told her if she wanted to compete, she should wear some foundation, which she started doing. But she had a weight problem and she wouldn't diet. She wore these big khaki skirts and striped blouses and that wasn't changing. She didn't have a body for a dress. So I told her to at least buy some nice underclothes."

In September 1974, John Labovitz, Hillary's friend from the Watergate Committee, stopped in Fayetteville to visit her. "She was kind of agonizing about whether she really wanted to do this—that is, cast her life in Arkansas," he said. Campaign workers noticed the strain on Hillary as well. "Both she and Bill went through fits of being on the outs with each other . . . I think both of them had misgivings about whether or not heading toward a marriage with the other one was the right thing to do," Erwin Davis said. "I refereed some of their arguments. Her main problem with Bill was she was just wondering why she followed a guy down here who was just such a one-dimensional person—lives, breathes and dies with politics. I [also] recall some snippy remarks by Hillary about Bill's girlfriend or the other women that he was seeing at the time. . . . She would disappear from the campaign headquarters and be gone for days at a time. The impression I got was she was sick and tired of the whole damn thing. . . . She had a bad complexion on her face, probably out of stress from moving to Arkansas and stress from wondering whether she ought to marry Bill."

Mary Lee Fray understood Hillary's conflicted feelings about Bill as well as anyone. Early in the campaign, she was struck by the devotion with which voters—especially women—were responding to Clinton. She had never seen anything like it in politics before. "You had these women, especially older married women, getting in their cars and following him from rally to rally, just to hear him. They were listening to the same speech over and over again." In the weeks that spring when she and Paul, her son Robbie, and their newborn baby lived with Clinton in his small one-bedroom rental house on the outskirts of town, Mary Lee saw the tender side of Bill that Hillary, and perhaps even the women on the campaign trail, had been drawn to. "He would make pots of tea, which he learned to do in London, and we would stay up all hours talking politics and drinking tea. When the baby woke everyone up, he never once complained. He would put the baby to sleep on his stomach. I can't imagine any other Arkansas politician doing that."

Still, Bill could be cold and uncaring, which is how she recalled his reaction to a violent altercation between herself and another campaign staffer. Mary Lee also began to feel that Bill was taking advantage of her and her husband. Having taken a leave of absence from the university to run for Congress, Clinton, who had no income, pestered Mary Lee to call her parents back in Virginia for money, even after the Frays moved into their own apartment. "Bill couldn't keep a checkbook. He never paid his own electric bill or his phone bill. He thought I was going to cook for him and pay the grocery bill. He would promise you the world and then forget about it."

Mary Lee thought Bill was using Hillary as well, asking her to write his state convention speech and even putting her to work selling sandwiches at the convention itself to raise money for the campaign. "She had feelings," Mary Lee said. "And she was hurt that he wasn't calling her his fiancée. He never did that. Her father and brother were down here working for him. He could have paraded her around at the state convention that year, but he didn't care."

Many observers, including biographer David Maraniss, have concluded that Bill Clinton exhibits the classic traits of a child reared by an abusive, alcoholic parent: a strong desire to smooth things over and to please; near-crippling dependencies on others; a volatile temper; low self-esteem; and addictive behavior in the form of compulsive politicking and sexual activity. In a dysfunctional household, such children learn to thrive in chaos, constantly changing their own behavior to keep things in balance and trying to please everybody through manipulation and lying. Commitments are made and broken at random. In extreme cases, truth and reality mean little. Outsiders are kept at bay and deceived in a family culture of concealment.

Clinton's family background is such a thick stew of personal indecency and salacious rumor that in 1992 when people claiming to be his half-siblings began suddenly to show up on the campaign door stoop, the Clinton campaign had to hire a private detective to research the candidate's genealogy. Bill's maternal grandfather, James Eldridge Cassidy, often referred to as an "ice man" from Hope, was also the local bootlegger. Bill Blythe, a traveling salesman from Texas whom Clinton claims as his natural father, had a string of marriages—probably four—before he met Virginia. Blythe was said to have been with a different woman almost every night.

The circumstances of Bill Blythe and Virginia Cassidy's marriage and Clinton's subsequent birth remain foggy. According to Meredith Oakley in her book *On the Make,* Bill Blythe was already married to Wanetta Ellen Alexander when he married Virginia on September 1, 1943. "Court records show that he and Wanetta did not divorce until March 1944," Oakley reported. "That being the case, the marriage of Virginia Cassidy and Bill Blythe, and their son's subsequent birth in 1946, was illegal under Arkansas law."[6] David Maraniss, too, questioned whether Blythe was Bill's natural father. By Maraniss's reckoning, nine months before Bill's birth date, Bill Blythe was still serving in the military in Italy and he wouldn't arrive home in Louisiana for another month. Virginia's explanation of the seemingly odd timing was that her labor was induced "weeks ahead of schedule because she had taken a fall and the doctor was concerned about her condition."

Bill's maternal grandmother, Edith Grisham Cassidy, raised him in his formative years, while Virginia attended nursing school out of state. Virginia soon married her second husband, Roger Clinton, whose name Bill eventually took, perhaps in order to "legitimize" the new family. Though he later campaigned as "the man from Hope," Bill spent most of his youth with Virginia and Roger in Hot Springs, where gambling casinos and prostitution houses made the city a popular spot for mobsters from all over the Midwest and South. Despite Bill's claim to have grown up poor, Maraniss portrayed the Clintons as relatively well off. Bill had a car in high school, played golf, and swam at the country club. Roger managed his brother Raymond's local Buick dealership, and Virginia worked as a freelance nurse-anesthetist and was said to minister to the local call girls as well.

Virginia was a doting, defensively protective mother. In her book *Leading with My Heart,* she told of how she had taught herself mental tricks to block out the unpleasant realities of life. Her husband Roger was a gambler, a womanizer, and a drunk. When Virginia divorced him, she claimed that he had physically abused her, once throwing her to the floor, stomping on her, pulling off her shoe and hitting her on the head with it.[7] Virginia fought a losing battle to blunt the impact of her husband's abusive behavior on her family. In Hillary's book *It Takes a Village,* she later noted the deforming effect Bill's and Roger Junior's upbringing may have had on their characters. She pondered whether Roger Senior was responsible for the drug addiction of young Roger, and hinted that she held the elder Clinton responsible for Bill's infidelity. This also suggests how Hillary may have rationalized the behavior throughout their marriage as a sickness, not a moral failing.

As the congressional campaign drew to a close, rumors about drug use in the campaign and Clinton's womanizing were flying through the district. Mary Lee Fray said Baptist preachers were getting up in the pulpits on Sunday and urging churchgoers not to vote for Bill Clinton. Clinton was also rumored to have been the long-haired, bearded mystery protester who climbed up a tree and displayed an anti-Nixon poster during the president's 1969 visit to Fayetteville for an Arkansas football game. At the time of the incident Clinton was in England, but the gossip persisted.

Arkansas politics are notoriously rumor-charged, and it was only a matter of time before Hillary felt the sting of unfounded stories about herself. The rumors, emanating from the Gas Lite bar, where Don Tyson and his cronies caroused, depicted Hillary as a lesbian and likely reflected a deep-dyed cultural prejudice against a woman who didn't wear panty hose, sexy sandals, or fit the southern male's image of how a woman should behave. According to Fray, Tyson had once told him that Hillary "should keep her mouth shut." Unaccustomed to having his authority challenged by a candidate's girlfriend, Fray too may have embraced this unflattering image of Hillary as a way of both explaining her assertiveness and justifying Clinton's own profligacy. "People were talking about Hillary and women. When I got the fourth telephone call about it, I went to Bill, but he brushed it off," Paul Fray said. Fray then confronted Hillary, who cursed Fray with the kind of salty language she may have picked up in college. "She was real mad. She said, 'It's nobody's goddamn business.' Then I told her we needed to address it, that the rumors were hurting Bill. And she said, 'Fuck this shit.' And I said, 'Hillary, you can't just cuss it away.'" According to Fray, Hillary refused to dignify the coarse accusations with a denial, which only fed the rumor mill further.

That unpleasant encounter between Hillary and Fray was the product of other tensions that had been building for weeks, a classic turf battle between two headstrong personalities—the candidate's handler, who knew his way around the politics of the South, and his girlfriend from the North, who didn't. Fray viewed Hillary as an uppity, Puritanical, Ivy League women's-libber. Their cultural differences led Fray and others on the campaign staff to view the Chicagoan in their midst as arrogant and rude. "Down here, they give you the peach pie first, then they pour the acid on it. Hillary did it the opposite," Mary Lee explained.

The Frays believed that Hillary regarded Paul, her future husband's best friend, as a sticky-fingered, white-trash political hack. (Her instincts were proven justified a few years later, in 1980, when Fray was compelled by the state to surrender his law license. In a 1977 incident, he had altered a court docket for a client, changing a drunk-driving record from conviction to dismissal, accepting a $500 bribe for his trouble. Though Arkansas' board of law examiners found Fray to be of "good moral character" in a 1984 review, the Supreme Court of Arkansas did not reinstate the license.) As election day neared, Hillary's suspicions about Fray's character were being borne out. There was hushed discussion in the headquarters about accepting money from the district's dairy interests, money that could be used to buy some ballot boxes in the Hammerschmidt stronghold in Fort Smith.

"I had it wired in Fort Smith with absentee ballots," Fray recalled. "But Hillary had a glass to the door and found out about it. She had her ideals about how campaigns should be run." Sticking by her Methodist creed and abjuring Alinsky's doctrine of seizing power "by any and all means," Hillary was not about to be tainted by petty Arkansas corruption. According to Fray, she had already nixed paying street money to turn out the black vote.

The showdown came on election night, when it appeared that Clinton was losing by a narrow margin and there was still time for Fray to get down to the Fort Smith ballot boxes and perhaps throw the election in Clinton's favor. In what aides later referred to as "the hen and rooster fight," Bill, Hillary, Paul, and Mary Lee went at it behind closed doors. The out-of-staters, Hillary and Mary Lee, were dead set against breaking the law. "I had the keys to the green and gold Monte Carlo, which was the only car fast enough to get to Fort Smith in time," Mary Lee remembered. "I also had a canvas camera bag that had the cash in it that was to be used to close down the campaign. And I was physically blocking the door. I knew they'd be sorry for what they'd do. You could cheat in a state race and get away with it, but in a federal, you'd have the federal marshals in there, and Paul was going to get arrested, and I told him, 'Bill Clinton won't know you then.' "

Hillary was just as adamant. "She wasn't going to Washington on a dirty, stolen election, she made that clear," Mary Lee said.

When it became clear that Fray would not be going to Fort Smith and that Clinton would lose by fewer than 10,000 votes, the fight degenerated into screaming and mud-slinging, with recriminations all around. Telephones and books sailed across the room, smashing windows. Fray blamed Hillary, Hillary blamed Fray, and Mary Lee blamed Bill. Bill and Hillary never blamed one another, but Hillary got an earful about Bill from Mary Lee. "I threw all the trash on Bill," Mary Lee said. "The deceit started with hiding the girlfriends. This is the first time Hillary found out about a lot of things."

Though Clinton lost the race, he had captured 48.5 percent of the vote against a strong incumbent as a virtual unknown in politics with no experience. In political circles in Arkansas he was called the Boy Wonder, and he attracted notice on the national scene as a rising star in the Democratic party. Hillary must have been struck by the immaturity Bill had displayed during the campaign, yet his powerful political appeal was equally striking. Whatever impact Mary Lee's revelations may have had on her, Hillary displayed a firm resolve to carry on and forgive her boyfriend any personal foibles, confident that she and Bill complemented one another in an extraordinary way. The knowledge that he truly needed her must have provided her with an enormous sense of power and security. Early the next morning, she came into the headquarters and began to close the office down while fielding calls from reporters as far away as New York and Washington. In an article for the law school's alumni magazine, Mark Grobmeyer, a law student of both Clintons, recalled that Hillary tried to make Bill feel better by "tap[ing] a note to Bill's desk after his defeat reminding him of all of the disappointments that Abraham Lincoln went through in his life only to ultimately be elected president of the United States."

During the campaign, whether for political or personal reasons, Bill had insisted that Hillary rent her own house near campus rather than move in with him. Soon after the election, in his disappointment about his defeat and with the adoring campaign volunteers gone, he moved in with Hillary. The Frays believed he was just trying to save rent money. "He was mooching off everyone in town. He had no income and was in debt," Mary Lee said.

When the Clintons returned to teaching law the next semester, colleagues on the faculty, as well as students, soon noted their contrasting styles. Robert Leflar, a professor at the law school, remembered Hillary as "specific, definite, even hard-boiled." Nobody ever said that about Bill. In the fall of 1993, the *Arkansas Law Record* published a collection of essays about the Clintons' years at the school. "Back then, as now, people were never indifferent about Hillary; you either liked her or you didn't, but no matter what, you grew to respect her," wrote Woody Bassett, who took classes taught by Bill and Hillary and later worked in several campaigns. "Bill was the eternal lounge rat. When Bill Clinton wasn't in the classroom, he was down in the lounge shooting the breeze with students . . . Hillary was tough, intelligent, and highly articulate."

Hillary did not seem to need electoral politics to fulfill her ambitions. She acted on her fervent commitment to public interest law by teaching, starting a legal clinic at the law school, and helping establish the area's first hotline for domestic abuse and rape victims. She lobbied for a bill in the legislature that would have required judges to rule on the admissibility of a rape victim's sexual history before the information was presented to a jury. She helped establish the much-needed Cummins Prison Project and worked on a high-profile death penalty case, filing a brief with the Arkansas Supreme Court arguing that capital punishment is unconstitutional because of its arbitrary application. The brief was credited with saving the life of Henry Giles, a retarded man convicted of murder.

According to the Frays, Bill often told Hillary that if he didn't make it in politics he would go into legal services with her, but he seemed to have no discernible interests other than getting elected to office. As he restlessly planned his next political move, his students complained that he was unprepared for class and late with his grades. Once, he lost an entire stack of student exams.

Bill and Hillary also grappled with personal decisions. Bill's friends believed he had mixed motives in asking Hillary to join him in Arkansas permanently. On the one hand, Mary Lee Fray said, Bill cared deeply about Hillary and always spoke of her in a special way: "He talked about the kindness of her heart and the beauty of her eyes. He always talked about her in a way that he didn't talk about all the other girlfriends and dates."

But Mary Lee also suspected that Bill's concern for Hillary arose from his belief that she could do something for him, just as she had at Yale. "Bill was treated like a prince by Virginia, even when he was older. She would lay out the towels like a hotel. The night before she left for work, she took the sticky buns out of the freezer, and she would take the bacon out of the package and separate a few slices in a container with a paper towel, because she knew he'd leave the package out on the table and it would spoil. Bill knew he needed that routine and that balance in his life, and Hillary could provide it." Of course, it wasn't so much a homemaker as a political nanny that Bill sought. Bill must have recognized it was Hillary's contributions that enabled him, a relative unknown, to nearly beat a popular incumbent.

Bill may have seen another benefit to marrying Hillary: marriage would quell the womanizing rumors that had hurt his image with the Arkansas electorate. Bill Morse, the Washington County organizer who traveled with Clinton, said that Clinton told him in December 1975 that he was going to marry Hillary: "He realized that if he'd announced an engagement during the race, it would have helped." In the spring of 1975, on a trip to eastern Arkansas, a Clinton supporter raised the subject of his living out of wedlock with Hillary. "Not for long," Clinton shot back. The man Bill Clinton considered his main competition on the political landscape, Harvard-educated state attorney general Jim Guy Tucker—described by Rex Nelson in the *Arkansas Democrat-Gazette* as "youthful, good looking, intelligent," and even "Kennedyesque" was also planning to marry in 1975.

After the academic year ended, Hillary returned to the East Coast for a visit, where she sought the advice of several friends on whether to settle down in Arkansas permanently with Bill or pursue career opportunities in the Washington Democratic policy and legal establishment. By her own account, Hillary's uncertainty appeared to center more on her professional interests and on Arkansas rather than on Bill, whom she loved and whose possible defects as a mate she seemed prepared to take in stride. "It nearly didn't happen at all. Making the decision to get married took time for me. Bill and I had begun dating in law school, but even after things got serious, I just could not bring myself to take the leap marriage requires. I never doubted my love for him, but I knew he was go-

ing to build his life in Arkansas," Hillary later wrote in one of her syndicated columns as first lady.

Hillary's words suggest that when she returned to Arkansas, she may
not have reached a decision. Suddenly, the gawky den mother from Yale
was almost literally swept off her feet by Bill, who surprised her with his
purchase of a little stone cottage in Fayetteville and a formal proposal of
marriage. She accepted on the spot. At the last minute, Hillary and her
mother rushed out to Dillard's department store to buy a Victorian lace
wedding dress.

Launching what would later become a full-fledged political partnership, Bill and Hillary turned their October 1975 wedding into a public
event. After a ceremony by a Methodist minister at their house, hundreds
of guests attended the lawn party at the home of Ann and Morriss Henry,
Democratic political organizers in Washington County, where the talk
centered on Bill's running for office again in 1976. Hillary, however, stole
the show with an announcement of her own. She was going to keep the
name Hillary Rodham rather than take the name Clinton. That morning Bill had broken the news to Virginia, who broke into tears. He also
told Paul Fray, who warned Clinton indignantly: "Hillary Rodham will be
your Waterloo."

In so many ways, of course, Hillary did not seem the type to be swept off
her feet. Throughout her early career, Hillary had proven to be determined, practical, calculating, and in full control of her own destiny—the
lawyer from day one, as her Wellesley classmate had put it. But Hillary
had occasionally displayed another less predictable, more emotional, and
more vulnerable side. This suggests her openness to being seduced by
someone like Bill Clinton. For the next ten years at least, Hillary would
struggle with the terms of both her private and public life in Arkansas. In
retrospect, even considering that the White House was the final prize, the
question would be whether she would have made the same choices had
she known of the future challenges she would face—in the form of Bill's
inherent character flaws, which for a long time she seemed willing to deny
or rationalize, as well as the encroaching squalor that defined the political culture of Arkansas.

4

Stranger in a Strange Land

By all accounts, Hillary's early years in Arkansas were full of disappointments and frustrations. Arkansas politicians, businessmen, and lawyers were a sharp departure from the social reformers of Wellesley College, the legal activists at Yale Law School, and the constitutional lawyers whose historic debates in the House Watergate Committee were, to Hillary, what law practice and public service were all about. In contrast, the Arkansans—fiscally and socially conservative, Southern Baptist, blue-collar, and poorly educated—while overwhelmingly Democratic, did not resemble Democrats like Burke Marshall or Marian Wright Edelman in the least.

Mentored by such civil rights stalwarts, Hillary now faced the prospect of life in a state with a disgraceful history of racial hatred. Arkansas was infamous for its response in 1957 to the Supreme Court's 1954 desegregation ruling in *Brown* v. *Board of Education*. When nine black students tried to enter Little Rock's Central High School, Governor Orval Faubus tried to thwart them by calling in the National Guard; President Eisenhower had to send in the Army to defend the students' right to attend the school.

Almost a third of Arkansas' small population of 2 million lived in the kind of grinding poverty that Hillary had never seen, even in the ghettos of Chicago or Boston. In 1977, per capita income in the state was only $5,073, forty-ninth in the nation. "Thank God for Mississippi" was a tongue-in-cheek refrain: but for that neighboring state, Arkansas would be last in the nation in everything.

Democratic Party bosses dispensed patronage and controlled the voting precincts in the predominantly rural state, flexing their influence from the prairies in the east near Tennessee to the Ozark Mountains in the northwest. In the bleak Mississippi Delta region of southeastern Arkansas, black preachers delivered votes to pols who learned fast which palms to grease. In the Third World economy of the Delta, a few dollars or a Coke and some cookies could usually buy a vote.

Lively discourse on the great issues of the day, like the debates on the Yale Quad, was nowhere to be found. Arkansas' one-party tradition meant that elections were settled in Democratic primaries with little contention over ideas or issues. The state had not sent a Republican to the Senate since Reconstruction, and since that time only two Republicans had won the governorship—most recently Winthrop Rockefeller, Nelson's younger brother, who fled his family back East and ran as a progressive on a platform of bringing Arkansas into the New South.

By the early 1970s, the Democratic Party was beginning to emerge from decades of Faubus's control. In what was called the Era of Pretty Faces, a new crop of up-and-coming politicians—Clinton among them—gravitated toward Senator J. William Fulbright as a mentor. Differences among them were mostly matters of age, personality, and style. Campaigning on issues like education, roads, and jobs, they forged a new political machine, which Clinton, edging out Governor David Pryor and Attorney General Jim Guy Tucker, came to dominate.[1]

Clinton was the best campaigner political observers in Arkansas had ever seen. That was saying something in a state that had produced more than its share of political giants, from Faubus to Fulbright to Wilbur Mills. Clinton's rare ability to seem sincere and empathize with voters set him apart from even the most accomplished politicians. People generally took an instant liking to the boyish candidate with the soaring rhetoric and boundless energy. "No one will love this state more, care more about our people's problems, or work harder to see that we become what we ought to be . . . ," Clinton would often say.

The effect of his oratory, first seen in the race against John Paul Hammerschmidt in 1974, inspired what became known as a "Cult of Bill." As he worked the Pink Tomato festivals and toured the state's black churches and nursing homes he recalled names with uncanny facility. He may have seemed like a country boy at Yale, but in Arkansas Clinton's appearances at rallies were likened to the effect of a rock star walking into a Wal-Mart.

Clinton was able to change his plan to stay in the conservative third district and try to beat Hammerschmidt again in 1976 when Attorney General Tucker decided to vacate his office in order to run for the congressional seat of the legendary Wilbur Mills. The powerful House Ways and Means Committee chairman had resigned after the exposure of his alcohol abuse and his escapades with stripper Fanne Foxe, the "Argentine Firecracker."

Clinton's only impediment to entering the 1976 race for attorney general was financial. With a salary of $6,000 a year, the state attorney general's position was considered a "charity" job. It was impossible to serve without independent means of support. With no family wealth or outside source of earnings, plus the burden of outstanding personal debts from student loans and the first campaign, Clinton was able to run only because he had Hillary's $18,000 annual college professor's salary to fall back on.

Though Bill had no competition in the general election, after winning the 1976 primary for attorney general he still needed to campaign for the rest of the Democratic ticket. But after the dramatic confrontation with Paul Fray over the aborted attempt to steal the '74 election, Hillary decided to refocus her political energies away from Arkansas and on her own career. Rather than staying in Arkansas and campaigning with Bill, she continued to build an independent, and at times, an even more influential political base for herself in the national Democratic party, pursuing the direction she had begun with her service on the Watergate Committee. Moving back to more familiar political territory in the Midwest, she worked in Jimmy Carter's presidential campaign as a deputy director in charge of field operations in Indianapolis. This was a rather extraordinary mark of Bill's support for Hillary's independence and no doubt an important reason for her continued attraction to him; in the middle of an election, few politicians would be happy about their spouses leaving the state to campaign elsewhere.

Having worked in a winning presidential campaign, Hillary likely passed up the chance to parlay her connections into a plum slot in the new administration in Washington. She eventually accepted a Carter presidential appointment to a seat on the board of the Legal Services Corporation, which allowed her to continue living in Arkansas and to travel to Washington several times a year for meetings. She returned to Arkansas after the November election, where Bill's first electoral victory meant abandoning the life she had made for herself in the laid-back college town of Fayetteville. There, she had seemed fairly content teaching law and running the local legal clinic. But Bill now had to work in the Capital, and commuting from Fayetteville was out of the question financially.

Thus, in 1976 Hillary uprooted herself and moved to Little Rock, joining the Rose Law Firm. Her starting salary of about $15,000 helped the couple buy a modest one-story brick home in Hillcrest, a desirable residential district in the hills above the city. Bill, meanwhile, began planning his next political race. Perhaps eyeing a move back east, Hillary preferred that he run for the Senate in 1978, but two strong contenders from the Pretty Face contingent—David Pryor, the incumbent governor, and Jim Guy Tucker, then a member of Congress—were thought likely to make that race.

Clinton decided to run for governor, and faced little competition ·for the Democratic nomination. His opponents were Frank Lady, a religious conservative who accused Clinton of being "the most liberal politician ever to come out of Arkansas," and a seventy-five-year-old turkey farmer, Monroe Schwarzlose. Though Hillary's public profile was virtually nonexistent, she drew criticism from both candidates. The first accusation was that Hillary had used her private position as a lawyer to influence the state government. Lady charged that Attorney General Clinton decided not to intervene in a utility-rate increase, proposed by a company controlled by the powerful Stephens family, because Hillary had done legal work for Stephens on an unrelated matter. Schwarzlose conjured up an image of Bill and Hillary as an obnoxious yuppie power couple. "We've had enough lawyers in the governor's mansion. One is enough. Two would be too much," Schwarzlose said. At the time, those charges barely registered, but they exposed the lines of attack that would be employed against her by political opponents in the future.

In a small state like Arkansas, where the gap between the very rich and everyone else was a canyon, the gubernatorial and Senate races turned on getting the financial backing of a very few kingmakers in backroom deals—Paul Fray's dairy interest flim-flam writ large. Clinton did what he had to do to get elected: In 1978 he began to court the kingmakers' support, and he soon mastered the favor-trading game.

Arkansas was run by a handful of business titans: the Stephens family, which owned Wall Street's largest brokerage firm and whose patriarch, known as "Mr. Witt," financed the Faubus machine for years; Sam Walton, the founder of the giant Wal-Mart retail chain; and chicken producer Don Tyson. Below the mega-rich—or the "Arkoromans," as some called them—was an elite white-collar professional class, centered in the capital city of 250,000, who ran their businesses, banks, bond houses, and law firms. Most of them had attended the University of Arkansas in Fayetteville and knew one another well.

With all of the money and power concentrated in the hands of a few, the elite did what it needed to in order to keep the money coming in and to stay in power. In the state's money-politics tradition, public and private money sloshed around in the same pot. Governors, who stood for election every other year, were especially dependent on these monied interests. Not too long before Clinton took office, the governor's compensation package was still known as "ten thousand a year and all you can steal."

As a mentor, Bill Clinton enlisted "Big Daddy" Don Tyson, a proverbial don of the Arkansas political mafia. Tyson has been described by the *Los Angeles Times* as "a driving force behind the political ascendancy of Bill Clinton."[2] Tyson operated his chicken empire in northwest Arkansas from a virtual replica of the Oval Office, except for the egg-shaped door knobs and the chicken head carved into the fireplace. Presiding over one of the strangest corporate cultures in America, Tyson insisted that everyone, from top executives down to the lowliest chicken pluckers, wear the same khaki-colored uniform with his or her name sewn in red thread on the breast pocket.

The uniforms were Tyson's only concession to anything resembling a socialist workers' paradise. The concepts of worker's rights and socially responsible corporate citizenship, which Hillary had been exposed to at Yale, were foreign to the state's oligarchs. To Hillary, Don Tyson must have represented the face of unbridled capitalism: a ruthless exploiter, a renowned union foe, and a heavy polluter who filled the local lakes and streams with chicken feces.

In a 1994 *New York Times* profile, Tyson defined Arkansas politics as "a series of unsentimental transactions between those who need votes and those who have money." He needed to stay in political favor because the poultry industry was heavily regulated by the state and he provided politicians with whatever it took to win their support. In the late 1970s, "when the legislature was in session, they all used to stay at what was then the Marion Hotel," one close associate of Don Tyson's recalled. "Well, you could buy and sell them. Don would call you up and ask if you were free for dinner. He'd say, 'Meet me at the Little Rock airport at five P.M. I want to surprise you.' His private plane would pull up and two of the best-looking women you've ever seen in the skimpiest costumes you've ever seen would pop out. The plane would take off and a couple of hours later it would land in Bimini, where Don had a big boat."

Tyson may have also embodied for Hillary the state's entrenched political and financial system and the absence of any sense of public morality among its leaders. When *60 Minutes* interviewed Tyson in 1994, Mike Wallace led off by saying: "We've spoken to people—and I'm sure you know this—who have called you, I quote, 'ruthless, amoral, unscrupulous, mean-spirited.' But they wouldn't come on camera and say that because they're afraid of you and your power." Such charges of personal corruption must have struck Hillary, who hailed from the suburban Midwest (and had rejected the drug culture both at Yale and in Fayetteville), as depraved. Her Methodist-inspired social conservatism and stiff personal moralism did not mesh with the culture in which she was now expected to live and thrive.

After winning the '78 primary, with Tyson's backing, Clinton was a shoo-in for governor; his GOP opponent, former legislator Lynn Lowe, was a virtual unknown. Before the November election, Tyson secured a promise from Clinton to raise the legal limit on truck weight on state roads from about 73,000 to 80,000 pounds. Most other states used the higher limit, making it harder for Arkansas' producers to compete, and costing them millions. Heavier trucks on the road, however, meant the expenditure of more public funds for maintenance, as well as more accidents. (As attorney general, Clinton had already delivered once for Tyson, intervening in a lawsuit to defend regulations that would enable the state's poultry producer to boost production significantly.)

Tyson was linked to another deal with Clinton that would raise allegations of influence peddling when it was disclosed more than a decade later, in 1994. Just before the November election, at the suggestion of Tyson's lawyer Jim Blair, Hillary—soon to be first lady of the state— began trading in the high-risk commodities futures market, turning a $1,000 investment into $100,000, a 10,000 percent return, in just nine months.

Bill Clinton had become friendly with Jim Blair during his 1974 race for Congress. That year, Blair was managing the senatorial campaign in which Senator Fulbright was defeated, but the Fulbright circle was still the place to be for a politician on the make. Eleven years older than Clinton, by the late seventies Blair was an established player, serving as legal counsel to the state party, and he soon became an important adviser to Bill. In 1977, Attorney General Clinton recommended Blair to President Carter for appointment to the Federal Home Loan Bank Board.

Blair was engaged to be married to Diane Kincaid, a University of Arkansas professor who had worked as a volunteer in the '74 Fayetteville campaign and had become close with Hillary. Kincaid was a Washington, D.C., native who had originally moved to Arkansas to marry lawyer-politician Hugh Kincaid. When the marriage didn't work out, she soon began dating Jim Blair. When Hillary was at odds with Paul Fray in the Fayetteville headquarters, she would sometimes work out of her rented house, where Kincaid would join her. When Kincaid and Blair married in 1979 Clinton officiated at their wedding, and a tuxedo-clad Hillary acted as "best person." The Clintons often vacationed at the Blairs' cottage on Beaver Lake, just outside Fayetteville.

Though the twenty-nine-year-old Hillary would not have known it, the sweetheart deal is commonplace in Arkansas, a state where even college coaches are routinely cut in on lucrative deals to keep them from accepting offers from out-of-state competitors. In the 1970s, lots of folks in northwest Arkansas in and around Tyson Foods were making millions in the commodities markets, trading through the Springdale office of the brokerage house of Refco, Inc. Hillary's broker at Refco was Robert "Red" Bone, a former thirteen-year employee of Tyson's, who had once lived with Tyson and was a current client of Blair's. The year before Hillary began trading with him, Bone had been barred from futures trading for a year on charges that he, Don Tyson, and Tyson Foods were manipulating the egg futures market. Hillary may not have known this history, but her friend Jim Blair, who was Bone's lawyer as well as Tyson's, surely did.

Playing the commodities market is an extremely risky proposition. Three-quarters of futures investors—even experienced ones—typically lose money. Yet a 1994 statement given to the press by Blair, who opened the account in Hillary's name and directed her commodities trades, suggested that her investment was a sure bet. Blair said he approached Hillary, telling her that "it was one of those rare chances to put aside some money," and that "she wouldn't have to be the expert. I'd give her advice."

In the commodities market, investors commit to buy or sell a certain quantity of a commodity at a stated price at some future date. They hope to make money by correctly guessing the way the commodity's price will move over that stretch of time. The investor puts up only a deposit—or margin—on each contract. Hillary often did not have the money on deposit to make the trades she was involved in—which affected contracts worth millions of dollars—and given the Clintons' limited net worth, it seems unlikely she could have covered the losses even if Refco did cover her margin calls.

By virtue of her marriage to Bill, Hillary was a privileged member of Arkansas' insider political class—where the normal rules of investment and risk evidently did not apply. There is no evidence, however, that Hillary knew Blair had arranged to get her special treatment from the brokerage. She probably had no idea of what the normal rules were: "Nobody called and asked me for anything," she later explained. Moreover, if she had suspected that Blair was manipulating her trades to buy influence, nothing in her personal history suggests that she would have gone along with the scheme. As Hillary later described her thinking, "I trusted Jim Blair and it worked out for me." All she knew was that Blair was a political mentor of Bill, and was engaged to be married to her best friend in Arkansas. Whether or not it dawned on Hillary that the investment was being directed by a lawyer for a company that was heavily regulated by the state, Bill—as an elected official—should have recognized this appearance of impropriety.

Like the commodities trades, the Whitewater real estate investment was a deal not uncommon in politics—especially among governors in the South, of both political parties—where a well-off businessperson wishes to make life comfortable and secure for a powerful politician. The investment was made at precisely the same time as the commodities trades—on the eve of the 1978 gubernatorial election—and seemed to have the same purpose: An Arkansas hustler, Jim McDougal, wanted to get close to the incoming governor. Hillary, at best, was an after-thought.

"I wanted to make some money for Bill Clinton," McDougal later explained. "I think I saw Bill and Hillary down at the Blackeyed Pea, you know, the restaurant, and I said, 'I've got this piece of land on the White River I'm going to buy. You want to go in with me? I'll take care of setting up the financing.' They said 'okay.' "

Calling himself a "political businessman," McDougal, like Jim Blair, was a mentor to Bill Clinton. He was well known in the state's governing circles since he had headed the Youth Campaign for Orval Faubus in 1960. He also bragged about having set up profitable real estate deals for insiders, including Senator Fulbright, whose money McDougal claimed to manage. McDougal met Clinton when McDougal was running Fulbright's Little Rock office and he took the chubby intern under his wing. Though he looked more like Daddy Warbucks, the slick-talking Mc-Dougal regaled the young Bill with his imitations of FDR, whose New Deal politics McDougal adored. McDougal once said that he despised the Republican Party "for starving the country for the last 100 years." In the mid-1970s, while he was working on a master's degree and teaching political science at Ouachita Baptist University, he met his future wife Susan, a drama student fifteen years his junior.

A few months before the November 1978 election, while McDougal was working in the Clinton campaign, the Whitewater Development Corporation was established. The McDougals and the Clintons were fifty-fifty partners in a 230-acre riverfront development project in the Ozark Mountains, a small slice of the largest land deal in the history of Marion County. The land, picked out by Susan and purchased for $203,000, was to be subdivided into forty-two lots for low-end vacation and retirement homes which, when sold, might bring about $47,500 profit to each couple. The Clintons planned to keep one lot for themselves, but it sold quickly because it was so nicely situated at the spot where the White River meets Crooked Creek.

Blair and McDougal were able to help Bill financially before he took the reins of power in an election that was a foregone conclusion. Bill beat Lynn Lowe in the 1978 gubernatorial election with 63 percent of the vote, becoming, at age thirty-two, the youngest governor in the United States since 1938, when thirty-one-year-old Harold Stassen became governor of Minnesota. Owing to his youth and charisma, the new governor immediately attracted the attention of the national news media and the powers that be in the Democratic Party, who even briefly considered him as a potential running mate for either Jimmy Carter's re-election bid or Ted Kennedy's challenge to Carter.

The Clintons chose "Diamonds and Denim" as their inaugural theme and Don Tyson threw a pre-inaugural bash at Little Rock's swank Camelot Hotel, perched on the banks of the muddy Arkansas River. In a nod to the old guard, Clinton invited Orval Faubus to an inaugural celebration. But before he was even sworn in, Clinton made a misstep that signaled the difficulties he would face during his first term. In an interview with the *New York Times*'s Howell Raines, Clinton seemed to express a view of his home state as in need of an enlightened government crusade—a view shared, if not inspired by, Hillary. Clinton attributed his win to a desire among Arkansans to no longer "be perceived, especially by themselves, as being backward." The remark was seen as ungracious and presumptuous.

One should not underestimate the intoxicating effect of Bill's rapid ascent on the ambitious young couple. To Hillary especially, it must have seemed a stunning confirmation of their virtue and merit as members of a moral elect, and may also have encouraged her to think of Bill as a rising star on the national scene. To consummate what they apparently believed was a popular mandate endorsing their crusading liberal spirit, the Clintons set out to recreate Camelot in Little Rock, eagerly sponsoring a panoply of then-fashionable enlightened political and social initiatives. Not surprisingly, their youthful arrogance and overreaching was immediately sensed and ironically opened up the ground beneath Clinton's feet just as he seemed to have attained his first real foothold in national politics.

"They brought in all these bright young people from out of state to try to cure all the ills in the state in one vast move, and you can't do that." Richard Herget, Clinton's 1980 campaign chairman, recalled. The three bearded aides who ran Clinton's first-term administration— Rudy Moore, Jr., Steve Smith, and John David Danner—were known variously as the "diaper brigade," the "children's crusade," or "the three stooges."

At thirty-five, Rudy Moore, Jr., was the oldest of the triumvirate. Moore had worked on Clinton's congressional race and chaired the '78 campaign. Like his two colleagues, he often showed up for work in cutoffs and a T-shirt. Moore and Steve Smith, the second member of the trio, were bound to have poor relations with the legislature, which was filled with cranky yellow-dog Democrats unsure of quite what to make of their new governor. Smith and Moore had both previously served in the body, where they led an unsuccessful Young Turks challenge to the entrenched establishment.

Smith, a professor, environmentalist, and ACLU activist who had briefly managed the 1974 campaign after Hillary ran off Paul Fray, was put in charge of development issues. He referred to the business community as "suits," and, in line with the "small is beautiful" slogan of the environmental movement, advocated using state sanctioning and funds to promote non-industrial development of small service businesses and agriculture. Smith also tried to block the timber companies from clearcutting Arkansas' renowned forests. He later told journalist David Osborne, "People like me [on the staff] were sort of smart ass, and angered a lot of people. We were after every dragon in the land . . . I used language like 'corporate criminals,' which really did not endear the governor to the timber companies."[3] Working with Jim McDougal, Clinton's Whitewater business partner, whom Clinton had appointed as a paid economic development aide, Smith advocated bringing a version of FDR's New Deal to Arkansas. New cabinet departments of energy and economic development were formed, and the state began to promote certain industries, creating opportunities for graft on a scale hitherto unseen.

Clinton's third aide, Berkeley lawyer John David Danner, had met the Clintons through his wife, Nancy "Peach" Pietrafesa, a community activist who was a friend of Hillary's from her Wellesley days. Pietrafesa, who like Hillary Rodham had elected to keep her own name, also worked in the governor's office. Danner and his wife alienated many state legislators with what was seen as pointy-headed liberal attitudinizing. Legislators also griped about Pietrafesa having kept her maiden name. In a reprise of Paul Fray's reaction to Hillary as a strong, independent woman, the legislators also engaged in contemptuous gossip about Hillary and Pietrafesa. When it was disclosed that Danner had spent federal money without legislative approval to train top-level state bureaucrats in such subjects as "how to tell what turns you on," he and his wife resigned.

Hillary was self-consciously leading her generation in keeping her maiden name, staking a claim to independence and an identity separate from her husband's. But as the old boys made clear in their effort to stigmatize Nancy Pietrafesa, Arkansas was not yet ready to accept the two-career "power couple," which was quickly becoming the norm on the East and West coasts. To Arkansans, Hillary, busy carving out her own professional niche rather than living in Bill's shadow, was a symbol of this alien culture, and as such she quickly became a political liability for Bill. In truth, the reaction of the Arkansas public and press to Hillary was not without foundation; to a certain extent, she did embody the elitist attitudes of the eastern liberal establishment to which she had successfully assimilated. The Arkansans' reaction of distrust and hostility would later be played out on a national scale, though curiously, Hillary herself seems never to have anticipated or understood it.

The issue of Hillary's decision to keep the name Rodham had arisen once in the 1976 campaign for attorney general, and Bill vigorously defended her choice, saying she was a "nationally recognized authority on children's rights" and had every right to maintain her own professional identity. During the 1978 campaign for governor, Hillary had made several joint appearances with Clinton and stood in for him at an important Labor Day event in Little Rock. She was not profiled in the state's major paper, the *Arkansas Gazette,* until two days before the election. The article, which identified her as Hillary Rodham, described "an accomplished speaker who frequently appears on Clinton's behalf and gives detailed answers to complex policy questions. She intends to be actively involved in policy making if Clinton is governor."

Not until after the election, when the newspapers began writing regularly about Hillary Rodham, did people begin to take notice of the fact that she had not taken her husband's name, and Hillary was compelled to defend her decision to the electorate. The conservative-leaning *Arkansas Democrat* ran an article headlined: "Ms. Rodham? Just An Old-Fashioned Girl," in which the new first lady explained that keeping her own name made her "feel like a real person." Hillary said, "We realized that being a governor's wife could be a full-time job. But I need to maintain my interests and my commitments. I need my own identity, too."

Unfortunately, the explanation, honest and forthright though it was, was not well received. *Arkansas Democrat* political columnist Meredith Oakley, a blunt-speaking native Arkansan who covered the Clintons for more than a decade, summed up the prevailing caricature of Hillary among voters during the first term: "People thought even his wife didn't like him enough to take his name. She didn't shave her legs. She was a ball-busting feminist."

Hillary's personal presentation only exacerbated that perception. Though she was the first lady of the state and a lawyer at a prestigious downtown law firm, Hillary still dressed like a Fayetteville flower child; people called her Bill's "hippie" wife. While Bill was forging ties with Don Tyson (an alleged polluter), Hillary, a committed environmentalist, shunned aerosol products, and like many feminists of the era, she rebelled against the social convention of shaving her legs and underarms.

Hillary's nonconformity was a scandal at the Rose Law Firm, where it was viewed as liberal East Coast haughtiness and disrespect. The firm's secretaries, who resented having to work for a woman in the first place, made cruel comments about Hillary's appearance behind her back, to which she could not have been oblivious. The comments likely amplified her sense of alienation and rejection by the locals, whom she may accordingly have judged in her own mind all the more harshly as country bumpkins.

"At first, she didn't wear stockings and the old ladies at the firm were horrified," said Hillary's former Rose secretary from the late 1970s. "She was a comic figure as a lady lawyer. Her hair was fried into an orphan Annie perm. She had one large eyebrow across her forehead that looked like a giant caterpillar. We laughed until we cried. She tried to look good when she went to court, and she would put on some awful plastic jewelry. She'd be wearing high heels she couldn't walk in. There wasn't one stereotypically womanly or feminine thing about her." The office staff considered Hillary's weight problem an endless source of amusement as well. "She was on a perpetual diet," the secretary said. "She would show up for work with a big bag of lettuce and eat out of it all day."

If Arkansans weren't taking to Hillary, the feeling was mutual. Hillary made little effort to hide her view of the locals as rubes and rednecks. She did nothing to court the local press, an attitude that left a lasting negative impression with some reporters. "She doesn't like to have to explain herself or be accountable," Meredith Oakley said. "Her view is it's none of the public's damn business. She wanted you to know her ideas, but she doesn't want you to know her and she doesn't want to know you."

For many Arkansans, angry that native son Bill appeared to have been swayed by the influence of East Coast liberal elites, Hillary—even more than Bill's trio of unpopular aides—became the convenient scapegoat. "One on one he [Bill] was one of the boys. But when she was around, the Georgetown and Yale stuff came through. He was a stiff shirt," said Larry Gleghorn, a state trooper who served on the security detail during Clinton's first term.

Much later, in a 1994 *American Spectator* article written by this author, loose-lipped Arkansas troopers (not including Gleghorn) caused political problems for the Clintons by going public with accounts of Clinton's womanizing at the Little Rock governor's mansion. At the time they were working for Clinton, however, the troopers were at one with the boss, whom they viewed as a somewhat more polished good old boy. The governor liked nothing more than pulling off the road with the boys and filling up at the Tastee Freeze drive-through. (Famous for never carrying money, Bill expected the troopers to pay.)

Hillary must have felt imprisoned in the governor's mansion—actually a nondescript neo-Colonial brick structure situated in the lowest-lying area of a decaying neighborhood on the edge of downtown Little Rock—with a contingent of hostile cops milling around day and night. For their part, the troopers may have sensed the remnants of anti-military, anti-police attitudes Hillary had expressed during the Black Panther protests at Yale. In any case, clearly sensing her personal discomfort and strongly disapproving of her liberal politics, they loved nothing more than frustrating her wishes and getting under her skin. Understandably, Hillary reacted by scooting off to work at the Rose Firm in her Oldsmobile Cutlass early each morning, not to return until after dark.

"She was a bitch day in and day out," said Gleghorn, now a captain in the Arkansas state police. "She always screamed we were taking the wrong route when we drove her to an event. She was a die-hard anti-smoker and most of us smoked. She hated it if we wore cowboy boots with our uniforms. It made her furious. On official trips, you'd go to their rooms and tell her, 'We need to leave in fifteen minutes,' and she'd snap, 'We know it.' Then they'd be late and she'd give us a good cussing."

The troopers mocked Bill's dependence on Hillary and his evident inability to stand up to her. The security staff was responsible for protecting Hillary as well as Bill, and she often bristled at the imposition on her privacy. Gleghorn finally complained to Clinton that the troopers couldn't perform their jobs properly without more cooperation from Hillary. "He said, 'You'll have to fight your own battles with her.' I think he feared her. He was always telling me that she was smarter than he was. Anyway, one day, I had a talk with her, right in front of him, and he loved it. I told her as far as I was concerned she was the property of the state of Arkansas and we were going to do our job and protect her until she got the law changed."

At the root of the tension between the troopers and Hillary was the troopers' role in facilitating Bill's extramarital affairs. The sordid history of Clinton's infidelities while he was governor and the culture of petty deceit it engendered was fully exposed only after Clinton took office as president in 1993, when troopers Roger Perry and Larry Patterson alleged in the *American Spectator,* and later in the *Los Angeles Times,* that as governor Clinton had improperly used them on dozens of occasions to facilitate his extramarital affairs. By their own account, the troopers pimped for Clinton, helped him orchestrate a cover-up of his almost daily amorous activities, and even made their own use of what they called "residuals"—Clinton's female rejects and leftovers, picked up at the bars the men would frequent.

For at least a decade, the troopers said, Clinton had been prone to extramarital affairs, conducting several at a time, as well as indulging in numerous one-night stands. The troopers alleged that while they were being paid by the state and driving state cars, they were regularly instructed by Clinton to approach women and to solicit their telephone numbers for the governor; to drive him to rendezvous points and guard him during sexual encounters (including one alleged incident with a state employee named Paula Jones, who sued Clinton for sexual harassment after the *Spectator* report was published); to secure hotel rooms and other meeting places for sex; to lend Clinton their state cars so he could slip away and visit women (some of whom were given state jobs, like Gennifer Flowers, whom the troopers confirmed had been romantically involved with Clinton since his first gubernatorial term); and to help Clinton hide his activities by keeping track of Hillary's whereabouts.

The troopers further alleged that they were eyewitnesses to some of the encounters, including incidents where oral sex was performed on

Clinton in parked cars on the grounds of the governor's mansion and in the parking lot of a local elementary school. According to the troopers, these clandestine sexual encounters occurred even after the presidential election, and they continued through Clinton's final days in Little Rock. In a subsequent *Spectator* article, trooper L. D. Brown told reporter Daniel Wattenberg that while he worked at the governor's mansion in the mid-1980s, he solicited sexual partners for Clinton during travels throughout the state. "Over a hundred at least," Brown said. "I'd hate to even try to guess." Brown said he and Clinton frequently rated women on a ten-point "grading" scale. Betraying a view of Clinton as just another traditional southern misogynist, the governor viewed women, Brown said, as "purely to be chased, dominated, conquered." (Neither of the Clintons specifically denied the troopers' accounts. Bill said he "did not do anything wrong" and Hillary denounced the stories as "terrible.")

It was the nature of Arkansas and the Clinton circle that nearly any witness with compromising information on Clinton was also in a position to be compromised. The troopers were angry that after years of service to the governor, Clinton had won the presidency and gone off to Washington without offering them incentives in the form of better jobs or raises to remain loyal. As they contemplated coming forward, visions of book deals and tabloid television stardom danced in their heads. After Patterson and Perry went public, the Clinton folk dug through their personnel files and publicized an incident from several years prior in which, after getting drunk at Little Rock's Bobbisox Lounge, the two of them wrecked a state car and allegedly conspired to defraud an insurance company. (The troopers denied the accusation.)

Bill's reckless personal behavior, including his serial infidelities, was the central fact of Hillary's shaky married life, and it would soon become a central fact of their political life as well. Surely, Hillary heard the same rumors that everyone else in Little Rock did: Clinton's affairs were whispered about even by high school students throughout the capital city. In the early years of their marriage, however, Hillary may have been unsure just what to believe. As she must have seen it, the sources of the gossip were either "beauty queens" of the type she had encountered in Fayetteville or the troopers themselves, whom she despised. For a while, anyway, it may have been easier to turn a blind eye. "Her greatest quote was, 'L.D., sometimes you have to make a leap of faith.'" Brown said.

On other occasions, Hillary seemed all too aware of what was going on.

In an anecdote the troopers related both to the *Spectator* and to the *Los Angeles Times,* Hillary once awoke in the middle of the night, flicked on the bedroom light, and called down to the guard house looking for Bill. When told Bill had gone out for a drive in the middle of the night, Hillary was said to have exclaimed, "The sorry damn son of a bitch!" Perry said he grabbed the cellular telephone, located Clinton at one of his girl-friends' homes, and told him to get back to the residence immediately. "He started saying, 'Oh God, God, God. What did you tell her?' " Perry recalled. When Clinton arrived home soon after, Hillary was waiting in the kitchen, where a wild screaming match ensued. When Perry entered the kitchen after the dust had settled, he said the room was a wreck, with a cabinet door kicked off its hinges.

The troopers seemed to feel that Bill was justified in slipping out of his marital bed at night to prowl the streets of Little Rock because they saw Hillary as an undesirable, foul-mouthed harridan who had brought the mistreatment and neglect on herself. Yet it seems fairer to conclude that Hillary's flaring temper was an understandable reaction to the hu-miliation to which she was subjected on a regular basis. Though the troopers were indifferent to her feelings, in the incidents they described Hillary was evidently pained by Bill's behavior and mortified that the guards knew the sordid details. In her bitter sarcasm about "rubes," it was possible to see not only a reaction to the redneck local culture (one of the leading Little Rock steakhouses was named "Sir Loins") and the pimping troopers under her roof, but also her disappointment over Bill's true nature. The politically idealistic and sensitive "new man" of their Yale days had turned out to be a compulsive philanderer "in bed" with the chicken king.

In deciding to join Little Rock's Rose Law Firm, Hillary veered from the public interest law path she had charted at Yale, the Children's Defense Fund, and the University of Arkansas. The oldest firm west of the Mississippi, Rose was considered the state's most prestigious.[4] It was named for American Bar Association founder U. M. Rose, a Kentuckian who had joined the partnership in 1865. Historically a staid white-shoe firm, Rose had been staffed for years with lawyers' lawyers, leaders of the state bar, and former and future state Supreme Court judges. Rose was the firm of choice for the Arkansas power elite, counting Stephens Inc., Wal-Mart, and Tyson Foods among its corporate clientele. Rose lawyers did routine corporate work but, when necessary, they quietly exerted their influence in the corridors of power.

This staid profile began to change in the mid-seventies under the leadership of managing partner C. Joseph Giroir, Jr., the first securities specialist in the state, who recognized the opportunity to build an aggressive commercial litigation and securities practice in the no longer sleepy Arkansas capital. "We organized the firm in a way that focused on institutional clients—mostly banking, corporate and securities clientele," Giroir said. "My perception of where the law was going was that the institutional clients [like Worthen Bank and Stephens Inc.] that had needed corporate securities work for a decade would grow and need a commercial and litigation practice.... Until the mid-seventies in Arkansas, most litigation was personal injury, insurance, and routine contract disputes."

A short, swaggering man who favored cowboy hats with his double-breasted suits and filled his office with ornate gold-leaf French furniture, Giroir was a lawyer-cum-business tycoon who devoted half of his time to tending to outside business interests—and eventually left the firm because of it. He personified a certain nouveau riche type in the eighties in Little Rock, when barrels of money were suddenly being made in highly competitive mergers and acquisitions and bond underwriting business. Doug Bonner, a former Rose lawyer who worked in Giroir's securities department, said, "Did you ever see the movie *Road House?* You know that guy that tried to run the town—Ben Gazzara played the character—that is what Joey Giroir was all about."

Under Giroir, the firm grew from seventeen lawyers in the mid-1970s to more than fifty lawyers a decade later, and Hillary was part of the hiring spurt. Giroir was willing to shake up the firm's culture, but his decision to retain the wife of the new attorney general was viewed as controversial among the older guard, who gave Hillary a somewhat chilly reception. Though her critics, both in the state and nationally, made political hay of the common perception that Hillary joined the Rose Firm by virtue of her political connection to Bill, the very opposite appears to be closer to the truth. Hillary wasn't hired because she was married to the newly elected attorney general, but rather in spite of it.

With power concentrated in so few hands, the potential for conflicts of interest in the Little Rock legal business was great. Though conflicts of interest were endemic and the concept of legal ethics appeared to be somewhat more elastic there than elsewhere, blatant conflicts were frowned upon, if only because they threatened to expose the insider system. In this respect, being married to a top politician was a handicap for an aspiring lawyer. "I think some thought she might prevent us from taking cases because her husband was attorney general and they felt like in certain cases where he was representing the state and we were representing another party, that we might be precluded from taking cases," Giroir said. J. Gaston Williamson, a partner at Rose, added: "Our firm historically was a non-political firm. When we first employed her, we debated long and hard over whether we would employ her. The fact that she was the wife of a politician was a strike against her."

In 1977, Hillary was recruited to the firm as an associate by Vincent W. Foster, Jr., who met her on the Fayetteville campus the year before when he was recruiting at the law school. They immediately hit it off due to Foster's pro bono activism in Arkansas' legal services community. Foster, who had spent his childhood in Hope, had been a friend of both Bill Clinton and Thomas Franklin "Mack" McLarty III, the future chairman of the Arkla oil and gas company. Foster was first in his law school class at Fayetteville, had received the top score on the bar exam, and joined Rose upon graduating. He developed a reputation for being one of the least political of Rose's senior lawyers, and also the one with the most integrity. "Vince was the Clint Eastwood of the legal profession in Arkansas," said Thomas Mars, who was hired by Foster and Hillary in the mid-1980s. "He was super-organized and meticulous. Everyone wanted to emulate his style."

"Vince Foster was one of the best lawyers I'd ever seen or been around—ever," maintained Phillip Raley, who was opposing counsel to Foster in several cases. "He's one of the finest people that I've ever been around. He was an absolute pleasure to work with if you were on the other side of the case—because you never, ever questioned what Vince said. . . . There was never any question that he would stand by his word. . . . He had a very, very good reputation in the community and he had a lot of things that physically helped him. He was tall, good-looking—all of that helps you in the courtroom."

If it hadn't been for Foster's impression on her, Hillary probably wouldn't have joined Rose. Her studies at Yale had sparked an interest in family law, which was not a priority at the firm, especially under Giroir.

Confronted with few opportunities to practice in areas that engaged her interest, during her first few years at Rose she was permitted to do outside legal work with William Wilson, Jr., who had an independent Little Rock law practice. Working with Wilson, Hillary was involved in a range of criminal defense, personal injury, child custody, and domestic abuse cases. Wilson, who described himself as a "dime store lawyer and mule farmer," had seen Hillary give a speech to the state bar association seeking funds for a local legal services project. "It was an all-male group in those days and the crowd was 90 percent against her," Wilson told the *Boston Globe*. "She was passionate, logical and well-informed. I thought to myself, 'That young lawyer has a good mouth on her.' "

The Rose Firm's stiff corporate culture and stifling paternalism was a poor fit for someone more at home on a college campus or working in public policy or public interest law. Hillary was the first woman to make partner in 1979, and there were no black partners at Rose even in the mid-1990s. In the converted YWCA building just east of downtown where Giroir had moved the firm, law clerks and support staff were forbidden to swim in the pool at the same time as the lawyers. Resembling a red brick schoolhouse or a hospital, and decorated in the faux-English style of Little Rock designer Kaki Hockersmith that was favored by the city's yuppie professionals, the Rose compound was an elite haven surrounded by a depressing sea of wig shops and clothing stores with names like "Mr. Cool's."

Hillary had little in common with her fellow partners, who lived in the hills above the city with their southern belle housewives in huge new homes with Georgian-style columns and circular driveways, played tennis at the Little Rock Country Club, and dined at LaScala, the white-tablecloth Italian restaurant in the upscale Heights neighborhood, where Rose partner William Kennedy III was a part-owner.

Hillary's sense of isolation may have been another source of her bond with Foster—a thoughtful, discreet man, whose low-key personal style stood in stark contrast to the showy southern-lawyer culture that Giroir and his protégé Bill Kennedy brought to the firm. Rather than eating lunch with the Rose cronies at LaScala, where Kennedy was known for his boorish table manners and stingy tipping, Foster preferred to eat alone at his desk. Over time, as Hillary coped with the demands of a mother, family breadwinner, and political wife, as well as the disappointments of working in a law firm run by southern white men who did not share her views or interests, Hillary grew much closer to Foster, both professionally and personally. "It was a very, very close friendship. There was a lot of mutual admiration. They had everything in common," said Thomas Mars.

A few months after Bill was elected governor in early 1979, Hillary made partner. At this point, it seems likely that the firm began to view her connections as a possible asset, which may explain why they tolerated her unusual arrangement with William Wilson. Still, there was concern that her political profile might cause more trouble for the firm than it was worth. "While there was certainly prestige involved [in having Hillary at the firm], there was no small amount of downside of her being associated with the firm because of her husband's occupation and position," said Rose partner Allen Bird. "We constantly had conflicts. We always had to work at issues in ways that normally lawyers don't have to worry about—how they will look, from policy points of view—that sort of thing."

Hillary, meanwhile, juggled her law practice with the political and social demands suddenly thrust on her as first lady of the state, ranging from public speaking to playing hostess at official state events . "I will tell you that she was as interested in fulfilling her duties as first lady of the state and doing whatever she could to help [Bill] as she was in making a living practicing law," Bird said.

Bill seemed to recognize that his success was in some measure attributable to Hillary. "Our vote was a vindication of what my wife and I have done and what we hope to do for the state," he had said upon winning election as governor in 1978. Hillary, however, showed little interest in public affairs in Arkansas and evidenced no desire to exercise political influence through her husband. In addition to her work at Rose, Hillary had more than a full schedule, traveling to Washington several times a year where she was now chairing the board of the Legal Services Corporation, an independent federally-funded agency that provides legal aid to the poor.

Keeping Bill focused on governing the state soon became a major distraction for Hillary. Within months of his taking office, local cartoonists were depicting their new governor as a young child on a tricycle. Paul Fray had fondly called Clinton "the boy" back in Fayetteville; his staff now began referring to him as "the baby," evoking not only his youth but his lack of certitude, chronic tardiness, frequent temper tantrums, and propensity to spend a good deal of his time playing pinball in the basement of the governor's mansion. According to her former secretary, Hillary started to spend a good deal of her day scolding Bill over the phone for being a wastrel. "They had a totally symbiotic relationship," Hillary's former secretary said. "They spoke several times a day, always about business. She did all the work, and he'd be back in the mansion hanging around with his friends, and she would say to him, 'What are you doing with them? They can't do anything for you.' "

As he often would in the future, Bill turned to Hillary when he fell into political trouble. In 1979, during an outcry over a decision by the State Health Department to begin reimbursing nurse practitioners with the state Medicaid funds, Clinton appointed Hillary to head a governor's advisory committee on health care in the state's rural areas. Dr. Robert Young, the director of the agency, and an outsider whose autocratic style was resented in the medical community, proposed making medical care available to those who lived in rural areas where doctors were scarce by having nurse practitioners serve as doctors. The medical society was up in arms over the proposal, anticipating the partitioning of their market share by paramedicals. Eager to quell the furor, Clinton asked Hillary to figure out how best to expand health care to Arkansas's poorest communities without cutting into doctors' fees.

Hillary's work on outside political activities was at first a source of friction between herself and Vincent Foster. "Integrity was his [Foster's] thing," said Hillary's former secretary, who also worked for Foster and Webster L. Hubbell, another Rose partner. "He was the only one who wrote out a voucher for personal photocopies. Everyone else, including Webb and Hillary, let the firm eat it. When he had a personal letter, it came out with a voucher for the stamp. He billed by the tenth of an hour. Webb [who eventually went to jail as a result of bilking his partners and clients] billed an hour for a ten-minute call. She had me doing tons of political work. Democratic fund-raising stuff. She was base-building. Vince would ask, 'What is all that on the floor?' I'd say, 'That's Miss Rodham's personal work.' She was yelled at by Vince for doing it. And then she yelled at me for telling."

Years later, Hillary's partners said that she had never developed her career to its full potential because she had become much more deeply involved in keeping Bill's political career on track in the 1980s. "Our regret is that it [politics] took . . . too much time away from her law practice. She would have been a much more successful lawyer had she not been a politician's wife," said J. Gaston Williamson. Bill Kennedy, by then the managing partner of the firm, told the *American Lawyer* in 1992: "We're very proud of Hillary, and if she had ever quit having two lives and concentrated on the law practice, she'd have been a superb lawyer."

Kennedy's statement implied that Hillary had not exactly been the dazzling super-lawyer that national media reports have universally described. The image of Hillary as a high-powered litigator has become so ingrained in the public consciousness that it is difficult to think of her career in other terms. Though Hillary was undoubtedly a highly accomplished legal activist and politico, a close inspection of the record finds little to support her reputation as one of the most accomplished lawyers of her generation.

No one at Rose questioned Hillary Rodham's abilities. "She was a good lawyer, as good a lawyer as any I've met, a smart person," said Thomas Mars, who worked with Hillary. Yet out of personal loyalty and Arkansas pride, firm members felt compelled to maintain the public pretense that Hillary had a busier practice than she really did, especially during the 1992 presidential campaign when nosy reporters from East Coast newspapers were snooping around for juicy material. "When people would call down here about her practice, like the *National* [*Law*] *Journal,* I'd just say how great she was," Mars said. "I never talked about how she was juggling lots of balls, political and personal. She wasn't in the office a whole lot."

Hillary's national reputation appears attributable mainly to her having been listed twice as a corporate litigator in the *National Law Journal's* survey of the nation's "100 Most Influential Lawyers," a list that included, among others, former Attorney General Richard Thornburgh, Harvard professors Alan Dershowitz and Lawrence Tribe, ACLU president Nadine Strossen, and Washington super-lawyer Lloyd Cutler. Though the rating was a tribute to her political skills, Hillary was not in this league as a practicing lawyer. Most reporters who wrote about her legal career during the '92 campaign reflexively cited the "top 100" honor without probing further. When an enterprising *Time* reporter did call to inquire, the editor of the *National Law Journal* said that Hillary had been singled out not for her legal work but because of her work with the American Bar Association to fight "gender bias" in the legal profession. She was cited "because of her record as a leader of a network of women lawyers who are working to educate judges nationwide on the issues of gender bias. . . . Hillary set in motion a lot of changes. She is a female partner of a law firm leading the way in changing the role of women in the profession," the editor said.

A careful evaluation of Hillary's legal career published by the *American Lawyer* in 1992 was a rare exception to its cursory coverage in the media. The investigation found that her reputation as a litigator was quite inflated; in fifteen years, she had tried only five cases, in family law, patent infringement, and intellectual property. The publication could identify only two regular clients of hers. "[C]ontrary to some press reports, she's simply spent too little time practicing to be considered that much of a lawyer," the report concluded.

Hillary handled no noteworthy cases during her legal career. Reporting that she was rarely seen in court, the *American Lawyer* observed that she tried to dodge the highly visible—and often the most interesting and challenging—cases in order to avoid potential conflicts or political fallout. The overwhelming majority of corporate cases get settled, and a good lawyer tries to keep the client out of court. Nonetheless, an attorney who opposed Hillary on a commercial matter in the late 1980s told the *Los Angeles Times* that she had led him to believe she wanted to go to trial, then offered to settle "on very favorable terms to our side" the night before their court appearance because she was worried about the impact that losing the case might have on her husband. "She had to take politics into account on each matter. She was afraid to tie it up and go to court. She ended up settling on most matters," the lawyer was quoted as saying. If in fact Hillary felt such political pressure, it was yet another example of how being married to the governor of the state made it difficult for her to establish a topflight legal practice.

Anyone in Hillary's position would have faced similar pressures. But Hillary seems not to have been terribly interested in practicing law at a firm like Rose anyway. Her love was policy, not law as it was traditionally practiced. Her intellectual development at Yale Law School had yielded a true commitment to public interest law as a means of forcing political change. Even while she worked as a partner at Rose and began to play political nanny to Bill, she found time to pursue this interest intensively. "It doesn't matter if Bill is a lawyer, attorney general, or governor—I'm still going to worry about these things," Hillary once said.

In 1977, she helped found a group called Arkansas Advocates for Children and Families, an advocacy organization that helped create the Governor's Commission on Early Childhood, assuring state money for new child care programs. She also lobbied for an overhaul of the state's child welfare system. Arkansas Advocates worked closely with Marian Wright Edelman's Children's Defense Fund. Her role in establishing the Little Rock children's organization showed that even while working at Rose, Hillary had not abandoned her political agenda. In the late 1970s she pursued her interest in family law further as chairman of the Legal Services Corporation, which supported Arkansas Advocates.

In contrast with the public policy cases that were her labor of love, Hillary's work at the Rose Firm usually involved routine and tedious legal matters. One of her first regular clients, for example, was the Little Rock Airport Commission. The position of counsel to the commission, which Hillary held for twelve years, didn't bring much money into the firm (about $30,000 a year), but it provided her with the beginnings of a steady client base as well as an introduction to Little Rock's insider system. In addition to working on lackluster cases, she also had to tolerate the comically condescending efforts of Little Rock's old guard to accommodate a woman lawyer in their midst and to ingratiate themselves with her husband.

The most influential member of the Airport Commission to participate in the decision to hire Hillary was Seth Ward, a gruff, multimillionaire businessman who was the father-in-law of Rose partner Webster Hubbell. Webb Hubbell, a one-time Arkansas Razorback offensive tackle and former mayor of Little Rock, was another good old boy—not as bright or meticulous as Foster, but well connected politically. He rose to his position in the Little Rock power structure by marrying Ward's daughter Suzanna, but his relationship with his rich father-in-law was tricky: Ward was fond of cracking that it cost him "a hundred thousand a year to keep Webb in politics." Hubbell was the firm's link to political circles in the capital. Said one Rose Firm lawyer: "Webb basically managed files. He had other roles."

Seth Ward abstained from voting on the airport attorney appointment because of Hubbell's position at Rose, but he had a lot of influence with the other commissioners. Hillary Rodham's appointment as counsel for the Airport Commission was surprising in a socially conservative town that typically kept women out of the power structure, especially considering that the longtime commission attorney was unceremoniously dumped to make room for her. Hillary's hiring was portrayed in public statements as an advance for women rather than as a political move. "This was a chance for us to get a woman on the staff and involve women more in airport operations," Ward said at the time. Commission chairman George Munsey commented, somewhat absurdly, "We felt we'd like to have the ladies involved in the overall operation of the airport."

When Hillary took leave from Rose in 1982 to campaign full time for Bill's reelection, another Little Rock lawyer, William Hamilton, was named to replace her as airport counsel. After Clinton won, Hamilton was axed to clear the decks for Hillary again. "We were out at a cocktail party at the Little Rock Country Club. We [Seth Ward and Hamilton] were standing around having a drink when Hillary walked up," Hamilton remembered. "Then Seth said, 'When are we going to have you back?' And she said, 'When did you want me? I didn't know you wanted me back.' This is all in front of me, which pissed me off. And he said, 'Well, how about Monday morning?' I just stood there like a dummy . . . what could I say? There wasn't any discussion—that was the end of it."

Hillary learned that in Arkansas it helped to have people like Seth Ward in your corner. Earlier in her career, she had instinctively networked with Burke Marshall and Marian Wright Edelman and John Doar. But here in Little Rock she did not yet know the character of the people with whom she was working, and what sorts of favors they would ask of her in the future.

5

Alinsky's Daughter

If Hillary was discouraged by her early experiences in Arkansas, she responded by tackling a wide range of challenges outside the state. Through her work with the Legal Services Corporation, the Children's Defense Fund, and the American Bar Association, Hillary maintained close contact with the East Coast confederates she had met at Wellesley, Yale, and the Watergate Committee, and gradually built her own reputation, independent from Bill's, as a lawyer-activist in power circles within the Democratic Party. She thus fulfilled her long-standing desire to be a public interest lawyer by becoming part of a movement of lawyers, activists, and bureaucrats working through the legal system and the government to advance social change.

Hillary's public interest legal career largely escaped notice in Arkansas, even as she solidified her left-liberal policy preferences and garnered important training as a political operative. It was a testament to her skills and determination that she was able to develop these national links—eventually becoming the chairman of the board of the Children's Defense Fund—from a remote home base in Arkansas, where she continued to practice law at Rose. Paradoxically, while Hillary foreclosed many career opportunities by moving to Arkansas in 1974, she ended up accomplishing more as a part-time public interest law advocate than most people would have achieved working at it full time. Indeed, she would ultimately become the symbolic leader of the liberal establishment.

Though less publicized than her links to the Children's Defense Fund, Hillary's service on the board of the Legal Services Corporation in Washington in the late 1970s thrust her onto the national scene. The publicly funded legal services movement was the perfect vehicle to accomplish the plans Hillary had broached with Saul Alinsky ten years before. She would now prove that the key to achieving real social progress was not Alinsky-style agitation but skillful bureaucratic manipulation from inside. This tactical difference with Alinsky is what made Hillary's radicalism much more effective, but also harder for the public to perceive.

In the legal services community as in the student protest movement and her prior stint in Washington on the Watergate Committee, Hillary was among like-minded people who saw themselves as waging a just and necessary war against a malignant conservative enemy. And as with her previous successes—from revolutionizing student life at Wellesley to helping to win Richard Nixon's resignation in the Watergate inquiry— her ultimate success in a political war with the Reagan administration bred in her a certain overconfidence and self-righteous assurance. It also permanently stamped her opponents as unenlightened or even evil— "the enemy"—in her mind. The opposition, meanwhile, formed their own stereotyped impression of Hillary as a high-handed, brusque, and obstinate intellectual elitist.

In December 1977, President Jimmy Carter, in whose campaign Hillary had worked, appointed her to the independent LSC board, a group of politically connected lawyers that distributes government legal aid money to local programs nationwide. Six months later, the Carter White House put out word that Hillary Rodham would be its candidate to chair the board, and soon after the board members elected her as the first woman in the organization's history to hold the post. "They decided it was time to show that a woman could chair the board," said fellow board member Cecilia Esquer, who nominated Hillary. Hillary's sense of excitement at the opportunity to prove herself, and by extension all women, by running a multi-million-dollar national organization at the very young age of thirty must have been palpable. Equally intoxicating must have been the chance to grasp the levers of government power and to exercise that power in the service of her strongly held ideas and beliefs.

As Esquer remembered her, Hillary epitomized the liberated woman of that period. The busy young lawyer commuted from Arkansas to Washington on a monthly basis, where she ran the two-day board meetings of the national corporation with efficiency and aplomb. She had, of course, kept her maiden name. When she gave birth to Chelsea in early 1980, "she was breast-feeding her at the first board meeting after she was born," Esquer said. Later that year, when Bill lost the governorship, he accompanied his wife to Washington and sat on the sidelines quietly minding Chelsea while Hillary conducted official business.

The question of whether the federal government should provide free legal services to the poor has been bitterly contested since the government first began spending $1 million a year on the program during the heyday of LBJ's Great Society in 1965. The LSC became an independent corporation by an act of Congress in 1974 and was given an annual budget of $90 million. By the end of Hillary's tenure, that budget had ballooned to over $300 million a year.

In the view of Roger Cramton, the Cornell law professor and chairman of the LSC board under President Gerald Ford, the original Great Society legal services program set forth objectives far beyond the goals of traditional legal aid. Previously, legal aid had been thought of as helping low-income people apply for government benefits, deal with landlords, or fight for child support. The LBJ program was run by professional activists whose idea of social justice meant litigating and lobbying to change laws, and extending the welfare state, as well as Alinsky-style organizing of the poor into political pressure groups.

When Congress wrote the law establishing the Legal Services Corporation as an independent entity in 1974, Cramton argued in an article in the *Villanova Law Review,* it sought to proscribe the blatantly political objectives of the old program—lobbying and organizing the poor—while preserving the use of a full range of legal techniques, including class action suits and impact litigation, for poverty lawyers seeking to ensure "equal access to justice" for the poor. Cramton concluded, however, that the somewhat ambiguous wording of the new law seemed to do little more than substitute "neutral rhetoric" for the "emotionally charged rhetoric" of the Great Society program. In effect, despite efforts to scale back the politicized activities of the programs, it could be argued that nothing had really changed.

Following Cramton's tenure under President Ford, Hillary's board quickly swung back to the 1960s approach of aggressively using the courts to expand the welfare system and increase government control over private property, and to conduct ideologically generated and driven litigations. Ample evidence of the goals of the LSC is contained in training manuals dating from Hillary's tenure, one of which described the LSC-funded attorney as "an arm of community organizations, that is, the lawyer was to function as part of a political effort, at times as a lawyer, at times as an organizer, an educator, teacher and PR man." An end to be attained through courts and legislatures was "power over the distribution of wealth, power over the means of production and distribution."

In Hillary's 1978 Senate confirmation testimony, she endorsed the use of legal services lawyers to "reform" laws and regulations the LSC deemed "unresponsive to the needs of the poor." During one LSC board meeting, according to the minutes, Hillary spoke of her embrace of the radical view of legal services: ". . . look what legal service does, it takes a Wellesley graduate and turns her into a union worker for legal services. I mean, you know, I mean, there's change in this society. People have to recognize that."

Soon after assuming the chairmanship of the board (at one meeting she referred to herself as "chair—whatever—person, thing, or whatever"), Hillary spoke at a planning retreat at the Airlie House in Airlie, Virginia. The traditional meaning of legal services—providing access to the legal system—was not enough to ensure the rights of the poor because the legal system does not necessarily produce "just results," she said. Referring to her fellow board member Mickey Kantor, who had been featured in the *Yale Review of Law and Social Action* in 1972 for his lobbying efforts on behalf of an independent LSC, Hillary observed, "After Mickey's reading of the [LSC] statute about people's access to the system of justice, I don't know if I want 'equal.' I mean, to some extent the people that we represent need more than equal access to resolve their difficulties, and I prefer to keep just the word 'access,' because I think that provides more of an opportunity for the kind of flexibility and creative use that we are talking about."

As Roger Cramton pointed out in his article, the statute governing the LSC and its mandate of service to the poor was revised in 1974 to state that the LSC was to pursue "equal access to justice." The standard indicated a scaling back of the 1960s radical activist goals of "law reform" and "social change." In minutes of the planning retreat, Hillary's blunt criticism of the new legal statute showed that she was not satisfied with providing standard legal services for low-income people, but was looking to extend this arsenal of legal firepower to manipulate the political and legal system. The LSC, in her view, should function as a liberal advocacy group, ensuring wealth redistribution to the poor and legal mandates of equal results, rather than simply assuring equal opportunity.

At Airlie House, Hillary went on to suggest that effecting social change through the courts alone might not be possible, "First, because I think that it is inevitable, in any society, that the legal system is principally an establishment, conservative system. And that good lawyers are better able to manipulate it than bad lawyers, for whomever their clients happen to be. But that it, by definition, stands for the established order." Reflecting the trendy left-wing thinking of the late 1970s, Hillary seemed to accept an idea of the law as illegitimate and up for grabs—a staple of the Critical Legal Studies view that law is an instrument of ruling-class domination rather than an inherently fair process of dispute resolution.

As a student at Wellesley, Hillary had shown her aptitude for using the bureaucratic power of the establishment to further her political goals. At the Airlie House retreat, Washington lawyer Steven Engelberg, a Carter-appointed LSC board member close to Hillary, warned the group that if the legal services staff went to Capitol Hill to ask for funds for the type of changes they really wanted to implement, the "established figures" in Congress would never agree. Engelberg advised the assembled advocates to avoid any talk of income redistribution or welfare and to speak only of providing low-income people with lawyers to help them out of run-of-the-mill legal jams. By adopting this strategy, Hillary was able to win big budget increases for the program. Thomas Ehrlich, a Stanford law professor who was president of the LSC during the early part of Hillary's board tenure, praised her ability to lobby Congress for more money. "She understood right away that you have to go up on the Hill and present the program in a very conservative way. She would say, 'Whatever you may think of Head Start or some other program, the Legal Services Corporation is a very conservative concept,'" Ehrlich recalled.

In later years, Hillary would characterize her work at the LSC as anything but radical. And she may have been sincere when she described the legal services movement as being above partisan politics. "I never thought that being for legal services, which I have been for 22 years, is 'liberal,' " she told the *Washington Post* in August 1992, calling legal services "a bedrock issue for equal justice and an absolute imperative to have available. I don't think that is liberal or conservative. I think that's how you make a justice system work. I view it as a very pragmatic response to people's needs."

However, a review of the cases undertaken by LSC lawyers during the late 1970s belies any claim that the program was an apolitical service organization. Indeed, the litigation undertaken during Hillary's tenure was so political that two officials from Clinton's home state, Democratic Senator Dale Bumpers and Republican Representative Ed Bethune, complained in a public statement in 1980 that LSC attorneys were looking "for too many cases which can effect an economic or social outcome."

Under LSC's administrative structure, specific litigation decisions are made by hundreds of local boards, and not at the national level.[1] In this sense, the national board existed as something of a front organization, especially on Capitol Hill, an acceptably mainstream presence behind which operated the far more radical grassroots activists employed at the local offices. With its authority to make grants to the local boards, however, the national board did set an overall policy direction and a tone as to what was permissible and desirable, and it exercised final control through its power of the purse.

During Hillary's tenure, an LSC grantee in Ann Arbor, Michigan sued to compel the federal government to define "black English" as a separate language under a section of the Equal Educational Opportunities Act of 1974, thereby forcing the state to provide all black residents with mandatory remedial language training. Another suit sought to turn over two-thirds of public lands in Maine to Indian tribes. In New York, an LSC grantee sued the New York City Transit Authority for its failure to employ former heroin addicts, claiming that such a failure was discriminatory toward blacks and Hispanics. Several affirmative action lawsuits sought to classify drug addicts, alcoholics, and gays as "handicapped."

In Ohio, a legal services program sued U.S. Steel to either prevent plant closures or force a sale of steel mills to a worker-community group. The local LSC grantee employed Saul Alinsky disciple Staughton Lynd to handle the case. When it came to trial, Ramsey Clark joined him at the plaintiff's table. And in a famous 1981 case, in Hartford, Connecticut, Jane Doe, a transsexual welfare recipient represented by the LSC grantee Neighborhood Legal Services, sued the state's welfare agency for denying payment for a sex-change operation. The state maintained the operation wasn't a legitimate medical expense.

California Rural Legal Assistance, a major LSC grantee, filed suit against the University of California to stop research aimed at improving agricultural productivity. The suit maintained that efforts to develop new farm machinery benefit "a narrow group of agribusiness interests with no valid public purpose, contribute to agricultural unemployment or the displacement of farm workers, or the demise of the small family farm, or the deterioration of the rural home and rural life." The editors of *The New Republic* responded with a stinging 1980 editorial: "To oppose research aimed at increasing productivity is simply insane . . . too often legal aid lawyers use poor people as guinea pigs in an attempt to impose through the courts some fanciful middle-class view of social justice."

Just how "fanciful" were some of the strategies for addressing the legal problems of the poor during Hillary's tenure? "I remember one case in southern Louisiana, filed against the state's Wildlife Commission, which had promulgated rules on oyster collecting that were said to be discriminatory against black oyster collectors," said Dennis Daherty, a former senior LSC staffer. "So the LSC gave a special grant for a three-day workshop for the oyster collectors in which Marxist speakers and folk singers described a pattern of oppression. They never did get a lawyer to represent them."

The legal concepts embedded in such litigation received Hillary's implicit support through a set of rules for grantees proposed by the LSC board and published in the *Federal Register* on March 23, 1981. The rules required that LSC grantees not discriminate against homosexuals; hire a fixed percentage of bilingual employees in certain areas; adopt hiring quotas to guarantee employment of women and minorities at levels that reflect "parity with the relevant labor market"; and include drug addicts and alcoholics under the definition of "handicapped," thus protecting them under anti-discrimination laws. (The rules were never adopted, due to opposition in 1981 by the new Republican-controlled Senate.)

While Hillary chaired the LSC, the organization forged close links with the National Lawyers Guild (NLG), which had been founded in 1937 with the assistance of the International Labor Defense, the American section of the International Class War Prisoners Aid Society, an agency of the Comintern. It remained an active affiliate of the International Association of Democratic Lawyers (IADL), an international Communist front controlled by the Communist Party of the Soviet Union. The IADL was described in a CIA report on Soviet propaganda operations published by the House Intelligence Committee in 1978 as "one of the most useful Communist front organizations at the service of the Soviet Communist Party." The report noted that at its 1975 conference in Algiers, "the real and ideological interests of the IADL were covered by the agenda . . . which considered law to be a function in the struggle against imperialism, colonialism, neocolonialism, racism and apartheid. Under the banner of anti-imperialism, the IADL's thrust . . . was to do battle with the large international companies as a way to gain adherents and backing in the developing world."

Through the years, the National Lawyers Guild had associated itself with many radical causes, including the Critical Legal Studies movement. A significant number of NLG activists were members of the Weather Underground's Prairie Fire Organizing Committee, a faction of Students for a Democratic Society that was committed to violent revolution. During the trial of leaders of the Baader-Meinhof terrorist gang in West Germany, NLG sent an observer team to express solidarity. In 1975, the NLG executive board voted to "provide legal support and resources" to aid the Palestine Liberation Organization.

The Guild—which has claimed that the American system of justice "is used to hound, attack, imprison, and execute the oppressed minorities, workers and political activists"—supplied legions of attorneys to local legal aid programs during Hillary's tenure. In the classifieds section of the Guild publication *Guild Notes* for November–December 1980, the overwhelming majority of employment advertisements were placed by federally funded legal services programs. By 1980, the NLG reported that an estimated one thousand of its members worked in the LSC system. A 1977 NLG conference in Seattle featured a presentation from "the Legal Services Task Force on the work of NLG members employed by this federally funded program." NLG members working within the Legal Services Corporation even started an employee association called the National Organization of Legal Services Workers. Under Hillary's LSC chairmanship, the Guild-affiliated National Conference of Black Lawyers was a direct grantee; according to a listing in the LSC board's annual report for 1977, the conference received six-figure grants during her board tenure.

Training manuals and conferences produced by the national corporation and distributed to local programs counseled lawyers not only to engage in the kind of partisan politicking prohibited by the LSC's charter, but also to harass opponents in the community, a reflection of Saul Alinsky's influence on an entire generation of activists. A handbook on *Tactical Investigations for People's Struggles,* for example, was filled with Marxist rhetoric and cartoons depicting the fictional "Chema Kill Corporation" founded by "Chester A. Prominent," who "oppresses the poor." Another manual, *Strategic and Tactical Research,* suggested the "use of muckraking" to "neutralize" opponents: "Muckraking kinds of research can put pressure on key people holding up legislation in committees of City Hall, state legislatures, or Congress." At a June 1981 LSC training conference in upstate New York, LSC workers were told to use personal information to "intimidate" targets. One speaker specifically cited the "tactical rules" of Saul Alinsky: " 'Whenever possible, go outside of the experience of the enemy,' to cause confusion, frustration and fear." Nailing a dead rat to a local official's door was suggested as one way of doing this.

Hillary herself led a pitched battle over the private bar's judicare programs, in which private lawyers provided services to the poor at a discounted rate and were then reimbursed by the government for the difference. "The irony is that we followed the socialist model in the legal services field from the very beginning, with the government hiring the lawyers," said Roger Cramton, the Ford LSC board chairman. "The [Rodham] board was not willing to reexamine that, and they had to be dragged kicking and screaming to include the private bar in any of the activities. The judicare model would have depoliticized legal services enormously," because regular lawyers rather than community activists would have been involved.[2]

As chairman of the board Hillary appears to have done everything in her power to suppress and defeat the judicare projects. "There was quite an opposition to judicare among the legal services people. Hillary was none too crazy about the idea," recalled Tom Greene, who was appointed by the LSC board in the late 1970s to study the impact of judicare demonstration programs of the private bar and report back on the feasibility of expanding them. "We looked at judicare and vouchers and other things. I visited several LSC offices and made a report on it and attended several LSC board meetings with Hillary as chairman. I thought judicare could work. But I was told [by the Rodham board] that the non-activist lawyers weren't specialized enough to provide legal services to the poor."

Throughout her whole career, Hillary never seemed to revisit her own intellectual assumptions or develop a talent for compromise. As a leading advocate of judicare, Republican Congressman F. James Sensenbrenner of Wisconsin, then the ranking minority member of the House subcommittee which oversaw the LSC, butted heads with Hillary over the issue. In the late 1970s, with the Democrats in control of the presidency and both houses of Congress, Hillary apparently saw no reason to entertain the Republican position. Though she could be exquisitely skilled in selling the program as "conservative" in courtesy calls on Capitol Hill, when challenged by a knowledgeable conservative critic seeking a fair hearing for an alternate proposal, Hillary was defensive and inflexible. She was emboldened as well by support from a powerful liberal press, which had long regarded the LSC as a sacred cow.

"In the two counties immediately north of Milwaukee, everybody, the local bar and the welfare advocacy organizations, favored a judicare approach," Congressman Sensenbrenner recalled. "Members of the private bar would do the work and they would be paid at less than the going rate. But Hillary and Dan Bradley [Hillary's handpicked LSC president] were insisting on opening federal programs in the counties. I sent a letter to Bradley representing the views of my constituency unanimously, and I got nowhere. They ignored it. Then, he and Hillary came over to meet with me. They weren't interested that everyone in the district was for judicare, that there wasn't the need for a legal services program in either Sheboygan or Ozaukee counties.

"When I made the argument for judicare—that it would be more cost-effective—they told me flat out that there would be a full-time staff office in the two counties so the LSC bureaucracy in Washington could control what these lawyers did. What Hillary was doing as chairman of the board was solidifying control by the government and the bureaucracy. And they were spending taxpayer money to do it. She tried the same with health care. Back then I reached the conclusion that she is a control freak," Sensenbrenner concluded. "She wants to utilize the power of the federal government to make sure she, her people, and her philosophy have control."

Though Sensenbrenner can be counted as a reasonable and informed foe, the tenor of the conservative attack on Legal Services in the late 1970s was set by New Right firebrand Howard Phillips, who so dominated the debate that Hillary may have seen him as the exemplar of the Republican view. During the Nixon administration, Phillips was appointed acting director of the Office of Economic Opportunity with orders from the White House to shut it down. The office housed the Great Society's legal services program before it became an independent entity. When Nixon bowed to pressure from Congress and decided to keep the office open, Phillips resigned and started a group called Conservatives for the Removal of the President. He founded the Conservative Caucus in 1974, campaigning against the establishment by Congress of the independent LSC. Phillips later founded the U.S. Taxpayers Party, which emphasizes a social-conservative agenda, including opposition to abortion and condemnation of homosexuality.

Just as he had failed to convince Nixon to gut the Office of Economic Opportunity earlier in the decade Phillips, a bushy-eyebrowed demagogue in the mold of Pat Buchanan had little success developing a persuasive case against government-funded legal services, even among Republicans on Capitol Hill. In 1981, while Bradley was president and Hillary was board chair, a Phillips-backed amendment to ban Legal Services lawyers from representing gays was brought to the floor of the House of Representatives by ultra-conservative Democratic Representative Larry McDonald of Georgia. "The extent of Howard's argument was 'queers shouldn't have lawyers,'" said a former Reagan administration official who worked in the legal services area during the transition from Hillary's board to President Reagan's board. "This is how [Hillary's] view of conservatives as venal and tactically and strategically stupid evolved. It is hard to imagine two settings [Watergate and the legal services struggle] in which conservatives were so dumb and so easily caricatured."

By 1980, Hillary had succeeded in tripling the federal budget for legal services and was presiding over a virtual revolution in the priorities of local legal services programs nationwide. Though relatively young and in-experienced, she had earned the respect of her professional colleagues. "She always did her homework. She had a presence and used humor well. I was impressed with Hillary. She could take a meeting and make it work," said Leona Vogt, a consultant who conducted management analyses of agency programs for the board. "She was a good executive, who took the job seriously. She was very good at taking the issue at hand and identify-ing it and dealing with it rationally. She could hold her own with anyone. She wouldn't be cowed."

Hillary's leadership skills—at least when exercised within friendly con-fines—enabled her to navigate a course despite divisions within the movement. While Republicans in Congress complained that the agency was too enmeshed in politics, radical lawyers in the field protested that the national board was not strong enough in its support of their agenda. Racial minority members of Hillary's own board formed a submovement. "A big part of her job was just keeping the lid on," said Vogt.

By 1980, there were more ominous signs on the horizon. After a strong primary challenge from Senator Ted Kennedy, President Carter had be-come a weakened incumbent. California governor Ronald Reagan, the Republican presidential nominee, had slashed state legal services for the poor. With her legacy thus imperiled and the local legal service activists who relied on her leadership threatened with defunding, Hillary saw lit-tle choice but to fight. She tried to fend off the expected Republican at-tack with a range of offensive maneuvers that were later found, by an impartial General Accounting Office investigation in the early 1980s, to have violated federal law in authorizing the expenditure of federal funds for lobbying and political organizing, a practice prohibited by the very 1974 law that established the LSC.

Though Hillary showed her mettle and more than lived up to the field workers' expectations, her fight to preserve legal services exemplified her growing acceptance of an ends-justifies-the-means political philoso-phy, or, as Saul Alinsky put it, "whatever works to get power to the peo-ple, use it." In her advocacy of the Black Panther cause and her desire to impeach Richard Nixon for war crimes, Hillary had stretched the sys-tem as far as she could. Now, she crossed the line in order to preserve what she believed was a noble and necessary enterprise endangered by mean-spirited attacks.

Sometimes partisans, particularly the young, will err out of inexperience and excess of zeal—and may be granted a measure of grace if the erring is both minor and infrequent. Young lawyers often exhibit a warrior mentality before being softened by maturity or wisdom. In violating the LSC guidelines proscribing the use of government funds and agencies for political lobbying, it might be said that Hillary Rodham was merely the bureaucratic overlord at the switch, as mistakes were made by faceless activists beneath her. Perhaps the impropriety never even occurred to her.

Yet her pattern of conduct suggests less the young hothead than the dedicated political operator, determined to use the system to advance her cause while exempting herself from any responsibility to abide by its rules and procedures. In the LSC case, she would be the no-holds-barred, hired-gun litigator and political street fighter that her Watergate mentor Bernard Nussbaum had prepared her to be.[3]

In 1980, the LSC funded a drive to defeat a tax-cutting measure on the California ballot known as Proposition 9, sponsored by Howard Jarvis, father of the 1978 Proposition 13 property tax revolt in California. The strategy was to marshal the votes of the legal services "client communities"—about 20 percent of the California population—and to turn out a large "no" vote against Proposition 9, which would preserve state funds for legal aid and, not coincidentally, spur turnout for Jimmy Carter's re-election. The U.S. Comptroller General, who heads Congress's independent investigative agency, the General Accounting Office (GAO), subsequently concluded that the conduct of legal services personnel who participated in the effort to defeat the California ballot measure was illegal. According to the GAO report, these were "the precise sort of activities that are prohibited by the statute's injunction against using corporate funds to oppose a ballot measure that is already on the ballot and where clients' legal rights are not at issue." (Mickey Kantor was chairman of the "No on 9" Committee at the time federal money was being funneled to it by his own LSC board.)

In addition to funding the "No on 9" campaign, the LSC spent millions in 1980 to defeat political opponents nationwide. A March 26, 1980, memo from top LSC official Clint Lyons, which was sent to all LSC programs throughout the United States, authorized each to use 1 percent of its taxpayer-funded budget for explicit political spending, which was prohibited. The Lyons memo stated that "this allocation was approved in December 1979 by the LSC Board of Directors."

After Reagan was elected president and the Republicans took control of the Senate, Reagan announced his intention to eliminate funding for the LSC altogether and Republicans in Congress launched investigations of alleged abuses of power during Hillary's tenure. "When Ronald Reagan came in, everybody shifted into a defensive 'everybody is out to get us' mode," recalled Leona Vogt. The left reacted to Reagan's election with a new sense of discipline and esprit de corps, and a renewed conviction of its moral and political vocation. Once again, Hillary was at the forefront of the action. Redoubling her efforts, she authorized a nationwide lobbying campaign—also later found to be illegal—to ensure the survival of legal aid programs and to resist Reaganism at every turn.

More than anyone, Hillary could be credited with preserving the embattled program and thus helping to institutionalize the progressive social movement in the federal government despite the election returns. "Hillary understood that you had to seek out constituencies and build support in the local communities so that it [the program] couldn't be destroyed by another administration," said Thomas Ehrlich, the former LSC president. "As it happened, Reagan came in, but the base that was built during her tenure enabled the program to survive. I credit her with that."

Within a month of Reagan's election, in December 1980 and January 1981, the LSC held eight regional "training" meetings for local LSC lawyers—in Boston, New York, Atlanta, Chicago, northern Virginia, Philadelphia, Denver, and San Francisco—to coordinate a grassroots political campaign for the preservation of "aggressive impact advocacy to improve the lives and power of poor people." The LSC enlisted the help of groups like the National Lawyers Guild and Americans for Democratic Action, and mounted telephone and direct-mail lobbying efforts nationwide.

At a training meeting in Denver, Alan Houseman, a top LSC executive, explained the challenge as Hillary and her cadre saw it. In a fairly hubristic expression of self-righteousness, Houseman described the legal services movement: "What is at stake is the survival of the committed, aggressive political staff. . . . What is at stake is not solely the survival of the Legal Services program. What is at stake is the survival of many social benefits—entitlement programs that we struggled, since 1965, to make real for poor people. . . . What is at stake is a number of other kinds of programs like affirmative action, civil rights programs. That, in the end, is what is at stake in this battle. Those, in the end, are far more important than legal services. Legal services is a tool to get them."

In preparing for the appointment of a Reagan-controlled board, and in anticipation of deep funding cuts and new restrictions on how federal money could be spent (if not outright elimination)—LSC executives took steps to get federal money out from under the control of the national LSC board. The sophisticated scheme involved the use of "mirror corporations" formed to hide the money trail. According to a Senate report, the New Haven Legal Assistance Association transferred its entire LSC grant of $543,000 to the South Central Connecticut Legal Services Corporation, a shell corporation outside the domain of the national board. That group merely screened cases and referred them back to New Haven, whose attorneys were paid by the shell corporation.

Technical assistance grants worth $2.7 million were moved from LSC-controlled regional support centers—which were coordinating much of the "survival" campaign—to the National Legal Aid and Defenders Association (NLADA), a private association of legal aid lawyers. A report commissioned by the NLADA openly referred to this process as "circumvention," and said the intention was to work in areas "which are likely to be blocked by LSC legislation or regulation" and to "solidify the political posture and the ideological glue of the system."

The Senate investigation showed that Clinton Lyons, director of the Office of Field Services at the LSC, and his deputy, Hulett "Bucky" Askew, were largely responsible for the transfer of the grants from LSC to the NLADA in 1981 and 1982. Lyons subsequently became the NLADA's executive director in 1983 and Askew worked for the organization as a highly paid consultant. Mickey Kantor, who sat on the LSC board with Hillary, had once lobbied on behalf of the NLADA. (Later, in 1993, in a show of appreciation for her efforts, the group gave an award to First Lady Hillary Rodham Clinton, who was praised at the ceremony in a speech by Attorney General Janet Reno.)

Relying on an expansive interpretation of the legislative intent behind the LSC charter, Hillary and her LSC lawyers argued that the board had not engaged in impermissible political activities. When Republicans in Congress asked the GAO to investigate, however, the GAO rejected the LSC's legal interpretation, concluding that the LSC "has itself engaged and allowed its grant recipients to engage in lobbying activities prohibited by federal law. . . . We believe the Corporation's construction [of the law] is improper. . . . In summary, through the use of recipient organizations and their contacts at the state and local level, LSC has developed an extensive lobbying campaign to support reauthorization legislation for the corporation and related appropriation measures being considered by the Congress. This activity violates the anti-lobbying statutory and appropriation restrictions described above."

As board chairman, Hillary approved these efforts to turn the LSC into a publicly funded political action committee. In Senate testimony following the GAO investigation, Franklin A. Curtis, the associate director of the agency, stated that LSC's former president Dan Bradley had acknowledged keeping the "board of directors informed of the survival effort through periodic communications. Board members also attended the regional project director meetings. The former president indicated that a January 9, 1981 memo to the board from the director of LSC's research institute accurately describes LSC's survival effort." In 1982 congressional testimony, Bradley, who left the agency when the Reagan administration came in, went further, conceding that the "survival" plan had been "stupid," "improper," and "probably illegal."

Hillary's final gambit was a personally led effort to thwart President Reagan's ability to appoint replacements to the LSC board. Disagreements within the Reagan White House about whether to appoint a board or simply to try to shut down the whole operation resulted in delays of more than a year before candidates were nominated, giving Hillary and her Carter-appointed board an entire year to implement their rear-guard strategy. When Congress refused to go along with Reagan's proposal to dismantle the LSC, the White House went ahead with plans to replace Hillary's board by appointing several lawyers during the congressional recess in late 1981. (Recess appointees may take office before Senate confirmation.)

The opposition's counteroffensive was two-pronged: a legal challenge to Reagan's authority to make recess appointees to the LSC board, and an all-out political assault on his nominees. In February 1982, the Carter board, now out of power, filed suit to prevent the Reagan board members from holding a meeting, alleging that their appointments were unlawful. Several members of the Carter board had themselves been so-called recess appointees in 1979, but the middle of a political war was evidently no time to quibble over technicalities. Hillary hired her Rose Law partner and fellow legal services devotee Vincent Foster to represent her in the case. William Harvey, the Reagan-appointed acting board chairman, recalled a conference call he had with Hillary shortly after he was named to the board. "I remember that [Dan] Bradley got on the phone with Rodham and said they shouldn't be doing the lawsuit. But Rodham wanted it. Bradley was probably afraid that we would uncover the intense political nature of their activities in deposition."

Meanwhile, the Reagan nominees were roasted on Capitol Hill and in the press. California Judge George Paras was labeled by Democratic Senator Thomas Eagleton of Missouri as a "14-carat-bigot" for referring to a fellow judge as a "professional Mexican." Conservative activist William Olson, another nominee, was attacked for having written the Reagan transition memo recommending abolition of the agency he was now slated to oversee. And William Harvey, an Indiana University law professor, was pilloried for having vetoed the establishment of a poverty law clinic at his law school.

In the end, Hillary could feel that she had used the legal process to whip yet another Republican president. Her lawsuit and the controversy surrounding the Reagan appointees threw sand in the gears of the new board and stalled its plan to rein in LSC-funded activities. Later, her lawsuit became moot when a Reagan-appointed board was finally confirmed by the Senate after more than a year. But it was a very different board from the one Reagan originally nominated. In the end, under political pressure, all eight Reagan nominees, strong conservatives who might have been expected to radically reverse Hillary's legacy, were withdrawn and replaced by moderates who made no drastic policy changes from the Rodham era.

When Hillary's term on the LSC board expired in 1982, she strengthened her ties to East Coast activist circles by joining the board of the New World Foundation, considered one of the nation's most left-leaning philanthropies. Based in New York, the organization was founded in 1954 by philanthropist Anita McCormick Blaine. Serving on New World's senior staff was Adrian W. DeWind, who during the 1970s was a member of the Committee for Public Justice, founded by Lillian Hellman. That group monitored alleged FBI abuses of the U.S. Communist Party and the Black Panthers.[4]

The New World Foundation is not a traditional philanthropy; it funds political movements rather than research, educational, or charitable efforts. The foundation's literature says that it "seeks to join others in the struggle for social justice and peace," and holds that "genuine world security will be accomplished through equitable and just relationships" instead of through military strength.

During Hillary's tenure, which lasted from 1982 through 1988 and included stints as vice chair and chair of the board of directors, the organization sharpened its focus on political activism. Hillary wrote in one annual report, "The New World Foundation has sought to use its resources to strengthen the bridge—between the system and the neediest and least represented—and to encourage other foundations to focus on the fragility of activists' efforts on behalf of the poor in general and people of color in particular. In this effort we have made mostly general support grants rather than special project grants, so as to provide core support to organizers and advocates."

The New World Foundation has given many grants to mainstream liberal groups like the Children's Defense Fund. But much of its money went to the hard left. The foundation supported the Christic Institute, which spent hundreds of thousands of dollars bringing charges against supporters of the Nicaraguan Contras that were later held in court to be frivolous. Many of the foundation grantees, such as the National Lawyers Guild and the Institute for Policy Studies, had ties to the Communist movement. Another grant recipient, the Africa Fund, lobbied on behalf of the most extremist elements within the African National Congress. Under Hillary's chairmanship, the foundation supported the Committee in Solidarity with the People of El Salvador, better known as CISPES, which was founded in New York City in 1980 by Farid Handal, brother of El Salvador's Communist Party chief Shafik Handal. Farid had come to the United States to mobilize American support for the FMLN, the major Communist guerrilla organization in El Salvador.

The New World Foundation was also a benefactor of Grassroots International, which described itself as a "people-to-people partnership for social change." While a New World grantee, this organization was giving money to two Palestinian groups with ties to the Communist faction of the PLO—the Union of Palestinian Working Women's Committees and the Union of Palestinian Medical Relief Committees.

Hillary appears to have gotten involved with the New World Foundation through Marian Wright Edelman; when Hillary joined the organization Edelman's husband Peter was a member of New World's board, as was the Democratic lawyer Vernon Jordan. When she signed onto the board in 1982, Hillary had already been serving since 1976 on the board of the Children's Defense Fund, where she had once worked as a young lawyer just out of Yale. She became chairman of the CDF board in 1986 and remained in the post until she stepped down during the 1992 presidential campaign.

Hillary has said that through her work with Edelman, "the world opened up to me and gave me a vision of what it ought to be." Her experiences with Edelman appeared to confirm her belief that reform could best be achieved coercively, through top-down government edicts. Edelman also solidified Hillary's belief that her public policy agenda was a higher calling that transcended partisan politics. Hillary's differences with Alinksy had turned on the question of working inside or outside the system; Hillary had decided to work on the inside. Edelman would provide her with a vision of big government as an instrument of virtue and moral progress, a crucial element of Hillary's intellectual seduction.

In the years that Hillary served on its board, the Children's Defense Fund grew into an influential, multi-million-dollar, non-profit lobbying and research organization. Representatives of the group lobbied both the executive branch and the Congress on a broad range of social welfare legislation, testified as experts on Capitol Hill, and issued widely cited statistical studies on such social problems as child poverty. Meanwhile, Hillary continued her war against the Reagan administration: CDF successfully fought off budget cuts in education, welfare, and child nutrition programs. Legislative victories during the 1980s including expanding Medicaid benefits to cover poor children, as well as a $5 billion a year child care bill, which offered subsidies for day care and tax credits for low- and moderate-income families; increased funding for Head Start; and provided funding to public schools to expand after-school care programs. Twenty years after Kenneth Keniston advocated a federal guaranteed income in the book Hillary had helped research at Yale, Edelman continued to advocate extending welfare benefits to married, working people with children to ensure "all Americans a decent income."[5]

A 1996 *Wall Street Journal* profile described Edelman as "an American Mother Teresa with accolades including 100 honorary degrees . . . and an Albert Schweitzer Humanitarian Prize." In a 1993 profile of Edelman and her organization in *The New Republic,* Mickey Kaus outlined its reputation in elite circles: "The Children's Defense Fund is by now one of the capital's best-known, best-connected lobbies. Large corporations (Chrysler, Coca-Cola, Morgan Guaranty Trust) proudly help finance its $9 million, 120-employee budget. Bloomingdales puts CDF's 1-800 number on its shopping bags at Christmas; Ben & Jerry's publicize the Fund on its Popsicles. News organizations eagerly disseminate the seemingly safe, authoritative data that are CDF's stock in trade." Noting that *Harper's Bazaar* had recently run a profile of Edelman, headlined "Saint Marian," which called her an "unrelenting visionary who has spent her life leading the crusade to help our nation's children," Kaus went on to describe the Edelman aura. "The *Washington Post* has chronicled her courageous role as a young lawyer in the civil rights movement, her interracial marriage to former Robert Kennedy aide Peter Edelman, her three sons' 'Baptist bar mitzvahs.' . . ."

Though she was an unreconstructed Great Society liberal, Edelman, the daughter of a preacher, was not a member of the cultural left. Rather, her public image was, as *Harper's Bazaar* put it, "America's Mother." The motto of the Children's Defense Fund is a child's prayer: "Dear Lord, be good to me. The sea is so wide and my boat is so small." One of Edelman's books, *Guide My Feet,* is a collection of prayers, which shows that Edelman subscribed to the kind of Bible-inspired social gospel activism to which Hillary had first been exposed by her Methodist mentor in Park Ridge. In another book, *The Measure of Our Success,* Edelman becomes a scolding national nanny, lecturing the public on the need for personal responsibility in daily life and shared values in forming public policy. In a series of lectures at Harvard University, Edelman denounced "messages of bliss without responsibility, frequently transmitted by mass media and rock music," as Mickey Kaus noted.

Kaus's article on Edelman was published in February 1993, a time when the Clinton White House was making many critical personnel and policy decisions. In the intramural debates within liberalism and the

Democratic Party, *The New Republic* had come to serve as a house organ for political centrists, who clustered around the Democratic Leadership Council and favored reforming the 1960s social welfare programs for which Edelman vigorously fought, including those providing unrestricted welfare payments to single mothers. In a shot across the bow against the ideas and strategies put forth by Edelman—and by extension, Hillary Rodham Clinton—Kaus portrayed Edelman as cynically manipulating public concern about "children" as a means of achieving more far-reaching political goals. He quoted Edelman as conceding that she hit upon the idea of using children's rights as a proxy issue when "the country was tired of the concerns of the 1960s. I got the idea that children might be a very effective way to broaden the base for change."

Edelman's success as a lobbyist, Kaus wrote, stemmed from her ability to turn all policy debates into debates about children. The strategy "requires that CDF reduce every issue of anti-poverty to a question of 'protecting children who can't speak for themselves.' Not only are Head Start, WIC [the Special Supplemental Food Program for Women, Infants, and Children] and immunization cast as children's issues, so are welfare, day care, housing and employment." The result, Kaus concluded, was to "corrupt what is a necessary national dialogue about poverty and the family."

Citing Nicholas Lemann's book *The Promised Land,* Kaus reported that when Martin Luther King, Jr., was assassinated he had been working on the Poor People's Campaign, an effort to get the nation's poor to converge in protest on Washington demanding more federal help for social programs. The idea, Lemann wrote, was to find "the magic formula that would convince the country as a whole to identify with poor blacks in the cities in the same way that it had identified with Rosa Parks in Montgomery . . . to see them as decent people who had been subjected to a wrong that could now be righted." (The protest in 1969 was not successful, nor was Edelman's personal visit with President Nixon in the White House to discuss these issues.)

"The CDF can be seen as Edelman's attempt to find King's magic formula, to give the fight against black poverty the same right/wrong cast as the fight for civil rights," Kaus continued. "Many of the organization's characteristics—its righteousness, its tendency to see the poverty debates as a conflict between good people and bad, between the 'helpless' and the forces of 'callous' neglect and 'greed'—parallel characteristics of the civil rights movement from which Edelman emerged. Like that movement, CDF says, 'We know what to do.' The only question is 'if America has the political will.' "

The CDF was thus able to position itself above the political fray and to condemn its opponents as mean-spirited partisans. In a 1996 *New Republic* article reviewing books by both Edelman and Hillary Rodham Clinton, liberal social critic Jean Bethke Elshtain objected to Edelman's use of the Bible for political purposes and compared the moral fervor, overheated presentation, and intellectual intolerance of the Christian left, which Edelman represented, to that of the Christian right. As Elshtain reported, in *Guide My Feet*, Edelman likened her political opponents to King Herod in the Christmas prayer. "That mentality . . . pretty much requires the demonization of one's opponents: they are not only wrong, they are godless."

"Really quite evil" is how Edelman once described a GOP welfare reform proposal she opposed. In the 1980s she commonly referred to Reagan reform proposals as "threatening the lives" of children. But it wasn't only Republicans who were stung by Edelman's ire. Wayward Democrats were targeted, too. Between 1988 and 1990, the Children's Defense Fund sought to pass a massive federal day care program that would have created a new central bureaucracy to supervise standardized, federally funded day care centers staffed by state-credentialed experts nationwide. When Democratic representatives Tom Downey of New York and George Miller of California voiced support for tax breaks or vouchers to allow parental choice in day care, Edelman accused them of "continuing [a] private guerrilla war to kill child care legislation" and being willing to "rob millions of children." Downey called the charge "inaccurate and immature," and House Speaker Tom Foley called Edelman a "bully."

Indeed, under Edelman's direction, the Children's Defense Fund— far from being a neutral children's advocacy group—fought hard for its own political agenda by joining a network of left-liberal groups in the rough-and-tumble-world of partisan politics. At the height of the 1980s U.S.-Soviet tensions, Edelman was a member of the board of SANE/FREEZE, a leading disarmament group, and she has been affiliated with the Washington School, a project of the Institute for Policy Studies. While Hillary chaired the board, CDF was a member of the Alliance for Justice, the group that fought to politicize the courts in the activist spirit of Yale Law School. The Alliance orchestrated campaigns against conservative jurists like Robert Bork, Clarence Thomas, and many other Reagan and Bush judicial nominees in an effort to preserve the power of the courts to enact liberal policies. (Bork was publicly opposed by then-Governor Clinton.)

The battle over Bork's confirmation to the Supreme Court was the defining event in the culture wars of the 1980s. To the political left, the brilliant Judge Bork, a strict constructionist of constitutional doctrine who opposed the Douglas view of law to which Hillary adhered, threatened to overturn decades of social progress ushered in by the Warren Court. Bork's opponents ran a slick campaign of distortion and innuendo, falsely presenting him as an advocate of back-alley abortions and mass sterilization to control pregnancies among female workers. This tactic of using public harassment and personal vilification was advocated by Saul Alinsky and the New Left as a means of defeating political opponents and seizing control of power. It was a style of politics first unleashed on the national stage by Hillary and her counterparts on the Watergate Committee, when partisan political warfare was increasingly fought not on the grounds of substantive policy difference but on real or imagined charges of personal ethical failings. Hillary's argument that Richard Nixon's prosecution of the war in Vietnam was not only the wrong policy but immoral and even criminal was the first stage in the criminalization of partisan political differences.

LSC activists carried these same tactics of personal destruction and character assassination into the late 1970s and 1980s in their neighborhood organizing efforts, and in the early campaign against Reagan LSC board nominees as morally unfit to hold office. Next came Bork; and the excesses of the Bork struggle produced the spectacle of the Clarence Thomas nomination for the Supreme Court. Thomas was not only a strict constructionist like Bork, but a black conservative as well; he threatened to break up the monopoly position of the American civil rights establishment on questions of race. Failing to stop Thomas on substantive grounds, the opposition resorted to accusing him of moral impropriety in the Anita Hill sexual harassment case. The opponents were willing to publicize the confidential, uncorroborated charges of a reluctant witness, thereby compromising the procedural rights of both accuser and accused in the effort to "get" Thomas. The manipulation of Anita Hill, in sum, was the political equivalent of the recommendation, in one of

Hillary's LSC training manuals, to nail a dead rat to a recalcitrant alderman's door.

Edelman's policy views and rhetorical style were echoed in several scholarly articles that Hillary penned in the late 1970s and 1980s addressing the broad rubric of children's rights. The general theme running through these writings is the desirability of transforming social relations and politicizing family life through bureaucratic and legal processes, and enhancing the paternalistic role of state agencies and trained experts in all spheres, especially those connected with children. The tone and substance of her writings are those not of a Marxist revolutionary but of a Swedish-style technocratic socialist.

In her *New Republic* review of *It Takes A Village,* Elshtain discerned clear signs of Edelman's influence on Hillary. Hillary's seriousness of purpose, brilliant articulation, and dogged persistence in advancing her causes sometimes gave way to hyperbolic rhetoric, uncompromising stances, and attempts to squelch debate within her own camp. Hillary's method, Elshtain wrote, "invites recourse to the courts and more generally it invites moralistic overreach, paternalism, and a limitless extension of sympathy that casts a pall over political debate because it transforms one's opponents into nasty depredators who mean to do children harm."

Hillary's articles would later prove highly controversial, a testament to what she and her ideas had come to represent to both the right wing of the Republican Party and the left wing of the Democratic Party. They were attacked in the 1992 campaign as "anti-family" by Republicans like Pat Buchanan and praised by liberals like historian Garry Wills, who called Hillary "one of the more important scholar-activists of the last two decades" in a 1992 essay in the *New York Review of Books.*

Hillary's first article, "Children Under the Law," published in 1973 in the *Harvard Education Review,* proposed changes in the laws governing children, whom she referred to as "child citizens." Declaring that "I want to be a voice for America's children," Hillary advocated a reversal of the presumption by the courts that children are incompetent before the law. Children, she argued, should have all of the procedural rights guaranteed to adults under the Constitution, and the legal presumption that there is an identity of interests between parents and children should be rejected. Under 18th century English common law, she wrote, children were "chattels of the family and wards of the state." But recent Warren Supreme Court cases on children's rights signified progress, in her view. She applauded several decisions of the Warren Court, including *Brown* v. *Board of Education,* which recognized that black schoolchildren had a constitutional right to attend integrated schools; a landmark decision extending procedural rights to juveniles called *In re Gault;* and a series of decisions upholding students' rights to grow long hair, refuse to salute the flag, and wear black armbands to protest the Vietnam War. (Since the 1970s, the courts have consistently resisted the legal reasoning in these cases and failed to extend children's rights.)

Hillary praised a dissent by Justice William O. Douglas from a Burger Court ruling in *Wisconsin* v. *Yoder,* a case involving Amish parents who challenged on religious grounds a Wisconsin statute forcing them to send their children to high school. While the Court's majority held for the parents, Douglas objected that the children themselves had not been consulted. Douglas argued that the children's views should have been weighed more heavily than the parents'. A child who aspired to become a "pianist or an astronaut or an oceanographer," he reasoned, would have to "break from the Amish tradition." If children were "harnessed to the Amish way of life," their lives were likely to be "stunted and deformed." Hillary hailed Douglas for basing his opinion "not only on available legal precedents, but on psychological and sociological findings that children of the relevant ages possess the moral and intellectual judgment necessary for making responsible decisions on matters of religion and education."

Hillary acknowledged that her advocacy of rights for children had an expressly political dimension. The children's rights movement, she wrote in "Children Under the Law," "highlights the political nature of questions about children's status. . . . The pretense that children's issues are somehow above or beyond politics endures and is reinforced by the belief that families are private, non-political units whose interests subsume those of children." Again betraying her view that the law was a social construct rather than a set of neutral principles, Hillary argued that the inferior position assigned to children under the law should be seen as "part of the organization and ideology of the political system itself."

As the social critic Christopher Lasch explained in *Harper's* magazine in October 1992, Hillary "regards the children's rights movement as a logical extension of earlier movements to give civil rights to slaves and women." Indeed, she had once written, "The basic rationale for depriving people of rights in a dependency relationship is that certain individuals are incapable of or undeserving of the right to take care of themselves and consequently need social institutions specifically designed to safeguard their position. . . . Along with the family, past and present examples of such arrangements include marriage, slavery and the Indian reservation system."

"In a society that finds appeals to individual rights irresistible, [Hillary's] position looks attractive at first," Christopher Lasch responded. "Who could object to principles that are designed to protect individuals against arbitrary authority—against the state as well as the family? A careful reading of [her] argument, however, shows that she objects to the family much more than she objects to the state. . . . Although she warns that the state's authority must be 'exercised only in warranted cases,' her writings leave the unmistakeable impression that it is the family that holds children back and the state that sets them free. . . . Her position amounts to a defense of bureaucracy disguised as a defense of individual autonomy."

Hillary devised a novel solution to the question of who decides when state intervention is appropriate in the event that a child may need to be removed from his or her family because of physical or emotional abuse. Stating that since state agencies and the courts often rely on "middle-class" values to judge a family's child-rearing practices, she suggested entrusting the decision to "boards composed of citizens representing identifiable constituencies—racial, religious, ethnic, geographical," which would be responsible for making recommendations on when parental rights should be terminated.

In 1977, Hillary contributed an essay entitled "Children's Rights: A Legal Perspective" to the book *Children's Rights: Contemporary Perspectives,* edited by Patricia A. Vardin and Ilene N. Brody. Here, she proposed a sliding scale for determining the competency of a child, based on "social and psychological realities." She noted that some experts warned that the move to declare children to be rights-bearing individuals would create a new class of rights that would be difficult to limit, but she did not share their concerns, maintaining that a minor's "[D]ecisions about motherhood and abortion, schooling, cosmetic surgery, treatment of venereal disease, or employment and others where the decision or lack of one will significantly affect the child's future should not be made unilaterally by parents. Children should have the right to be permitted to decide their own future if they are competent." Taking a leaf from Douglas and the judicial activists, she went on to raise the prospect of children adjudicating their rights "to grow up in a world at peace" under a United Nations declaration or to fight "future technological changes that may damage him or her." She also suggested that "children and adults might have special standing to question the proliferation of nuclear power or junk food. . . ."

"The notion that children are fully capable of speaking for themselves . . . makes it possible for ventriloquists to speak through them and thus to disguise their own objectives as the child's," Lasch responded. These ventriloquists would be people like Hillary, filling the ranks of government bureaucracies. Hillary wrote that she was searching for a "theory that adequately explains the state's appropriate role in child rearing. . . . It has taken a considerably longer time to reach a stage where we recognize that each family at some time needs a certain amount of assistance from the government to care for the needs of its members." For Hillary, the "infallible index of progress," as Lasch put it, is a proliferation of state-managed and funded children's programs, from Head Start to day care to child immunization.

In a 1978 article in *Public Welfare,* Hillary reviewed the Kenneth Keniston book she had helped research at Yale. "Certain myths . . . serve only to inhibit the development of a realistic family policy in this country," she opined. "The myth of the housewife whose life centers only on her home is effectively dispelled by statistics demonstrating that the average school child now has a working mother. The myth, or perhaps more accurately, the prejudice, that each family should be self-sufficient is challenged in a compelling chapter on the 'stacked deck' faced by the poor, minority, or handicapped children who are born into a situation of inequality and, most of them, kept there for the rest of their lives. . . . Collective action is needed on the community, state and federal level to wrest from [technology, television, nuclear plants, automobiles, drugs] and those who profit from their use the extraordinary power they hold over all us, but particularly over our children."

In a fourth article, Hillary addressed even more concretely her view of the role of government in family policy. "Children's Policies: Abandonment and Neglect" was a book review of Gilbert Steiner's *The Children's Cause,* written by Hillary for the *Yale Law Journal* in 1977. Here, she took legislators to task for failing to involve the government more directly in family policy, deplored President Nixon's veto of the 1971 Comprehensive Child Development Act, and recommended the establishment of a congressional committee and a new federal executive department for children's needs. "Politicians, not wishing to appear as advocates of interference with the family, balk at turning their Boys Town rhetoric into public commitments on any but the safest of issues. Besides, for most public officials, the idea of a federal policy for children is alien. . . . Policy makers are simply not accustomed to thinking about children's needs in the same way they think about missile development, dam construction, or even old-age assistance."

Hillary faulted the liberal scholar Gilbert Steiner for his "cautious attitude about government involvement in child-rearing . . ." Steiner argued that the burden of proof should be on the proponents of legal competence for children to show why parents aren't competent to raise their children. Hillary disagreed: "Legislators and executives take risks of all kinds when they decide to build a nuclear plant or introduce a deadly pesticide or advocate no-fault insurance." Saluting the "generals in the War on Poverty," she dismissed out of hand a study Steiner cited that questioned the effectiveness of the Head Start program. "Apparently, we share so much apprehension about potential harm to cherished, albeit fantasized, family values that programs on children must demonstrate immediate success or risk extinction, even in the face of subsequent evidence of achievement."

Lasch wrote that the corollary of Hillary's advocacy of children's competence was that parents were not qualified to raise their own children without help from the state. "Criticism of parents' incompetence has always been the child savers' stock in trade. Such arguments played an important part in the progressive movement, which laid the foundation of the welfare state," Lasch explained.

> Then as now criticism was directed against allegedly benighted backward people who clung to their ancestral ways and resisted the assimilation into the dominant culture of the Enlightenment. The urban masses, said William Gladden, an early exponent of the social gospel, had to be "civilized, educated, inspired with new ideas." . . . The therapeutic campaign against backward, "traditional" families has a long history, which alone should make us skeptical about the desirability of another campaign

along the same lines. After years of bureaucratic experimentation, we are entitled to wonder whether a "comprehensive child care program"— [Hillary's] panacea—is what the country really needs. Previous efforts to rescue children from "undesirable" families have produced very little in the way of desirable results. A negative verdict on those efforts hardly rests on a "rush to judgment." It rests on experience stretching back to the turn of the century.[6]

Hillary displayed her leadership potential in helping to put this liberal legal theory into practice at the national level. In his analysis for *Harper's,* Christopher Lasch drew the connection between her call for court-conferred children's rights and an expansion of the welfare state and the feminist movement. "Empowering" children through the courts and establishing a government role in caring for them facilitated the conditions for female professional success. "The movement for children's rights . . . amounts to another stage in the long struggle against patriarchy," Lasch wrote.

By the late 1980s, as feminism became the dominant ideological tendency on the left, Hillary worked to eradicate "gender bias" in the legal system through the American Bar Association (ABA). Since she had been active in the association's section on individual rights and responsibilities, the home of the legal activists within the bar, Hillary was a natural choice to chair a special ABA commission, established in 1987, on women in the legal profession. The commission was yet another opportunity for Hillary the culture warrior, working inside the system rather than taking to the streets, to influence the traditional American legal system by forcing on it the group identity politics of contemporary liberalism. Significantly, her work also brought her the professional recognition and national acclaim that had eluded her as a practicing attorney at the Rose Law Firm. In 1988 and 1991, citing Hillary as one of the top one hundred influential lawyers in the United States, the *National Journal* stated that the ranking was heavily based on Hillary's work on the ABA women's commission.

The commission was established to further the ABA's Goal IX, which "calls upon the association to promote equal participating of women and minorities in the legal profession." Hillary's commission worked for four years, held numerous public hearings, produced voluminous reports to the ABA's House of Delegates, and distributed professional manuals on sexual harassment, parental leave, and day care to the ABA membership.

One commission report examined the ABA itself, documenting "the existence of a glass ceiling within the association." Commission-sponsored events included a meeting in Los Angeles entitled "From Adam's Rib to L.A. Law: The Image of Women Lawyers in Television and Film" and an ABA program called "Real World Solutions to the Mommy Track Debate." The commission also created the Margaret Brent Women's Lawyers of Achievement Award, named after America's first woman lawyer. The award was immediately politicized when Anita Hill was named its first recipient. Hillary spoke at the awards lunch.

In its various reports and public hearings, the commission's recommendations for eradicating "gender bias in the courts" ranged from adopting quotas for the promotion of more women as senior partners in law firms and in the judiciary to schemes to include more women on juries dealing with discrimination and harassment cases because of their supposed unique gender perspective. Through its work, the committee promoted within the legal profession a feminist critique of the law as a servant of patriarchal power, which treated women as male property. In this view, notions of logic, objectivity, equality under law, and the common good are all regarded as reflections of the patriarchal bias.

The theory had been germinating among Fem Crits at the elite law schools, including Yale, in the 1970s, and it was promoted throughout the 1980s by groups like the National Organization for Women and the NAACP Legal Defense and Educational Fund, whose activists worked closely with Hillary on ABA commission projects. Some feminist scholars and activists posit distinct differences between male and female ways of thinking, moral reasoning, and social and political behavior. Ann Scales of the University of New Mexico, for example, extends the argument to undermine the fundamental premise of legal reasoning that truth can be objectively determined by logical analysis. "Feminist analysis begins with the principle that objective reality is a myth. It recognizes that patriarchal myths are projections of the male psyche," she wrote in the *Yale Law Review* in 1986. "Male and female perceptions of value are not shared and are perhaps not even perceptible to each other." Hillary herself gave a presentation to an annual ABA convention in 1991 purporting to demonstrate "how men and women use the English language differently," according to an ABA publication.

Under Hillary's chairmanship the ABA commission also embraced this branch of feminist theory in the area of sexual harassment, aiming to replace the objective legal standard of the gender-neutral person with the subjective reaction of the female complainant. The gender-neutral person enshrined in current law, these feminists argue, is a patriarchal artifact intended to perpetuate male power. "Sexual harassment is trivialized by some as normal behavior growing out of the natural attraction between the sexes, and mistakenly assumed by others to encompass only a supervisor's quid pro quo demand for sex in exchange for hiring or promotion," one ABA commission manual stated. "In fact, illegal sexual harassment encompasses a range of behaviors on the part of supervisors and co-workers, and on occasion customers and clients as well. These behaviors may or may not affect the harassed workers' employment status, but they often affect her psychological well-being."

The most important legacy of Hillary's commission was the establishment of highly controversial "gender bias task forces" to remedy discrimination in federal and state courts and local bar associations nationwide. The task forces are underwritten by federal or state funds and are routinely composed of lawyers and judges who share the same politically correct agenda as Hillary. Though these task forces have been strongly resisted by conservative judges and lawyers as threats to the independence of the judiciary, they have acquired significant power within the legal system.

The ABA adopted its official policy on "Gender and Race Bias Task Forces" in August 1991 as Hillary's commission wound down its operations. The policy states: "Resolved, that the American Bar Association supports the enactment of authoritative measures, requiring studies of the existence of bias in the federal judicial system, including bias based on race, ethnicity, gender, age, sexual orientation and disability, and the extent to which bias may affect litigants, witnesses, attorneys and all those who work in the judicial branch." The task forces were intended to examine "employment data, case assignments and other factors to determine whether, for example, women and minorities are represented in key appointed or civil service jobs." Working under the auspices of various federal and state courts, the task forces have investigated the hiring practices of judges and even questioned judges about how confidential judicial deliberations on specific cases are conducted. The stated objective is to determine whether particular judges showed "bias" in either their personnel practices or in their handling of specific cases.

Conservative critics have attacked the ABA task forces on several grounds. For one thing, "bias" is never defined. The task forces send out detailed questionnaires that are filled out by people who work in the court system or appear before it and are often returned anonymously, filled with unverified charges. "To take just one example," the *Wall Street Journal* observed in a 1996 editorial, "the task force wants to know whether the respondents have ever 'observed' counsel or judges patronize someone because of his or her race or gender. How a respondent is supposed to determine the motivation behind a patronizing remark is never explained. . . ." Critics have also charged that the end goal of the task forces is to enforce proportional representation by gender and race in all court personnel decisions, including the selection of judges.

Perhaps the most serious threat to the independence of the judiciary is the prospect that the unprecedented Orwellian probes into the way legal cases are decided could put political pressure on judges to decide cases in a particular way. "Court employees are told to break down defendants, lawyers and other parties by race and sex. We doubt it's much in anyone's interest to formalize inside the court system the same group-identity obsessions that now rule politics and academia," the *Wall Street Journal* commented, adding, "It's a short step to the dangerous view that a minority defendant can get a 'fair' trial only from a minority judge and a minority jury, or that outcomes of trials ought to be scrutinized for bias."[7]

Hillary's pursuit of her ideological commitments had been remarkably steadfast and consistent throughout the 1970s and 1980s. During those years, every major initiative of the left-wing legal activists—fought tooth and nail by the right—bore the stamp of Hillary Rodham. These beliefs and activities were the one consistent thread in a life of personal and political turbulence and turmoil. Had Hillary worked for groups like the LSC, CDF, and ABA as a full-time staff attorney and activist rather than as a part-time board member as she juggled her commitments in Little Rock, it is possible to imagine that she would have had an even greater impact on American politics and culture. But this was not how Hillary's influence would reach its full force. For as the 1980s wore on, she was increasingly preoccupied not with her own commitments to legal advocacy and public interest law but with Bill Clinton's political career as governor of Arkansas and then as a potential candidate for the presidency.

Starting in 1980 with the political events in Arkansas, where Governor Clinton faced his first re-election campaign, Hillary would be permanently drawn into Clinton's political orbit.

6

The Real Comeback Kid

The specter of Ronald Reagan haunted Hillary not only at the Legal Services Corporation in Washington, but also at home in Arkansas, where President Carter's unpopularity threatened to deflate support for Bill's first re-election campaign as governor. The country's increasingly conservative mood did not bode well for the young man whose administration resembled a 1960s-style New Politics movement run by the "diaper brigade."[1]

At this point, Hillary's political energies were directly engaged only at the national level, where she was successfully fending off the Republican threat to federal legal services and serving on the board of the Children's Defense Fund. Aside from heading up the rural health care initiative and scolding Bill by telephone from her Rose Firm office, few of Hillary's talents were focused on making Bill's first term as governor a success, and he was paying dearly for her absence.

The national trend toward conservatism was amplified in Arkansas in 1980 by a newspaper war between the established liberal paper and a reinvigorated conservative tabloid. For years, the *Arkansas Gazette* had been the dominant newspaper in circulation, owing to its quality and prestige; it was also much more liberal than its readership. In contrast, the *Arkansas Democrat,* a small-circulation afternoon tabloid, didn't have the money or the staff to do much more than rewrite the morning paper. In 1975, the *Democrat* was purchased by the scion of a prominent publishing family, and John Robert Starr, a retired Associated Press bureau chief in Little Rock, was hired to run it. The curmudgeonly Starr staffed the paper with acerbic political writers like Meredith Oakley and began writing a biting daily column himself. (The war ended in 1991, when the two papers merged to form today's *Arkansas Democrat-Gazette.*)

By 1980, the *Democrat* was portraying the Clinton administration as filled with arrogant big-government types with "wild ideas," as Starr put it in one column. Exposés ran on one state project that spent a half-million dollars training fifty people in depressed areas to chop firewood. Starr awarded his reporting staff a series of "Sweet William" prizes for the biggest boondoggles they could uncover. In 1980, after Clinton raised the state's budget to over $1 billion for the first time, Starr tagged the governor "Billion Dollar Bill." When Clinton was caught driving himself at 80 mph to a speaking engagement while state troopers were out vigilantly enforcing the new 55-mph speed limit, Starr gave the story big play, as he did the revelation that Hillary's car hadn't been properly assessed in 1977 or 1978. For the latter, Bill blamed a staffer in the attorney general's office, who he said was supposed to have taken care of Hillary's car, inadvertently revealing the couple's use of state employees for their personal business.

But Clinton was not just under attack from the populist right. Those in the state who favored more sweeping reform criticized the governor for failing to face down the state's special interests. After Clinton gave a speech that summer to the Democratic National Convention in which he claimed to be governing in the reformist tradition of Dale Bumpers and David Pryor—both of whom had tried to decentralize state power— he was blasted in an angry editorial in the *Pine Bluff Commercial,* the daily serving an industrial city south of Little Rock, whose editors had begun to lose faith in Clinton's integrity after his inaugural invitation to Orval Faubus. In the editorial, Pulitzer Prize–winning columnist Paul Greenberg tagged Clinton "Slick Willie," a phrase that would follow him into the 1992 campaign.

Clinton had worries on three fronts: crime, Cubans, and car tags. On crime, Clinton's liberalism was most evident in his refusal to schedule executions and his commutation of the life sentences of forty-four prisoners in his first term, many of them convicted murderers. One of them soon killed again, inciting a public uproar.

The crime issue was exacerbated by the events surrounding the 1980 Mariel boatlift, when Fidel Castro deported many thousands of Cubans to the U.S., including a number of mental patients and criminals. This created social and economic mayhem in Southern Florida. In May, President Carter ordered that about twenty thousand refugees be sent to Arkansas' Fort Chafee, a federal installation near Fort Smith that had been a relocation camp for Vietnamese refugees in 1975. Carter promised that the U.S. military would maintain order at the camp; but when hundreds of refugees rioted and escaped into the foothills of Fort Smith, the military stood by and did nothing. Carter not only refused to intervene but sent more Cuban refugees to the site later that year. Though Clinton eventually called in the National Guard, he was blamed for losing control of the situation and for failing to stand up to Carter.

The third concern, car tags, had its origins in Clinton's effort to repair his relations with the Arkansas oligarchy, which had lately become strained. Earlier in his term, Clinton had reneged on his promise to Tyson that he would raise the weight limit for trucks traveling on state roads, concluding that the required road maintenance was too costly. Clinton later followed his aides' advice to pay for new state road projects by raising license fees for heavy trucks. When Tyson came in to complain about the new legislation, Clinton aide Rudy Moore left the chicken mogul cooling his heels for quite a while, enraging Tyson. In an apparent effort to get back in Tyson's good graces, Clinton overruled the recommendations of his advisers and instead doubled fees for transferring vehicle titles and raised the cost of registration for cars and pickup trucks. Those who had older, heavier cars—disproportionately the rural poor—had to pay the higher fees, setting off an anti-tax backlash.

In the Democratic primary that spring of 1980, turkey farmer Monroe Schwarzlose, now seventy-nine, challenged Clinton once again. No one paid much attention to the old campaigner, least of all Bill and Hillary, but on election day Schwarzlose's garnering of 31 percent of the vote was a warning that the incumbent was in serious trouble. Despite Clinton's apparent vulnerability, the Republican Party hadn't yet produced the strong candidates or organized their constituents to the degree that was necessary to take on the Democrats in general elections. It took a defection from the Democratic Party to produce a legitimate challenger to Clinton: A wealthy investment banker named Frank White, a Democratic protégé of David Pryor, switched parties and declared his intention to run against Clinton in November.

Noticeably absent from the campaign was Hillary, who, as chair of the LSC, was spending much of her time flying back and forth to Washington, coordinating the election-year political efforts of the legal services movement. She was also busy with the duties of motherhood: In February 1980, she gave birth to daughter Chelsea, whose name was derived from "Chelsea Morning," a Joni Mitchell song popularized by Judy Collins in the early 1970s. Hillary approached pregnancy in the same determined way that she addressed every challenge, eating the proper diet and taking Bill to Lamaze childbirth classes. (She ultimately had the baby by caesarean section.) The new mother surprised local politicos by refusing to turn Chelsea's birth into a media event. Hillary's desire to protect her family's privacy took priority over politics: A week passed before the press office of the governor even released a photo of the new family.

Perhaps she should have exploited Chelsea's birth for political advantage after all, for the Republicans were quietly attempting to capitalize on Hillary Rodham's reputation as a snobby careerist from the North with an Orphan Annie perm and Coke-bottle glasses. Though she did her best to skirt the issue by introducing herself as "Hillary—Governor Clinton's wife," there seems little doubt that Hillary's decision not to take Clinton's name was a *sub rosa* issue in the election. Arkansas political analysts believe that it cost Bill crucial support in the race, which he lost by less than 2 percent of the vote. "Any one of the issues could have accounted for the two percent," political consultant Jerry Russell acknowledged. "But you have to figure at least two percent didn't like that she kept her maiden name, so I've always said that the name cost him the election."

As a contrast to Hillary, Frank White trotted out his wife Gay. The epitome of the traditional Arkansas political wife, Gay White was a homemaker who lunched at the Little Rock Country Club, spoke of her strong Christian faith, and volunteered her time at the Fellowship Bible Church. With her big hair and ruby red lips, she trailed after her husband on stops throughout the state, beaming à la Nancy Reagan as she stood dutifully behind Frank on the speaker's platform.

Up until 1980, Hillary had pursued a career entirely independent of

Bill; none of her public interest legal work, either nationally or in Arkansas, had helped his political career one iota. Her politically risky decision to keep her maiden name as the wife of a politician in a conservative southern state underscored the fact that she had independent interests to which she fervently clung and which Bill fully supported. Caught between two sets of cultural expectations—between what she expected of herself as a professional woman and committed feminist and the expectations of the voters of Arkansas—she firmly refused to change her name to help Bill win re-election. "I was her worst critic over that," said Richard Herget, who managed the 1980 Clinton campaign and whose views were a good barometer of the Arkansas political establishment. A major insurance broker, Herget had been a supporter of Faubus, Fulbright, and Pryor, and has also been described as the best friend of Mack McLarty. "I think that issue cost us the election," he said. "And boy, if Hillary and I didn't tangle on that one. I think Hillary just felt very strongly that she wanted to maintain a professional identity of her own, and I can understand that.

"I made a speech one time to a Democratic women's club during the campaign. And the average age of the attendee was in the sixties. And I asked this group of ladies, afterward, before they opened up for questions, I said, 'Let me ask you a question.' I said, 'How do you feel about the issue of Hillary Rodham, you know, not being Hillary Clinton?' And, oh God, I wish I hadn't asked it. They unloaded on me. 'She's not good enough to take his name,' and that sort of thing. You've got to remember that this is the conservative South. Hillary just wasn't that in touch back then."

Whether Hillary's active involvement in the 1980 re-election campaign would have changed the outcome is an open question. Plainly her ability, displayed in the 1974 congressional campaign, to fine-tune Bill's political message and keep him focused was sorely missed. On the other hand, her public image was already exacting a toll even in her absence, and she did not seem to have an innate feel for the Arkansas electorate. As election day approached, White was still 15 points behind in the polls, but he had raised enough money to blanket local TV stations with ads depicting rioting Cuban refugees. Hillary couldn't understand why the issue resonated so strongly with voters. She told friends that she regarded the ads, which featured black Cubans, as racist. Veteran Arkansas legislator Pat Flanagin remembered a conversation with Hillary just before the election in which he told her that people were upset by the car-tag tax hike and the influx of Cuban refugees. "Hillary's response was, 'No, our polls don't show us that,' and, 'Well, there's no reason for them to be upset.' Only later did they decide, 'We need to listen to those folks.' "

Coddled by the one-party political machine, Clinton also appears to have considered himself invincible as White, gradually siphoned off one-time business supporters alienated by Clinton's new taxes, new regulations, and broken promises. And although the *Arkansas Democrat* had a policy of making no official endorsements, White also benefited enormously from John Robert Starr's relentless attacks on the incumbent governor. On election night, White did the unthinkable, upsetting Clinton with 51.9 percent of the vote.

Friends of the Clintons later told reporters that Bill had broken down, bawling uncontrollably both on the eve of the election when he saw defeat coming, and again on election night, when he faced the first big setback of his life. The following day the Clintons commiserated over lunch with their friends Jim and Diane Blair. As Diane Blair later recounted in *The Clintons of Arkansas,* Clinton "was half-laughing, half-crying over the country song on the café jukebox, 'I Feel So Bad I Don't Know Whether to Kill Myself or Go Bowling.' "

Little has been made of the differing approaches the Clintons seem to have taken regarding the disaster of Bill's loss in 1980, much less of the predominant role Hillary played throughout the ensuing period of recovery. Clinton's electoral defeat was Hillary's first taste of real loss, and it came at Bill's hands, not her own. She may have even felt partly responsible for having been so resistant to the idea of changing her name. Reeling from the shocking defeat, Hillary's instinctive reaction was to quickly regroup, meet the concerns of the voters head-on, and develop a pragmatic new strategy to resuscitate her husband's endangered career. Simply put, Hillary assumed responsibility for the political rehabilitation of Bill—pulling together a new political machine and moving Bill to the center in accord with the prevailing political winds of the Reaganite 1980s.

Before the Clintons had even vacated the governor's mansion, Hillary—always willing to retrench tactically in the face of adversity—advocated a forthright apology to the voters for several of the unpopular liberal initiatives of the first term. She counseled Bill to demonstrate his

contrition by immediately repealing the hike in car-tag fees before sur-
rendering office to White.

Bill, in contrast, was seemingly in denial, psychologically unable to accept the verdict of the electorate. In his first post-election interview with
the *Arkansas Gazette,* he claimed the voters had not really wanted to remove him from office, merely to send him a message by shaving down
his margin of victory. His last speech to the Arkansas general assembly
was "unrepentant," as Starr put it. "He admitted no mistakes."

If Bill had trouble acknowledging the failings of his first administration, Hillary surely did not. "Hillary was significantly responsible for his
comeback," Jerry Russell said, recalling her Arkansas political debut. Both
Clinton and White had agreed to appear at a seminar analyzing the election returns at the University of Arkansas–Little Rock in February 1981,
just weeks after White's stunning upset. But Clinton backed out when
faced with the prospect of publicly discussing the details of his defeat.

Making a pivotal concession by no longer keeping her distance from
Arkansas politics, Hillary boldly stepped up to the plate. When the conference began, Russell said, "they announced 'the governor could not
be here with us today.' And Hillary got up and did a wonderful job of
talking about how they weren't paying attention to the voters. She said
they had been overconfident and hadn't listened to the people. It was a
very candid analysis. Frank White's presentation had been very funny
and it was a hard act to follow. But Hillary was able to do it. She looked
at everybody square in the eyes and said, 'We made mistakes.' And they
never made the same mistakes again." The local media was impressed:
the *Arkansas Gazette* described the speech as "spunky and eloquent."

Bill, in contrast, utterly fell apart. The wounded ex-governor entertained several job offers that would have entailed leaving Arkansas—the
chairmanship of the Democratic National Committee (no prize after
Carter's devastating loss to Ronald Reagan); directorship of Norman
Lear's new left-wing lobby, People for the American Way; presidency of
the University of Louisville; or partnership in a Washington law firm. But
he couldn't seem to pull himself together to meet any of those challenges. Instead, he took a token job as "of counsel" to a Little Rock law
firm, Wright, Lindsey & Jennings, which was arranged by Bruce Lindsey,
the son of one of the firm's founders who would later become an important player in the Clinton operation. According to a later account in
the *Wall Street Journal,* Lindsey had called Clift Lane, former owner of

Lane Processing, Inc., a major poultry company, to line up a retainer arrangement with the firm to help pay Clinton's salary. "They wanted to help Bill out because he was out of a job," Lane was quoted as saying, adding that he did not remember the firm having done any significant legal work while on retainer.

Visitors to Clinton's office found him in a deep funk, obsessed with the voters' rejection of him rather than focused on the future. He spent long hours roaming through the aisles in the Food Emporium in the Heights, the city's yuppified residential enclave, stopping strangers to inquire why they had turned him out of office. In an interview with the *Washington Post* in 1992, Hillary referred to the forays as "confessionals in the supermarket aisles."

In retrospect, friends speculated that the Clintons' marital turmoil during the campaign may have contributed to Bill's defeat—the candidate was visibly distracted, and rumors of Clinton's philandering may have been part of the reason Hillary devoted her professional attentions elsewhere. "As I look back," Rudy Moore, one of Clinton's main aides during his first term, wrote in *The Clintons of Arkansas*, "it is more evident that Bill Clinton was not the same person psychologically in 1980 that he had been before or that he had been since. It must have been something personal, perhaps in his relationship with Hillary, but he was ambivalent and preoccupied. . . . His re-election campaign reflected it."[2]

Once again, speculation about an alleged Clinton affair swept through the Capitol in 1979 and 1980, the period when Hillary was pregnant with Chelsea and then stayed home caring for the baby. Gennifer Flowers, the ex-nightclub singer who came forward during the '92 campaign with allegations of a long-term affair that she said began in 1977, has said the local media began inquiring about her relationship with Bill at about this time.

By some accounts, Clinton pursued extramarital affairs more indiscriminately after the election. In interviews during the 1992 campaign, Clinton hinted that "trouble" in his marriage began after his gubernatorial defeat. David Maraniss reported that soon after Clinton's loss at the polls, he sat on the floor of the couple's new home, a simple west side frame house, playing with Chelsea and singing, "I want a div-or-or-or-orce." Clinton's sexual appetite appeared to have a deeply rooted psychological dimension in which political failure seemed only to enhance his need for personal approval. In their book *The Comeback Kid*, Charles

F. Allen and Jonathan Portis described a man whose vision of himself was apparently distorted by his own extreme neediness, which encompassed an inability to assume responsibility for his compulsive seduction of women. "Clinton is known to have asked several confidantes: 'What am I supposed to do about these women who throw themselves at me?' His friends warned him to resist the temptation and to consider the effect that an affair would have on his family, not to mention his political future."

Such concerns, of course, weighed more heavily on Hillary than anyone. When Bill lost the Fayetteville race and Mary Lee Fray spilled the beans about Bill's girlfriends, Hillary had come into the campaign headquarters early the next morning and dealt with the press on Bill's behalf. Now, however, Hillary was not Bill's girlfriend, but his wife and the mother of his child. With Bill's extramarital affairs escalating and his open talk of divorce, Hillary naturally had doubts about the future of the marriage. So, in 1981, Hillary stepped back and carefully evaluated her position, just as she had done when she returned to the East Coast after the '74 campaign to solicit advice from friends about whether she should permanently settle in Arkansas.

For Hillary, channeling her workaholic energy into Bill's political career would mean a drastic change in her own career path. Thus, if she was going to take charge both of her marriage and of Bill's possible comeback effort, she would need as much information as possible. Some say that Hillary was particularly aggressive about tracking down information on Bill's alleged affairs during this period.

Former Little Rock private investigator Ivan Duda claims that Hillary asked him to report to her on whether Bill was having extramarital affairs during this period when he was out of office. "She wanted me to get dirt on Bill, to find out who he was fooling around with," Duda said. He claims to have reported to Hillary the names of about eight women he thought Bill was involved with, including one woman who worked at the Rose Firm. "That one really hurt and made her furious," Duda recalled. (Duda—who acknowledged that he later had his private investigator's license revoked by a Clinton-appointed board, after being cited twice for carrying a badge, which was prohibited by board rules—said that he has no proof of the transaction because Hillary gave him only cash to cover expenses.)

As Hillary mapped out her future, she also considered taking a job as president of Hendrix College, a liberal arts school affiliated with the United Methodist Church, located in Conway, Arkansas, thirty miles outside Little Rock. The university job would have corrected the professional detour Hillary had taken, away from teaching and legal services, when she joined the Rose Firm, where she still appeared unfulfilled and unchallenged by her work. But the college presidency would have precluded her putting together Bill's comeback effort, and she soon decided against it.

After a period of contemplation, unprepared to admit failure or concede defeat, Hillary resolved to commit herself to fighting both for her marriage and Bill's political future, which may well have become fused in her mind as a single pursuit. Her decision provides a strong rebuttal to the popular depiction of Hillary as a latter-day Lady Macbeth, artfully using Bill as a vehicle to advance her own agenda. This is a woman, after all, who had already handed Ronald Reagan a major defeat in the legal services battle in Washington. Clearly, she did not need Bill to exert power and influence in the political sphere. A more likely interpretation is that Hillary concluded that orchestrating Bill's return to the state house was the surest way of holding her emotionally fragile husband and new baby together as a family unit. Bill clearly had a bleak future if it wasn't in politics. There is no sign that Hillary acted out of grander political calculations or ambitions, nor in the end did she make adequate provision for her own future, should her efforts have failed. She therefore could not allow herself to fail.

At this juncture, the story of the Clintons' marriage became one of an enigmatic partnership the likes of which have rarely, if ever, been seen in American politics. Drawn further into Bill's political world (and inevitably compromised by it), Hillary became Bill's watchdog, policy adviser, and problem solver, in addition to playing the roles of wife, mother, and family breadwinner. As Hillary picked up the pieces of Bill's career, the couple's relationship grew into a unique symbiosis—their friend Max Brantley of the *Arkansas Times* called it a "co-candidacy"—that they would take all the way to the White House.

But the arrangement had an unintended consequence: Bill's political career began to swallow Hillary up. Left to her own devices, Hillary Rodham might well have emerged as a political figure in her own right, perhaps parlaying a successful tenure as chairman of the LSC into a future cabinet slot in a Democratic administration, a seat on the federal bench, the presidency of a college, or a bid for elective office. The co-candidacy, by contrast, was not the high-achieving path to a Supreme Court seat that Dorothy Rodham had raised Hillary to pursue, nor was it quite the progressive partnership—where she and Bill would venture forth to change the world together while Hillary maintained her own sphere—that she may have envisioned at Yale. Instead, Hillary, who was in so many ways a paradigm of the modern feminist movement, would now become that most regressive of female stereotypes: the power behind the throne.

Within a few months of the 1980 defeat, Hillary took charge of assembling Bill's comeback team. Texas native Betsey Wright, who had met both Clintons in the '72 McGovern campaign, flew to Little Rock from Washington, where she had spent most of the 1970s as an organizer in the women's movement. After the McGovern campaign, Hillary had urged Wright to go to Washington, where she joined Hillary's Wellesley roommate Jan Piercy in founding the National Women's Education Fund, a nonprofit organization devoted to increasing women's representation in elected office and other leadership positions. The group trained women in fundraising and campaign techniques. "Do not overdo make-up but be sure to add more for TV," one manual advised.

Without Wright's belief in Hillary's dedication and commitment—she had initially been more intrigued by Hillary's political promise than by Bill's—it is doubtful she would have relocated to Little Rock to work for Bill. Hers was a partnership with Hillary. From the time Wright came on board, "most everybody in Arkansas thought that Hillary and Betsey Wright ran Bill Clinton," according to former governor White. In political circles, Hillary, Betsey, and press secretary Joan Roberts were known as "the Valkyries." Like Hillary, Betsey seemed ready to accept responsibility for Bill and devoted herself to his political success. Wright wasn't romantically interested in Bill, so Hillary could trust her around her husband without fear of a sexual relationship. Together, Hillary and Wright were an effective political team, with Wright handling the nuts and bolts of the operation. In the two years preceding the '82 election, Wright, a heavyset chain smoker with a famously foul mouth and a temper to match, built the political organization that Clinton lacked. Ensconcing herself in a cubicle outside Bill's office at Wright, Lindsey & Jennings, she worked day and night to computerize the vast set of Bill's handwritten note cards listing his contacts and contributors since 1974. When Bill was re-elected, Wright became his chief of staff, raising money, dispensing jobs, handling constituents, and overseeing the day-to-day legislative agenda.

Hillary also brought political consultant Dick Morris into the Clinton inner circle at this time. Though working as a hired gun for both Democratic and Republican candidates later made him known as a political chameleon, Morris got his start in the same left-wing anti-war political circles of the Democratic Party as the Clintons, Betsey Wright, and two other longtime friends of the Clintons, Susan Thomases and Harold Ickes—both of whom had first met Bill in the summer of 1970, working in Washington for Project Pursestrings, an effort to cut off funding for the Vietnam War. In the late 1960s, Morris and Ickes were on opposite sides of a factional dispute between groups of left-wing reformers in New York City politics. Morris, the newcomer, was known as a shrewd tactician; Ickes, while pragmatic, was more issues-oriented. Ickes and Morris worked for McCarthy and McGovern as well.

Morris had first met Clinton when he was attorney general in the mid-1970s. By then, Morris had established himself in New York as a political consultant. After Clinton decided to seek the governorship in 1978 and drew only token opposition, Morris had given Clinton shrewd tactical advice about how to help Governor David Pryor defeat Jim Guy Tucker in the 1978 Senate primary, who Clinton saw as the main threat to his dominant position in the Arkansas state Democratic Party. Morris's subsequent work for conservative Paula Hawkins in her race for the Florida Senate in 1980 didn't stop Hillary, when she belatedly realized that Clinton was in trouble, from calling in Morris in the closing days of the '80 race. By then, however, it was too late and Clinton went down to defeat. For the 1982 comeback, Hillary again sought Morris's help. The pair evidently concluded that Clinton would never again be elected governor of Arkansas as a liberal. The strategy they settled on was for Clinton to adopt much of the critique of his own first term that had been advanced by the Republican opposition and conservative critics like John Robert Starr. "Most of the ideas were Morris's, some were Hillary's, and she made sure they were implemented," said one adviser to the 1982 Clinton campaign. "Hillary is a person of action."

According to Clinton biographer David Maraniss, Hillary and Morris shared the same "dark" view of politics. Morris was especially attuned to the need to create "enemies" in political combat, a slick political consultant's analog to Saul Alinsky's notion of "mass jujitsu." The formula was a success, and as a result Morris established a political bond with Hillary while growing personally closer to Bill. He became a permanent fixture in the Clinton entourage in subsequent gubernatorial re-election campaigns.

As discussion turned to an announcement of Bill's candidacy in early 1982, Hillary and Morris planned two television spots and scheduled them to air just before Clinton was to kick off his campaign. The ads— filmed by a Little Rock advertising man, David Watkins, who referred to Clinton as "the greatest seducer who ever lived"—were intended to establish Bill in the new centrist mold and to portray him as having embraced the core principles of the Republican opposition. One ad renounced the car-tag fees and other taxes imposed in his first term, and included a spot where Clinton pledged not to propose any new taxes in a second term. The second ad portrayed Clinton as tough on crime. Hillary advocated an explicit apology for the first term, but Clinton resisted. "Bill would have debated the ads forever and there would have been no ads," said the Clinton adviser. "Hillary made it happen." Though in the end he didn't actually use the word "apologize," Clinton did look soulfully into the camera, and say: "I learned that you can't lead without listening."

In his uncertainty about the move to the center, it is not clear whether Clinton was simply so personally wounded that he was blinded to the brilliance of the strategy, or whether he was clinging to Hillary's authentic views out of a sentimental attachment to the couple's McGovernite history. At his best, Bill was a quick study, ambitious organizer, and unparalleled campaigner. He could also be a brilliant synthesizer of ideas, perhaps more so than Hillary—Yale's Guido Calabresi had likened his considerable intellect to an all-encompassing "hot bath." But as the debate over the television ads revealed, Bill was too much of a procrastinator to put his ideas into practice without Hillary's bracing "cold shower." Bill's unusual dependence on his wife and the duo of political advisers, Morris and Wright, suggested a troubling inability to define his own political identity. This fundamental weakness—and the constant interventions by Hillary that were needed to keep him on course—was the

root cause of the zig-zagging and flip-flopping of his public policy pronouncements in the years to come.

In the 1982 primary, Bill defeated Jim Guy Tucker, the man Morris had
helped him outmaneuver in 1978. Tucker was the first real opponent
Clinton ever had from the Democratic party in a statewide race. Just
twenty-seven years old, Tucker, who hailed from a political family, had
gone to Harvard, worked at the Rose Law Firm, and been elected Pulaski County prosecutor. When he took Wilbur Mills's seat on the House
Ways and Means Committee, political columnist Rex Nelson wrote: "Future senatorial material. Maybe even presidential." Former Attorney
General Joe Purcell, conservative state senator Kim Hendren, and the
ever present Monroe Schwarzlose were also vying to oppose White, whose
own missteps had encouraged the Democrats to think that a comeback
was possible. The Democratic nominee would have plenty of ammunition: Among other flaps, White was forced to admit that he had signed
a bill mandating the teaching of creation science in the public schools
without even reading it first.

Having won the primary, the Clinton team turned its attentions to
November. The key to Clinton's victory would hinge on turning out the
black vote. In the '74 campaign for Congress, Hillary had recoiled at the
notion of paying money to obtain black votes, and Clinton had lost the
election. The pattern was repeated in 1980. "They [the Clinton cam-
paign] didn't haul the black vote. You know what I'm saying? And it cost
about a quarter-million dollars to get the black vote out in East Arkansas,"
Clinton's opponent Frank White said. "They didn't think they had to do
that to beat me. And when they found they were in trouble, it was too
late to do it."[3]

As in many southern states with large rural black populations—Georgia, Mississippi, and Louisiana, among others—Arkansas politicians
spent money to turn out the black vote. Historically, the practice was not
confined to the South or to blacks or even to Democrats. The rural white
vote was for sale in parts of the South and street money poured into black
communities in some large cities of the Northeast. Although under
Arkansas law it was permissible to spend small amounts of money to get
out the vote, excessive amounts of cash—or "street money"—was said to
change hands.

Until 1965, Arkansas had a poll tax that made it prohibitively expensive for blacks to vote. In the days before its repeal, politicians or their operatives gave money to white landowners or employers to pay the poll tax for their black workers, who were then transported to the polls and told how to vote. This was how Democratic candidates who supported segregation, such as Orval Faubus, routinely drew substantial black support. In 1966, the first year after the poll tax was repealed, Republican Winthrop Rockefeller, running as a liberal against the candidate of the Faubus machine, cut deeply into the black vote. Rockefeller, it was said, had an unorthodox approach to attracting votes: He reportedly distributed thousands of bicycles to poor black children, who were instructed to tell their parents to vote for him.

Blacks make up about 16 percent of the electorate in Arkansas, and with the exception of Rockefeller's quixotic candidacy, almost all of that vote goes to the Democrats. The turnout of black voters on election day can vary widely depending on how much effort is mounted by a candidate to get them to the polls. By the time Clinton was a statewide candidate in the mid-1970s, distributing "get out the vote" money was common practice and an open secret in the Democratic Party. Republicans would probably have done the same, but they didn't have a network of operatives in place in the communities who knew how to get the job done, nor did anyone other than Rockefeller have the cash.

The black vote was even more important to Clinton than to most other Democrats because he tended to run poorly among white male voters. In 1982, while Betsey Wright and other political operatives headed the effort in Little Rock, victory hinged on the ability of local operators like Bert Dickey, a farmer from the town of Earle in northeastern Arkansas, to turn out the vote. According to Frank White, Clinton won the '82 election in Bert Dickey's predominantly black eastern district, where Dickey's family had long been politically active. Dickey's grandfather was on the state racing commission and an uncle was a local banker. The family business was farming and they owned the local John Deere dealership.

Over the years, Dickey traveled with Clinton, contributed personally to his campaigns, and held fund-raisers for him at his home. In return for his efforts on Clinton's behalf, Dickey said, he sought appointment to the state's Fish and Game Commission in 1984. Patronage jobs in the swollen state bureaucracy, numbering about five thousand, were highly coveted. The plum appointments were to the more than two hundred powerful state boards and commissions, all of whose members were named by the governor. Many of the posts had terms longer than the governor's in order to keep them nominally independent, but because Clinton ended up governing for five terms, he was able to gain control of most every patronage slot in the state. Commissioners were paid little more than per diem expenses. But the payoff might come later—especially with posts on key commissions like Highways or Fish and Game, which controlled development issues.

Dickey said Clinton initially agreed to give him the Fish and Game post, but an hour before the appointment was to be announced he received a call from the governor's office telling him the post was going to someone else. Again in 1988, Dickey said Clinton promised him a job with the state vocational education system if he earned an advanced degree. Dickey studied for a doctoral degree in technological and adult education at the University of Tennessee, but he withdrew when he concluded that Clinton would not keep his word: "He kept lying to me, but I kept wanting to believe him."

According to Dickey, who retains a raft of detailed notes and ledgers to bolster his claims, beginning in the '82 Clinton campaign, he and others passed on amounts of cash ranging from $500 to $1,000 to the local "power brokers" in the black community—ministers, morticians, realtors—who acted as pass-throughs to drivers and other workers who physically turned out the vote, earning, he estimated, about $25 apiece per day. Rounded up and handed a palm card printed by the Clinton campaign, the voters might get $2 apiece or a Coke and cookies, and a ride to the polls.

Though Earle was a town of only about 3,500 in Arkansas' predominantly black first district, one of four in the state, Dickey eventually was responsible for all 24 counties in the district, which lay in the poverty-stricken Mississippi Delta region. "The proof was in the pudding. Credibility is built up over time," Dickey explained. "They use you again and again. And you get more money the more they're sure you can deliver the vote." At this high point, Dickey said, he "easily" handled $100,000 in cash for the gubernatorial primary, and another $100,000 in the general election.

Where did all the money come from? According to Dickey, he raised some of it himself by selling "quick and ready access to the governor's office" or, he claims, actual appointments to local boards and commissions, depending on the amount of the contribution. Dickey passed on the money to aides who assessed the campaign's overall financial needs and distributed it back down to him in big sacks, often adding tens of thousands to the amount Dickey had raised himself.

Dickey recalls that there were contributions far exceeding the legal campaign contribution limit of $1,500. "Fifteen hundred might get you a free season pass to the race track, that's about it," Dickey said. Some small cash contributions were given directly to Clinton at fund-raisers, he said. "You'd fold up a hundred-dollar bill or two and just go by, shake hands, palm it, slick as you ever saw. That was done quite a bit."

Dickey did have a good idea of how some of the collected cash flowed so that it could be spent on the books. In the '82 race, Dickey alleges, "I was asked [by a high-level Clinton aide he declined to name] if my wife and I wanted to give $1,500 each to Clinton. And I said no. And they said, 'How about $100?' And I said okay. Then, they gave me $2,800 in cash, told me to deposit it, and write the campaign two checks for $1,500. Then they told me if anybody asks where I got the cash, tell them that I sold a piece of farm equipment to somebody off the side of the road for cash." (Others involved in the Clinton campaigns have denied that any wrongdoing occurred in the use or reporting of campaign funds.)

So it was that a rough division of labor was established for the co-candidacy: Hillary would be deeply involved in campaign strategy, honing the message, and representing Bill in public forums, but it was Bill who dealt with the seamier side of Arkansas politics. Bill was the political organizer par excellence who knew where the money and votes were.

Bill's increasing dependence on Hillary took various forms. In *The Clintons of Arkansas*, Rudy Moore observed that "the chief criticism" about Bill was that "he told people what they wanted to hear and then didn't follow through on his commitments." This was not, in Moore's view anyway, because Clinton was empty or unserious: "He simply wanted to help every person he could, and he hated to disappoint anybody if he thought there was any merit at all in what they wanted." Bill therefore tended to be reluctant to make tough political choices that helped some but hurt others. Making decisions was "against Bill's nature. And that is where Hillary often provided some balance."[4]

If she still viewed her husband's constituents as "rubes," by 1982 Hillary had learned to mask her true feelings, hold her nose, and work the local fish fries for votes. On leave from the Rose Law Firm for the year, she was an instant hit as a regular stand-in for Bill on the stump. Hillary also accompanied Bill to a series of private meetings with local opinion makers to help him make his case. "I had a newspaper in western Arkansas and I had a critical editorial about some actions he took as governor when he was making a campaign appearance in 1982," newspaper publisher Garrick Feldman recalled. "And his campaign people called me and asked me to meet with them both. They wanted to explain whatever it was he did. I remember sitting between him and Hillary, and she was backing him up, trying to explain their position, saying he was sincere about his actions and telling me that my criticism was unfair."

At the same time that he moved to the center and tried to regain business backing, Clinton made a calculated return to the populist theme of lower utility rates which he had sounded as attorney general, exploiting White's image as a rich investment banker bought and paid for by special interests. "He was campaigning that year on utility reform, because Frank White had passed the biggest electric-rate increase in the state's history," recalled John Brummett, then an *Arkansas Gazette* reporter. "If he forgot to mention the issue in a speech, she was there to whisper to him and make sure he mentioned it. He was very focused and stayed on message that year, and the people who knew what was going on in the inside gave her the credit. Once a play is set, she is a good disciplinarian."

A stout mustachioed man who fancied himself a local Jimmy Breslin, Brummett was a friendly critic of Clinton's from the populist left. He tended to romanticize Clinton's unpopular first term as more principled than his subsequent tenure in the state house, and he faulted Hillary for the turnabout. Since Hillary was credited by insiders like Brummett as having had stronger ideological commitments than Bill, they tended to see her pragmatism as a cynical betrayal of ideals. She therefore bore the brunt of criticism from Bill's disappointed supporters who felt abandoned by his rightward shift. Bill, on the other hand, was seen as standing for so little in the first place that his flip-flopping was more easily forgiven. Whereas Bill was expected to be nothing more than a political animal, Hillary was seen as having a character flaw when she acted like a politician. The more adept she was at playing the game, the harsher the criticism.

"I've seen her explain legal issues to him," Brummett recalled. "There was one case, the Wayne Cryts case, where I saw her give him a very good ten-minute briefing on it, concluding with a moderate political position he could take. [Cryts, an officer of the American Agriculture Movement in Arkansas, was jailed in 1972 for refusing to name the seventy farmers who helped him remove bushels of soybeans from a grain elevator that had gone bankrupt in a dispute over who owned it.] Her general view of the world is fairly liberal, but in the end she's just as pragmatic as he is, and more coldly so. Whatever would keep him in office, she'd do."

What critics like Brummett failed to recognize was that Hillary's pragmatism was a tactic, not a philosophy. She was anything but insincere in her beliefs; over the long haul, she had no intention of conceding the substantive issues or bedrock principles to the other side. Nor, as Brummett implied, did the pragmatism come easily to Hillary. While pursuing her political goals through public interest law, Hillary had never really been compelled to compromise her beliefs. She had always worked within elite left-liberal environs, where her convictions were unchallenged by her colleagues—the Wellesley College student government, the Watergate Committee, and the LSC and Children's Defense Fund boards. Now, enmeshed for the first time in elective politics in a conservative southern state, she struggled to justify the new centrist emphasis necessary for political survival in terms of the Reverend Jones's philosophical teachings, which had been reinforced by all of her experiences in the 1960s and 1970s.

During this period, Hillary once again became a regular churchgoer, joining the First United Methodist Church in Little Rock, serving on the board and providing free legal services. Hillary's work with the Little Rock church led her to travel the state giving talks on why she was a Methodist, speaking eloquently of the eighteenth-century British reformer John Wesley and his social gospel message. The theme of one such talk, at a Baptist church in North Little Rock, was "Women, Armed with the Christian Sword—To Build an Army for the Lord." When the Reverend Jones visited Hillary in Little Rock in the early 1980s, he recalled, she peppered him with questions about the morality of the death penalty. Having once written a legal brief against the death penalty that was credited with saving the life of the mentally retarded Henry Giles, Hillary seemed troubled about Bill's embrace of capital punishment as an element of his move to the center. At the time of Jones's visit, Clinton had been re-elected and faced a decision about carrying out a death sentence for a serial rapist. Hillary, who clearly thought the death penalty was barbaric, appeared to be seeking guidance from Jones on the issue. Jones gave her the assurances she sought. "She asked me what I thought of capital punishment," Jones recalled. "And I said in the Judeo-Christian tradition you can't rule it out, because there is fairly strong support for punitive justice. Punishment is an aspect of a theology of justice. . . . And I said just as I believe in the Just War theory that one can justify war . . . I think you can talk about justifiable capital punishment. She said, I agree with that. And she said, 'It is agonizing, but I think there are some people who have forfeited their right to life.' And then I said, 'And I don't support capital punishment as a deterrent but as something some people deserve.' And she agreed with that. But she agonized over it." Jones's accommodating answer highlights his own elastic view of traditional religious doctrines and suggests the role that Hillary's religious beliefs may have played in helping her to square her pragmatic instincts with her moralistic principles.

In the '80 race, Frank White had injected religion into the campaign, often mentioning his membership in a non-denominational fundamentalist church. After his defeat Clinton also began regularly attending services at Little Rock's Immanuel Baptist Church. While Hillary genuinely seemed to be seeking spiritual guidance and a renewed sense of purpose, Clinton's churchgoing was widely seen as politically directed, since he chose to attend a Sunday service that was televised throughout the state. He sang in the choir, standing behind the minister directly in the sights of the television cameras.

In another move that some of Bill's supporters viewed as hypocritical, Hillary began to assiduously court *Arkansas Democrat* editor John Robert Starr. To some of the local liberals, opposition to Starr was on a moral par with opposition to the death penalty. The columnist had a reputation as a bully who was willing to engage in *ad hominem* attacks to score rhetorical points, not the least of which was his contemptuous treatment of "Sweet William" and "Billion Dollar Bill" in the 1980 race. Many observers believed that Starr's ranting against Clinton had cost him that election.

Perceiving Starr's support as absolutely critical to the effort to remake Clinton's image, Hillary cultivated the controversial editor, engaging with the press in a way that she had refused to during the first term, when she did not view herself as part of Clinton's political machine. Now, she treated the irascible conservative columnist to a series of private lunches during which she laid out what Bill would do in a second term, and carefully gauged Starr's reaction. Knowing that Starr was married to a schoolteacher, Hillary cannily broached the subject of a governor's initiative to reform Arkansas' schools in his second term. In courting Starr, Hillary revealed a side of herself that the public rarely saw. She had a lively sense of humor, a hearty laugh, and even a flirtatiousness that many men found appealing. Like Bill, she now proved that she could be a seducer as well.

Max Brantley, a former *Arkansas Gazette* columnist who now edits the left-wing alternative newspaper *Arkansas Times,* has been described as "the strongest Clinton supporter among major columnists" in Little Rock. He and his wife Ellen, who attended Wellesley with Hillary and who was appointed to a state judgeship by Clinton, were personal as well as political friends. Brantley was strongly critical of Hillary's efforts to neutralize Starr. "There were people like us [Brantley and his wife] who like the Clintons and liked them politically, and hated Starr, and understood pragmatically why you have to do that, because he was a force as a daily columnist in one of the statewide dailies," Brantley said. "She kissed his ass. It was just disgusting. But, it worked." Starr barely wrote a bad word about Clinton during the 1982 election—or thereafter.

In truth, Brantley was condemning Hillary for having done exactly what any determined politician making a bid for a political comeback would have done. But to Starr, Hillary had more to offer than a typical politician. Even as she was ostensibly selling Starr on the virtues of her husband, it was Hillary's own commitment, strength of character, and willingness to work hard to achieve her goals that Starr came to believe in. He and Hillary worked together on the effort to reform Arkansas' schools in Bill's second term, and Starr would even promote her as a candidate for governor in 1990. Like many in the old boy establishment who gave Hillary a chance, and got to know her well in her various endeavors through the coming years, Starr ended up laying aside their political and cultural differences and embracing Hillary far more enthusiastically than native son Bill. "The difference between Bill and Hillary," Starr said in retrospect, "is that deep down Hillary is a good person."

Having repositioned Bill, the final step on the road to re-election was Hillary's own dramatic makeover. "The Hillary Question is still with Bill Clinton and like a snowball racing down a slope it is getting larger and larger and larger in the voters' minds," reported the *Arkansas Gazette* shortly before the 1982 campaign kicked off. "As tacky a question as it may seem to many, the Hillary issue is one of too many well-known reasons that Bill Clinton lost his bid for re-election two years ago. The Hillary question—the difference in their last names—is no secret to the voting public." The advice Mary Lee Fray had given Hillary almost a decade before in Fayetteville about wearing nail polish and sexy sandals and repeating the views of her husband had turned out to be on target. "After the defeat, one of the things they realized was that in Arkansas they expect the little woman to be there by the man's side," said Rex Nelson, the *Arkansas Democrat-Gazette* political editor. (The irony was that Hillary was really supplying the views, which she was then required to repeat as if they were his.)

As Clinton prepared to announce his re-election and the *mea culpa* television ads blanketed the state, Hillary bowed to pressure and issued her own *mea culpa,* inviting guests to a series of meet-and-greets with Mr. and Mrs. Bill Clinton. When the moment of truth arrived, Hillary understandably tried to finesse her name change, since it was something she had resisted rather courageously for years. In making the announcement, Hillary explained that she had been Hillary Rodham as a practicing lawyer; now, taking leave from the Rose Firm to campaign full time, she was free to be Mrs. Bill Clinton. Clinton chimed in with the claim that Hillary had always used his name socially, which wasn't true. One of Hillary's favorite anecdotes, in fact, concerned the time that the couple had gone to a function at the Carter White House as Bill Clinton and Hillary Rodham. Bill had been taken aside and admonished by a presidential aide for bringing a woman other than his wife to the affair.

Hillary's announcement made headlines across the state and nationally. The *Washington Post* reported that Hillary Rodham, as she was known in Washington when she chaired the Legal Services Corporation until

1981, "will not only give up her law practice to campaign full time, she also will stop using her maiden name and henceforth be known as Mrs. Bill Clinton." Hillary explained to the *Arkansas Democrat* that she had retained the name because "it was important to me that I be judged on my merits and that Bill be judged on his merits," and conceded that she had not been "at all prepared about the concern people expressed about this decision which we had made personally."

Clinton told *The New Yorker* in 1994 that the impetus for the change came solely from Hillary. "In one of my conversations with the president," wrote Connie Bruck, "he emphasized the point that not only had he not requested her to change her name but he had at first resisted her changing it. She understood that it was part of a picture that we had painted for the voters that made them feel alienated from us. And she said to me—I never will forget . . . I respect her so much for this, because she came in to see me, and she said, 'We've got to talk about this name deal.' She said, 'I couldn't bear it—if we're going to do this, let's try to win. I couldn't bear it if this costs you the election. It's just not that big a deal to me anymore.' "[5]

Other published accounts have suggested that Bill—later described by Hillary as "the only man in Arkansas who didn't ask me to change my name"—was privately complaining to supporters that the issue was costing him politically. Perhaps Clinton felt unable to confront Hillary on the subject himself, allowing his friends and supporters to act as his surrogates. In an interview with the *Washington Post,* Hillary acknowledged that a campaign mounted by Bill's supporters had produced the difficult decision. "It became a kind of growing concern among his supporters, who came to see me in droves, or called me on the phone and related story after story, and said, 'We really wish you would think about this.' "

In retrospect, Hillary's decision to yield to political reality and help seal Bill's re-election may be little more than a sign of how much he meant to her. Many politicians make symbolic gestures to alter negative public perceptions—George Bush's supposed fondness for pork rinds, Michael Dukakis in a tank, and Bob Dole without a tie are but three obvious examples. Dick Morris's GOP senatorial candidate Paula Hawkins had a face-lift before running in 1980. Hillary's decision to take Bill's name, however, seemed a change of a different order because she had been so principled about the matter all along. Her close friends knew this. "I teared up. I had a lump in my throat," Betsey Wright was quoted as saying of the announcement.

Her name wasn't all Hillary felt compelled to change for the sake of political expedience: She also called family friends and asked them how to dress for the people of Arkansas. She wore her hair straight, lightened it, held it in place with a headband, and began wearing contact lenses and knit power-suits. There were even reports that she adopted a phony southern accent, as Meredith Oakley put it, "peppering her remarks with colloquial references to 'y'all.' "

"Hillary was a different woman then than I think she is now," said Doug Bowman, who worked with Hillary at the Rose Firm in the late 1970s. "The transformation occurred as Bill continued politically. When Bill lost the governorship to Frank White, [she] glamorized physically, and lost weight and became a different person. She used to be Hillary Rodham in the days I worked at the firm. Then all of a sudden she was Mrs. Clinton."

The personal sacrifice Hillary made was not insignificant. Though it has been mentioned as only a footnote in most accounts of the Clintons' political history, the change from Hillary Rodham to Mrs. Clinton was actually of great moment, and not only as political symbolism. As she apparently resolved the cultural tension with Arkansas in favor of the local mores, only one obscure news report in the *Times-News* of McGehee, a town of five thousand residents in East Arkansas' poor Delta region, appears to have picked up on her ambivalence. Asked if she had legally changed her name to Hillary Clinton, the *Times-News* reported, " 'No,' came the ice-cold answer from Arkansas' former first lady." Indeed, Hillary's true feelings could be gauged by her decision not to change her name legally, to continue practicing law as Hillary Rodham, and to keep signing her tax returns "Hillary Rodham."

That Hillary's physical appearance should have become a political issue must have been quite painful for her. One acquaintance, whom she called for sartorial advice at this time, said that during the conversation Hillary was on the verge of tears. Hillary had always been carefree about her appearance and never seemed to think of it as a way to advance her interests. She had been raised by her parents in a very frugal household with an austere Puritan aesthetic. Dorothy, moreover, had taught her to value substance over style. Hillary herself once explained: "I don't vest my identity in my hair or my clothes. I view that as what you have to do to get up in the morning and go out in the world."

Whether this attitude was a product of her upbringing or was instead a method of rationalizing deep-seated insecurities about her looks is impossible to know. Though Hillary was the prototype of a smart, successful woman who had it all, her physical appearance had always been something of an Achilles heel. In mocking Hillary's attempts to look pleasing—dieting, perming her hair, and wearing plastic jewelry and heels—her Rose Firm secretary's point was not that Hillary didn't care about how she looked, but rather that she was awkward and unsure about how to put herself together. Bill's perpetual philandering and cruel asides must have made her self-esteem all the harder to maintain. When a male friend of theirs asked Bill in the early 1980s why he had begun dating Hillary at Yale, he was astonished when Bill guffawed and said it was because there were so few women at the law school to choose from.

Perhaps in reaction to the southern belle culture and Bill's weakness for beauty queens, Hillary later tried to show her daughter that her physical appearance was unimportant, much as Dorothy Rodham had done by buying Hillary a frumpy prom dress. According to Chelsea's former nanny, Becky Brown, "I remember after my interview at the mansion, Robyn Dickey [the mansion administrator] told me that Hillary had asked her if she thought I was the type who was into clothes and makeup. She told Robyn she didn't want anyone around Chelsea who was into clothes. One time Chelsea was in a play circus at school, dressed as a clown, and the teachers decided to let the kids wear their costume home and show their parents. I'll never forget that Chelsea cried and cried until they took her makeup off her. She said she had to get the makeup off before she got home and her mother saw it." (Hillary also refused to let Chelsea pierce her ears.)

In softening her image in 1981, Hillary wished to be seen by the public in her role as mother, something she had scrupulously avoided exploiting in the 1980 re-election campaign. "She began to change the things that were liabilities. She traveled a lot, getting off the plane and yanking that child onto the tarmac. She worked very hard to do the things that were traditional and appropriate," said columnist John Brummett.

The local political establishment seemed satisfied that Hillary Rodham had surrendered to convention and appeared to subordinate her preference for autonomy to Bill's career. Suddenly, the local press began singing her praises: "Mrs. Clinton is almost certainly the best speaker among politicians' wives," the *Arkansas Gazette* gushed in an article before election day. "She is an Illinois native, perhaps a little brisker, a little more outspoken than the traditional Southern governor's lady. . . . The name change indicates that she's working at softening her image a bit . . . and succeeding, apparently. She has become a good hand-shaking campaigner in the traditional Arkansas style." Judging from Hillary's response to friendly Rotarians, "she could melt willingly enough when the occasion demanded." The newspaper described her new role as "the traditional one for candidates' wives—to be at her husband's side, gaze raptly at him as he speaks, to enthusiastically greet well-wishers afterward. The fact that she has become accomplished at what is a rather passive role for a person of her background and temperament probably is a tribute to self-discipline. Her spirit shows when she speaks on her husband's behalf."

Reinvented as Mrs. Bill Clinton, Hillary soon learned that she could be more than a behind-the-scenes political operative. For the first time, she could be deployed as an effective weapon to openly fight Bill's opponents, who quickly found that they couldn't counter-punch a lady. "She spoke for him at a day parade," Frank White recalled. "And you know, she jumped all over me, said I wasn't being truthful about her husband and his record. This was a new thing in Arkansas politics. She comes in, lays waste to the opponents, and you know it's kind of difficult to get up there and let a woman have it." When the incumbent Republican governor refused challenges to debate Clinton, Hillary pulled two-year-old Chelsea into the political fray, publicly taunting White: "Frank White would probably try to avoid being in the same room as Chelsea. Chelsea could debate him and win."

Hillary's confrontation with White illustrated how adept she was in turning the very thing that had been a liability—her reputation as a "ball-busting feminist," as Meredith Oakley had indelicately put it—into a major asset. During the first Clinton term, when Hillary Rodham was seen as too ambitious and aggressive in advancing her own career, that image hurt Bill. Now that she was exercising her talents on Bill's behalf as Mrs. Clinton, she was very successful. Instead of treating the Arkansas mores as obstacles to be overcome or set aside, Hillary was now deftly turning them against the Arkansas voters and press.

Bill Clinton was elected to a second term as governor with 54.7 percent of the vote. Neil McDonald, the campus coordinator for the 1974 Clinton campaign in Fayetteville, was stunned when the woman he remembered as Bill's abrasive four-eyed Yankee girlfriend appeared at the inaugural ball as the gracious Southern political wife, even requesting that the orchestra play a honky-tonk country music tune following a rendition of "Happy Days Are Here Again." The diamonds-and-denim theme of the first Clinton inaugural was replaced by a more traditional formality. Hillary wore a silk chantilly lace gown that was described by the *Arkansas Democrat* as a "feminine creation . . . innocent . . . yet sophisticated . . . soft and wispy." The *Gazette* said Hillary would be "the belle of the ball." Hillary—once ridiculed as a hippie—was quoted as saying the owner of the Little Rock shop where she bought the gown should "be ready for a call from Nancy Reagan."

In the end, it was hard not to think that Hillary had lost a bit of herself in this image-making process. Hillary was not a phony and she should not have had to play the part to advance Bill's career. Though in the short term Hillary made the right political decision for Bill, in the longer term, an honest effort to educate the public about her choice to keep her own name might have been the better solution. For with the name change, Hillary's image became a matter of political spin, and it is fair to assume that she began to feel somewhat untrue to herself as a result. Indeed, the struggle with her image that she now began was one that she would never really win—witness the wild oscillations between tough-talking super-lawyer and apron-clad cookie-baker in the '92 campaign, and her monthly makeovers as first lady. Over time, as she became a national figure, these shifting image changes would subtly undermine Hillary's stature by conveying an uncertain impression that the electorate received, correctly or not, as either a sign of confusion or lack of confidence about who she really is, or worse, an effort to hide her true self from the public.

That Bill had Hillary to thank for the resurrection of his political career would be an understatement. Though Bill has been praised for his remarkable political resilience and improbable buoyancy, Hillary would seem to better deserve the label "comeback kid." But for Hillary, what had begun as an instinctive maneuver to help her foundering mate and preserve her family would now become a full-time occupation. Although she managed to maintain her connections to the national Democratic Party establishment, Hillary Clinton gradually lost her independence and separate identity as she shifted all of the intelligence, vigor, and commitment she had brought to her various causes to the endless task of keeping her husband politically viable. Over the years, the co-candidacy itself—the personal political power of Bill and Hillary—would become the new cause.

7

Joan of Arkansas

In the first few months of his second term, after his hard-fought come-back, Clinton again appeared distracted. In February 1983, he suffered a humiliating defeat when the legislature refused to back his plan to eliminate the public service commission and place utility regulation under the governor's control. At the close of the legislature's regular session in the spring of 1983, Clinton gave an interview to the *Arkansas Gazette*, which headlined the article: "Wasn't Weak, Vacillating, Clinton Says of His Stands."

Bill's lack of focus in the first few months of 1983 must have worried Hillary. In 1982, she had taken leave from her law practice, organized his political team, and essentially gotten him re-elected. Now with her own career on the back burner, she had a considerable stake in his success. If Bill failed again, her sacrifices would be for naught.

In consultation with the team that forged the comeback campaign—Betsey Wright and Dick Morris—the Clintons decided to pick one strong issue to cement the repositioning of Bill as a moderate centrist and to provide a platform for his re-election in 1984. The issue they chose, re-forming Arkansas' school system, presented an opportunity to shed once

157

and for all the image of out-of-touch liberalism of the first Clinton term and also co-opt opposition on the traditionalist right. As part of that effort, the three left-wing aides who had set the agenda in the first term were banished, replaced, in effect, by Hillary, Wright, and Morris.

Education reform was the hot button issue of the early 1980s among Republicans and reform-minded Democrats eager to take on the entrenched interests of the educational establishment, especially the teachers' unions. President Reagan's National Commission on Educational Excellence had issued a widely publicized report that spring decrying a "rising tide of mediocrity" in America's schools. A new wave of both Republican and Democratic governors, from Lamar Alexander in Tennessee to Richard Riley in South Carolina, had launched education reform initiatives in their states. Hillary and Morris wanted to position Clinton as part of this movement.[1]

A month after Reagan's commission rendered its report, Clinton asked the state board of education to appoint a committee to propose sweeping new standards for the Arkansas schools, among the worst in the nation. Though he had many well-qualified educators to choose from, Clinton made the unusual move of naming Hillary to chair the committee. By his own account, the idea was hers: "When he [Clinton] reflected later on how it came about, Clinton joined the crowd and gave credit to his wife," Roy Reed, a former *Arkansas Gazette* reporter and friend of Clinton wrote in *The Clintons of Arkansas.*

> He recalled the day when her role was decided. "We [Bill and Hillary] were sitting around talking about it, and I said, 'This could be the most important thing we'll ever do. Who should I name the chairman of the Standards Committee? The chairman is the key.' Either the first or second day we talked about this—we talk about a lot of things like this— she [Hillary] said, 'I think I'd like to be it. Maybe I'll do it.' " He reminded her that she had just taken eight months away from her law practice to help him get re-elected. She was a partner in one of the most prestigious firms in Little Rock. She said "Yeah, but this may be the most important thing you ever do, and you have to do it right."

Implicit in Hillary's comment was a recognition that a top-to-bottom reform of Arkansas's school system would be an extremely difficult challenge, and one which Bill might not be able to meet without her help. Arkansas was ranked last among the fifty states in the number of high school graduates entering college. Of the nearly 370 school districts, about half had no foreign language or physics instruction, slightly more than 100 had no mathematics, and 91 had no chemistry. As a result, the state's students performed abysmally on standardized tests.

Complicating the task further were entrenched interests that could be counted on to fiercely resist change. These interests included the politically powerful Arkansas teachers' union, which had supported Clinton's opponent, Jim Guy Tucker, in the '82 primary; hundreds of rural school boards; and many parents. The reform proposal would undoubtedly cost money, which meant new taxes in the traditionally low-tax state. The job, therefore, called for qualities that Hillary apparently believed she possessed and Bill lacked. Foremost among these was an almost Nixonian resolve—a willingness not to be liked, indeed to make enemies—if that was what it took to get the job done.

As in the 1982 gubernatorial campaign, Hillary again cleverly turned the tables on the Arkansans who had rejected her as Hillary Rodham. Because she was now being presented as helping her husband reform the schools, a realm where women were traditionally prominent, rather than pursuing her own agenda, the Arkansas public registered no objection to her wielding significant policy power. "When we think of school teachers we think of women," said Richard Herget, the 1980 Clinton campaign chairman, "and so if you're going to take on a feminine institution, and that's school teachers, what better person to have do it than the governor's wife?" (Although Hillary's appointment was not at all controversial in Arkansas, when the Clintons imported the co-candidacy to Washington, they would be blindsided by the skepticism of many who viewed the novel power-sharing arrangement as an abuse of public trust.)

Heading the reform initiative served Hillary's needs as well as Bill's. Her legal work at the Rose Firm—serving, for example, as counsel to the Little Rock Airport Commission—wasn't engaging her passion for public policy and social reform. Nor was her talent for operating in politics deployed to full advantage in her new role as traditional political wife on the campaign hustings. Now she had a chance to fulfill her obligations as first lady while doing work she found meaningful and rewarding: pursuing a child-centered social policy initiative at home. In discussions after the election with John Robert Starr, the conservative

Democratic editor whom she had transformed from a critic of her husband into a personal supporter and sounding board, Hillary revealed a
strong desire to enter the Arkansas policy arena in a formal way. "In one
of our meetings that we had—I had lunch with her maybe a half-dozen
times—and in one of those I asked, 'What do you want?' " Starr recalled.
"And she said, 'I want to run something.' "

Though up to now she had pursued it outside of Arkansas, Hillary
had a genuine commitment to the pursuit of a far-ranging social agenda,
including education and health. Enlightened institutional reforms
would mean better teachers and better results for kids, she firmly believed. Bill shared this belief, and indeed the co-candidacy was partly
based upon a fervent mutual interest in public policy and a conviction
that intelligence and expertise could resolve social problems. This lifelong interest, creating a bond of surprising strength, goes back to the
first phase of their relationship at Yale—a love affair born in the seminar. However, while Bill enjoyed a good debate and displayed an awesome command of policy details, he was not the ideologue of the pair,
nor did he necessarily share Hillary's commitment to making her ideas
a reality. Still, to the extent that she believed he really cared about helping people, Bill maintained a hold on her affections and loyalty.

As she promoted the reform plan throughout the state, Hillary sometimes spoke as if she were leading, with serene resolve, a crusade to bring
Arkansas out of the Dark Ages. In one newspaper interview, Hillary acknowledged her relatively privileged background and lack of exposure
to Arkansas' intractable economic and social problems, but she seemed
unaware that her tone could easily have been interpreted as patronizing.
Sounding like a visitor to a Third World country, she said, "Here you have
a much clearer, up-close sense of what it means to raise kids on $10,000
a year. I feel like the move [to Arkansas] represented a re-entrance to
the human condition." At another point, she seemed to blame Arkansans
for lacking the right priorities. The state's residents, she scolded, had to
overcome the backward mindset "that you could build a wall around
Arkansas and it wouldn't matter" and begin "giving sufficient attention
to quality education."

The education reform effort was a battle that Hillary would ultimately
win. Her greatest early triumph, it plainly fulfilled her self-conception as
a crusading progressive reformer. Regrettably, however, the lessons she
seemingly drew from this victory over the forces of reaction and igno-

rance would only set her up for a fall in the great health care debate of 1993.

Hillary worked hard to create the impression that the impetus for education reforms sprang not from the Ivory Tower but from a grass-roots clamor among Arkansans for better schools. In the summer of 1983, Hillary's committee held seventy-five public hearings, one in every Arkansas county. Traveling and speaking throughout Bill's home state, she transformed herself into a respected figure, more admired than her husband in many quarters. State senator Lu Hardin, who represented the small town of Russellville at the time, vividly remembered a speech Hillary gave to local leaders. "My wife Mary was with me and I remember getting in the car, after visiting with Hillary briefly afterwards, and Mary said it was one of the most persuasive speeches she had ever heard. She was ready to sign up and help."

In her speeches, Hillary sounded some of the same centrist, values-oriented themes of the New Democrat philosophy that Bill would later embrace. She seemed instinctively to recognize the need to present the education plan in a way that would appeal to the culturally conservative elements in the state. Complicating one-dimensional portraits of Hillary as a 1960s-style leftist, she sounded the themes of personal responsibility and discipline that reflected the work ethic of her midwestern upbringing, her Methodist heritage and training under Don Jones, and the religiously inspired social activism of her mentor Marian Wright Edelman. One could hear in these speeches the same young woman who had rejected the libertinism of the cultural left in the 1960s.

Much of what she had to say could have been mistaken for the public moralizing and traditionalism of Dan Quayle or William Bennett, years before they appeared on the national scene. Hillary often made the point that lasting reform in the schools could not be achieved unless families were made stronger and more stable and society returned to "shared values." In one such talk, she averred, "The first purpose of school is to educate, not to provide entertainment or opportunities to socialize. Discipline holds no mystery. When it is firm, clearly understood, fairly administered and perceived to be so, it works. When it isn't, it doesn't." In an interview with a local news station, Hillary went further, linking the decline in educational standards to the Vietnam War protests of the

1960s and the subsequent turmoil that caused "our entire social foundation [to be] shaken." The basic recommendation of her commission, she said, would be "a return to the traditional definition of education, of requiring that teachers teach and students learn, and that schools do what they are supposed to do, which is transmit knowledge and the ability to apply it." She went on to say that "people have lost a lot of confidence in themselves and in their institutions, whether it be government or churches or public schools. Now, I believe that we are coming out of that period where we are once again understanding that as a nation we have to expect something of ourselves."

Hillary's belief that government should play the primary role in rebuilding the social foundation, however, set her apart from both the New Democrats and the cultural conservatives, who argued that government had caused much of the problem in the first place. Hillary's approach, by contrast, would lead to a kind of nanny-state despotism that even some on the left, wary of placing too much power in the hands of self-anointed virtuecrats, found discomfiting. Underneath the traditional values packaging, Hillary's plan to reform the schools required that every local school conform to a set of elaborate, state-imposed "standards" designed by Hillary and an elite cadre of education experts and policy wonks. As evident in her scholarly writings in the area of children's rights and her work at the Legal Services Corporation, Hillary saw government power as a vehicle for social progress. Her basic view of Arkansans themselves as backward and benighted can only have strengthened her commitment to getting children away from their parents at a young age and into centrally planned schools, with uniform curriculums, run by accredited experts.

Many of Hillary's proposed standards were inspired by the findings of the Reagan commission—mandatory kindergarten, smaller classes, more course requirements, a lower age for mandatory school attendance, and competency tests that students had to pass to be promoted out of third, sixth, and eighth grades. She also sought to eliminate overcrowded classrooms so teachers would have no "excuse," as she put it, for substandard teaching.

But whereas the Reagan plan favored decentralization, Hillary's plan imposed centralized command and control: Under the standards she proposed, any school that failed to meet requirements crafted by state planners could be dissolved or annexed. School districts would be required to raise taxes to meet the standards or they would be shut down.

Because fewer schools would make more efficient use of limited resources, many Arkansas educators had long viewed consolidating schools and school districts as desirable. School consolidation had already come to many parts of the South in the 1960s and 1970s as a result of court-ordered integration, but it had yet to reach the most desolate areas, where poor transportation and rural geography made commuting impracticable. Until Hillary came along, no one had the courage—and perhaps the naïveté—to tackle the project head-on. With her plan to break up the local school districts, the Yale-educated lawyer from the North threatened to disrupt a long-established southern way of life.

In the past, consolidation proposals had been defeated by local school board members and school bureaucrats who stood to lose their petty fiefdoms. School districts in Arkansas were the ultimate patronage machines, dispensing jobs, such as school secretary and janitor, that were highly valued in the community. Consolidation would force thousands of school bureaucrats back into the classroom where they would actually have to work for a living. People in wealthier industrial areas opposed consolidation as well, because they did not want their tax dollars spent educating poor farmers' children.

Finally, while it might have seemed an afterthought to someone of Hillary's background, local schools were the central focus of civic life in the many rural towns, where the high school football game was the high point of the week. Soon enough, the locals began to grumble that Hillary wanted to take away Friday night football! Hillary didn't help matters with her advertisements touting minimum competency tests for all students "no matter how good an athlete they are." Arkansas needed to become at least as "fanatic" about mathematics and science as it was about football, she said on one occasion. "This isn't only for the benefit of the students who don't participate in sports and cheerleading, but it's also for the benefit of those who do participate because high school activities don't last forever and life goes on after seventeen."

These public forays notwithstanding, those close to the process said that Hillary was committed to a specific program of reforms even before she convened the town meetings. She really had no intention of carrying out the people's wishes, whatever these might be; she saw her role as putting them on an enlightened path. "Hillary was behind the idea of asking the public for their input, to get over the perception that all they cared about was what their advisers think," said *Arkansas Democrat-Gazette*

editor Rex Nelson. As the newspaper's political editor, Nelson closely followed Hillary's role in the reform effort and wrote a short biography of
the first lady after Clinton won the presidency. "She'd already made up
her mind, but she went out and convinced the public that she got the
idea from them," he said.

Democrat Pat Flanagin of East Arkansas had spent years studying the
Arkansas education system and sat on the legislative committee that considered Hillary's plan. Flanagin agreed with Nelson's view that she was
not interested in hearing contending opinions, noting that she even
moved to cut off debate when objections or criticisms were raised.
"Hillary's package was a damned sacred cow. If you questioned it, you
were brow-beaten with a don't question attitude," Flanagin said. At the
same time, however, "Hillary would privately admit that some of the criticisms were valid. [She would say] are you going to be against the standards? Are you going to be against education? As if questioning the
details of their proposal was synonymous with being opposed to educational reform in the state." (The idea that criticism equals opposition to
reform presaged Hillary's posture in the health care debate years later.)

Perhaps Hillary wished to avoid scrutiny of the "details" because the
plan's fine print reflected some of the progressive ideas that she had
imported to Arkansas from liberal precincts back East. The curriculum
proposal had a few multiculturalist flourishes of the sort that would later
generate tremendous controversy over the issue of political correctness.
In the history section, for example, emphasis was shifted to newly trendy
social history at the expense of learning about great events and individuals. In a 1988 survey on the impact of Hillary's reforms conducted by
Little Rock's liberal Winthrop Rockefeller Foundation, one teacher complained that the standards watered down basics in the curriculum to
make way for fluffier "innovative" approaches. "I feel remorse also because of the things they left out that I included before the standards.
Some committee came up with these things that were important in American history, other things were left out. I don't understand how one person can decide, for example, to leave out the entire War of 1812."[2]

Schools were required to provide classes in journalism, music, consumer education, arts and crafts, and "global studies," the latter being a
course in world history that emphasized the "diversity of culture patterns," devoting as much time to African as to European societies. In
many globalized curriculums, Dick and Jane books become Juan and

Maria books; world history becomes "galactic" history; and the pledge of allegiance is translated into a different language every day. When Hillary was asked about the global studies requirement in a public hearing, she brushed aside questions, telling the audience it was a "sophisticated" new approach.

Hillary's standards were also larded with "support programs" such as "guidance and counseling" and "media services." Dr. Bill Van Zandt, who served on Hillary's committee, said he helped her "develop data that would substantiate the need for [certain] aspects of the curriculum," including mandating that counselors be placed not only in junior highs, but in elementary schools to teach "personal growth and development. . . . Traditionally, these aren't part of elementary curriculum. . . . That was a big step to redefine the curriculum."

Hillary also pushed for more female administrators in the schools. Women, she seemed to believe, had more to contribute to education simply because they were women. "One thing which I think would improve the quality of education probably about 100 percent in five years is to increase by one hundred fold the number of women superintendents and principals. I don't say that facetiously. . . . The principal, who is often a fellow who took night courses and wrote a thesis at the school of education about basketball theory and is working his way to be superintendent, doesn't have a clue about how to get the most out of his teachers, how to encourage that development, that spark, that enthusiasm."

Kim Hendren, the conservative state senator who opposed Clinton in the '82 Democratic primary, queried him on "how much social liberalism was packaged into Hillary's education standards. His response was '[T]hat is where she is from.' " Dorothy English, a conservative activist, also raised objections with the governor. "We were fighting the mandatory kindergarten, which we didn't want," said English. The opponents of mandatory kindergarten wanted to have as much opportunity to school their children at home as possible. "He said that if it wasn't mandatory, parents won't insist that their kids go. And I asked if the state knows better than the parents and he said yes. Finally, in frustration, he said, 'Look, I can't change this, it's Hillary's bill.' "

When the standards were approved, Hillary used her political capital to push through other innovations, including an outcome-based education plan that set uniform learning goals to be measured by standardized tests. Critics argued that this was a cookie-cutter approach to education that encouraged teachers to "teach the test" and nothing more. The Governor's School for the Gifted and Talented, where both Hillary and Betsey Wright taught, brought together top students from around the state for summer programs at Hendrix College. The school served as a platform for some of the most radical academic theorists in the country. In March 1993, conservative social critic Thomas Sowell charged that the curriculum subjected students to a "one-sided barrage of films, lectures, and readings favoring homosexuality, 'animal liberation,' pacifism, and a whole string of other causes dear to the left and far left." The list of readings for the summer 1991 session of the school included an essay titled "The Spiritual, Political Journey of a Feminist Free Thinker," by Emily Culpepper, who assailed the "androcentrism" of Christianity, said the "concept" of Jesus was "inescapably hierarchical," and described the crucifixion scene as "necrophilic" and "sadomasochistic." Among the scheduled speakers that summer was Dr. Mary Daly, a Boston College professor, who spoke on the topic: "Recalling the Courage to Sail; the Voyage of a Radical Feminist Philosopher." Daly came to fame in the late sixties when she was fired from her teaching post after arguing in *The Church and the Second Sex* for the integration of women in church leadership, but was reinstated and given tenure after students protested. Though still at the Catholic college, Daly has renounced Christianity and its "patriarchal caste system." Later, she argued in her book *Gyn/Ecology* that medicine was dominated by a patriarchy dedicated to the castration of women; the book became a cause célèbre and theoretical centerpiece of the extreme edge of militant feminism.

Hillary frequently linked the problems facing the schools to other social problems, such as teenage pregnancy—which, in her words, was "one of the most common reasons" girls drop out of school—when she became chairman of the Arkansas Adolescent Pregnancy Child Watch Project in 1986. The state's teen pregnancy rate was the second highest in the nation. Working with Joycelyn Elders, Clinton's state director of health, Hillary helped establish school-based health clinics, which distributed condoms and other contraceptives to young students and were advocated nationally by the Children's Defense Fund. "Of course, Hillary and Joycelyn Elders were very much in support of [the clinics]," legislator Pat Flanagin recalled. "She [Hillary] felt like Arkansas should be leading in something other than chicken and VD."

Again parting company with some segments of the left, when she spoke publicly on teen pregnancy Hillary frequently emphasized a traditional social message of abstinence rather than birth control. "Society bombards kids with sexual messages on television, in music, everywhere they turn, but families and churches aren't doing enough to help them withstand the pressure to have sex. Adults are not fulfilling their responsibility to talk to young people about the future, about how they should view their lives, about self-discipline and other values they should have. I don't know how we got off the track, but it is not happening in the families of our kids. Adults don't feel comfortable telling their children not to do things, or they don't know how to communicate that message effectively [as] I'm trying to do."

"Not birth control, but self-control" should be encouraged, she continued. "It's all right to say no . . . for children to engage in sexual activity . . . violates every traditional moral code and it unleashes emotions and feelings and experiences that children are not equipped to deal with."[3]

Though Hillary's staged public meetings and emphasis on values went a long way to neutralizing potential conservative opposition to her projects, the fact remained that Arkansas was a one-party state where the opposition was unorganized, unsophisticated, and easily dismissed as reactionary or self-interested. Operating in this unusual political vacuum seemed only to confirm Hillary's hubristic sense of moral and intellectual superiority—even invincibility. Had she been the wife of the governor in California or Texas, Hillary might have learned the art of compromise by contending with a vigorous Republican party, a range of powerful interest groups, and a critical press. Arkansas, by contrast, had little to teach her about democratic politics.

If Hillary met with less opposition in promoting the plan than might have been expected, there was a good deal of controversy over how the reforms would be financed. Before the standards were even proposed, Clinton faced a revenue shortfall for education. In May 1983, the Arkansas Supreme Court had ruled unconstitutional a formula for distributing state funds to school districts that gave more money to schools in areas with higher tax bases. Clinton's dilemma was figuring out how to get more money to the poorer districts without taking money away from the wealthier ones, in effect equalizing downward. As part of the Hillary and Dick Morris–designed '82 comeback strategy Clinton had promised not to raise taxes. His solution was to fold the revenues already needed into the tax proposals for Hillary's reforms. Clinton simply asked for twice as much money.

The Arkansas Department of Education projected that the standards would cost $200 million to implement, with the state hiring 3,781 more teachers, nurses, counselors, and librarians and building more than two thousand new classrooms. Teacher salaries, which averaged $12,000 a year, would also be raised. To pay for the new proposals and cope with the mandate from the supreme court, Clinton floated three different tax increases: a sales tax, a severance tax on natural gas, and a corporate income tax. Under the Arkansas constitution only half of the legislature was needed to pass a sales tax, while a 75 percent vote was needed to raise taxes. So Clinton proposed a sales tax hike, even though it was the most regressive of the three possible sources of revenue.

The sales tax increase—the first in twenty-six years in the state—promised to be an uphill fight. The Clintons decided that the best chance of passage was to present it as a necessary element in a reform effort opposed by entrenched special interests. Since a state budget formula allocated for teachers' salaries about 70 percent of any money raised, the Clinton plan proposed tying the tax increase to a minimum competency test for teachers.

In a page from the playbook of Dick Morris—who has been quoted as saying he believes in identifying an enemy in politics and demonizing it—the education plan was positioned against the one powerful interest group opposing the plan, the teachers' union. There was little down side for the Clintons, since the union had not supported Bill in the 1982 Democratic primary and had never been popular in the right-to-work state anyway. Whether or not Morris had ever studied Saul Alinsky, the strategy was one that the old master would have approved. "Before men can act an issue must be polarized," Alinsky had once written. "Men will act when they are convinced that their cause is 100 percent on the side of the angels and that the opposition are 100 percent of the devil. He knows that there can be no action until issues are polarized to this degree." Alinsky's thirteenth tactical rule in *Rules for Radicals* was: "Pick the target, freeze it, personalize it, and polarize it."

Though she may have been less cynical about it than Alinsky or Morris, the idea held great appeal for Hillary as well. "She made it very clear that there had to be a bad guy in this," Richard Herget said. "Any time you're going to try to turn an institution upside down, there's going to be a good guy and a bad guy. The Clintons painted themselves as the good guy. The bad guys were the school teachers."

By proposing the teacher test, the Clintons showed how adept they were at capturing Republican territory and exploiting it to their political advantage. In his memoir *Yellow Dogs and Dark Horses,* John Robert Starr wrote that he was the first to suggest to the Clintons, in meetings at the governor's mansion in the spring of 1983, that a teacher test be included in the reform plan as a way of justifying the new taxes to a public whose reflexively anti-tax mood Starr well understood. Frank White, whom Clinton had defeated in the '82 race, had also been on record as supporting the idea of linking any tax increase for education to a teacher test.

Teacher testing had come in and out of favor since the turn of the century, but the idea was all but abandoned in the late 1960s and early 1970s because of perceived racial bias in the tests. By the early 1980s, as the public began to fear that American schools were falling behind those of other nations, the idea of testing new teachers came back into vogue among centrist and conservative school reformers. By early 1983, teacher testing proposals were pending in eighteen states, mostly in the conservative South. The Clinton plan would go well beyond these proposals, however, by aiming to test teachers who were already in the classroom.

After his defeat in 1980, Clinton, who had always been fascinated by public opinion polls, began to live by them. Clinton's ability to translate poll data into positions that tap into the mood of the electorate was another important asset that he brought to the co-candidacy. Clinton's instincts in this regard brought needed balance to Hillary's often brittle, headstrong approach, which at its worst could seem dismissive and contemptuous of the sentiments of the average voter. "Hillary's qualities are what you see in a corporate boardroom," said one longtime friend of the couple. "She's a leader and a good political player. But her political judgment is that of a mere mortal. Bill is indecisive, but he's a far better politician."

Once Starr suggested the teacher test, Clinton commissioned opinion polls on the subject from Morris. "Clinton had done polling and knew if we were going to do this [pass the reforms] we needed to raise taxes. The poll found that to get an increase in the sales tax, 50 percent would support it for education, but 85 percent would support it with a teacher test," said former state legislator Charlie Cole Chaffin, a member of Hillary's standards committee who was for years the only woman in the Arkansas legislature. "You weren't going to sell a sales tax without giving the people something for it," Cole Chaffin continued. "And since by law most of the money was going to the teachers, you had to hold them accountable. You had to precisely say what the tax was for."

Armed with the results, Morris pushed the idea of the test with both Clintons. Once they embraced it, Hillary sought to protect the teacher test from potential opponents by shielding it from public view, the teachers' lobby, and even her own standards committee. Although Hillary held public meetings around the state ostensibly to poll the public on what should be in the plan, the teacher test was rarely, if ever, mentioned. The secret process recalled the criticism leveled by Jerry Zeifman, the lawyer who worked with Hillary on the Watergate committee. Zeifman had warned that Hillary's and Bernard Nussbaum's restrictive procedural rules were designed to cut off the Judiciary Committee members and staff from access to information about the progress of the investigation and thereby hijack the impeachment process.

When Hillary announced the plan that fall in a legislative address, she suddenly sprang the test on everyone, calling it "the real heart" of the reform package. Charlie Cole Chaffin said she did not recall the test ever being discussed in the standards committee, save perhaps once in passing. Had she been asked her opinion during committee deliberations, she said, she would not have supported it. Committee member Jim Price, who also would have opposed the idea if given the opportunity, added, "I saw it as a political ploy." By end-running her own committee, she placed her fellow members in the awkward position of having to go along with the chairman on an idea some of them did not favor or else publicly cross her, which no one seemed prepared to do.

In proposing the teacher test, the Clintons were taking on not only Arkansas teachers, but also the national education establishment, which saw the proposal as a political gimmick designed to scapegoat teachers. The idea of testing teachers who were already in the classroom was vigorously fought by the national teachers' unions every time the subject was raised, and Arkansas was no exception. The unions feared that if the test passed in one state, it would quickly be implemented in others. Following Hillary's announcement, the Arkansas union threatened to go on strike and prepared a lawsuit to stop the test. Soon bumper stickers appeared targeting both Bill and Hillary with the slogan: "No More Clintons."

Hillary, however, personally bore the brunt of the teachers' wrath. "Lower than a snake's belly" was how one school librarian described her in a news account. Charlie Cole Chaffin recalled, "Hillary was treated real ugly in some schools. In [predominantly black] East Arkansas, teachers slammed their doors as she walked down the halls." Hillary's friend Diane Blair later told the *Washington Post* of an especially hostile response Hillary received when she visited one Arkansas school in 1984: "A number of teachers were enraged that they were being asked to do this demeaning thing of taking a test to see if they were fit to be in the classroom. And a lot of their antagonism was vented in a very tangible way toward Hillary." Yet the heated reaction only seemed to confirm her sense of mission. "Once sometime in 1984, I remember walking through a crowd with her at a school," said Blair, "and you could hear teachers hissing at her. She just shook her head and said, 'I get this all over the state. It's heartbreaking. It's hard. But some day they'll understand.' "

Hillary did not back down, nor did she mince words in the face of the outcry from the teachers: The tests, she declared, were a necessary means of purging "incompetent" teachers. At the height of the controversy, Hillary accepted an invitation to debate teacher testing with the director of education of the Rand Corporation, a prominent think tank, before the annual convention of the American Federation of Teachers, an AFL-CIO affiliate, where she delivered a vigorous and persuasive defense of the test and lambasted Arkansas teachers who opposed it as shortsighted and self-interested. (The National Education Association, the leading national teachers' union, mounted an unsuccessful court challenge to the Arkansas test.)

In addition to earning the enmity of the teachers' unions, Hillary was willing to run the risk of being criticized for playing racial politics. Racial minorities tended to fail standardized teacher tests at higher rates than whites. Throughout the South, where black teachers had only recently been hired to teach in desegregated schools, many viewed competency tests as a way of disqualifying blacks from teaching. Some liberals were disillusioned by what they saw as Hillary's willingness to pander to the prejudices of middle-class white voters, a charge that would later be leveled against Dick Morris as well. "There was a great schism," said Kai Erickson, former executive director of the Arkansas Education Association. "The idea of a teacher test was understood to have appeal to those white parents who felt that black teachers were not competent. The black teachers, though, felt that it was racist." Hillary viewed the test as a necessary means to pass the tax, which would then fund the reforms. Being a pragmatic operator, she may have decided to adopt the test—even if she agreed with critics who saw it as a deeply flawed approach that appealed to the baser elements of the Arkansas populace—in order to achieve her desired end.

Shortly after the standards were announced and the tax increase and teacher test were formally proposed in the fall of 1983, Clinton called the legislature into special session. The governor often lobbied members personally for his projects, but when Hillary came to the Capitol, people noticed. "The legislators liked dealing with her better than with Bill because she was more professional and reliable," said Doug Wood, who served in the legislature at the time. If there was a touch of sexism in the way older men in particular seemed impressed by the "novelty" of an articulate, driven young woman who spoke her mind, Hillary appeared to play along and use it to her advantage. Hillary also convinced the so-called Good Suits Club—one hundred or so of Little Rock's political and financial movers and shakers—to make the education standards its major project. "The establishment really bought into what she was doing," said Blant Hurt, a Little Rock journalist who was critical of Hillary's plan. "There was a lot of interest from a collection of businessmen—Don Tyson, people like that—[who] helped sell it." Tyson, Sam Walton, and others contributed to a political fund, administered by Betsey Wright, which collected private donations to finance an advertising and direct-mail campaign to promote the initiative.

Though a loyalist of the teachers' groups, state senator Jay Bradford was nevertheless persuaded to abandon his supporters after Hillary wore him down in a memorable telephone call to his office. "She talked me into voting for her," said Bradford, who was generally supportive of Clinton but was prepared to vote against the governor when the vote on the teachers' test came up. "I was saying, 'Look, I've helped you on eight issues, I'm gonna sit out on this one.' But she's so persuasive and effective that she got me right off the bench and I went to the well again."

With time running out in the special session, the Clinton bill remained bottled up in the legislature's education committee for weeks. By this point, both the tax and the test were generating significant opposition. "He [Bill] couldn't get his bill out of committee, just couldn't get it out," said longtime state representative Lloyd George, the education committee chairman and a cattle farmer from the town of Danville. "Hillary came in and spoke to us for about an hour and a half one day," George recalled. As Clinton sat quietly in the audience, "She answered questions. That's when I made my remark, when I said, 'Hell, we elected the wrong Clinton.' We took a vote that day and got his education program out of the education committee. Hillary got it out."

According to George—like John Robert Starr a tough old curmudgeon not easily moved or impressed Hillary's arm-twisting made the difference on this and many subsequent occasions, notably including an effort to reform the state's juvenile justice programs. "Hillary would come around the Capitol working for her husband, selling his programs. If there were committee members who weren't seeing things right on Bill's program, Hillary would hunt them out." At one point George suggested a "Clinton for Governor" bumper sticker with the kicker: "Hillary, that is."

Following Hillary's appearance, George's committee voted unanimously to support the new standards, with the exception of mandatory kindergarten. (Schools were required to evaluate those who had not attended kindergarten before enrolling them in first grade.) In short order, the legislature approved the majority of reforms in the package, including the one cent sales tax increase that would generate approximately $155 million to fund the reforms. The teacher test, on which support for the tax increase was built, passed by only one vote. The state board of education soon approved the standards as well.

Press reports noted that Clinton's efforts in the education reform bill stood in sharp contrast to his usual political style of compromise. Observers attributed the resolve to Hillary, particularly on the teacher test. At the end of the day, the Clintons won a spectacular—if perilously narrow—victory. However, the question of whether that victory reinforced

Hillary's high-handed style and inflated her view of her own political acumen would bear heavily on her later undertakings.

The education initiative achieved mixed results for Arkansas schools. No one questioned Hillary's good intentions, nor did anyone doubt that merely putting education on the state's agenda was a good beginning. Perhaps the most tangible improvement was that most school districts were now offering four foreign languages and advanced math, subjects students rarely had an opportunity to study in the past. "I know she's a lawyer but I think we should get her an honorary Ph.D. in education. She's the best thing that's come along for education in Arkansas in the last fifty years," L. D. Harris of Blytheville, an educator who served on the standards committee with Hillary, was quoted as saying at the time.

However, critics claimed that some strong local schools and some curriculums were sacrificed in the name of uniformity. "As Arkansas' education czar, she approached her job as a social engineer who centralizes and bureaucratizes, rather than as a market liberal who respects local autonomy and defers to the wisdom of market forces," Blant Hurt wrote in a 1992 *Wall Street Journal* article. Hurt's judgment was backed up by a 1988 Winthrop Rockefeller Foundation survey of parents, teachers, and administrators in seventy-three school districts. "Thus far, the Arkansas school reform effort has by-passed teachers," the foundation concluded. "From their perspective, it has had a heavy, top-down regulatory quality. The result is a serious, large demoralization of the teaching force . . . they feel constrained by what they perceive to be a strangle-hold of mandates, needless paperwork and limited encouragement."

According to the survey:

> While the new course offerings in some districts have expanded and enriched curriculum, in other districts the reforms are perceived to have had an opposite effect. In the view of one respondent, "Districts with rich curriculum have had to shrink." Loss of local control over some aspects of curriculum was cited as having a detrimental effect on local curriculum development. Examples were given of excellent programs which had been eliminated or altered to meet reform requirements. This was reported to be most true in large districts where model programs had been eliminated in order to meet the standard. Several teachers shared

this point of view; one said the reforms have "pulled our general standards down." Another teacher said, "We used to have it great, now it's ho-hum. The standards did not pull us up to meet everybody else but pulled us down to meet everybody else."

As the reforms were implemented, the Arkansas education bureaucracy predictably ballooned. "More time spent filling out paperwork meant less time teaching children," Hurt noted in the *Wall Street Journal.* "In September 1987, Benny Gooden, superintendent of Fort Smith School District, complained of the 'intolerable bureaucracy.' He claimed it took 11 pounds of paperwork between March and July of that year just to prove his district had complied with the state's education standards. 'We kept a copy of everything, of course, and weighed it.' "

In the view of liberal critics like Rockefeller Fountation director Tom McRae, however, the new layers of bureaucracy were but one problem. They objected more strongly to the tight political control from the governor. "I think that the flaw really came in that the governor's office and Hillary after its passage tried to micro-manage it in the Department of Education because they simply did not trust the bureaucracy," said McRae, a liberal Democrat who supported Clinton at the time the survey was completed but decided to challenge him for the Democratic gubernatorial nomination in 1990. "There are stories about how, after the Clintons left for Washington, Betty Tucker [wife of Clinton's successor as governor, Jim Guy Tucker] would get calls from people—people in middle-level positions [in the Department of Education]—asking what to do about fairly low-level, mundane kinds of things with regard to the standards. The suspicion was that the department had been micro-managed out of the governor's bedroom."

Lack of funding for the new standards was another commonly cited problem. The money raised for the ambitious reforms turned out to be inadequate. Under the tax bill passed by the legislature in 1983, by mid-1985 all proceeds from the increase reverted to the state's general fund. "At that point, only because 54 percent of every dollar is required to go to education, was it an increase for education," said McRae. Clinton "got the largest single tax increase in state history on the basis that it would be dedicated to education but the total increase wasn't." When the state fell into a recession, many of the improvements were put on hold; Clinton had to go back to the legislature in 1987 and again in 1989 for more tax increases. In 1991, the Arkansas sales tax was boosted yet again to raise an additional $145 million for education.

Still, from 1984 to 1992, education spending in Arkansas more than doubled and the state had little to show for it. The *Wall Street Journal* analysis by Blant Hurt showed that the standards failed to raise student test scores: "By 1992, Arkansas' ACT [American College Test] scores were up, but the new average was a result of the 'enhanced' ACT test implemented in 1990 that resulted in score-inflation in all states. Adjusted accordingly, the 1992 ACT test scores are exactly the same as they were in 1972. This places Arkansas near the bottom of the test-score rankings among the 28 states using the ACT. . . . The trouble extends to the lower grade levels as well. In May 1991, a record 22% of the Little Rock School District's eighth graders failed the state's Minimum Performance Test." In May 1991 there were still over three hundred school districts in the state (down from 347 in 1982). In 1992, almost 60 percent of all Arkansas college freshmen needed remedial courses in math, reading, and English composition.

As critics had contended, the teacher competency test seemed useful primarily as a political device. In retrospect, it is possible to surmise that Hillary was willing to be accused of race-baiting because she knew the full force of the test would never be brought to bear on teachers. The state set the passing grade at such a low level that in practice the test had no teeth. There was, in fact, a serious competency problem in the classroom, as Hillary had claimed. More than 10 percent of teachers failed the test the first time they took it. But these teachers were permitted to remain in the classroom. The state paid for remedial training and let them retake the test for up to two years until almost all of them passed. Of about thirty thousand teachers, approximately 3 percent ultimately lost their jobs.

Despite the illusion of success, the Clintons' main contribution to education was in atmospherics, not real reform. Even the Clintons' friend and political ally Max Brantley conceded, "The teacher test is a cynical ploy. It was a meaningless test. It did little to improve the quality of teaching." More than anything, Brantley said, the Clintons "made it fashionable in Arkansas politics to be for education."

Education reform resulted in a political bonanza for the Clintons. Hillary fully repaired her image with both the Little Rock political establishment and the voters of Arkansas. She was named "Headliner of the Year" by the Arkansas Press Association in 1983. Countless other awards were heaped on her in the mid-1980s, including Young Mother of the Year by the Arkansas Association of American Mothers, Public Citizen of the Year by the Arkansas chapter of the National Association of Social Workers, and Woman of the Year by the *Arkansas Democrat*. She received an honorary doctorate from the University of Arkansas at Little Rock in recognition of her work in education and on children's issues and was chosen to give a prestigious commencement speech at the Fayetteville campus. She joined the board of the Arkansas Children's Hospital. She accompanied Clinton on trade missions to the Far East. Bill even named her to head a new policy planning group for the state, the Commission on Arkansas' Future.

Though he had reservations about the results, Brantley agreed that the effort burnished Hillary's image: "She quickly got command of the topic, used her considerable energy to go everywhere she had to go to sell it, won tens of thousands of friends in the process, made her reputation single-handedly through that effort as a forceful, decisive person who had good instincts and good intentions."

At an April 1986 Little Rock dinner in Hillary's honor, Bill, as he has done consistently throughout the partnership, paid tribute to her as "far better organized, more in control, more intelligent and more eloquent." Saluting her commitment to social activism, Clinton called Hillary his role model: "She did a lot of volunteer work when she was a young person. When she came to Arkansas, she started a legal services clinic there. When I became governor, she'd already gotten some women together who were family advocates and formed a group called the Arkansas Advocates for Children and Families. She's been my role model, because it's been so much more a part of the fabric of her everyday life than it has been of mine."

Though he didn't mention it, Clinton may have been grateful to Hillary not only for her inspiration but for her political calculations. The idea of finding one issue for Bill to run on again in 1984 and 1986 was a masterstroke. The kicker was that the standards were designed to take effect in 1987—through two election cycles in which the standards could serve as a ready-made platform for Clinton. The Republicans in Arkansas, never strong, were barely heard from again after Clinton moved to the center. Bill's strongest prospective opponent in 1984, Frank White, sat out the election because "he realized that the education issue made Clinton too strong to handle," John Robert Starr said. "If he had not come up with the education program, he'd have served one more term and then we'd have beat him again." Clinton coasted easily to victory that year and again in 1986, when Frank White tried to make a comeback. In the Democratic primary, Clinton handily defeated the aging Orval Faubus, who campaigned on the side of the small rural schools resisting consolidation, and he went on to win the general election by convincing voters that White could weaken the standards.

The reforms also made Clinton a serious political figure on the national scene. Though Hillary had taken the heat for the test and pushed it through the legislature, Clinton was admired throughout the region as the only governor who had been tough enough to face down the teachers and get a competency requirement enacted. Just as the teachers' union had feared, other states, including Texas and Georgia, soon followed suit with competency tests of their own, and Clinton was seen as a trendsetter. With appearances on *Face the Nation* and *Donahue,* Clinton came into national focus for the first time as a moderate Democrat who had courageously bucked one of his party's traditional liberal special-interest constituencies.

With Bill's political position in the state secured, both Clintons began to turn their attention to the question of a run for the presidency. There were, of course, signs from the beginning that Bill's vaulting political ambition had been part of what attracted Hillary to him. She had mentioned to Bernard Nussbaum as early as 1974 that her boyfriend was going to run for president one day. Nor had she been in Arkansas long when she saw that Bill's political future was of interest to politicians and press outside the state. Even in his failed first run for Congress, Hillary had fielded calls from the *New York Times* and the *Washington Post* the day after the election. By 1980, Clinton had been mentioned as a possible running mate for Jimmy Carter or Ted Kennedy. That same year, according to Cecelia Esquer, a fellow LSC board member of Hillary's from Arizona, Hillary quizzed her for political intelligence on Bruce Babbitt, a potential Clinton competitor in the national party.

Clinton's defeat later that year seemed to wipe him off the political map. But Hillary Rodham would not have married a loser. She was smart and ambitious and wanted nothing but the best. After the comeback victory in 1982 and re-election in 1984 and 1986, their best, Hillary must now have realized, was president.

Hillary's efforts on the education front not only secured Bill's position in Arkansas politics but appeared to bear fruit almost immediately as the couple became stars in the Democratic firmament, clearing the way for Bill's path to the Democratic presidential nomination. In addition to returning Clinton to the statehouse in 1986, voters approved a change in the state's Constitution that gave the governor a four-year term. With the Arkansas legislature meeting for only a few months every other year, over the next several years Governor Clinton was able to solidify his ties to business leaders like Don Tyson, put the state on automatic pilot, and position himself for a national race. Within a week of the November '86 gubernatorial election, *Newsweek* was touting Clinton as a potential candidate for president in 1988.

The "two-for-one" concept that would give the Clintons so much trouble in the '92 campaign also came into public view as they became known in Democratic Party circles as the quintessential baby-boomer power couple. For the first time, two tracks fully converged—Bill's ambition, charisma, and talents as a political organizer and Hillary's focus, decisiveness, and commitment to social change. In political circles, they became known as a team, "Bill and Hillary Clinton," not "Bill Clinton and his wife." On the heels of Hillary's victory in getting the education plan passed by the Arkansas legislature in 1984, *Esquire*'s registry of "the best of the new generation" included both Bill and Hillary, listed separately. In 1986 when Bill became chairman of the Education Commission of the States, a Denver-based nonprofit organization of educators and legislators, Hillary accompanied him to the annual convention and led a session on government programs for young people who had dropped out of school because of drugs or teen pregnancy.

Also on the strength of Hillary's education plan, Bill was soon elected vice chairman of the National Governors Association and co-chaired, with NGA chairman Lamar Alexander, a task force to develop a five-year plan for reforming America's schools, which included national teaching standards and higher teachers' salaries. Clinton's link to the Republican Alexander furthered his goal of positioning himself for a national audience as a moderate-sounding southern Democrat. Secretary of Education William Bennett called the report "the single most important event in American education in the last five years" and remarked that Alexander and Clinton could be the "Packwood and Rostenkowski of education reform."

Hillary was as busy as Bill in expanding her political portfolio outside Arkansas. She was elected to chair the Children's Defense Fund board in 1987 and headed the New World Foundation that year as well. Also that year, she brought Marian Wright Edelman to Arkansas to celebrate the tenth anniversary of the group Arkansas Advocates for Children and Families, which she had helped found. She was appointed to the William T. Grant Foundation's Commission on Work, Family and Citizenship, a national organization that was conducting a study of how government and business could help solve the problems of at-risk youth. She served on the board of the New York–based Child Care Action Campaign. And she was named to the National Association of State Boards of Education's Task Force on Early Childhood Education, which was studying ways to ease the effects of school reforms on the very young. At a time when family issues such as education and welfare reform were also at the top of most governors' agendas, Hillary attended southern and national governors' meetings in Washington, D.C., Miami, and Idaho, accompanying Clinton, who had been elected chair of the NGA later in 1986. In an unusual move, Bill sent Hillary as his designee to the Southern Governors Association Task Force on Infant Mortality, where she spoke at one meeting as an expert on infant mortality. Bill, meanwhile, took up one of Hillary's causes, chairing a panel on teen pregnancy and drug abuse.

The wife of former Mississippi governor Ray Mabus recalled Hillary's active participation in the wives association of the governors conference, which Hillary chaired while Bill was NGA president. "Everyone looked to Hillary as an example," said Julie Mabus, who chaired the wives group in the late 1980s. "More than the rest of us, she was very much a part of Bill's political life. I was interested in child care and I remember picking her brain on that, about the HIPPY program she set up in Arkansas. I looked up to her." (HIPPY, the Home Instruction Program for Preschool Youngsters, was a variation of the national Head Start program. It taught mothers to impart basic skills to preschool children at home.)

Hillary was also becoming a recognized figure in national feminist circles, heading the Little Rock host committee for the Great American Family Tour, led by Democratic Representative Patricia Schroeder of Colorado, who launched an exploratory bid for the presidency in 1988. The tour culminated with a Washington rally, which Hillary attended, sponsored by the Coalition of Labor Union Women and designed to highlight the inadequacies of the Reagan administration's family leave and child care policies.

Perhaps the capstone to the Clintons' efforts—participation in the ultimate baby-boomer networking confab known as Renaissance Weekend—also came via Hillary's education reform initiative. As a southern governor pursuing education reform, Clinton became close to South Carolina Governor Richard Riley. Riley, in turn, was close to Phil and Linda Lader, a prominent South Carolina couple who founded the weekend in 1981 with the idea of using the New Year's holiday as a time for self-reflection rather than aimless partying. At Riley's suggestion, the Clintons were invited to the weekend for the first time in 1984, and they became fixtures at the event, which grew in notoriety through the 1980s, attracting policy wonks from politics, business, academia, and the arts such as David Gergen, Lamar Alexander, and Marian Wright Edelman as well as journalists like Art Buchwald and Joe Klein. The attendees participated in such panel discussions as, "If These Were My Last Remarks . . . ," "Building Your Inner Life," and "You'd Never Guess: What Only My Friends Know About Me." Self-help topics have included "How to Survive a Vasectomy," and "Brides-to-Be, Changing Your Name?" Hillary participated in panels including "Conversations with Some Challenging Women" and "Hard Choices." Bill spoke on "What I've Learned."

Hillary had now tied her political future inextricably to Bill's. But immersion in Arkansas politics and attachment to Bill's political machine had certain less salutary consequences that were only beginning to manifest themselves. Bill would soon draw Hillary into using her position as a Rose Firm lawyer to further the cause of the co-candidacy. The Republicans, whom Hillary had paralyzed politically, needed to exploit every advantage that came their way. They were eager to expose what they saw as the less attractive underbelly of the Clintons' political partnership: Hillary's behind-the-scenes activities at Rose. This time, the partisan allegations would go well beyond complaints about her name and potshots at her physical appearance: In Clinton's 1986 rematch against

Frank White, Hillary's reputation and integrity would be called seriously into question, with charges that she was using her influence with her husband to benefit her private legal clients and line her own pockets. Hillary was now in the line of fire—the target of a concerted assault on her personal integrity from which she would never really recover.

8

Wifewater?

The political scandal involving the Clintons' Whitewater real estate investment and their dealings with the McDougals troubled Madison Guaranty S&L has come to focus almost exclusively on Hillary Clinton, who was cast as an unethical wheeler-dealer lawyer and the driving force behind corrupt financial deals and tawdry influence peddling in Little Rock.

Not surprisingly, Republicans have been eager to exploit this portrayal for political gain as they have made Hillary the prime target of their Whitewater investigations: "Well, we know Hillary Clinton is a pivotal player in this [Whitewater]. . . . She is at the heart of this whole investigation," said GOP Senator Rod Grams of Minnesota. "I mean, everything kind of runs through her office and out of her office."

But it is really the mainstream media's harsh portrait of Hillary that has stuck in the popular imagination. Hillary was described as a "hard-edged, even mean-spirited money-grubber" by the *Wall Street Journal*'s Al Hunt, summarizing approvingly the view of Hillary advanced in James Stewart's 1996 book *Blood Sport*. The *Washington Post* reported that *Time* magazine's excerpt of the Stewart book "features a cover photo of Hillary

Rodham Clinton looking like a Gothic fiend. At first glance, she's a vampire—ghastly white skin, scarlet lips, teeth slightly bared—coming at us cloaked all in black. In that eternal cliché of suggested guilt, her glance is averted. But study the image for a minute and you'll notice that the red 'M' in 'TIME' forms two perfect horns on the first lady's head. This is no mere bloodsucker: it's Satanella."[1]

Everyone from the denizens of Washington's political salons to the casual man-on-the-street observer seemed to agree. Noting that Stewart's book "fails to come up with a smoking gun," Charles Peters, editor of the *Washington Monthly*, wrote, "it does confirm the impression we have had that, to the extent there was behavior that if not criminal was certainly embarrassing, the principal sinner had been Hillary Clinton." In a March 1996 piece headlined "First Lady Bears the Brunt of Unfavorable Opinion on Whitewater," the *Washington Post* took a random sampling of voter opinion. Beverly Hill, a 36-year-old Democratic civil servant from central Kentucky, was quoted as saying that while she did not believe that President Clinton had done anything illegal in Whitewater, she thought Hillary had broken the law. "I don't know that I can put my finger on any one thing but I thought maybe she knew some things he didn't."

The *New Republic*'s major foray into Whitewater reportage focused on Hillary and the Rose Law Firm in a 1994 cover story by *Mother Jones* writer L. J. Davis entitled "The Name of Rose: An Arkansas Thriller." *Time* informed its readers: "From the start, Whitewater has been more about Hillary than her husband." The *Economist* labeled the whole scandal "Wifewater," while the publication *Tax Notes* wondered if Bill might be "an innocent spouse." Talk show host John McLaughlin exclaimed: "Whitewater translates into Hillary!" And a joke about Hillary going to jail became a staple punch line of David Letterman's nightly Top Ten List. ("Top Ten Highlights of Hillary Clinton's Appearance on *Larry King Live*: Number 3: 'Revealed that if she's going to prison, she's taking fat boy down with her.' ")

Even the most left-leaning columnists and magazines, which might have been expected to defend Hillary out of ideological solidarity, helped to publicize the prevalent caricatures. Indeed, the notion of Hillary as a greedy yuppie was the one thing left-liberal opinion simply could not abide, and it did her more damage with her own supporters than any other single charge. As standard bearers of the 1960s generation in American politics, the Clintons, especially Hillary, were expected to be above and beyond the self-interested power-games and coarse ambitions of the older generation. Columnist Jack Newfield wrote that Hillary resembled "an Ozark Leona Helmsley, with her executive acumen, self-righteousness and potential Whitewater tax liability." The *Nation* chimed in with an editorial explicitly suggesting a parallel between Hillary and Richard Nixon: "What did Hillary know and when did she know it?"

This image of Hillary as a cynical and avaricious baby boomer had its roots in a bitter political campaign in Arkansas known as "Rocky III." Republican Frank White, bidding for a comeback in the 1986 gubernatorial race, decided to run a campaign against Hillary rather than Bill. "The term 'Billary' was first used by me in '86," said White's campaign consultant, Darrell Glascock. "At first, I used the term on my home answering machine as a joke, but it got in the papers and then everybody started calling to hear the message. Clinton called, and on the message, he said, 'Well, you're working for Porky Pig.' "[2]

Due to Hillary's education reform effort, Bill was invulnerable to political attack; his candidacy was never really threatened by White. "White's poll numbers suggested that there was no way for him to beat Bill Clinton," Glascock conceded. "So the theory behind the campaign was to finally expose what everybody on the inside already knew was going on in Arkansas for years."

When White's pledge to "re-examine" Hillary's popular education standards fell flat, he turned his guns on Hillary's legal practice and the Clintons' finances. The first strike came when White proclaimed that when he was governor, his wife had not held a paying job: "Gay was a full-time First Lady." Next came the commercials: "I made a television ad that rolled a list of ADFA [the Arkansas Development Finance Authority, a billion-dollar economic development agency] bond deals during Clinton's governorship in which the Rose firm either was the bond attorney or the attorney for the issuer," Glascock said. "This showed that Rose had a piece of the action on virtually every bond deal since ADFA was founded. We asked why that was. Then we showed a shot of the Rose firm and said, 'This is where Hillary Clinton works.' And then we showed the governor's mansion and said, 'This is where Hillary Clinton lives.' Then it said, 'Power corrupts. Absolute power corrupts absolutely.' "

Glascock said the Hillary ad backfired because direct attacks on the first lady did not play well with the Arkansas electorate: "Jumping on a guy's wife is really touchy. This was branded a 'dirty campaign,' a 'negative campaign.' Frank White would go home every night and his wife Gay would be crying about phone calls about the terrible negative campaign and saying she couldn't go to the country club and then White pulled the ads."

If Hillary had been subjected to more rigorous scrutiny in Arkansas, she might have been better prepared for the questions raised by the national press in the 1992 campaign. Columnist John Brummett, a sometime critic of Hillary, agreed that raising tough questions about her legal practice was taboo in Little Rock political circles. "We under-covered her in Arkansas," Brummett said, recalling a controversy over a plan by the powerful investment firm Stephens Inc. to sell thirty-two nursing homes to a Texas company, financed with an $81 million tax-exempt bond issue from ADFA. Stephens, a Rose client, stood to earn tens of millions, and the firm would have reaped huge fees. Critics said the homes weren't worth anywhere near $81 million. "The Stephens were owners of Beverly Enterprises [the chain of nursing homes] and they were losing money and wanted to work out a state bond issue and Rose was going to do it." Brummett said. "Bill Clinton was very quiet about it. I asked at a news conference whether his wife had lobbied him and it was like I broke some kind of rule. Jaws dropped. So he answered that yes she's talked to him about it, but no she didn't try to get him to do what she wanted. If you invoked Hillary at all, you got 'That's his wife. Leave her alone. Let her have her career.' Then at the next dinner party in the Heights, all the professional women would be after you."

Glascock was surely right that voters didn't respond to the effort to make Hillary a political issue. But the ad really failed because it was not the kind of responsible criticism that Brummett had in mind. Rather, the picture of Hillary's career painted by the White ad was a lie.

Contrary to the claims of the ad, Rose did not have a piece of every bond issue since 1983; it was merely counsel on six of twenty. While Rose's state bond work did increase after Hillary joined the firm, as the ad claimed, this coincided with a big increase in the state's overall bond activity during that period. According to the *Daily Record*, a Little Rock business publication, Rose ranked last among Arkansas' four big law firms in obtaining bond work from ADFA between 1983 and 1991. Worse yet, White's ad grossly inflated the dollar amount of Hillary's earnings from the bond business, claiming that Hillary made $500,000, or about three times what the entire firm took in from the business in seven years. (Years later, L. J. Davis repeated White's figures in his Whitewater reportage in the *New Republic.*)

Meanwhile, Clinton turned the anti-Hillary ads to his advantage, seizing the opportunity to strike a chivalrous pose: "I don't think there is any conflict of interest. It's not the first time White has attacked Hillary. I just wish he was man enough to debate her. . . . Frank has always had this obsession with trying to put down Hillary. I don't understand it." The Clinton campaign mocked White for picking on a woman by distributing bumper stickers with the message: "Frank White for First Lady." Hillary, meanwhile, delivered a detailed rebuttal, challenging White to disclose his own tax returns and reveal his earnings from state business while he was employed at the Stephens investment firm, which he refused to do.

A decade later, in early 1996, when the issue first raised by Frank White was still dogging her in the Whitewater affair, Hillary responded to a question on a radio call-in show: "You know, one of the—sort of the undercurrents of this series of questions about us is that I somehow must have used my law practice inappropriately to make money for my family. Well, as I have said, if I intended to do that, which I certainly did not, I didn't do a very good job of it."

Indeed, Hillary was the lowest paid partner at the Rose Firm. She started as a $15,000-a-year associate in 1977 and by the mid-1980s was bringing home only $50,000 to $70,000 a year from the firm. Not until 1990 did she make slightly more than $100,000 from her law practice. Though she, Vince Foster, and Webb Hubbell were senior partners in the litigation section, Hillary's commitments outside the firm were so extensive that she was making only about a third of what other colleagues on her level were making.[3]

Hillary's role as family breadwinner and financial manager, well-known to the public, was sometimes the occasion for political humor. In the 1986 primary, former Arkansas governor Orval Faubus challenged Clinton to release his income tax returns for the last several years. As a way of deflecting the issue, Clinton joked that he'd have to ask Hillary about it first. During Clinton's 1982 comeback, Senator Dale Bumpers had roasted Clinton with the line: "You see Bill sitting down there. If he looks tired, I can explain. He worked all day on his income tax return. He would have finished it except when he got to the bottom line, it called for the signature of the head of household and he couldn't find Hillary."

As with every young family, money was a concern for the Clintons. "We obviously wanted enough financial security to send our daughter to college and put money away for our old age and help our parents," Hillary has said. What was unusual—even in an era when most baby-boomer households had two incomes and women were assuming more financial responsibilities—was the extent to which this worry was laid exclusively on Hillary. Trooper L. D. Brown, who frequently chauffeured the Clintons to various engagements, recalled that a frustrated Hillary would sometimes complain to Bill: "I'm the one who has to make all the money!" Bill acted like a kid on an allowance, and Hillary clearly felt the pressure of being the adult in the family. "I'll always feel I'm sixteen," Bill had said. "And Hillary was born at age forty."

Certainly Hillary did not lead the life of a greedy yuppie. She was never extravagant, still driving an old Oldsmobile Cutlass and shopping at Dillards even when she was making six figures. One of her main holdings was part ownership of a Little Rock condominium she had bought with her parents, who had moved to Arkansas from Illinois in 1987, after Hugh Rodham's first stroke. The Clintons were the first couple in recent history to occupy the White House while owning no home of their own.

Whatever concern Hillary had for money came from necessity. As governor of Arkansas, the most Bill would ever make in a year was $35,000. Except by virtue of his public office, Clinton never provided for his family. True, public office had its perks: the Clintons lived in public housing with a generous $50,000 annual "food fund," a cook, a driver, free child care, even the free gardening services of prison convicts. Yet all of this could be revoked in an instant by the voters, who passed their judgment every two years. If Clinton had lost the governorship again, Hillary would have had an emotionally unstable political has-been on her hands. With no family money on either side, she would have had to figure out how to make ends meet. This is to say nothing of the always lurking possibility that the marriage would simply crumble under the strain of Bill's philandering, leaving Hillary alone and with a daughter to support.

Hillary's spotty career at Rose was a casualty of her commitment to politics. During the 1980s, Hillary wasn't racking up billables at the Rose Firm; she was channeling her considerable energy instead into the political co-candidacy. She had played a crucial role in putting together

Bill's 1982 re-election comeback, and in 1983 she devoted much of the year to getting the education reform package through the legislature. She also campaigned for him extensively in 1984 and 1986. Since Rose's compensation system was strongly based on production, meaning actual hours billed to clients, Hillary's low earnings reflected her regular absences from the firm.

Her partners estimated that on average she spent less than three quarters of her time on firm business. Joe Giroir said he asked Hillary to become the firm's administrative partner in 1982, a job that carried significant management duties and would have been a big promotion. Vince Foster was the administrative partner at the time, but he did not care much for managing people and wanted to be relieved of those duties. The job would have been especially suited to Hillary's talents as an organizer and facilitator, but Giroir recalled that she declined the position because she was preoccupied with Bill's re-election bid.

According to Giroir, the firm did not assign important cases to Hillary because it could never be sure that she would be available to see them through. Instead Hillary worked as a kind of junior partner, with Vince Foster as the lead attorney. "After a while, we had to assign her to sort of assist Vince," Giroir said. Even in the rare instances when she was ostensibly carrying the ball in negotiations or court, Foster was working hard behind the scenes to support her. Phillip Raley was opposing counsel to Hillary in a 1991 copyright infringement case involving two baking products companies. Though Foster was not listed as counsel in the case, Raley said he did much of the work. Jim Simpson, a partner with Friday, Eldridge & Clark, Little Rock's largest law firm, also said he had knowledge of several cases where Hillary was the counsel of record but Foster was the guiding hand. In one such case, Simpson represented Planters, the peanut company, in a suit against a Little Rock warehouse where hundreds of thousands of peanuts had spoiled. The case was settled the day before trial. "In that one she did what she seemed to do in all of them, and that was about midstream through the case she'd appear, act as if she was going to take a big role and then probably [after three months]— we would never see her again. She's adept at jumping into something, dealing with it quickly and jumping out. She's a tremendously quick study . . . being knowledgeable on that issue for 30 minutes or an hour and then never dealing with it again."

Hillary, then, was far from the center of the action at Rose. The charge that she used her position to bring state business to Rose—made famous in a 1992 presidential debate when California Governor Jerry Brown claimed that Clinton was "funneling money to his wife's law firm"—appears to be unfounded. If anything, the firm seems to have lost money from state business because of Hillary's affiliation, validating the reservations of some Rose partners who hadn't wanted to employ the wife of the attorney general back in 1977. When Brown raised charges of conflict of interest, a Clinton spokesman said Rose "let her [Hillary] do charity work in the children's defense, education and women's issues precisely because she was married to the governor."

Rose ranked well behind two other Little Rock firms in its volume of business with the state. "To avoid the appearance of undue influence, there was state business that we didn't go after as we would have if Hillary wasn't at the firm," Joe Giroir said. Former Rose lawyer Charles Owen added: "While Hillary was a partner at the firm, and her husband was governor of the state, we were going through great pains to avoid any ethical impropriety whatsoever." On a percentage basis, the firm had less state business in 1985 (only about 2 percent of total revenues) then it did in 1970. According to figures compiled by *Arkansas Democrat-Gazette* political editor Rex Nelson, from July 1, 1990 until March 1992, Rose received only $4,226.75 in state fees.

Hillary had nonetheless anticipated that political opponents would accuse her of capitalizing on her relationship with Bill, so she took an extra step to preempt this charge: She hired her friend Susan Thomases, who was then the administrative partner of a major New York law firm, to figure out a way of deducting fees taken in by the firm which were generated from business with the state when figuring her personal earnings at the end of each year.

Hillary has also been criticized for using her position as the wife of the governor to entice private clients with the promise, implicit or explicit, that they would get special treatment when appearing before state regulators. "Rose proves to be a handy prism for observing a Gothic, sometimes darkly humorous tale . . . [of] the uses to which an agreeable state government can be put," L. J. Davis wrote in the *New Republic*.

Yet Joe Giroir was, by far, the leading rainmaker at the firm. He had brought in most of the big clients, including Stephens, Inc., Worthen Bank, Wal-Mart, and Tyson Foods long before the Clintons arrived on the political scene. Many of these clients did have various matters pending before state regulators and the Arkansas legislature over the years, but if Rose was engaged in the sort of influence peddling described by L. J. Davis, it had been going on for decades. The firm did not need to employ the wife of the governor to enhance its clout.

Hillary, in any case, did not appear before the state for any of these clients. In fact, complaints about her emanating from within the firm itself stood the critics' charges on their head: Some lawyers complained that Hillary did not devote enough time to trading on her name to attract big-money clients. Hillary was pressured by her partners to give up the divorce and child custody work she enjoyed for more lucrative corporate cases. But she was basically content to do enough work to keep her head above water and collect a reasonable paycheck to support her family. Her passions lay outside the offices of the Rose Firm and beyond the monetary rewards of practicing corporate law. "She brought in some business because of who she was," Joe Giroir said dryly, "but not much."

Rose alumnus Carol Arnold, who worked closely with Hillary as an associate and then a partner in the litigation division, recalled that Hillary refused to use her influence to open doors to the governor's office for Rose clients. Arnold said she once went to Hillary because she had an important client who wanted to see Bill Clinton. "I went in and said 'Hillary, we need to talk to the governor,' and she said, 'Well, you have to call Betsey Wright and ask for an appointment.' "

Of course, by the mid-1980s, with Clinton re-elected twice, it seems reasonable to assume that the governor's wife's name on the law firm's marquee may have created the impression for potential clients of special entree to the state government or star status in the courtroom. The perception may have become more important to the firm by 1987, when Giroir left the firm after a power struggle and Rose's prestige began to fade. "Without her having to do anything, people just knew who she was and it was a natural thing for people to think, whether they should or not, because she was the first lady of the state that that somehow would do them some good," said Jim Simpson of the Friday firm, a Rose competitor.

Law firms around the country, of course, strike all kinds of arrangements with prominent people, especially out-of-power politicians, whose presence at the firm, the partners believe, will be good for business. The lawyers get origination fees, referral fees, some even get flat retainers, often for doing no actual legal work. Others don't even bring any business in and are maintained solely for their name value.

Hillary's relationship with Rose, then, was hardly out of the ordinary. In fact, she was less able than many attorneys to profit from her connections. The Rose Firm had an unusual compensation system—based on a five-year moving average of the percentage of an individual attorney's collections as a percentage of all of the firm's collections—that established only a weak link between new business brought in and a partner's compensation.

What seemed to be inspiring some of the criticism was Hillary's status as "wife of." When men like Joe Giroir brought in business because of their connections, they were handsomely rewarded and highly praised. Hillary, by contrast, was made to suffer for the suspicion that she was trading on her husband's name and reputation rather than her own. Anyone trying to practice law while married to the governor of a small state would likely have been subject to similar criticism.

Perhaps because some judged Hillary by the rules of the Arkansas system, she couldn't win. "She is a very bright, articulate, strong-willed person," said Arkansas lawyer Phillip Raley. "The fact that she was the wife of the governor, well, it's a small state and that wields a lot of influence and power. If you're working for the other side of a case and it doesn't pan out for you, you're going to be thinking in the back of your mind about intangibles—you don't know what is going through the minds of decision makers who may very well be depending for their future on her husband—whether that is in fact a reality, there's no way to know."

By that standard, Hillary should not have bothered hanging out her shingle at all, simply because she was the governor's wife. This was the approach taken by Marilyn Quayle, another well-known lawyer and political wife, who has publicly faulted Hillary's legal ethics. "If the press had done its job when Jerry Brown first brought it up, we wouldn't be in this position," she told the *New York Times* in 1996. Quayle didn't mention that in order to avoid the appearance of conflicts she abandoned her profession while her husband Dan was serving in the Senate. Even if Hillary had wanted to forgo practicing law altogether to pursue her political avocation, she could not have afforded the luxury.

By focusing on Hillary's supposed venality, critics like Frank White and Jerry Brown—and most of the press corps—overlooked the more salient question of whether she had allowed her career as a lawyer to become an appendage of the political co-candidacy. In the handful of matters where critics raised credible questions about her legal ethics, Hillary appeared to be motivated not by an interest in making money but rather by a wish to serve the interests of the political team. Having devoted herself to Bill's comeback in the early 1980s, when his political interests were at stake Hillary was now willing to risk the appearance of conflicts of interest in representing clients before the state government. Still, she did not share in any fees such work generated. Really, the arrangement looks more like the opposite of greed: Call it not getting paid for a living.

One such case involved the Grand Gulf, or "Grand Goof," nuclear power plant project, located near Port Gibson, Mississippi, and built at a cost of around $3.4 billion, a budget overrun of more than 400 percent. The plant, owned by Middle South Utilities, had the capacity to supply power to Arkansas, Mississippi, Missouri, and Louisiana. When federal regulators intervened to settle a disagreement among the states about who would buy how much power and at what price, Arkansas' utility company, Arkansas Power and Light, was forced to buy more power than it wanted, at a very high price. The company's plan to pass the construction costs on to consumers by raising rates was vetoed by the Clinton-appointed Public Service Commission, which wanted to spare consumers the increased costs. AP&L sued the PSC, charging that the commission was trying to force the utility into bankruptcy. A document surfaced in which a PSC attorney said that in the event of bankruptcy, the state "could pick up AP&L at a bargain price."

The case put Clinton in the delicate political position of having to either support an unpopular rate increase or oppose a powerful utility company. In a move that raised eyebrows even among friends and supporters, Bill asked Hillary to represent the state in the suit. When Frank White homed in on the issue in a television commercial, Rose disclosed that it was paid $115,000 by the state. Hillary did not see a dime of the money under the segregated partnership draw set up for her by Susan Thomases, but there was still the appearance of impropriety in her representation. According to Clinton biographer David Maraniss, when Dick Morris raised with Bill the question of whether he had exposed Hillary to conflict-of-interest charges, Clinton responded that he needed Hillary on the case because "anybody else would mangle it." When Morris's wife, an attorney, was told Hillary had taken the case, she said, "She's got to be out of her mind!"[4]

Hillary's intervention appears to have redounded to Bill's political benefit. AP&L formally supported White and took the public position that it was opposed to the settlement, which allowed AP&L to pass on only 80 percent of the cost to consumers. But insiders said that AP&L was not displeased with the outcome of the case. When Clinton announced his presidential candidacy in 1991, Jerry Maulden, the long-time AP&L president, was one of his first large-scale donors.

In another instance of Hillary using her position for political advantage, she brought her former college roommate Jan Piercy to Arkansas to help Bill fulfill a major campaign pledge to revitalize poverty-stricken areas in rural central and eastern Arkansas through increased capitalization. Piercy, who had worked with Betsey Wright in the women's movement in the 1970s, was now an executive at a Chicago development bank that was bringing investment and entrepreneurship to the city's South Side.

With state funding, support from Rose client Stephens Inc., and a grant from the MacArthur Foundation, where Piercy was a consultant, the Southern Development Bancorp was formed. Hillary was named an unpaid member of the board and the company's legal counsel. This put her in a sticky position when the company, as part of its plan to start operations in Arkansas, sought (and later received) approval from a bank regulator appointed by Clinton to buy the Elk Horn Bank in Arkadelphia. The legal fees collected by Rose didn't amount to much—somewhere between $100,000 and $150,000 over six years—but Hillary's representation raised conflict-of-interest questions that she was apparently willing to countenance as the price of launching the policy initiative. When reporters asked Southern Development president George Surgeon whether Hillary had been retained because of her political clout, he replied, "Oh, yes. Absolutely!"

Hillary's controversial representation of Madison Guaranty Savings and Loan, owned by her Whitewater real estate partners Jim and Susan McDougal, also fits her pattern of stepping in to protect Bill's political interests rather than to make money. Since the mid-1980s, the S&L has been the subject of intensive investigations by federal bank regulators and federal agencies charged with cleaning up the S&L crisis; by independent counsels Robert Fiske and Kenneth Starr; by House and Senate committees; and by the press. In May 1996, the McDougals, along with their former partner Governor Jim Guy Tucker, were convicted on multiple counts of mail fraud and conspiracy in connection with their looting of Madison Guaranty. The public's interpretation of Hillary's dealings with the McDougals lies at the heart of the assault from all quarters on her ethics, character, and reputation.

Whitewater in Arkansas boiled down to graft—a pattern of influence peddling and favor trading that while not necessarily illegal was clearly a violation of the public trust. Given that this intersection of politics and money had always been Bill's domain, it seems odd that Whitewater would come to be much more strongly associated with Hillary, an upright Methodist and principled political leftist who never fully adapted to the slick Arkansas culture in which Bill had learned to thrive.[5]

Much of the following narrative is drawn from a voluminous record compiled by the Senate Whitewater Committee and released in June 1996, as well as an earlier report by the Resolution Trust Corporation. Read carefully, the documents tell a story that turns much of the conventional interpretation of Whitewater on its head.

It all began in 1977 when, following the common practice of the state that in politics you make money, Attorney General Clinton personally invested with McDougal in a little-noticed real estate venture that pre-dated Whitewater. Personal wealth was never a priority for Clinton, but he was not one to turn his back on a sure thing. Clinton put in about $11,000 and realized a 75 percent return in eighteen months. It was due to this initial success that Bill, not Hillary, was impressed by McDougal's talent for investing and readily agreed to enter the Whitewater partnership when the McDougals suggested it in 1978. The Clintons expected to share equally with the McDougals in any profits but would also be liable for the debt if the McDougals could not make their payments.

The initial $200,000 investment was a no-cash deal, with McDougal appearing to use Clinton's status as the soon-to-be governor to line up financing. According to testimony by Don Denton, then an officer of the bank that made the main Whitewater loan and later a Madison Guaranty executive, the bank's lobbyist instructed him to make a loan he otherwise would not have made because Clinton was an "up and coming political star, a . . . rising star in the state."

In the early stages of the investment, Bill was more involved than Hillary, who demonstrated little interest in it. During a meeting attended by Clinton, his accountant Gaines Norton, and McDougal, in which the structure of the investment was discussed, Norton warned the two men that the tax deductions they were considering were illegal. According to Norton's later Senate testimony, after the meeting, Clinton took him aside and said that he "had to rely on his partner to structure [the deal] tax-wise properly," and "to back off and leave the issue alone." By instructing his accountant to "back off," Bill foolishly placed both his own and Hillary's fate in the hands of McDougal.

From the beginning, Whitewater was a losing investment. During the early years of the investment, the Clintons contributed their fair share— more than $35,000—to service the debt on the property. The properties finally began selling in mid-1981, and McDougal wrote the Clintons with good news: "Things are looking pretty good at Whitewater, as our receivables run about equal to what we owe." Hillary fired off a tongue-in-cheek reply, "If Reaganomics works at all, Whitewater could become the Western Hemisphere's mecca."

The real estate boom soon went bust again, and the McDougals, perhaps embarrassed at bringing the governor into a bad deal and wanting to maintain his favor, never asked the Clintons to make further payments on Whitewater's loans. Nor did they appear to inform the Clintons that sales were not covering the payments. Ultimately, the partnership lost about $200,000. Though the Clintons were fifty-fifty partners, the McDougals covered about three-quarters of the losses.

The Clintons have claimed that they were "passive investors" in Whitewater and have said they assumed the debt was being serviced legitimately. "I mean, we gave whatever money we were requested to give by Jim McDougal," Hillary later explained. "We did whatever he asked us. We saw no records. We saw no documents. He was someone who had been in the real estate business with many people we knew, including Senator Fulbright, and we just assumed that whatever he needed he would ask for, and we didn't have any information to the contrary."

As custodian of the family financial records, Hillary corresponded with McDougal during this period and the paper trail appears to back up her claim that she and Bill were passive participants. Her communications with McDougal suggest that Hillary was content to let McDougal operate the partnership and leave her in the dark on the details. In June 1982, for example, a loan taken out in Hillary's name to build a model home on the Whitewater property came due and she defaulted on it.

Hillary wrote a bank official that he should "speak with Mr. or Mrs. Mc-Dougal, who have made all the arrangements for this loan." Seeking renewal on another loan the following year, Hillary wrote McDougal that her request to the bank "fell on deaf ears. . . . Will you please ask someone to take care of this for us?" (While Hillary attempted to deal with the past due loans, Bill posed for the cover of *Arkansas Young Democrats* magazine with McDougal, who ran unsuccessfully for Congress in 1982 with the help of Tyson lawyer and infamous commodities trader Jim Blair.)

Hillary's hands-off approach turned out to be a terrible mistake. According to a report by the Resolution Trust Corporation—the federal agency established to handle the S&L crisis that reviewed Madison's books and issued a report in early 1996 on the Clintons' potential civil liability—the McDougals did not keep adequate records nor did they follow routine corporate procedure concerning Whitewater. They kept Hillary ill-informed about the investment and at times outright deceived her about how they were using the corporate shell to their own advantage. For example, McDougal did not inform Hillary until 1986 that in 1985 he had sold off several Whitewater lots in exchange for repayment of an outstanding loan and an airplane, which he put in his own name. Not until November 1986, in a letter to the Clintons offering to buy out their share of the Whitewater partnership, did McDougal inform them of the disproportionate burden he had carried for the preceding four years. He also wrote menacingly of "the high potential for embarrassment to you" if the fact that he had assumed the Whitewater mortgage payments was ever to become public. Backing up the Clintons' claim that they were passive investors, the RTC investigators concluded, "There is no basis to assert that the Clintons knew anything of substance about the McDougals' advances to Whitewater, the source of those advances, or the source of the funds used to make payments on the bank debt. . . . There is no basis to charge the Clintons with any kind of primary liability for fraud or intentional misconduct."

While the view of Bill as inept in dealing with money is widely accepted, Hillary's professed ignorance of Whitewater's finances and her apparent willingness to let someone else act in her name does not seem to square with her image as a detail-oriented lawyer and hard-driving taskmaster. Thus both liberals like Maureen Dowd of the *New York Times* and conservative critics like columnist Tony Snow have found the "passive investor" claim hard to accept. Snow called it "the amnesia defense." And Dowd wrote a satirical column about Bill calling a press conference to ask for Hillary's resignation as first lady: "At the time that she took over the job of First Lady, I had not gone over the Whitewater files. In retrospect, I wish I had. I trusted that she would exercise full and careful judgment in the handling of these matters, and I must confess that I paid little or no attention to supervising her in this area. Last night, as a matter of fairness to her, I read the files again in good detail, keeping in mind the high ethical standards I have set for my Administration. I have to tell you that, had I gone over these records before the inauguration, I would not have brought Hillary to Washington with me."[6]

Contrary to these insinuations, there is nothing in the record to suggest that Hillary knew much more than Bill about the McDougals' business practices or the particulars of their management of the Whitewater investment. Hillary, it seems, was no different from many talented and ambitious people who have little interest in or aptitude for finance. "If you knew the Clintons, they were the last goddamn people on earth you'd consult on a business deal," McDougal has said.

Wearing so many different hats and working the equivalent of three full-time jobs, more interested in policy and politics than money, Hillary was open to just the type of easy investment opportunity that McDougal seemed to offer. Whitewater was supposed to be the same kind of set-up that had earned the Clintons huge commodities profits in the late 1970s; the difference was that Whitewater never made money. Over time, it is possible that Hillary developed a sense of entitlement about her finances stemming from the financial and career sacrifices she was making, for example, in volunteering the better part of a year to reforming the state's school system. When things started to go sour, Hillary wanted McDougal to "handle it" and she asked few questions about how her obligations were being met.

If anything, the evidence suggests that Bill, far more than Hillary, was the real insider when it came to Whitewater and Madison Guaranty. By the early 1980s, in an era of thrift deregulation to finance speculative real-estate deals, his friends the McDougals had taken control of Madison Guaranty S&L and had begun to borrow heavily from it. The McDougals were running a classic S&L scam: Money was siphoned out of the institution through a complex series of fraudulent loans and real estate deals for the benefit of the McDougals, their relatives, and Arkansas political insiders. A 1986 examination of Madison's books by the Federal Home Loan Bank Board found that McDougal's control over Madison "enabled [him] to use corporate resources to develop large land developments [and] to divert substantial amounts of funds from the projects to himself and others." By the time Madison was closed in 1989, the S&L had run up $60 million in losses—including about $17 million in loans to insiders—that had to be eaten by taxpayers, who insured the deposits.

The real estate projects were not meant to make a profit but rather to fake the S&Ls' earnings, which in turn allowed the deposit base to keep rising. In the 1980s such schemes were quite common, and they worked until regulators caught on and cracked down on deposit growth, inducing cash-flow shortages that would cause the schemes to collapse. To postpone the day of reckoning, the S&L operators needed political clout to fend off the bank examiners. This is where McDougal's relationship with Bill Clinton—whose debt in Whitewater he was carrying and whose campaigns he had generously supported—came in handy. The heart of the Whitewater scandal was Clinton's apparent willingness to use his public office to help his private business partner and political supporter.

McDougal had held his first Clinton fund-raiser in the comeback race in '82. In April 1985, at Clinton's request, the McDougals threw a lavish fund-raiser at Madison Guaranty's art deco headquarters that raised $32,000. Between fifty and a hundred Madison employees and stockholders, including the McDougals and Susan McDougal's two brothers, helped Clinton pay off a personal loan for a campaign debt from the '84 race. Notably, Hillary did not attend either event. Whether Madison depositor funds were illegally diverted to Clinton's political coffers is still under investigation; one former Clinton aide has been quoted as saying that Clinton sometimes referred to "McDollars" and spoke openly of Madison as a "cash cow." (Clinton's personal lawyer has denied such allegations as "false, anonymous and scurrilous.")

There is little question but that the McDougals received the kind of protection and favoritism that was common under Clinton's gubernatorial administration, where people who loaned the governor money or contributed to his campaigns received state jobs, state business, special consideration by regulators, or favorable bills signed into law. The Senate Whitewater investigation uncovered a long list of public favors won by McDougal and Madison Guaranty during the period in which he was making the Clintons' Whitewater payments. In 1984, Clinton instructed two state agencies to lease space from Madison Guaranty even though less expensive space was readily available. According to testimony given to the Senate Whitewater Committee, when a state official objected that one of the spaces was too small and was situated in a dangerous neighborhood, he was told by the governor's office that the contract was going to Madison anyway because the McDougals were "friends" of Clinton.

In 1986, state regulators tried to get McDougal to improve the sewage treatment at Maple Creek Farms, a Madison development south of Little Rock. When McDougal complained to Clinton that the regulators were "incompetent bureaucrats" and "SOBs," the regulators were summoned to a meeting with McDougal in Clinton's office. According to the Senate testimony of one official, Clinton called him and pointed out that McDougal had been "a supporter of mine since I ran for Congress and has never asked me for anything." Though an internal staff memo warned Clinton that "all of the soil is not suitable for septic tanks," Clinton had the matter reassigned to other staffers.

Seeking to change a state law that prohibited the sale of alcohol at a manufacturing facility where he planned to build a yuppie brew pub, McDougal wrote Clinton chief of staff Betsey Wright: "Governor Clinton has made a commitment concerning this bill which I need to discuss with you at your convenience." The law was soon amended by a Clinton-appointed board.

In 1987, Clinton vetoed a water bill that favored the interests of a utility owned by two business associates of McDougal. He reversed the veto after the pair reminded the governor of contributions they had made at an April 1985 Madison Guaranty fund-raiser.

Perhaps most important to McDougal, especially as the feds closed in on Madison's lending practices, was his influence over the appointment of state bank regulators. A memo about appointments, handwritten on governor's office stationery, which was produced to the Senate Whitewater committee read, "Banking Board—ask McDougal."

In late 1983, a Federal Home Loan Bank Board investigation of Madison's books concluded that the S&L was in an "insolvent position" and warned that "viability of the institution is jeopardized." The board told McDougal he needed to raise more capital to stay in business, scheduled a second audit for early 1986, and made him agree to make no more loans to himself or his wife. To satisfy the examiners, McDougal decided to seek state approval for a novel plan to issue a class of preferred stock to raise capital for the faltering S&L. The stock was to be non-voting so that McDougal would retain control of the institution. The plan needed approval from the Arkansas Securities Commission, which was responsible for monitoring S&Ls in the state. In early 1985, McDougal recommended that Clinton appoint John Latham, chairman of Madison Guaranty, to the state savings and loan board that regulated Madison and would have to approve the stock deal. Latham had actually devised the stock plan for McDougal. "Bill we are down to about 15 state-chartered savings and loan institutions and I am about the only one around who has any interest in this board," McDougal wrote Clinton.

McDougal called another regulator and business associate, William Lyon, and asked if he would be willing to move from the state bank board to the S&L board in anticipation of a vote on the preferred stock deal. Lyon testified that when he balked, telling McDougal he thought the plan was a "rip-off of stockholders," McDougal told Lyon he would get Clinton to remove him from the bank board. A month later, Clinton called Lyon and asked for his resignation. McDougal left a message on December 22, 1984, for Clinton regarding the appointment of a new state securities commissioner, who had the authority to approve Madison's stock plan: "Re Beverly Bassett, on Securities Commission." Soon thereafter Clinton announced Bassett's appointment. (Bassett denies ever having met McDougal or that McDougal had anything to do with her appointment.)

Bassett's brother Woody, a Fayetteville lawyer and former student of Clinton's, was a campaign finance chairman in several Clinton gubernatorial campaigns. Beverly had also been a student of Bill's; she was one of the Fayetteville volunteers swept up in the "Cult of Bill" during the 1974 congressional campaign. Bassett went to work for Bill in the attorney general's office when she graduated from law school. By the mid-1980s, she was dating Archie Schaffer, a top Tyson Foods executive whom she later married, and was practicing law at the firm of Mitchell, Williams, Selig, Jackson & Tucker, where McDougal was a client. One of the name partners, future governor Jim Guy Tucker, was McDougal's lawyer and also his business partner in several ventures. While at the firm, Bassett did some work for Madison, seeking approval from the state securities commissioner for several Madison land deals even though she had described to Tucker in an internal memo Madison's "willful and not just negligent oversight" in complying with state laws at one land development project. Although her predecessor approved the deals, Bassett, within days of being appointed to the job by Clinton, sent out the notices of approval.

Hillary made a cameo appearance as a lawyer for Madison Guaranty before Beverly Bassett's commission, which had to approve McDougal's stock plan. In doing so, Hillary left herself open to the charge that she was abetting the classic S&L offense of the 1980s: leaning on bank regulators to keep afloat insolvent S&Ls run by political contributors. The practice was at the heart of the famous "Keating Five" scandal involving S&L kingpin Charles Keating and five U.S. senators. Since the government sometimes pursues law firms for civil liability in its efforts to recover S&L losses, the issue of her representation of Madison would dog Hillary for years afterwards, following her to the White House.

How Hillary came to represent Madison is a matter of intense dispute. The widely accepted account is Jim McDougal's, who told the *Los Angeles Times* in an oft-cited 1993 interview that in August 1984, Bill Clinton stopped by his office during a morning jog, plopped his sweaty body into McDougal's new leather desk chair, and complained about the Clinton family finances, a subject not usually a concern of Bill's. McDougal said he agreed to hire Hillary and pay her a retainer of $2,000 a month. "I asked him how much he needed, and Clinton said 'about $2,000 a month,' " McDougal told the *Times.* "I hired Hillary because Bill came in whimpering they needed help." Both Clintons have denied McDougal's account.[7]

As the Resolution Trust Corporation investigators noted in their report, this story—repeated in the *New York Times,* the *Washington Post* and in James Stewart's *Blood Sport*—implies that the retainer was, if not an illegal gratuity, then at least some sort of improper *quid pro quo* through which Hillary lined her pocketbook. The RTC emphatically rejected McDougal's account and backed up the Clintons' denials: "The purported recollections of Jim McDougal are inconsistent with those of others [interviewed] and upon analysis make little sense." The investigators found McDougal's use of the word "retainer" to be misleading. The fee arrangement was not intended to keep Hillary on call for unspecified reasons, as the word implies, but rather as an advance against McDougal's bill for specific work and expenses. The advance was necessary because Rose had represented McDougal earlier in the 1980s on an unrelated matter and McDougal had been very late in settling his bill.

Moreover, the RTC investigators' findings showed that Hillary, as the billing attorney on the account, made only about $20 a month from the Madison business, which could not possibly have helped the Clinton family financially.

The conversation between McDougal and Clinton could well have taken place, but it does not appear to have been the driving force behind the retention of Rose. The documentary record clearly shows that McDougal hired Rose not in August 1984, as he recalled, but in April 1985. If McDougal had been responding to Clinton's pleas for financial help, why did he wait eight months? Perhaps because by then there was something in it for McDougal, who did not appear to have $2,000 a month to toss around without a purpose. In the spring of 1985, the stock plan was very much on his mind.

Documents show that on April 3 Davis Fitzhugh, Madison's in-house counsel, called the Arkansas Securities Commission and floated the idea of the preferred stock deal to Charles Handley, Bassett's second in command. Handley told Fitzhugh he thought an S&L could only issue common stock, not preferred stock, but he invited Fitzhugh to submit a formal proposal anyway. Fitzhugh reported the bad news in an April 16 memo to Madison executive John Latham, who was serving on the securities commission board. McDougal clearly wasn't happy, writing Latham on April 18: "I want this preferred stock matter cleared up immediately as I need to go to Washington to sell stock."

A file marked "Madison Guaranty—Sale of Stock" had been opened at the Mitchell firm, McDougal's regular counsel, in early February. Something caused McDougal abruptly to switch the project to Rose. When McDougal heard that Handley was dubious about the plan, he may have panicked and concluded that the added firepower and prestige of the Rose Firm might be the only way of tipping the scales in his favor. On April 23, McDougal and Latham met with Hillary and retained the Rose Firm. As the RTC investigators explained it: "Sitting on the periphery of politics, McDougal wanted to be known as someone who had friends in high places. In the Clintons' case, he wanted to say something like this: 'They are friends of mine. We go way back. They have invested with me. I work for the governor. His wife is my lawyer.' "

On April 30, the Rose Firm submitted a plan to the Arkansas Securities Department for Madison's recapitalization. The plan was written by Richard Massey, a young Rose associate in securities law. As Hillary later explained, she had no expertise in this area and was merely the billing partner on the account. Before she took the business, Massey had suggested to Latham, whom he knew from school, that Madison hire Rose to try to win approval of the stock plan. McDougal then acted on the suggestion when he sensed the preferred stock deal was in trouble.

The April 30 letter was signed "the Rose Law Firm," but the last sentence pointedly stated: "Should you require further information or assistance, please advise Hillary Rodham Clinton or Richard Massey of this firm." The day before the proposal was submitted, records show, Hillary telephoned Bassett and the two spoke briefly. That telephone call has been the focus of Republican and media suspicions that Hillary was improperly using her influence with Bassett, an appointee of her husband's, on McDougal's behalf. Notwithstanding the opinion of a staff lawyer who informed Bassett that he didn't think the stock issuance was permissible under Arkansas law, Bassett and her assistant disagreed and she soon notified Rose that the plan could proceed. The familiar salutation Bassett used in the letter to Rose, "Dear Hillary," was later interpreted as drawing Hillary into a conspiracy to keep Madison afloat.

If the critics' suspicions are correct, a far more serious abuse of power may already have been committed by Bill, who, if McDougal is to be believed, appointed Bassett on his recommendation. Bassett is on record pointing out that she was an FOB, not a friend of Hillary. "Although I knew Hillary Clinton, and we were cordial with one another, we are not personal friends," Bassett said. If Bassett was in McDougal's pocket, Hillary's role was really superfluous—at most a little extra insurance that Bassett got the message. (Bassett denies giving McDougal or the Rose Firm special treatment.)

Thus Hillary could well have been the outsider in any wink-and-nod understanding between Clinton, McDougal, and Bassett, all of whom were in a better position to have had knowledge about McDougal's dubious banking practices than she. According to press reports, Clinton had been told as early as 1983 by one of Bassett's predecessors of problems with risky loans at another bank McDougal then owned. Bassett, of course, had worked as a lawyer for McDougal. As a state regulator, she would have been privy to the federal audit of Madison.

Clinton might also have had knowledge of what was going on at the S&L through his friendship with the McDougals, and in particular Susan, with whom he was quite close. Susan cut quite a racy profile in Little

Rock, appearing on television ads for Madison real estate projects clad in hot pants and sitting astride a white horse. She also kept the books at Madison. Madison executive Don Denton later told RTC investigators that McDougal ran the S&L "to the extent that he knew how." He was the "head honcho" only "when Susan wasn't there." (Susan's two brothers—David Henley, a realtor, and Jim, a Baptist minister—were indicted in 1990 along with McDougal on charges related to misapplying Madison finds. Charges against David Henley were dismissed; Jim Henley and McDougal were acquitted.)

In the end, however, McDougal did not get what he wanted: While Bassett approved the plan in principle, she set net worth requirements that Madison would have to meet before the stock could be issued. The financial condition of the S&L deteriorated so rapidly in the summer of 1985 that no stock was ever issued. Thus, McDougal did not stay in business any longer than he otherwise would have as a result of Hillary's or Bassett's actions.

Though the plan was not implemented, there is still the question of whether Hillary violated ethics guidelines in representing her business partner before a regulator who was a subordinate of her husband. In the late 1960s, the American Bar Association adopted a standard for lawyers saying that even the appearance of impropriety was to be avoided. Because appearances are subjective, the ABA dropped the controversial standard for lawyers (but not for judges) in its 1983 Model Rules, which were adopted in Arkansas in 1986. At a minimum, therefore, in 1985 Hillary may well have been in violation of the appearance-of-impropriety standard.[8]

Once before, in her aggressive posture at the Legal Services Corporation, Hillary seemed to skirt the rules for what she saw as noble ends, the first clear blow against her strict Methodist creed of abiding by the rules and standards of the system. Her representation of Madison may well have been the second blow.

Why, it must be asked, did Hillary put her reputation at risk by taking Madison as a client? One answer might be that in 1984, Hillary was for the first time a senior billing partner at the firm. Having just returned from the campaign trail, she may have been under pressure to bring in business. But Madison does not appear to have been an especially attractive or lucrative client. It seems more likely that Hillary was helping Bill repay a political debt to McDougal. Hillary was surely aware that on

April 4, 1985—the day after Madison executive Fitzhugh called Charles Handley to check on the preferred stock deal and three weeks before Hillary was hired to push it through—McDougal had held a fundraiser for Clinton in the lobby of Madison Guaranty.

Hillary, of course, may not have believed she was doing anything wrong; she had already learned from Saul Alinsky and the Critical Legal Studies perspective that legal constraints may be socio-political devices— merely the rules of a game to be manipulated, particularly by those in power. Hillary's episode with McDougal suggests that the concentrated power in a one-party state like Arkansas had its own seductive appeal and bred a certain moral arrogance and carelessness about any appearance of impropriety or possible ethical lapse.

Bill Clinton's own sense of ethics could be seen in his turning to Webb Hubbell to help draft a proposed disclosure law for public officials and their family members that was specifically designed to reveal just the kind of potential conflicts present in the Madison situation. According to the *New York Times,* the effect of a watered-down version of the law that Hubbell had a hand in drafting—passed by voters in 1988 after the original version (which did not exempt Clinton) failed to pass the state Senate—was to "exempt Mr. Clinton from having to report in detail on the potentially complex questions of which of his wife's or the Rose Firm's cases require disclosure." By the time of the 1992 campaign, Hubbell had been designated head of Rose's conflicts committee, putting him in charge of fielding media calls about Hillary's law practice. "He was the authority. The person who would give you guidance," said former Rose associate B. Michael Bennett. "Which is kind of ironic considering what happened [i.e., the later exposure of Hubbell's fraudulent billing practices]."

The Rose Firm remained on retainer from Madison for about fourteen months, continuing to work on the preferred-stock deal and on other regulatory issues before the state. Although much of the work was done by other attorneys at the firm, Hillary played a second cameo role on a set of real estate transactions for a Madison real estate subsidiary. The transactions, which related to a proposed real estate development known to many as Castle Grande, were a major part of the federal criminal case that led to the convictions of the McDougals and Tucker in 1996.

Hillary's involvement was not publicly known until Rose Firm billing records were discovered in the White House book room and released to the White House special counsel and Senate Whitewater committee in early 1996. The belated disclosure produced a media feeding frenzy: "Examiner Describes 'Sham' Dealings at Madison" (*Washington Post*), "Records Raise Questions About First Lady's Role" (*Los Angeles Times*), and "Papers Point to Hillary in 'Sham Deal' " (*Washington Times*). Once again, Hillary was tarnished by the improprieties of her Arkansas associates.

The Castle Grande development was a thousand-acre piece of property south of Little Rock, which McDougal intended to develop as an "upscale working class" industrial park, combining mobile homes, shops, and a truck stop. Because Arkansas S&L regulations limited how much Madison could put into speculative real estate, McDougal arranged to make a $1.15 million non-recourse loan to one of its employees and have him buy a portion of the property from the seller, the Industrial Development Corporation (IDC). The employee involved was none other than Seth Ward, Webb Hubbell's father-in-law, who had gone to work for McDougal in retirement as a part-time adviser. McDougal planned to divide up the IDC parcels and sell them off at inflated prices to insiders, including Jim Guy Tucker and Senator Fulbright, with loans from Madison. Ward was to get a commission on the deals as well as other perks, including use of a red Mercedes-Benz. (About $4 million in losses from the Castle Grande project were passed on to U.S. taxpayers.)

Federal bank examiners later labeled the purchase of the property from IDC a "fictitious" transaction, a means of hiding the true ownership through a straw purchaser, Seth Ward, to evade the regulation. Several of Hillary's colleagues at Rose were involved in the closing of the original purchase. When the deal was investigated by the Resolution Trust Corporation to determine whether the firm had aided and abetted a fraud, no evidence was found that anyone knew of the fraudulent aspects of the scheme, with the possible exception of partner Webb Hubbell (Hubbell denies knowledge). The multimillionaire Ward certainly appeared to have the financial wherewithal to be in a legitimate partnership with McDougal. The RTC investigators concluded: "It simply would not be persuasive to argue that, for $21,000, McDougal corrupted the Rose Law Firm and convinced half a dozen lawyers, most of whom he did not know, to join him in a scheme to violate the law." The

RTC did, however, criticize the firm for getting involved with Castle Grande at all. "At the time it assisted Madison Guaranty with the Castle Grande deal, Rose Law Firm was aware of regulatory concerns about the soundness of the institution [Madison Guaranty], particularly its net worth," the RTC said. This would have been especially true for Hillary, since she presumably reviewed Massey's work on the preferred stock deal.

When the properties began selling, McDougal couldn't come up with the cash to pay Ward's commission. McDougal also may have feared that if the commissions were paid, federal regulators, then conducting a second audit on Madison's books, would discover the straw purchaser arrangement. Webb Hubbell told the RTC that Ward "had a sense Madison was having trouble" and was "very anxious" about whether he was going to be paid everything he thought he was owed. Ward, of course, was not just Hubbell's father-in-law and sometime Rose client, he was also the man who had helped Hillary get one of her first clients, the Little Rock airport commission, back in the late 1970s when she was a young Rose lawyer. Ward, with whom Hillary still spoke regularly on airport commission business, was known to visit the Rose Firm unannounced and commandeer the use of secretaries and telephones whenever he pleased. "Ward had a habit of dropping by and demanding product immediately," the RTC investigators wrote.

In May 1986, Seth Ward dropped by and asked Hillary to draft a document for him giving Madison an option to buy back one of the parcels he owned, Holman Acres, for $400,000. It was later valued at $47,000. Evidence suggests that Hubbell was supposed to draft the option but was out of town that day and Ward simply used Hillary as a pinch hitter. The RTC investigators looked into whether the option on the property was a fraudulent way for Madison to continue to disguise the "fictitious transaction" and secure Ward's commissions in the event Madison failed. But they could not decide definitively whether the option had any relationship to the disputed commissions or if McDougal had simply wanted to secure the option on Holman Acres, which was considered the "prize property" of the lots.

The Republican majority on the Senate Whitewater committee argued that the option was designed to conceal Ward's commissions, and they suggested that Hillary knew of the scheme at the time. Madison executive Don Denton told the committee of an April 1986 telephone call with Hillary, a month before she drafted the option, in which he claimed to have warned her that the Castle Grande transactions might be improper. Denton said Hillary had "summarily dismissed" his concerns. The Democrats countered that Denton's testimony lacked credibility. On June 3, 1996 Denton had told the RTC that he had no recollection of the call; in a second interview on June 11, Denton recalled the conversation in some detail.

In any event, the RTC concluded that even if the option was tied to a sham transaction, Hillary would not have known it. The report noted that Hillary was not a real estate lawyer, that the option was hastily and poorly written, and that she billed Madison only two hours for drafting it. Even the name of the property was misidentified in Hillary's draft, indicating that she had seen none of the underlying documents, which might have clued her into the "straw man" aspect of the deal and Ward's commission arrangement with Madison. "The option did not assist in the closing of the acquisition. It . . . was created many months after the transaction closed. The option . . . does not prove any awareness on the part of its author of Ward's arrangements with Madison Financial. . . . While Mrs. Clinton seems to have had some role in drafting the May 1, 1986 option, nothing proves that she did so knowing it to be wrong, and the theories that tie this option to wrongdoing or to the straw man arrangements are strained at best," the RTC concluded.

In their minority report, the Democrats on the Senate Whitewater committee made an even stronger point in exonerating Hillary of any knowledge of the alleged fraudulent aspects of the deal: Seth Ward himself has consistently maintained for more than a decade (twice in court) that the May option was unrelated to the commissions he claimed were due him from Madison. If this was Ward's position, why would he have told Hillary anything different at the time the option was being drawn up?

While the possibility that Hillary was in on the tawdry details can't be completely discounted, nothing in Hillary's past indicates that she would knowingly participate in a sham deal. Rather, she likely felt indebted to both Seth Ward and Webb Hubbell—who, like Foster, was her protector at the firm, covering for her when political duty called. The debt had been repaid once, when Bill named Hubbell to a vacancy on the Arkansas Supreme Court, and now she was willing to go to bat for him again, covering his work when he was out of town. But even if one accepts her professed ignorance of the purpose of the option, which would clear her of charges of wrongdoing, the troubling impression of Hillary's passivity remains. This impression contradicts the take-charge stance that Hillary seemed to adopt in the political sphere. One wonders whether Hillary had simply resigned herself to keeping certain seamy aspects of Arkansas life at arm's length; she may have concluded it was better not to know.

While such an arm's length posture in the representation of Madison might absolve Hillary of any complicity in McDougal's dealings, it does raise the question of how she approached her professional responsibilities as a lawyer. Richard Massey, Hillary's subordinate, testified that she had never informed him of her business relationship with McDougal. In the case of the Castle Grande option, Hillary appears to have done what Seth Ward asked her to do, apparently failing to give adequate consideration to how the option might affect her client, Madison Guaranty. As with the Whitewater investment itself, Hillary's approach toward Castle Grande—a stark contrast with her engaged attitude toward the "co-candidacy" and her pursuit of public interest matters—seems to have kept her at a comfortable distance from the questionable dealings around her. Whether her stance was the product of naïveté or guile, Hillary's judgment would be faulted in either case.

Bill's insider status, by contrast, was more certain. This could be seen in another alleged deal to keep Madison afloat, one in which Hillary does not appear to have played any part. David Hale was first introduced to Clinton by Hillary's old nemesis Paul Fray in the early 1970s. Hale ran Capital Management Services, a firm set up to make taxpayer-insured loans to the economically or socially disadvantaged. But Hale, whose own attorney called him the "Heidi Fleiss of loans," diverted millions to Madison insiders like McDougal and Jim Guy Tucker and other members of the Democratic party elite, leaving little money for legitimate loans. Taxpayers ended up paying about $3.5 million for these bogus loans, some of which were funded through the federal Small Business Administration, which licensed Capital Management.

Later, in the Whitewater investigation in which he cooperated, Hale pleaded guilty to two felonies. In testimony at the trial, Hale alleged that in early 1986 McDougal told him he needed money and that the "political family" needed to be cleaned up. Hale said that he, McDougal, and

Tucker then conspired in a plan to make a fraudulent $300,000 loan to Susan McDougal. Next, Hale said, he met with McDougal and Clinton "to talk about getting the loan ready and consummated." According to Hale, Clinton offered to provide his Whitewater property as security for the loan. Clinton allegedly told Hale, "Be sure—my name cannot show up on this." The $300,000 loan went to Susan McDougal, doing business as Master Marketing. Susan never repaid it. When much of the loan's proceeds disappeared, Hale said, Bill later asked him, "Do you know what that whore Susan did with the money?" Clinton denied under oath that he had ever met with Hale or that a loan was ever mentioned to him.

If Hale's account is true, it raises the question of why Clinton would have gone out on a limb for the McDougals. Was he simply helping a contributor, or paying the McDougals back for carrying his losses in Whitewater? Or did Susan have special leverage with Bill? In any event, if Hale is to be believed, Bill made the worst judgment in the Whitewater affair, abetting a fraud and digging the Clintons deeper into a hole. As a consequence of the Hale loan, about $50,000 found its way into the Whitewater account—meaning that a company co-owned by the Clintons received money generated by a fraudulent transaction.

Hale, of course, is a convicted felon and has credibility problems as a witness. But his word is not completely uncorroborated. The Senate Whitewater committee produced testimony from William Watt, a Hale business associate, about a phone call from Hale in which Hale said Clinton asked him, "Did you get my deal done? Did you help my friends?" If Clinton knew the loan was a fraud, as Hale claimed, he could be subject to charges of conspiracy and criminal solicitation—far more serious allegations than all of the Whitewater charges leveled so far against Hillary put together.

If Hillary hadn't known the extent of McDougal's problems before, by 1986 the picture was becoming all too clear. She had been a lawyer for Bill's friend and supporter, who was, quite possibly, an S&L crook. During the second federal audit of Madison in 1986, which declared the institution insolvent, one examiner produced a handwritten note that listed "Bill Clinton," but not Hillary, as a potential Madison insider, raising the prospect that either Bill's campaign or the Whitewater partnership had benefited from Madison's shoddy practices.

When Bassett got notice for a July meeting of the Federal Home Loan Bank board at which action against the McDougals was expected, she fired off a note to a top Clinton aide, effectively tipping off a potential insider as to the progress of an investigation: "Madison Guaranty is in pretty serious trouble. Because of Bill's relationship with McDougal, we probably ought to talk about it." On July 11, 1986, the McDougals were removed from the savings and loan association at a meeting of the Federal Home Loan Bank Board in Dallas attended by Bassett.

On July 14, Betsey Wright wrote a note to Clinton which said: "Whitewater stock, McDougal's company, do you still have? Pursuant to Jim's current problems, if so I'm worried about it." That same day, Hillary had a letter hand-delivered to McDougal terminating Rose's representation and returning part of the unused retainer. The letter pointedly noted the representation "has been for isolated matters and has not been continuous or significant." Hillary appeared to believe her involvement with Madison and McDougal had come to an end, but its legacy would come back to haunt her years later.

Indeed, by now, it was becoming clear that Hillary's main problem in Arkansas was not her own unseemly indiscretions, sleazy associations, or grave character flaws, but those of her husband: In a figurative sense, she had married the mob.

Another of Bill's shady associations that ended up soiling Hillary's reputation involved Dan Lasater, a high-flying Little Rock millionaire bond daddy and one of Bill's closest friends and important supporters. Lasater had met Clinton in the early 1980s through his mother Virginia, whose box at the Hot Springs race track was next to Lasater's. He befriended both Bill and Roger Clinton; Roger soon became part of Lasater's Little Rock cocaine circle. Lasater was famous for his parties, where silver ashtrays of cocaine were sprinkled among trays of hors d'oeuvres and the entertainment was provided by a troupe of women known locally as "Lasater's girls."[9]

When the FBI investigated Lasater's drug connections in the mid-1980s, he admitted to giving away cocaine on more than 180 occasions, including using it to lure a sixteen-year-old girl into a sexual relationship. "I was introduced to cocaine use by Dan Lasater when I was 16 or 17 years old and a student at North Little Rock 'Ole Main' High School," said the girl in a sworn police affidavit. "I was a virgin until two months after I met Dan Lasater. Lasater plied me with cocaine for sexual favors. . . . Dan

Hillary Rodham poses for *Life* magazine after gaining fame for her Wellesley commencement speech in 1969.

In their youth, Bill and Hillary imbibed the heady influences of the 1960s. Bill's mentors were politicians: JFK, Sen. J. William Fulbright, and (above center), George McGovern, whose Texas campaign Clinton managed in 1972. Hillary's most significant early influence was religious: the social gospel activism of the Reverend Don Jones (below) has leavened her leftism with a distinctly conservative tinge.

Other important figures in Hillary's life included grassroots political organizer Saul Alinsky (above right), crusading lawyer John Doar, who hired Hillary to work on the Watergate impeachment inquiry, and Children's Defense Fund founder Marian Wright Edelman (right).

Travis Doster/*Springdale-Morning News*/Sipa Press

John Sykes/*Arkansas Democrat-Gazette*

Bill's political career in Arkansas got off to a rocky start. Above, Clinton and campaign manager Paul Fray (center) grimly assess precinct reports in his failed 1974 congressional bid. Following his marriage to Hillary in 1975, Bill went on to a rapid rise in Arkansas politics, and became one of the youngest governors in America in 1978. At left, Bill and Hillary attend a prayer service on Inauguration day, 1979.

Hillary appears to have had some difficulty in adjusting to the role of political wife. Above, Hillary watches Bill field questions at a press conference during his first term. At right, Bill Clinton and "Hillary Rodham" attend a dinner at the Carter White House in 1979 during Hillary's tenure as head of the Legal Services Corporation.

Bill's star rose quickly in the Democratic firmament. At left, he appears with New Jersey Governor Brendan Byrne as spokesman for Democratic governors at a National Governor's Conference in 1979. Below, Bill and Hillary pose with week-old Chelsea despite Hillary's reluctance to exploit the birth for political gain.

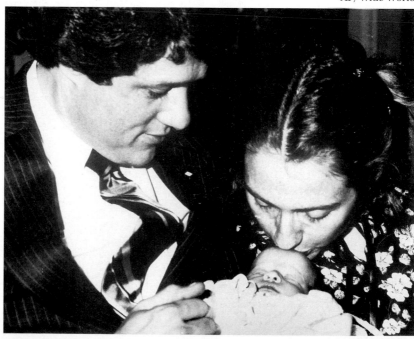

Travis Doster/*Springdale-Morning News*/Sipa Press

Bill's meteoric rise did not last long. After one term in office, voters voiced their discomfort with his too-liberal agenda, handing him a narrow defeat. At right, Clinton glumly pulls the lever for himself in 1980. Not for the first or last time, Hillary took charge of Bill's political career, repositioning him as a centrist and guiding him to re-election in 1982. Below, Bill and Hillary celebrate his victory in the Democratic primary.

AP/Wide World

John Sykes/*Arkansas Democrat-Gazette*

During the years of Clinton's governorship, Bill and Hillary forged a close-knit political family. Top, Bill and long-time chief of staff (and self-described "bimbo" monitor) Betsy Wright—equally a booster of Hillary's. Right, Hillary's law partner and close friend Vincent W. Foster, whose suicide rocked the Clinton White House in its early months. Bottom, Foster's wife Lisa, Hillary, Foster, and two unidentified guests at a Little Rock function.

H. Wilson/*Arkansas Democrat-Gazette*/Sipa Press

Sygma

Above, Clinton and Rose Law partner Webster L. Hubbell, a trusted confidant of both Bill and Hillary. In 1994, Hubbell pleaded guilty to charges of skimming from his overcharging of Rose clients and was sentenced to two years in jail. Below, "Chicken King" Don Tyson, one of the wealthiest men in Arkansas, was Bill's first political patron.

In the 1980s, Clinton secured his political base, winning re-election three times in six years. At left, Clinton discusses his record in 1983. Below right, Clinton attends Arkansas National Guard training exercises in full regalia. Meanwhile Hillary, now known as Mrs. Bill Clinton, underwent a series of makeovers, coloring her hair and adopting contact lenses as in the photo at left.

Building on the phenom-
enal success of Hillary's
education reform initia-
tive, Bill's national profile
as a centrist "New
Democrat" continued to
rise. At right, Bill and
Hillary attend a dinner at
the Reagan White House
in 1986. Hillary's efforts
to position Bill for a 1988
presidential run went awry
when Bill unexpectedly
took himself out of the
running at a Little Rock
press conference in July
1987. Hillary, in a rare
moment of public
emotion, wipes away a
tear in the photo below.

John Sykes/*Arkansas Democrat-Gazette*

Hitting the campaign trail in 1992, Hillary came into her own. Above, she whips up the crowd at a Clinton-Gore rally in Providence, RI. At left, Bill and Hillary jog for the cameras through Colonial Williamsburg.

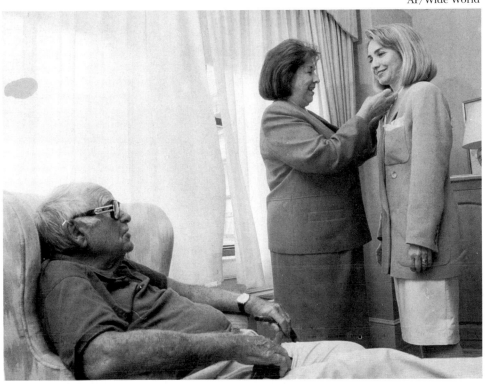

Above, Hillary savors imminent victory in a New York hotel room with her parents, Hugh and Dorothy Rodham, during the 1992 Democratic National Convention. Below, in a confident display of her authority and influence, Hillary Rodham Clinton publicly counsels her husband in fulfillment of their campaign slogan, "two-for-one."

As Hillary had feared, it did not take long for the scandals of Arkansas to find their way to Washington. At left, Susan Thomases, Hillary's "enforcer," frustrates the Senate Whitewater committee, failing to answer questions pertaining to Vincent Foster's suicide. Below, top White House aides are sworn in before testimony. From left to right: Harold M. Ickes, George Stephanopoulos, John D. Podesta, and Bruce R. Lindsey.

William Jordan/Gamma-Liaison

On the heels of her grand jury appearance, Hillary embarked on a promotional tour for her bestselling book, *It Takes a Village.* Above, opponents harass her with accusatory epithets. Below, an equally impassioned supporter poses for a photo-op with Hillary.

Oswaldo Jiminez/Sipa Press

Hillary Rodham Clinton talks to reporters outside the U.S. District Court in Washington on Friday, January 26, 1996 after testifying before a grand jury investigating Whitewater. Mrs. Clinton testified for about four hours. The independent counsel's inquiry continues at this time. Despite the obvious distraction of the investigation, Hillary continues to play an active role in the 1996 presidential campaign, and her influence would almost certainly increase in a second Clinton Administration.

Lasater personally gave me cocaine 10 to 15 times. He made it available to me 50 to 60 times." At least two other witnesses in the investigation recalled the girl, by name, as being part of Lasater's cocaine set, and one witness identified two different occasions when Lasater plied high school girls with the drug—once at a "graduation party" at which three to five young women used the drug. Michael Drake, a former Lasater employee, told the Senate Whitewater committee that Lasater used cocaine "to manipulate people," and Lasater himself admitted in Senate testimony to giving cocaine to employees.

As he had with McDougal, Clinton became indebted to Lasater in a variety of ways. Lasater and his employees were major campaign contributors over the years. Clinton also traveled on Lasater's corporate jet. In the spring of 1985, Lasater provided his jet to transport celebrities to a charity fund-raiser that Hillary promoted. In 1983, at Bill's request, Lasater gave Roger Clinton a job in his Florida horse stable, according to an FBI interview of Lasater. Lasater also told the FBI that he had loaned Roger $8,000 to pay off cocaine debts after Roger told him the coke dealers were "threatening him, his mother and brother."

In return, Clinton greased the wheels of government for Lasater's benefit. Lasater furnished Clinton with a list of suggested appointees to the Arkansas Housing Development Agency, the agency that would decide whether to choose Lasater as an underwriter for state bond business. The Whitewater committee disclosed a note Clinton had written to Betsey Wright referring to Lasater & Company that said "need to fill their recs for [the housing agency]." According to testimony from AHDA board member Charles Stout, shortly before an AHDA board meeting in 1983, Bob Nash, an economic development aide, called and instructed Stout to cut Lasater in for 15 percent on a pending bond issue and any future issues. Lasater had never before participated as an AHDA underwriter. "I said 'Bob, that's not right, the governor's office is not to interfere with this agency.' And he said, 'Well, that's the way we want it anyway,' " Stout testified. Between 1983 and 1986, Lasater & Company participated as an underwriter in $637 million worth of state bond offerings.

In early 1985, Hot Springs lawyer Sam Anderson, a childhood friend of Roger Clinton, went on trial for cocaine distribution. Anderson testified in court that Lasater was a possible target in a cocaine sting operation. Though Clinton denies it, he appears to have pushed for Lasater to be chosen to underwrite a bond issue to improve the state police radio system. After Anderson's public revelation, Lieutenant Colonel Tommy Goodwin told the Senate Whitewater committee that Clinton had come to him seeking information about the investigation. "Colonel Goodwin agreed that Governor Clinton's focus was not on Mr. Lasater's use of cocaine [which Clinton knew of]; rather it was directed toward determining whether he was going to be arrested for such use while his company was handling the police radio transaction," the committee report stated. Following a series of maneuvers by Clinton and his staff, which appeared to give Lasater an unfair advantage in the bidding process, Lasater was chosen as the underwriter and reaped substantial fees.

Bill's links to the drug world, including his close association with Lasater, threatened his political position once Roger Clinton was indicted in 1984 by a federal grand jury on five counts of drug trafficking. William Wilson, the "dimestore lawyer" with whom Hillary had worked in the late 1970s, was brought in as Roger's criminal lawyer. According to Meredith Oakley's book *On the Make,* before the November election in 1984, Roger pleaded not guilty to the charges, only to change his plea three days after his brother was safely re-elected. While Roger served a jail term, he was named a co-conspirator in a case brought against Lasater, and he testified against him. Lasater ultimately pleaded guilty to the felony of "knowingly and intentionally conspiring to distribute cocaine," and was sentenced to thirty months in jail.

When the pending Lasater drug investigation and his state bond deal surfaced before the 1986 election, Hillary sealed off the inquiry. A last-minute television ad aired by the White campaign highlighted the Clinton–Lasater connection. When a reporter asked Bill a question about the Lasater drug investigation at a press conference, he appeared dumbstruck; Hillary, sitting in the audience, jumped to her feet and upbraided the reporter. Lasater was under investigation but no charges had been filed, Hillary asserted. She went on to give a lecture about the rights of the accused and said it was wrong to comment on an ongoing investigation.

Clinton's ties to Lasater seem to have been a constant political worry. When federal regulators seized First American Bank in Chicago, a federally insured S&L, Lasater was sued for $3.3 million for using the bank's funds for personal trading. When the Rose Firm was hired by the Federal Savings and Loan Insurance Corporation to represent it in the case against Lasater, both Vince Foster and Hillary worked on the case, which was quietly settled under seal for $200,000. Lasater was represented by Wright, Lindsey & Jennings, the firm of Clinton handler Bruce Lindsey.

When Hillary's role in the Lasater case was first revealed in 1994, the pattern of media coverage was already well established from Whitewater. Bill's long history with Lasater was barely mentioned in the mainstream press, while Hillary's representation of the FSLIC—for which she billed only two hours—was branded a "glaring conflict of interest," as the *Chicago Tribune* put it. Though a subsequent federal investigation found no evidence to allege a conflict of interest on Hillary's part, the damage in terms of public perception was done.

By 1987, as the Clintons made plans for Bill to announce his presidential candidacy it was evident that Hillary had done far more for Bill than honing his political identity as a moderate centrist who would run on the promise of being the "education president." Though she left the money-politics sphere to Bill and was careful not to abuse her position at the Rose Firm for personal gain, as Bill's national prospects brightened and he turned to her for help, Hillary had seemed willing to use her position—and risk her own reputation—for the sake of the co-candidacy.

Though she did not appear to violate any laws or conflict-of-interest rules (except perhaps the appearance-of-impropriety standard), Hillary had become inextricably linked with the least savory aspects of the Arkansas political system through her marriage and political partnership. When one's partner is dirty, there is inevitably guilt by association. But first, the Clintons had to arrive on the national stage. And it soon appeared that the more deeply Hillary fell into the Arkansas muck, the more insistent she became on escaping from it.

9

Partners for Life

Having worked hard to position her husband for the presidency and having subordinated her legal career in the process, Hillary was about to find out that her loyalty to Bill and the political co-candidacy had not been repaid in kind. In April 1987, Clinton went to New Hampshire to test the political waters, giving a speech to the state Democratic party. The Clinton speech followed one by Gary Hart, the presumptive Democratic front-runner, who officially announced his candidacy in May. Within a few weeks, the *Miami Herald* reported that a team of five journalists had determined that a woman from Miami named Donna Rice had spent a Friday and Saturday night with Hart at his Capitol Hill town house. Hart had invited reporters to follow him to disprove widespread rumors of his womanizing, and the Hart camp denounced the story as scurrilous.

Three days after the *Herald* story ran, CBS aired a video on the evening news "showing Hart accompanied by an unidentified woman—apparently not Donna Rice—on the yacht docked in Fort Lauderdale, Fla., in late March [1987]." (Rice was in fact the woman in the photo aboard the yacht *Monkey Business*.) Hart aides then received a call from a *Washing-*

217

ton Post reporter who presented them with evidence of yet another extramarital liaison, and suggested that Hart drop out of the race or the story would run. Hart announced his withdrawal the next day.

Publishing the *Miami Herald* story was a departure for the press, which had disregarded the sexual peccadilloes of presidents like John F. Kennedy and Lyndon B. Johnson. But since the 1960s, the press had grown far less cozy with those who sought political power. Print and electronic media outlets proliferated, making it harder for a few top editors in New York and Washington to control the flow of information, and the growing presence of women in the newsroom made it more difficult for male reporters to shrug off politicians' abusive behavior toward women.

In the case of Gary Hart, press corps insiders were of the opinion that his womanizing was so indiscriminate as to raise broader questions about his judgment and stability. Thus it was in the interest of the liberal establishment, of which the press was an important part, to remove Hart from the equation and clear the decks for a Democrat who could withstand the scrutiny of a presidential race.

Still, the Hart coverage prompted a round of journalistic navel gazing. Charles McDowell, a veteran Washington columnist for the *Richmond Times-Dispatch,* said, "I don't like it," and, "I suspect there must be better ways of getting at issues of character." Ben Bradlee of the *Washington Post,* however, praised the *Herald,* saying "More power to 'em." In a carefully worded column, David Broder, also of the *Post,* endorsed the *Herald* story: "What was at issue was Hart's truthfulness, his self-discipline, his sense of responsibility to other people—indeed, his willingness to face hard choices and realities. . . . The fundamental character questions raised by Hart's actions in this incident remain unchanged, and if they are not vital in judging a potential president, I don't know what would be."

Ellen Goodman of the *Boston Globe* gave the strongest endorsement of the *Herald* story:

> The old-boy tolerance of dalliance—men will be men—has been changed by the admission of women into the system: the gentlewoman's disagreement. More importantly, a slogan of the women's movement— the personal is political—had become a common sensibility. We are more willing to admit the importance of something we call character. And less willing to accept a character that is split between public and private life. But I don't believe that journalists have become obsessed with the candidates' sex lives. The profession has, rather, taken sex out of the

exempt category. . . . What if a reporter can prove that a candidate is a liar? Is he or she allowed to follow every lead, except the one that might prove the candidate had lied about fidelity? . . . "Womanizing" [is], however, a fair topic for reporters, because it revealed something about a man's capacity for deception, vulnerability to exposure, fascination with risk-taking.[1]

Ironically, when Hart withdrew, Clinton, who shared these same vulnerabilities, faced increased pressures to run. In taking on the teachers' union in Arkansas, Hillary and Dick Morris had positioned Bill as a candidate closer to Hart's neoliberalism than to the traditional interest group politics of the fading Walter Mondale wing of the party. In a field of candidates—later dubbed the Seven Dwarfs—that included old-style liberals like Massachusetts Governor Michael Dukakis, Senator Paul Simon of Illinois, and the Reverend Jesse Jackson, Clinton was seen as Hart's natural heir. However, the establishment media's new "Gary Hart standard" must have unnerved the Clintons. Until then, they had no reason to expect that Clinton's womanizing would present a potential roadblock to their ambitions for higher office.

Despite widespread talk of Clinton affairs in their newsrooms, the Arkansas press never once broached the subject in print. "The reporters knew all about it," said Darrell Glascock, the political operative who ran Frank White's 1986 campaign against Clinton. "Hell, half of them went out drinking with Bill and Gennifer [Flowers]."

Even at the height of the competition between the *Gazette* and the *Democrat*, reporters and editors were still part of the political insider class in Little Rock and found it hard to report such allegations about a likeable politician they knew on a first-name basis. Clinton had always been considered someone with national political potential; local reporters protected him out of a combination of self-interest—some wanted to follow Clinton to Washington in communications jobs or otherwise capitalize on his fame—and Arkansas pride.

"There were strong rumors about Bill and the various women," said Erwin Davis, a one-time Clinton campaign worker who ran for governor in the Republican primary in 1984, "but the Arkansas press has to obey the rules of the one-party state, and that means don't say anything negative about the Democrats in office. And so if you have a governor who is womanizing, then the Arkansas press would not report it . . . but everybody's pet dog knew the situation and knew that as soon as he went national, elements of the national press would not be so cowardly as not to print that stuff. And he learned that the national press was certainly a horse of a different color than the state press."

In his book *High Wire,* John Brummett later wrote that Clinton's womanizing was "such commonly accepted speculation among insiders that the Bar Association in Little Rock, in its biennial spoof called *The Gridiron,* featured in 1988 two lawyers portraying Gary Hart and Bill Clinton who sang, 'To All the Girls We've Loved Before.' " "He made no attempt to hide his womanizing. His leering at pretty women around the Capitol was disgusting," said former *Arkansas Gazette* reporter Carol Griffee, one of the deans of state-house reporting in the capital. "It was just so obvious it made me sick."

Bill left it to Hillary to deflect the rampant speculation about his affairs. Rather than deny the rumors, she contended that the subject was none of the reporters' business. "She had always insisted on this zone of privacy whenever the rumors about him came up," John Brummett said. But the Hart precedent seemed to abolish the zone of privacy for all candidates. What had previously been a problem in the Clinton marriage was now a political problem. "All of a sudden he [Bill] was having some strange conversations about the Gary Hart thing, asking legislators if a candidate admitted that he had caused pain in his marriage, would that be enough," Brummett recalled.

The most direct evidence of Clinton's concern on this score comes from Meredith Oakley's *On the Make,* in which she quoted her boss John Robert Starr's recollection of a conversation with Clinton: "We were talking about the Gary Hart factor in politics, . . . and I [Starr] asked him [Clinton] something to the effect of 'Well, you haven't ever done anything like that, have you?' You know [I was] expecting a negative answer, be it a lie or the truth. And he said, 'Yes, I have.' And I was somewhat taken aback, and I said, 'You mean, since you've been married to Hillary?' And he said, 'Yes. Do you want to know about it? . . . And I, to my eternal regret, said, 'No.' I just didn't want to know."[2]

As Bill entertained doubts about whether he could survive the heightened level of scrutiny, Hillary continued to make preparations for a July announcement undaunted by—perhaps not yet even fully aware of—the extent of her husband's vulnerability.

A trio of Hillary's liberal friends and associates was already being positioned to form the nucleus of a national campaign staff: Carl Wagner,

Susan Thomases, and Harold Ickes. The three had first met Bill Clinton in the summer of 1970 in Washington, when they all worked together on Project Pursestrings, an effort to cut off congressional funding for the Vietnam War. They were veterans of the internecine wars within the Democratic Party of the 1970s and 1980s, in which they took up the cause of the party's most leftist faction in the campaigns of Eugene McCarthy in '68, George McGovern in '72, and Ted Kennedy's challenge to President Carter in 1980.

Susan Thomases—who had lived with Ickes for five years in the 1960s—visited Bill in Fayetteville during his 1974 congressional race against Hammerschmidt. That's when she first met Hillary. The two became fast friends, sharing interests in law, public policy, and children's welfare. Before attending law school, Thomases had worked in New York City setting up child care centers for poor families. Hillary invited Thomases to join the Children's Defense Fund board in 1982.[3]

Since the early 1980s, Susan Thomases was the administrative partner of Willkie Farr & Gallagher, a prestigious New York law firm named for GOP presidential candidate Wendell Willkie, but now linked to the state's leading Democrats. She was the third woman in the firm's history elected to partnership. Her political résumé was impressive as well: She was the scheduler for Vice President Mondale in 1976, and in New Jersey managed Bill Bradley's first New Jersey Senate race in 1978—as one of the first female campaign managers in the country.

The hard-charging Thomases was often seen in her office holding two different telephone conversations at once, one on her desk phone and the other on a hand-held cellular. She had the sort of personality often found among lawyers in big firms: solicitous of those who are senior to them and abrasive toward underlings. Like Hillary before she was cast as a political wife, Thomases seemed to regard her appearance as an afterthought. She had a mop of frizzy black hair shot through with gray and wore tinted aviator-style glasses. Secretaries in her firm talked about how she would let her Chanel shoes get run down at the heels.

Though her first connection had been to Bill, by 1987 Thomases was a troubleshooter, adviser, and lawyer principally to Hillary. Hillary had turned to Thomases for advice when she was considering whether she should take Bill's name in the 1982 comeback bid, and Thomases had advised her again in the mid-1980s when Hillary set up her separate compensation system at the Rose Law Firm.

One Democratic lawyer who knows both women well speculated that Hillary may have admired Thomases and even romanticized her career as the sort that she herself could have achieved had she not gone to Arkansas. They had begun on the same track. Both were the only daughters in families of boys, both had strong mothers. Hillary went to Wellesley and Yale, and Thomases attended Connecticut College and Columbia University Law School. But by the 1980s, Thomases was a high-powered New York lawyer making a half million dollars a year, while Hillary's earning power was substantially eroded by her political work for Bill. Thomases lived on Park Avenue, had a summer house in Newport, Rhode Island, and was on a first-name basis with the top political figures in New York. She was living in a sophisticated world that Hillary, tied down in Little Rock, could engage with only at a distance. Thomases was anything but the traditional political wife: she kept her own name after marrying a carpenter-turned-artist, William Bettridge, who stayed home and took on many of the child-care responsibilities.

But something more than mere personal loyalty had solidified Thomases' position as Hillary's most trusted adviser; Thomases was also loyal to the idea of Hillary as the embodiment of an ideology. She viewed Hillary as symbol and role model for a new generation of women, a view to which many Democratic feminists would subscribe as Hillary's national profile rose. The two women also shared a certain moralistic rigidity toward those who did not share their political outlook. One former Willkie Farr associate first met Thomases at a 1989 cocktail party for new associates. The young associate approached the intimidating Thomases and introduced herself. In an effort to make conversation, she remarked that she had worked in politics while going to law school and had heard that Thomases was very active politically as well. "Oh?" Thomases inquired, her interest piqued. "Who have you worked for?" When the woman answered that she had worked on a Republican congressional campaign in Pennsylvania, Thomases broke in, saying, "You worked for a Republican? Pfffff. I don't want to have this conversation," and stalked off. She never spoke to the embarrassed associate again in the three years the associate worked for the firm.

Harold Ickes, another member of Clinton's national campaign triumvirate, was the son of Harold Ickes, Sr., FDR's Interior Secretary, who was known as "Honest Harold" and credited with cleaning up the Teapot Dome scandal. Harold Junior had risked his life as a civil rights organizer in Mississippi in the 1960s, was active in anti–Vietnam War protests and had a long history of involvement in progressive politics in New York where he joined a Long Island firm as a labor union lawyer.

Harold the younger doesn't seem to have lived up to his father's reputation for integrity, however. Though he was strongly motivated by issues, Ickes also seemed to embrace a "by whatever means necessary" philosophy of politics. Although Ickes has denied any wrongdoing, his ethics have been questioned in a variety of cases in New York: his firm's representation of union boss Anthony Amodeo, who allegedly had ties to organized crime; his dual role as David Dinkins's mayoral campaign counsel and as lawyer-lobbyist for companies seeking city contracts from Dinkins; and his work for the city's Off-Track Betting Corp., which has been plagued by allegations of political patronage.[4]

Working in New York politics for the 1970 Democratic gubernatorial ticket of Arthur Goldberg and Basil Patterson, Ickes may have undertaken a surveillance operation against his own campaign. As reported by this author in the *American Spectator* in 1994, one Saturday morning in September, a New York City policeman was patroling his beat in a radio car when he spotted a man he described as unkempt and shabbily dressed emerging from the Goldberg-Patterson campaign headquarters. According to the now-retired officer, that man was Harold Ickes. According to the officer's contemporaneous notes, Ickes had a large brown paper bag tucked under his arm as he hurried across Fifth Avenue. The officer, John Mackie, gave chase and took possession of the bag, which contained thirty-four different sets of keys, numerous checkbooks and registers, and a number of telephone and address books, each written in a different hand. There was also a large flashlight of the type that Mackie said is commonly used in burglaries. When Mackie informed Ickes that he would have to go down to the precinct station for further investigation, "Ickes began to harass me by calling me a lousy fucking cop." Mackie took Ickes into the station, where he was released after a Democratic campaign official vouched for him.

Ickes cultivated the image of a tough guy, often retelling the story of the unfortunate foe whose leg he had bitten during a confrontation in the early 1970s. He also had a hearing impairment from a punctured eardrum in his left ear. Though the lore is that the injury had been inflicted in heroic political battle, in truth it had been caused by a buffoonish accident: while doing some carpentry work in a friend's kitchen Ickes was scratching his inner ear with a screwdriver when the maid's door swung open and jammed the tool into his head, according to a political associate of Ickes' in New York.

Ickes' labor union work and political commitments drew Hillary to him, forming a lasting bond. (Even today in her capacity as first lady Hillary tries not to stay in a non-union hotel.) Ickes served as delegate selector for George McGovern at the 1972 convention, a key position which he used methodically to disenfranchise traditional blue-collar Democrats in favor of student and feminist activists. Working with Susan Thomases, he floor-managed for Ted Kennedy's bitter fight to wrest control of the Democratic nomination from Jimmy Carter. When Clinton decided not to run in 1988, Ickes joined Jesse Jackson's campaign as a key adviser. His client list included such prominent liberals as former *New York Times* executive editor Max Frankel, feminist author Letty Cottin Pogrebin, future commerce secretary Ron Brown, and the Children's Defense Fund.

In the same year that Bill Clinton ran the McGovern campaign in Texas, labor union consultant Carl Wagner managed the Michigan effort. Wagner went on to supervise Ickes in the 1980 Ted Kennedy campaign. "They [Ickes, Thomases and Wagner] were the left of the left," said David Ifshin, a neoconservative Democrat who clashed with Thomases and Ickes in the '92 Clinton campaign. They were also known for a willingness to employ scorched-earth tactics and for terrible tempers. "In fact," Ifshin said, "Wally Chalmers, an old [Ted] Kennedy person, was going around in 1987 saying not to get involved with the Clinton campaign because all the people around Clinton—Susan, Harold, and Carl—were psychopaths."

In early July 1987, Hillary was quoted as saying that an announcement of Bill's presidential candidacy would be made within two weeks. *Newsweek* also reported that Clinton had decided to run. Hugh and Dorothy Rodham purchased a condominium in Little Rock, a sign that Hillary was planning to hit the campaign trail and wanted her parents nearby for Chelsea. The Clinton exploratory committee scheduled a news conference for July 15 and rented a ballroom at the Excelsior Hotel. Television networks planned to fly their correspondents into Little Rock, and about four hundred Clinton supporters were invited to pack the room. Key supporters flew in from Los Angeles, Washington, and New York, including Mickey Kantor, who had served on the Legal Services Corporation board with Hillary and was now a lawyer and major Democratic fund-raiser in Los Angeles; former Hart and McGovern supporters Sandy Berger and John Holum; and Thomases, Ickes, and Wagner. They gathered for a small luncheon at the governor's mansion the day before the formal announcement.

A few days before the luncheon, however, Betsey Wright threw a wrench into the works. By 1987, Wright had come to be regarded by some Clinton intimates as emotionally unstable and even dangerous in her fierce loyalty to the Clintons. Working side by side with Bill every day through the years, Wright had almost as much sway with him as Hillary did. If Hillary was Bill's political nanny, Betsey was the bossy older sister.

Only Hillary could stand up to Betsey. Aides vividly remembered one argument about the '87 race when Hillary, poking a finger into Betsey's chest, backed the taller, heavier woman across an entire parking lot. "In '87, I think there was a war of wills between the women. Hillary wanted him to run and Betsey didn't. That was the split. It wasn't between Clinton and Betsey," said GOP strategist Darrell Glascock, who knew Wright well as a fellow political operative.

Wright may have wanted Clinton to be president as much as Hillary did, but her extensive political intelligence network gave her knowledge of Clinton's private life that Hillary likely did not have. In advising Bill not to run, Wright seemed most concerned with protecting Hillary and Chelsea from public embarrassment. Clinton had used several loose-lipped intermediaries on the state payroll to facilitate his private affairs, compromising himself and creating an issue—abuse of public office— that the press might well uncover. According to Maraniss's biography, Clinton and Wright had an eleventh-hour meeting at her Little Rock home in which she convinced him not to run because of the womanizing issue. "Then she started listing the names of women he had allegedly had affairs with and the places where they were said to have occurred," Maraniss wrote. " 'Now,' she concluded, 'I want you to tell me the truth about every one.' She went over the list twice with Clinton, according to her later account, the second time trying to determine whether any of the women might tell their stories to the press. At the end of the process, she suggested that he should not get into the race. He owed it to Hillary and Chelsea not to."[5]

Bill decided to heed Wright's dire warnings, but there was too little time before the scheduled conference to get word to all the invited guests, supporters, and media people who were en route to Arkansas. At the lunch at the governor's mansion, Clinton broke the news to his supporters—mostly Hillary's friends—and then called the Associated Press in Little Rock to leak word.

The next day, Bill and Hillary appeared as scheduled for the news conference. Bill said he was not yet ready to make the personal commitment and sacrifice a national race would require. His aides noticed that for the first time anyone could remember, Bill seemed in control and Hillary did not. As Clinton spoke, Hillary wiped away tears.

Little Rock's political junkies were not satisfied with the official explanations. Rumors abounded that Clinton had gotten a call from a *New York Times* reporter pursuing a story about an alleged affair with a woman he had appointed to a state position. Another account had it that the *Arkansas Democrat* had planned an exposé on his affairs for the day of Clinton's announcement.

Visibly upset, even humiliated, by her husband's decision not to run, Hillary was especially distraught about the painful reason for it. Her friends say Hillary questioned many of the decisions she had made in her life and seriously considered divorcing Bill in the wake of Bill's announcement. "In conversations with him and her, and in conversations my wife had with Hillary, this was the first time she acknowledged knowing of his extramarital activities," said one close friend of the Clintons, who first met the couple in 1982. "I think Chelsea has been the most underestimated factor in their lives. If it hadn't been for Chelsea, I think they would have divorced then."

Hillary, then thirty-nine, sought advice from friends not only about whether to stay with Bill but also about what to do with the rest of her life if there was to be no presidential run. She knew now that there would be no more children. "Even today, the one thing that can make Hillary cry is a discussion of why there were no more children," said the same friend. "We had lots of discussions [about her discontentment]. She saw herself as the breadwinner and that was not what she wanted to do with her life. She was most interested in the public policy issues. When he decided not to run, this created a big problem. She was already a partner in the law firm, there was going to be no second kid, and he was going to be governor of Arkansas forever. It was like, 'I'm in this rut.' The infidelity only fueled the fire. Neither one [of the Clintons] has tremen dous control over their emotions and feelings. When they were having an argument, you knew it, and it was a very bad time."

Paula Blanchard, a first lady from Michigan who made the decision to leave her husband, Governor Jim Blanchard, in 1987 under similar circumstances recalled Hillary's unusual reaction to the news of their breakup. Governor Blanchard and Clinton were close friends. "I'll never forget the day we were at a National Governor's Association meeting and I took a few of the first ladies who had been my closest friends, including Hillary, aside to a room to break the news that I was leaving Jim," Paula Blanchard remembered. "Well, everybody got up, hugged me, consoled me, and said they were so sorry, and some were crying. Hillary just sat there totally blank. She didn't say one word to me and then got up and left."

During this period of disaffection from Bill, Hillary was clearly growing closer to law partner Vince Foster, who appeared to be everything Bill was not: cautious, reliable, and trustworthy. Whether Hillary herself may have had an affair at this time with Foster has long been a subject of speculation. Even if the relationship was not consummated, Hillary and Foster had a very close emotional bond that went well beyond a professional association.

Rumors about the two of them had been common in Little Rock for years. One state legislator remembered being in the "quiet room in the legislature hearing some comments about Hillary and Vince Foster as lovers. People were sitting around looking at a newspaper article about Hillary's dad's funeral [in 1993] and a photo with Hillary and Vince standing side by side. And the comment was, 'Well, they sure got a good picture of the lovers.' "

After Foster's tragic suicide in July 1993, John Phillip Carroll, the senior partner in the litigation section at Rose, told the FBI that Foster had feared such rumors might surface during the '92 campaign. "Asked about possible stress points in Foster's life, Carroll advised that before the election, Foster told Carroll about the rumor that he believed was about to hit the press that he and Hillary Rodham Clinton were having an affair," the FBI interview summary stated. "He advised Carroll that he was having his telephone number changed and would not be at the office for a couple of days. He seemed shocked and concerned about it. He was making the changes because he did not want to run into the press.

He was telling Carroll in order to give Carroll and others at the law firm some kind of forewarning as to what was coming."

As it turned out, Foster had little reason for concern. The press displayed even more reticence in covering this aspect of Hillary's life than it did toward Bill's. When the Troopergate story alleging Bill's affairs broke in late 1993, the article was widely discussed and debated, but the troopers' additional claims about a Hillary-Vince liaison were disregarded. The troopers said that they had personally witnessed Foster fondling Hillary on various social occasions and claimed that Vince showed up at the governor's mansion "like clockwork" whenever Bill was out of town and stayed until the wee hours of the morning. The troopers also said they sometimes drove Hillary and Vince to a cabin kept by the Rose Firm in the nearby mountain resort of Heber Springs, where the two spent significant amounts of time together.

Many of the Clintons' supporters vigorously contested this aspect of the troopers' tale. Commenting on the troopers' account of public fondling, Little Rock journalist Gene Lyons wrote in the *New York Review of Books:* "The idea that Foster, whose reticence and sense of propriety were well known, would have done anything of the kind is almost as grotesque to his friends as the notion of Mrs. Clinton's permitting it."

During this period when she was entertaining second thoughts about her marriage and growing closer to Foster, Hillary appeared for the first time to put real energy into her law practice at the Rose Firm. Previously, making money had not been one of her driving concerns. Faced with the prospect of single motherhood, however, it made sense for Hillary to try to boost her income and put aside a nest egg that would allow her to move out of the governor's mansion with Chelsea and support herself, should that become necessary. Clinton couldn't be expected to contribute much in the way of child support on his $35,000-a-year governor's salary. In the event of a divorce, she could expect little from him but the financial neglect of a deadbeat dad.

As with everything she did, when Hillary set her mind to being a player at Rose, she had little trouble succeeding, taking a place alongside Vince Foster and Webb Hubbell as one of the three leading partners in the litigation section of the firm known as "the Trinity." As a result, many Rose women began to see Hillary as their mentor in a man's world. "I don't know that you'd say she had a 'reputation,' but I do know that she was at times demanding," said Sarah Hood Teed, a former Rose associate in the tax section. "But I've worked for other attorneys in the firm that were equally as demanding or more so based on the situation, and I'd be the same way if I was in her shoes because there's just times when the work's gotta be done, and it's gotta be done now, and it's gotta be done right."

Thomas Mars, a former associate at Rose who worked closely with Hillary, also remembered Hillary as a hard-driving boss, more than holding her own in turf battles. "I was working on files for other attorneys and I was getting there at three A.M. to make sure all the work got done," he said. Because Hillary had been absent from the firm so often, she had "lost her exclusive right to use me as her associate. I had been told to start working for other attorneys, too. When she found out about it, she became very territorial about me. She came in and told me I needed to know who was on first, and who was on second around here." Yet Mars did not appreciate what he described as Hillary's sometimes caustic asides. "She could charm your socks off, but she could also burn your ass. Once, in a conference with other lawyers, I made a point and she sneered at me with a reference to 'all your vast experience,' " Mars said. "I was young, but I did have some experience. It was embarrassing."

During her time away for Bill's re-election campaigns and the education reform effort, a problem had been festering at the Rose Firm that no one had addressed until Hillary turned her attention to it. The litigators—Vince, Webb, and Hillary, among others—were unhappy with the firm's compensation system, which allowed the corporate-securities lawyers to charge clients large premiums that they kept for themselves, even if substantial litigation work was involved. By the mid-1980s, first-year securities partners were making more than the senior litigation partner, and managing partner Joe Giroir earned at least four times what the top litigation partner was making.[6]

Giroir was also getting rich from buying and selling stocks in several Arkansas banks. In 1985, he was elected to the board of the Worthen Banking Corporation, a Rose client. During a major shareholder suit, Giroir's conflict led Worthen to drop Rose, a big blow to the firm. As a shareholder in another bank, Giroir was sued by the Federal Savings and Loan Insurance Corporation, which had become a top Rose client, for issuing a legal opinion on a loan from which he stood to benefit.

Playing on concern in the partnership that Giroir's outside involvements were costing Rose lucrative business and placing the firm in conflicted positions, the Trinity, led by Hillary, made a move in 1987 to oust the longtime managing partner. To pull off their coup, the three forged an alliance with Giroir's protégé Bill Kennedy, who stood to inherit the corporate department from Giroir. The number-one producer in the firm, Kennedy owed much of his success to his older mentor. Giroir had thrown much business Kennedy's way, including Rose client Beverly Enterprises, a giant nursing home operator with facilities in several states. Kennedy was the lawyer on a multi-million-dollar Beverly land deal that a judge said generated "unconscionable" profits for the client and the firm, and raised the cost of care to elderly, infirm nursing-home residents.

Recruited by the Trinity to aid their takeover plan, Kennedy was now ready to turn the screws on Giroir, just as he had with the elderly nursing-home residents. "They [the Trinity] used Bill. He was a soldier," said one person close to Kennedy.

After Giroir quit under fire, taking other attorneys and several major clients with him, the pressure at the firm to bring in new business increased tremendously, and Hillary did what she could to fill the role of rainmaker. She also joined the newly formed executive committee that made the firm's day-to-day management decisions in Giroir's wake. Kennedy, meanwhile, was named to the new position of chief operating officer.

One consequence of the power struggle was a change in the formula for figuring compensation away from its strict production-based scheme. The new formula allowed up to 20 percent of a partner's draw to be based on such subjective factors as "enhancing the firm's reputation," ability to generate business, client and associate management, and civic, bar association, and pro bono activities. More than anyone, Hillary, as the wife of the governor and pro bono legal activist at the Children's Defense Fund and the ABA commission on women, stood to benefit from the change. Her income rose steadily in the late 1980s, finally topping six figures by 1990.

Hillary also began to supplement her law firm income by accepting appointment to the boards of several large corporations, including Wal-Mart and TCBY (The Country's Best Yogurt). She told friends she sought the board work not so much for the extra income (she was paid $15,000 a year by Wal-Mart, hardly cashing in by Arkansas standards) but because she was bored at the Rose Firm and sought a new challenge in learning about business. The companies, in turn, were clearly eager to have the state's first lady flacking for them, performing such tasks as cutting ribbons at the opening of Wal-Mart stores across the state.

When Hillary joined the TCBY board in 1989, former vice president and director Erik Wulff seemed to have more in mind for her than ribbon-cutting. He was quoted as saying that the company's president, Frank Hickingbotham, had pulled off a savvy political ploy, "making sure he was in good grace with the people in power." After Hillary joined the board, the yogurt company became a Rose client, paying $275,000 in legal fees in 1991 alone.

Hillary also earned $31,000 a year—practically Bill's entire annual salary as governor—serving (beginning in 1990) on the board of Lafarge Corporation, the American subsidiary of a French company that is the second largest producer of cement in the United States. Lafarge has several plants in neighboring states but none in Arkansas. Hillary was criticized by environmental groups for working with a company that has been fined repeatedly by state and federal environmental regulators for burning hazardous waste. The affiliation with Lafarge was a measure of how far Hillary—who had once refused to use aerosol products in order to protect the environment—was now willing to bend in order to bring in extra income and build up her résumé after years of neglect. The position at Lafarge was likely attractive to her precisely because the company did no business in Arkansas; she had been chosen for the board for reasons other than her Arkansas political connections. James Affleck, who served on the Lafarge board with Hillary, said the board had no women on it at the time and was seeking to appoint one.

The other companies whose boards Hillary joined—Wal-Mart and TCBY—were at various times represented by the Rose Firm. Hillary's board work contravened the firm's advice to its lawyers that they minimize outside business relationships with clients—the very admonition that Hillary's allies had used against Giroir. Confident as she was of her own rectitude and ability to withstand temptation, Hillary apparently did not see the need to steer clear of potential conflicts of interest or hold herself to the same rules that she applied to others.

With Hillary largely absent from the Arkansas political scene in the late 1980s, Bill hit a rough patch that was reminiscent of his first term, when Hillary was occupied in Washington chairing the Legal Services Corporation and his administration was run by three woolly-minded liberal aides. A consistent pattern could now be discerned in the relationship: When Hillary pulled away, Bill faltered. "I do know that after the education standards were implemented in 1987 and Bill decided not to run, she went back to work for the law firm and quit advising Bill," John Robert Starr recalled. "And his damn administration went to hell."

Clinton was a skilled campaigner, but governing was not his strong suit. People complained that he was unprepared for legislative sessions, chronically late, and ignored the business of the state. He left Arkansas more than one hundred times in 1989 alone. After eight years, Clinton's record was also catching up with him: 20 percent of Arkansans were still living below the poverty line, teachers were the lowest paid in the nation, and the schools were still near the bottom in national rankings. Clinton had increased state spending 111 percent since his first term, and the state was suffering from revenue shortfalls as a consequence. Prohibited by the state constitution from deficit spending, Clinton asked the legislature for a $200 million tax-and-spend package in 1989. He tried to use the same creative strategy he had used to raise taxes in 1983, hiding the increase in a grand education-oriented policy initiative called Moving Arkansas Forward into the Twenty-first Century. But this time Hillary was not available to launch the idea and it went nowhere.[7]

Reporting on a visit to the state in 1990, the *Washington Post*'s David Broder, evidently keeping tabs on Clinton as a potential Democratic presidential contender, reported that "at home Clinton has had a rocky time. The legislature repeatedly has refused to pass his school-finance program because it involved higher taxes. Teachers unions, angry at his requiring competency testing of their members, withheld their endorsement in the primary. In a state desperate for jobs, the Clinton administration approved a big loan to a company in the middle of a labor dispute—angering the unions enough that the governor lost their endorsement."

The final blow to Clinton came when Betsey Wright quit his staff in the fall of 1989. Trying to fill the void left by Hillary, Wright had become even more of a workaholic since Clinton declined to run in 1987. Wright has never talked publicly about why she left, but one former top Clinton aide said she quit when Clinton began to see state legislators without clearing the appointments first with Wright. Exhausted and under great stress, Wright could not handle losing control over Bill.

As Wright departed, Hillary appeared to renew her commitment to her marriage and political partnership. Back in 1981, she had moved instinctively to pull her husband out of his depression and organize his comeback campaign. This time, Hillary had had a couple of years to mull over her options. When she recommitted, it was presumably with more calculated intentions.

"There was a 'come to Jesus' following the bitterness of the 1987 decision not to run," said a friend who spoke often with Hillary during this period. "They were either going to separate or spend the rest of their lives together. They decided to make a run in '92 and to do whatever it took to get there. They seemed at peace with it and they grew closer. You could see in certain moments when no one else was around that they would do things like hold each other's hands. I'd see them, you know, when they had turned a corner and didn't know anybody was watching."

What really happened between Bill and Hillary is impossible to know. Some of Hillary's friends tended to see her as falling for Bill all over again. As John Robert Starr put it in one interview, "Bill is very persuasive, particularly when he's acting pitiful. I can easily see him throwing himself on her mercy and convincing her that this would never happen again, and that what he did was relatively innocent."

Her critics, on the other hand, tended to see her decision to rejoin the marriage as a cynical act of power-seeking. "The deal was that he wouldn't do anything really stupid, like get photographed on a boat off Bimini, and she would stand by him if it came out," John Brummett believed. Max Brantley, who had criticized Hillary's courtship of Starr back in the 1982 campaign, called her decision to stick by Bill a "pact with the devil," in a 1994 interview with the *New Yorker*.

The truth was probably somewhere in the middle. Though she likely still loved Bill, she seemed willing to abandon her earlier visions of a romantic marriage, and instead make a very attractive compromise for a chance at the White House.

More than political ambition, however, seemed to be weighing on Hillary's mind as she decided to stay with Bill. Hillary had never embraced the permissive values of the counterculture and she held a strong belief that divorce should only be a last resort, especially when a child was involved. Describing her decision to settle for a flawed marriage, Hillary told *Glamour* magazine in 1992: "No marriage is perfect, but just because it isn't perfect doesn't mean the only solution is to walk off and leave it." In her book *It Takes a Village*, she wrote: "My strong feelings about divorce and its effects on children have caused me to bite my tongue more than a few times during my own marriage . . . One of the many difficulties with divorce is that it becomes a public matter. It goes to court. Painful child custody decisions must be made. Regardless of individual feelings, everyone involved in the process, especially a parent, has an obligation to temper the pain children will inevitably experience."[8] Thus it may have been not only her pragmatism and ambition, but also her idealism, integrity, and strength of character in staying married to someone who shared none of these traits, that worked both for and against Hillary. In any case, by late 1989 it was clear that she was back on board. That fall, she took a major role in a national summit at Monticello called by President Bush to reverse "the decline of our educational system." While other governors' wives went sightseeing, Hillary attended the conference and sat in on governors' meetings.

The final step in cementing Hillary's and Dick Morris's 1982 strategy of remaking Bill into an electable southern centrist came in 1990. Bill was picked for a two-year term to head the Democratic Leadership Council (DLC)—the group founded in 1985 to work for the election of moderate Democrats and to stimulate new ideas in the party. Chosen on a platform of education reform and job creation, Clinton drafted a DLC "party credo" that included goals of higher student test scores, lower dropout rates, and more choice for parents.

In early 1990, *Newsweek*'s Eleanor Clift picked Clinton as one of three rising stars of the new Democratic Party, along with Virginia governor Doug Wilder and Senator Al Gore of Tennessee. Yet even as Clinton's star was rising nationally, within the state his political capital continued to fall to its lowest point since 1980. He faced a tough primary in 1990 from Attorney General Steve Clark, and for the first time since Frank White's upset victory in 1980, the Republicans were determined to field a winning candidate in the general election. If Clinton ran for governor and lost, he would be finished as a presidential contender and his political career would probably be over.

In light of such bleak prospects at the state level, some of Clinton's advisers urged him to give up the governor's mansion and run for president as the head of the Democratic Leadership Council. But this would have meant losing his grip on the state party and its fund-raising apparatus. The Clintons thus considered running Hillary for governor as a way of holding onto these resources for a national race. Notably, the idea of Hillary running for governor was only considered as a means to help Bill win the presidency, not as a move to bolster her independent career, which she had surrendered to the co-candidacy years ago. A top Democratic operative in Washington received a call from Clinton early in 1990, soliciting his advice on whether Hillary should run for the state house. "The idea was he could have gone out and done the Jimmy Carter thing for two years running for president. He was scared to do that without a base. But he would have the base if he had Hillary there," John Robert Starr said.

The Clintons weren't the only ones who thought Hillary might be a stronger candidate than Bill. Power broker Witt Stephens was actively promoting the idea behind the scenes. Columnist Paul Greenberg had taken to referring to the "Governors Clinton." Even erstwhile Hillary critics like John Brummett were open to the suggestion: "Let me put it this way. For all his skills, Bill Clinton is the second-best politician in his family; the second-best speaker; the second-strongest personality. Dare I say it? Oh, why not? He would be the second-best governor. As he says himself, he 'overmarried.'"

The polls, however, were discouraging: When it became clear that Hillary couldn't win the race, Clinton declared for re-election with a hastily improvised Shermanesque pledge not to seek the presidency in 1992. Though the young and telegenic Steve Clark pulled out of the race amid allegations that he had misused his state credit cards for personal expenses and created fictitious records to cover it, Clinton still faced a surprisingly strong challenge from Tom McRae. A tall, patrician, Harvard-educated nonpolitician who reminded people of Abe Lincoln, McRae headed the liberal Winthrop Rockefeller Foundation, which had criticized Hillary's education reform package and other aspects of the Clinton record. Having served on the foundation's board, Hillary was quite familiar with its work.

On a day when he knew Clinton would be out of the state, McRae had planned to stage a mock debate with Clinton to attack his record. At the beginning of the news conference he unveiled a cartoon depicting a nude Clinton, his hands over his crotch, with the tag line: "The Emperor Has No Clothes." Hillary had shrewdly anticipated McRae's attack. Employing the same tactics that she used to knock over Frank White in two prior campaigns, Hillary, lying in wait in the audience, suddenly shouted,

"Get off it, Tom," and proceeded to quote from Rockefeller Foundation reports that had praised the very aspects of Clinton's record that McRae was now criticizing. "I went through all your reports because I've really been disappointed in you as a candidate and I've been really disappointed in you as a person, Tom," Hillary added.

McRae said later that he felt unfairly ambushed and unable to respond sharply because of Hillary's status and gender. "It was pretty much a no-win situation for me. One, I wasn't running against her. And there's certainly nothing to be gained, in a southern state, by taking on someone's wife," he maintained.

But Hillary's counterattack boomeranged. For many Arkansans she had overstepped the line, bringing the image of the "ball-busting" Hillary Rodham back to popular consciousness. Far from applauding her assertiveness and command of the facts, many voters recoiled from it. "I was complaining to my media person," recalled McRae, "and he said, 'Get her to do it again.' My name recognition in a three- or four-day period went—according to one poll—from something like 20 percent to 40 percent. It was probably the biggest single boost I got in the whole campaign in terms of a single event." McRae went on: "It seemed to help me a lot in the rural counties, probably for all the wrong reasons. For the next several weeks people I had never seen before, particularly rural women, would run up to me and hug me and say, 'Oh, I didn't know you were such a gentleman and she was so rude.' On the other hand, a lot of her friends in Little Rock thought it was wonderful—that she was worth her mettle and that she was tough."

The ploy seemed to backfire as well by exposing the true nature of the co-candidacy. Meredith Oakley wrote in the *Arkansas Democrat* that the incident showed Clinton "not only lacking fire in the belly but steel in the spine" and accused him of sending his wife "to do his dirty work for him." *Arkansas Gazette* columnist Deborah Mathis also disapproved. "Find a certain place and stay there," she admonished Hillary in a column. "Political trenches are no place for a lady."

Hillary, however, could not be blamed for the damage Bill had done himself in failing to deliver for the state in his third term. He won the primary against McRae with 54 percent of the vote, the narrowest lead since his comeback in 1982.

Although he was struggling for popularity on the home front, Bill's star was still rising on the national level and the GOP opposition recognized him as a threat. McRae had softened Bill up for the Republicans, who were secretly plotting to resurrect the Gary Hart factor, hoping that revelations of his personal conduct would cost him the governorship or at least wound him as a contender for the presidency in 1992. Former congressman Tommy Robinson and millionaire businessman Sheffield Nelson knew Clinton's vulnerabilities very well. Both were former Democratic insiders and Clinton appointees who had recently switched to the Republican party because Clinton looked beatable.

As Clinton's director of public safety in his first term, Robinson had been in charge of the state police, which enabled him to collect intelligence on Clinton's womanizing. Robinson soon ran for sheriff of Pulaski County, where Little Rock is located, and through a combination of tough talk on crime and media savvy, "Captain Hotdog" became the most popular political figure in the state, surpassing even Clinton. By 1989, Robinson had served three terms in Congress and was out of sync with the national Democratic party in Washington. With great fanfare, President Bush announced in the White House Rose Garden that Robinson was switching parties.

At that time, the legendary Republican strategist Lee Atwater was planning to make the Republican party dominant in the South by persuading so-called Boll Weevil Democrats like Robinson to switch parties. Moderate-seeming pols like Clinton weren't making his job any easier. Using John Paul Hammerschmidt, Clinton's old congressional opponent who was still in office, as an intermediary, Atwater had promised Robinson that if he ran for governor, he would have the full backing of the Republican National Committee (RNC).

According to Rex Nelson of the *Arkansas Democrat-Gazette,* who worked for Robinson's 1990 gubernatorial campaign, Atwater encouraged Robinson to go for Clinton's jugular: "A weak opposition could never capitalize on Clinton's character flaws. But Tommy might have used the womanizing issue in 1990." Nelson recalled: "I remember a meeting in October 1989, in Lee Atwater's office in Washington, when he was the RNC chairman. They planned to get us to raise the womanizing issue against Clinton, to tar him with everything. Atwater told us, 'Boys, I don't care who the governor of Arkansas is. My job is to get the president re-elected. I've already beat a northeast liberal governor. I know how to do that. What scares me is a moderate southerner. I want you to raise all those issues so that he'll be so damaged that even if he is re-elected, he can't get nominated in 1992.' Then Atwater got a brain tumor and there just wasn't much [RNC] interest in the race after that."

Soon after Betsey Wright quit his staff, Clinton helped her become head of the state Democratic party of Arkansas. Rex Nelson credited Hillary and Betsey with developing a plan to deliver the Republican nomination to Sheffield Nelson, who they believed would be a far weaker and less threatening candidate than Robinson in the November election. "Hillary and Betsey came up with the idea of encouraging Democrats to cross over into the Republican primary and vote for Nelson. They took Tommy out and delivered the election to Clinton," Rex Nelson said.

Sheffield Nelson was born to a poor family in rural Arkansas and had worked his way through school. He began working for the Stephens family at Arkla, the oil and gas company, in 1963, and he was chosen a decade later by Witt Stephens to head the company. Nelson split with the Stephenses in the early 1980s in an acrimonious dispute over a deal he entered into as president of Arkla with the Arkoma Production Company, a gas-drilling production firm owned by Nelson's friend Jerry Jones, now owner of the Dallas Cowboys. The deal turned out to be a bad one for Arkla, which was locked into a contract with Arkoma to pay part of the costs of a development project. Natural gas prices plummeted, and Arkla was forced to buy out Arkoma at an exorbitant price to stanch the losses.

Until he switched parties in 1989, Nelson was a longtime supporter of Democratic candidates, including Clinton and senators Pryor and Bumpers. He backed Ted Kennedy's challenge to Jimmy Carter in 1980 and chaired the state Democratic party during the 1980s. Clinton named Nelson to the Arkansas Industrial Development Corporation board in the mid-1980s. But as a result of the bitter 1990 race, Nelson and Clinton became sworn enemies. Compounding the ill-will was the Stephens' role: They had backed Robinson in the GOP primary but had now switched to Clinton, with whom they had an uneasy relationship, in order to beat Nelson.

Going into the final week of the campaign, Clinton was ahead by 15 points and Nelson had not yet found an effective line of attack. In a replay of Frank White's attacks on her, Nelson went after Hillary for profiting from work Rose did for the state. By then, Hillary was not only declining fees from state business but even paying the firm for the overhead costs of her office to avoid any criticism. Yet Nelson persisted, charging that "there are certainly profits from state money that have come to

the bottom line of her firm and go into her profit-sharing accounts."
(Tommy Robinson had targeted Hillary more directly, accusing her of
having been "the real governor for the past decade," and noting that he
"had put up with her tirades" when he held a position in the Clinton administration.)

In the closing days, Nelson aired an ad that finally seemed to resonate
with the voters. Splicing together parts of a speech Clinton had given to
the legislature, the ad showed him repeating the words "raise and spend,
raise and spend, raise and spend." Determined to avoid repeating her
grave mistake of 1980—when they were blindsided by voter wrath over
Clinton's liberal spending—the Clintons called in Dick Morris to run a
tracking poll. The poll showed Clinton had fallen 10 points in the few
days after the ads began. Clinton panicked and ran a rebuttal ad across
the state the weekend before the election.

The ad was financed through large personal loans the Clintons had
taken out in 1990 to add to Bill's campaign war chest. Although uncon-
cerned with personal and family wealth, Bill took a keen interest in
money for his campaigns. Hillary kept the family books but knew little
about the financing of Clinton's campaigns. Hillary's role appeared to
be cosigning for the loans; she owned about two-thirds of the couple's
assets and her annual income was at least three times the size of her
husband's.

The job of working with Bill to raise and manage funds had been filled
by Betsey Wright, who was now gone from the staff. Bruce Lindsey, the
campaign treasurer, was struggling to fill her shoes. In 1990, the Clintons took out $285,000 in personal loans from the rural Perry County
Bank, run by Herby Branscum, Jr., a former chairman of the Arkansas
Democratic party known as "Boss Hogg." Lindsey made last-minute cash
withdrawals from Branscum's bank that went to help pay for $50,000
worth of last-minute TV ads to answer Nelson's charges as well as to finance a turn-out-the-vote effort in the black community.

Branscum and his associate at the bank, Robert M. Hill, were later
indicted and acquitted in the Whitewater investigation on charges of
concealing the campaign's last-minute withdrawals, allegedly to keep
Clinton's opponents in the dark about the expenditures. The withdrawals were not reported to the federal agencies that require disclosure
of transactions involving more than $10,000 per day to prevent money
laundering. Lindsey was named an unindicted co-conspirator in the case.

Branscum and Hill were also accused of stealing bank funds to cover personal contributions they made to Clinton. The jury deadlocked on the charges of improper reimbursement, resulting in a mistrial.

Shortly after Hill delivered the contributions to Clinton to help him pay off the 1990 campaign debt, Branscum was appointed to the powerful state Highway Commission and Hill was named to a state bank board. Clinton, who testified by videotape for the defendants, denied that the appointments were made as quid pro quos for either the contributions or the alleged concealment of the cash withdrawals.

Despite Morris's worrisome poll, Clinton won re-election with a strong 57 to 42 percent showing. Though Clinton had closed the door on a presidential run in the election just ended, a few weeks later the governor-elect convened a lunch at the mansion for a few out-of-state Democrats to discuss a 1992 presidential bid. The only person from Arkansas in attendance was Lindsey, a close adviser of Bill's ever since Bruce had arranged for him to come into his father's law firm in 1981. Like Clinton, Lindsey had been active in the anti-war movement on his campus at Rhodes College in Tennessee and at Georgetown Law School. His father, Robert, was a founding partner in the influential firm of Wright, Lindsey & Jennings, and in his heyday was highly placed in Little Rock's old guard establishment. Lindsey would become known as Clinton's "shadow" in the 1992 race and in the White House. "Lindsey's like the plumber who fixes the faucet when the family is at work and slips the key back through the mail slot." Said the *Washington Post* in a 1994 profile: "No one saw him, but the problem is gone."

In preparation for the lunch, Lindsey had checked the actual wording of Clinton's campaign pledge not to run. He had thought there was more wiggle room than there was. Hillary, meanwhile, was unhappy that Bill had made a pledge that ran counter to her plan to run him in 1992. According to David Maraniss, Hillary, in a conversation with two friends after a meeting of the Wal-Mart board, came up with the idea of Bill touring the state ostensibly to seek voters' advice on whether he could be released from the pledge. This was dubbed "The Secret Tour"; no one was surprised when Clinton later announced that the people had blessed his intention to go back on his word.

The discussion at the mansion that day focused on political damage control. David Ifshin, a Washington lawyer and longtime Democratic operative who attended the mansion lunch, argued that the shortsighted pack journalists in the national press corps always covered the previous campaign. In 1988, the press had missed a huge story: Michael Dukakis's "Massachusetts Miracle" had been a hoax. While Dukakis touted the state as a model of economic development, it was essentially bankrupt. Next time around, Ifshin argued, the press would intensely scrutinize all aspects of the candidate's record in his home state to compensate for its failures in 1988.

"We knew Arkansas had some problems," Ifshin said. "You know, there are a lot of state capitals where you wouldn't want to set loose a special prosecutor, and Little Rock was one of them." Ifshin suggested that Clinton hire "three guys under the auspices of a PAC and one of the things they do is opposition research on Clinton. Have your answers out front and ready. Get it out of your way. Don't be on the defensive," Ifshin added. When Ifshin suggested this, "Bruce gave Clinton a knowing look and laughed."

Though they did not bring in outsiders, as Ifshin suggested, Clinton and his close associates did undertake opposition research on themselves. "In the spring of 1990, Clinton asked me to come to the mansion," said Darrell Glascock, the Republican operative who managed White's race against Clinton in 1986 and had announced his own candidacy for lieutenant governor that year. When Glascock arrived at the governor's mansion, he was ushered into a meeting with Clinton and Vincent Foster, perhaps attending as proxy for Hillary, who may not have wanted to hear the details for herself. "He had called me in to find out what everybody knew and said he was putting together a team to answer it all," Glascock said. Glascock, who had produced the 1986 Lasater ad, said that while he would not divulge his sources, he told Clinton of allegations he had collected about cocaine use by Clinton. The charges were not surfaced, Glascock said, because the sources would not prepare sworn affidavits. Clinton and Foster also inquired about the names of women whom Clinton was said to have been involved with. "On the women, I told them Sheffield [Nelson] had a list, and Tommy [Robinson] had a list. Hell, everybody had a list. They [Clinton and Foster] made one, too, and then they were going to get affidavits from them [the women] denying it. So that if any of them ever came out in the future, they could discredit them by saying, 'Look, she's denied it once.' " (The propriety of spending campaign money on damage control efforts has been under investigation by the Whitewater independent counsel, according to press reports. "There can be a reasonable inference they weren't just concerned about the 1990 governor's election but elections to come," Hickman Ewing, one of the Whitewater prosecutors, told *USA Today*.)

The Clintons also continued to prepare seven-year-old Chelsea for any damaging charges that might surface against Bill, a process they had initiated during the bitter 1986 gubernatorial race against White. "[W]e started at the dinner table to say to her that an election was happening . . . and then [told] her that in elections people say things about each other that are not very nice sometimes, even mean. And I remember her eyes just getting wide and welling up with tears, like 'why would anybody do that?'" Hillary said in a National Public Radio interview as she promoted *It Takes a Village*. The Clintons staged mock debates in which Chelsea played her father and Bill played an opponent. "She'd say, 'I'm Bill Clinton, and I'm trying to help people, so please vote for me,'" Hillary said. "Then I'd say, 'Well, now your daddy's going to be one of his opponents.' And Bill would say, 'Bill Clinton's a terrible person. He is mean to people.' And Chelsea would say, 'That's not true!' And I said, 'But honey, that's what's going to happen.' "

Hillary, meanwhile, was struggling with damage control on other fronts. One big headache was the Clintons' relationship with the McDougals. In the early 1980s Jim McDougal might have been seen as just another high-rolling S&L kingpin in an era of lax regulation; since then, the regulators had cracked down, the S&L scandal was in full force, and the language of the regulators was in wide use. What may have looked to Hillary like legitimate real estate projects at the time were now "sham deals."

By this time, Jim McDougal, who had lost control of Madison Guaranty in 1986, was destitute, living in a trailer in Arkadelphia and suffering from depression. He, along with Susan McDougal's brothers, would soon be indicted (and later exonerated) on fraud charges stemming from a series of loans in the Castle Grande transactions. Susan, meanwhile, had left Jim and fled to California, where she would subsequently be charged with embezzling money from the conductor Zubin Mehta and his wife, whose finances she was managing. (Susan McDougal has pleaded not guilty and denies she stole anything from the Mehtas.)

In *Blood Sport,* James Stewart challenged Hillary's claim that she was a "passive investor" in Whitewater by highlighting her role in managing the partnership's business affairs in the late 1980s. But Hillary's effort to pay off the debt and close out the books on a moribund investment did not constitute active investing, nor had she ever hidden her actions. In fact, she told Resolution Trust Corporation investigators in 1995 that she had "spent a great deal of time and money in the last several years [leading up to 1991] trying to understand the corporation's activities and pay certain of its liabilities such as real estate taxes, corporate franchise taxes and accounting fees incident to tax preparation."

A more questionable action had been taken by Hillary in 1988, when she ordered her Rose law firm records on Madison destroyed. At the time, federal regulators were investigating the collapse of the S&L, a former Rose client, and Seth Ward was suing Madison over the Castle Grande commissions. The destruction of the records came as part of a firmwide effort to consolidate files. But Hillary chose to destroy the files—including one on Castle Grande and one marked "Ward option"—rather than maintain them on microfiche. The Senate Whitewater committee suggested that the destruction of records during the litigation may have been a violation of legal ethics or possibly of the law if Hillary knew the documents were material to the investigation or the litigation. She denied any knowledge. "Because the *Ward* v. *Madison* case was ongoing at the time, Mrs. Clinton might well have destroyed evidence relevant to the case," the committee concluded. "Indeed, the May 1 option drafted by Mrs. Clinton was an important piece of evidence in the trial. It seems reasonable to assume, moreover, that Mrs. Clinton was aware of the *Ward* v. *Madison* litigation, involving as it did her former clients. Moreover, Webster Hubbell, her law partner and close friend, attended at least some of the trial." The RTC investigation of the Rose Firm, however, found that Hillary had no motive to dispose of the files since she did nothing wrong in drawing up the Ward option: "The worst that might be said is that Mrs. Clinton should have checked with her client before discarding files that belonged to it."

Whatever Hillary's reason for disposing of the files, it seemed clear that the Clintons could ill afford public disclosure of any association with Bill's fallen friends the McDougals as the presidential campaign geared up. Though Hillary may not have known it at the time she was acting as

Madison's lawyer, it was now evident that Madison was a nest of fraudulent loans and sham deals and that Hillary and her husband may have been in business with felons. Even if there was no underlying wrongdoing by Hillary in either the Whitewater or Castle Grande matters, a fear of the unknown—Did McDougal pump Madison funds into Whitewater? What was the purpose of that Ward option?—might have been enough to cause Hillary to launch a damage control effort to protect the Clinton presidential campaign from major political embarrassment.

In mid-1991, Hillary hired her Rose partner Bill Kennedy to investigate McDougal's murky financial maneuvers relating to Whitewater, which meant interviewing the rural bankers and real estate appraisers McDougal had dealt with in order to keep the partnership afloat. Though he had worked with the Trinity against Joe Giroir, Bill Kennedy was never close to Hillary. Still, she viewed him as someone who could get the job done. The heavyset, baby-faced Kennedy was the top billing partner at Rose, a position one did not attain in Little Rock by playing softball.

Kennedy may have done more than work on Whitewater for Hillary in 1991. He also may have been instrumental in neutralizing the first of the Clinton womanizing stories. By the summer of 1991, Clinton's impending candidacy was widely rumored in Little Rock. When Clinton publicly hinted for the first time that he was seriously considering a run, questions about his personal life cropped up immediately. He told reporters that the subject was "none of [their] business" and he accused them of being "the moral police of the country." "I think the people who ran in '88 kind of resented it and chose not to answer those kinds of questions and I would expect most people who run in '92 won't."

Though Gennifer Flowers was the first woman to come forward and publicly allege an affair with Clinton in mid-January 1992, another potentially incriminating story had actually been published several weeks before in *Penthouse,* but escaped notice in the traditional media outlets. Connie Hamzy, known locally as "Sweet, Sweet Connie," was a Little Rock rock 'n' roll groupie. In the early 1970s, she had published an article in *Cosmopolitan* recounting her experiences sexually servicing various rock musicians. In 1991, she was commissioned to update the piece for *Penthouse.* The writer who was working with Hamzy, *USA Today* columnist Melanie Wells, was poring over the handwritten diaries Hamzy had kept at the time, when she came across an anecdote about Governor Bill Clinton back in 1984.

According to Hamzy's notes, she was lying by the pool in a purple bikini at the North Little Rock Hilton—stalking members of the band Rush—when a man on Bill Clinton's security detail approached her and said that Clinton, who had just given a speech to a manufacturers' association, wanted to meet her. Hamzy entered the hotel where, according to her diary, Clinton told her, "I want to get with you," pulling her into a dark hallway leading to the hotel laundry room. "He was feeling me, and he was hard, and we were ready to do it, when we heard somebody coming and we stopped," Hamzy said. Clinton was apparently concerned enough about the incident to do little favors for Hamzy in the ensuing years. "One time I was trying to get tags for my car and they said I didn't have the right paperwork," she said. "I called the governor's mansion and they gave me an instant release."

According to Hamzy, a few years after the incident with Clinton, she met Bill Kennedy. "I met him [Kennedy] one day in 1987 when we both lived in the Quapaw Quarter," Hamzy said, referring to the historic district in downtown Little Rock that houses the governor's mansion, several blocks of impressive Victorian and Greek Revival–style homes, and a number of dilapidated apartment houses on the outer edges. Kennedy was single at the time. "He was out in the snow trying to turn his water off because his pipes had frozen. He invited me in and things went from there." Kennedy helped Hamzy make a few extra dollars by buying some of the dolls she made by hand, even taking them into the Rose Firm and hawking them to his partners.

Hamzy claims that Kennedy was aware that she was preparing her *Penthouse* article. "He even looked at my contract," she said. When Hamzy's story, "Confessions of a Rock 'n' Roll Groupie," was published in January 1992 in *Penthouse,* the Clinton team was ready to shoot it down the moment it hit the newsstands. Clinton press secretary Mike Gauldin called the Hamzy allegations "baseless and malicious lies." In what became a familiar pattern, *CNN Headline News* picked up the story but quickly dropped it. Clinton adviser George Stephanopoulos released an affidavit from a legislator who had been traveling with Clinton on the day in question, saying that Hamzy had accosted Clinton, not the other way around. According to legislator Jimmie Don McKissack, Hamzy yanked down her bikini top and "[Clinton] turned red. She reached for his groin. . . . We left immediately." Hamzy later concluded that Kennedy must have given the Clinton camp advance warning about the article. The version of events put out by the Clinton camp infuriated her: "Sex makes the world go 'round. But lyin' don't," she said.

The Hamzy story must have been one of the lurking allegations that Clinton had in mind when he decided not to run in 1987. But now he was better prepared. A few weeks before his October 1991 announcement he arranged to appear with Hillary at Washington's Sperling Breakfast, named for its host, former *Christian Science Monitor* Washington bureau chief Godfrey Sperling. The Sperling sessions were attended by the city's hotshot political reporters. In these circles, and within the Democratic Party, Clinton's zipper problem was as much an open secret as Gary Hart's had been. That fall, when a Colorado congressional colleague asked Representative Pat Schroeder of Colorado what she knew about Bill Clinton of Arkansas, Schroeder quipped that Clinton wouldn't be nominated unless his campaign found a way to keep every woman in Denver quiet.

The event was carefully orchestrated by the Clintons to give them the chance to allay concerns about his private life. "What you need to know about me is we have been together for almost twenty years and have been married almost sixteen, and we are committed to our marriage and its obligations, to our child and to each other," Clinton said. "We love each other very much. Like nearly anybody that's been together for twenty years, our relationship has not been perfect or free of difficulties. But we feel good about where we are. We believe in our obligations. And we intend to be together thirty or forty years from now, regardless of whether I run for president or not. And I think that ought to be enough." The most telling moment may have been when Bill looked at Hillary and said, "If she would run, I would gladly withdraw."[9]

Hillary's appearance at the Sperling Breakfast, which was described as "unusual" by the *Boston Globe,* showed that she would stand by Clinton in the event of revelations of extramarital affairs. Her presence sent the signal that it was safe to support Clinton because he would not be another Gary Hart, whose wife Lee had seemed less than fully supportive in the wake of the Rice story. Hillary, of course, was more than a political wife. She had rescued Bill from political oblivion by engineering his comeback victory in 1982. With the education reform initiative she had repositioned him as a New Democrat and then got the legislation passed through her own efforts. The education initiative sealed his re-election bids in 1984 and 1986. Though devastated in 1987 by his decision not to run for president, she approached the marriage two years later with a renewed sense of purpose and resolve. If Hillary was going to become the power behind the mightiest throne in the world, she was going to have to make it happen.

One close Clinton aide said that Bill, while ambitious, simply did not have "the fire in the belly" to make the '92 run. "He said he could have been just as happy staying governor."

That summer, Hillary called one prominent Boston Democrat in an attempt to line up financial support. "She wanted to talk about what Dukakis had done and it was clear she wasn't hearing the name of the big money in New England for the first time," the Democrat said. "She said, 'Bill is going to run. . . . What's Bob Farmer doing?'" In August, Farmer, one of the chief Democratic party fund-raisers, became chairman of Clinton's exploratory committee. She also asked Little Rock ad man David Watkins to open up Little Rock headquarters for the Clinton exploratory committee. "We need an adult down there," she had told him.

Hillary seemed eager to take on George Bush. In a speech to the Arkansas Federation for Democratic Women, she said, "We have to be ready, and if we are, I believe George Bush will get a well-deserved retirement when he tries to run for re-election. . . . If we can take on those challenges, I think the Democratic Party can take the lead. What's really reassuring is that George Bush doesn't really have a clue as to what's going on."

Hillary was the most prominently quoted spouse in a *Washington Post* feature that summer on the wives of potential Democratic candidates. The article focused on the women—public broadcasting executive Sharon Rockefeller, and lawyers Ruth Harkin and Niki Tsongas—as "a new generation of political leaders confronting questions their predecessors rarely considered." Though the article noted that the Democratic nomination might not be worth much given Bush's strong approval ratings, Hillary sounded upbeat about the challenge. As to whether Bill would run, she said: "That is a very tough decision, one my husband backed away from before and one he is still struggling with." Hillary's wording was a reminder that she had not backed away from the decision in 1987, nor was she agonizing over the choice in 1991. She had stayed in the marriage so that they could make the run.

The presidency would be the fulfillment of the long and hopeful journey that Hillary had begun back at Yale Law School. Despite the personal difficulties and disillusionments of the intervening years, Hillary still seemed to believe that their partnership could produce the kind of social change for which she had been fighting all her life. "I keep remembering the day Hillary came into a Defense Fund board meeting and told us, 'Well, Bill and I are going to run," Lucy Hackney, a CDF board member, has said. "And we knew right then that we were going to be the friends of the president of the country and his wife."

Because Bill was apparently driven more by a need for self-gratification than by any fixed set of beliefs, he relied heavily on Hillary's judgment, principles, and sense of higher purpose in making his decisions. She had the fire in the belly. "Well, he laid out this scenario about how he could make a race," said Max Brantley, recalling a discussion he had with Bill at the Little Rock airport in 1991. "He said, 'Hillary really thinks it'll work.' And that was kind of like: Here's the case, and then here's the clincher. The clear feeling was that (a) he valued what she said and (b) she had laid out a lot of this case I just heard him say."

"It was at the ballpark in the spring of 1991 that I first thought Bill would run for president," wrote James "Skip" Rutherford, former chairman of the state Democratic party and deputy director of Clinton's presidential campaign in *The Clintons of Arkansas*. "Hillary and I were sitting in the bleachers, and she kept saying that it was important for someone to have the courage to carry a different message to the American people in 1992. The Democrats needed a message and a messenger, she said. I knew she must be saying that to Bill, too."[10]

Clinton himself credited Hillary with his decision to run. In her 1994 *New Yorker* interview with him, Connie Bruck wrote that Clinton

> stated repeatedly that he had to "give her credit" for the insight she had had that for him 1992 would be the year of opportunity. "She always thought that the right kind of Democrat would have an opportunity to be elected in '92—always. I mean, from the beginning of [Bush's] term, when he took office, she told me that," the President said. "And when he got up to seventy per cent and then ninety per cent or whatever in the polls after the Gulf War, she never wavered in her conviction that '92 was a good year for the right sort of Democrat to challenge the estab-

lished orthodoxy of the Democratic Party, and also challenge the incumbent President. It was amazing. . . . And I've got to give her credit for that. That's one where instinct was right, and I didn't feel that way for the longest time. . . ."[11]

Clinton went on to tell Bruck that Hillary possessed a "sixth sense."
As the day approached for Clinton to announce his candidacy, there was still no campaign: No campaign manager, no finance person, no general counsel, no spokesman, not even an office. Hillary had to file the papers for Bill to enter the New Hampshire and Texas primaries herself.

Image makers, however, were on hand coaching Clinton for the announcement. According to a person familiar with the sessions, Clinton viewed tapes of John F. Kennedy's speeches in an effort to emulate his style and gestures. As Bill practiced, Hillary sat nearby with her nose in a briefing book, seeming to pay little heed. Bill had trouble getting down one particular hand motion of JFK's, but he came back the next day and announced excitedly that he had figured out how to do it—by imagining himself sticking a bank card into a money machine. Hillary, meanwhile, was instructed to stand behind Bill as he spoke and look at him with a "Nancy Reagan gaze."

Just before the announcement a group of about forty Clinton aides and Democratic campaign operatives convened in Little Rock. Among those present were a few old friends like Anne Wexler (the lobbyist), Mickey Kantor, and Robert Reich; Al From of the Democratic Leadership Council; media consultant Frank Greer; New Hampshire Democratic chairman J. Joseph Grandmaison, David Ifshin; and Susan Thomases and Harold Ickes.

Among the assembled group, Thomases was not known to be an especially gifted political strategist. "Of twenty ideas she has, nineteen are bad," Ifshin said. Most of the candidates Thomases had worked for were defeated, and within Democratic circles some blamed her for New Jersey Senator Bill Bradley's near loss to a virtually unknown Republican opponent in 1990. Thomases publicly excoriated Bradley afterwards for not relying enough on her advice, an unheard-of practice for a political operative. "Bill Bradley as a person is very smart, but he is not politically very hip," Thomases had said. Thomases didn't do much to help her reputation when the group gathered before Clinton's announcement. "Susan stood up and gave an unforgettable speech about how she didn't really have time to devote to the campaign and how we needed to hire a campaign staff because she couldn't do it," Ifshin recalled. "Essentially, she was giving a speech about herself. And I was thinking 'Who are you? And who cares whether you're involved or not?'"

Ifshin, of course, knew exactly who Susan Thomases was. They had clashed before. Back in 1972, Ifshin appeared at the same McGovern platform hearings that Hillary had, backing a minority plank on a guaranteed-income proposal. As an anti-war activist heading the National Student Association, Ifshin made a notorious anti-war radio address broadcast into North Vietnam criticizing U.S. policy. But Ifshin later re-examined these commitments in a way that neither Hillary nor Thomases and Ickes were willing to do. After spending time in an Israeli kibbutz during the Yom Kippur War, Ifshin came back to the United States believing in a strong defense policy. He soon allied himself with the Henry "Scoop" Jackson wing of the party and with the neoconservative Coalition for a Democratic Majority. An expert in campaign finance laws, he was active in the Mondale campaign in 1984, where he clashed with both Thomases and Ickes over the party's supportive stance toward Jesse Jackson. (Ifshin died of cancer in April 1996.)

Thomases soon made it clear that she was a force to be reckoned with due to her connection to Hillary. Following Clinton's announcement in Little Rock, the group of forty broke up and a smaller group met in Bruce Lindsey's downtown law office. At the smaller gathering, "Susan took the floor and announced that the most important asset in this campaign is Hillary," said Ifshin. "She gave a ten-minute monologue about Hillary and Hillary's staffing needs." (Hillary soon had a campaign staff of eighteen, including her own issues director and political consultant.)

Thomases' performance foretold the story of the '92 campaign. By virtue of her long-standing ties to the Clintons, Thomases appreciated something that Ifshin, the out-of-state adviser, did not: The centrality of Hillary to the political operation. New to the Clinton inner circle and stunned by Thomases' braggadocio, Ifshin later asked Bruce Lindsey about Thomases' role in the operation and what could be expected from Hillary in the coming months. "Bruce told me, 'We all know Hillary has to have her little friends around.' He said it with a smile and his voice was dripping with sarcasm."

10

Damage Control

When Bill and Hillary addressed the deans of the journalistic establishment at the Sperling Breakfast in Washington, they faced a sympathetic audience. Many in the press corps, increasingly dominated by
younger, Ivy League–educated liberals, viewed Clinton as "one of us,"
a product of the 1960s not only politically but culturally. Clinton was a
"liberal, semi-hip contemporary who seems to share their [reporters']
values," as the *Boston Globe* described the candidate. Eleanor Clift of *Newsweek* candidly said: "Truth is, the press is willing to cut Clinton some slack
because they like him and what he has to say." *Washington Monthly* editor
Charles Peters, who had once worked for John F. Kennedy, said: "The appeal of Clinton is similar to what went on with Kennedy, who was tremendously seductive. And the effect that had on the reporting and the
suppression of criticism helped us a lot in the Kennedy campaign."

Five years after Gary Hart was taken down—leading to the nomination of a weaker Democratic candidate and loss of the White House to
George Bush—the press was having second thoughts about how far it
should go in covering a public figure's private behavior. Two things made
Clinton's case different from Hart's, and both hinged on Hillary.

After decades of ideological politics in the Democratic Party, Clinton appeared to be a young and attractive candidate who could run a credible campaign at the head of the ticket. Clinton's appealing, articulate, and accomplished wife made the couple seem the very model of a socially advanced, baby-boomer power couple. Hillary's bona fides as a liberal activist were a subtle reassurance to the press that Clinton embodied the best of both worlds: A candidate who was moderate enough to get elected, but who had close ties to traditional liberal groups like the Children's Defense Fund. Hillary's presence at Clinton's side at the Sperling Breakfast was also a clear signal that she would support him in the face of allegations of womanizing. Had Bill appeared alone to discuss the subject, it would not have packed nearly the punch of the united front.

From the outset, the Clintons knew that damage control was going to be the single most important function of the campaign and that Hillary would therefore have to oversee it personally. What no one anticipated was the role the tabloid press would play in forcing the infidelity issue into public view. After the precedent-setting Gary Hart coverage in 1987, the genie was not going back in the bottle. The root of the scandal could be traced back to the 1990 governor's race in Arkansas, when a libel suit was filed against Clinton by former state employee Larry Nichols. Nichols claimed he was forced to resign from his job as marketing director at the Arkansas Development Finance Authority after being falsely accused of using state telephones to call Contra leaders in Nicaragua. He was really pushed out, he said, because he had gathered information on Clinton's purported use of state money to conduct his amorous affairs with Gennifer Flowers; with his press secretary, Susie Whitacre; as well as with newspaper columnist Deborah Mathis and two former beauty queens, Elizabeth Ward and Lencola Sullivan.

The Nichols lawsuit was ignored by the Arkansas press in 1990, but it had a long shelf life. Dozens of reporters came upon the legal papers when scouring public records in Arkansas, though only the weekly tabloid *Star* ran with a story. Clinton scoffed at the story as "old news" and noted that the *Star* had published stories saying, "Martians walk on earth and cows have human heads." Only the New York tabloids touched the story—"Wild Bill," said the *New York Post*, while the *Daily News* made the dread connection: "I'm No Gary Hart." (A month later, Nichols quietly dropped the suit and retracted the charges.)

The Flowers story was on everyone's lips, however, and Hillary was the first to address it directly, in a speech in New Hampshire two days after it broke. Evidently the Clinton campaign made a strategic decision that Hillary would take the lead in deflecting the womanizing stories, just as she had deflected rumors in Arkansas by invoking the "zone of privacy." "Is anything about our marriage as important to the people of New Hampshire as the question of whether they will be able to keep their own families together?" Hillary inquired. "That's an issue [faithfulness] that we are very comfortable with within our marriage. . . . We love each other. We support each other. . . . We've stood by each other through thick and thin." As Bill stayed mum, Hillary launched another strike in *Women's Wear Daily:* "We've had to deal with lots of dirt and negative advertising. We've learned our lesson about how you stand up, answer your critics and then just counterpunch as hard as you can."

When the media bypassed the Nichols story, the Clinton campaign breathed a sigh of relief. But the *Star* was only warming up. Before the story was published, John Hudges, a former aide to Clinton nemesis Sheffield Nelson, who had worked with Gennifer Flowers at a local television station, introduced a *Star* reporter to Flowers. Since she believed she would be named in the tabloid anyway, Flowers struck a deal reportedly worth $150,000 for an exclusive interview with the newspaper about her "decade-long affair" with Clinton, and turned over corroborating tapes of conversations with Bill dating back to 1990. This formed the basis for a second story, "My 12-year Affair with Bill Clinton: the Secret Love Tapes that Prove It."

The crucial question was whether the establishment media would consider the story newsworthy. Adding to their sense of fear and exasperation, the newer members of Clinton's entourage didn't know whether or not to believe it. The day the *Star* story broke, NBC alone among the networks mentioned it in passing in a profile of candidate Clinton. *The New York Times* noted it briefly in an Associated Press story buried deep inside the paper. The *Washington Post* led an inside piece with Clinton saying the story was "just not true."

In what would become a pattern with Clinton sex stories, the press covered the story indirectly: media critics and political reporters wrote about the controversy in their own newsrooms, mulling over whether allegations of infidelity were relevant to judging a candidate's fitness for public office. This allowed them to publicize the tabloid allegations through the tasteful prism of a journalism seminar. "I'm quite ashamed of my profession," *New York Times* editor Max Frankel said of the Flowers story. Ted Koppel's *Nightline* did a segment on whether or not the story should be covered, thus indirectly airing the charges to millions of viewers.

Since putative front-runner Mario Cuomo had announced in December 1991 that he would not run for president, it was all the more important for the liberal press to close ranks behind Clinton. The campaign season had already begun, and the Democrats had no better hope of winning the White House than Bill Clinton. In a reversal of his take on the Gary Hart–Donna Rice story, David Broder, in a *Washington Post* column headlined: "Odd Way to Choose a President," bemoaned the "ransacking of personal histories." Ellen Goodman of the *Boston Globe* changed her tune as well: "This may have the aura of a rerun, but it is not *Monkey Business* in 1988. It is private business in 1992 . . . in the vast debate over private lives, most Americans want to put the sex card back into the full deck."

Poll results in the wake of this episode clearly showed that the Flowers allegations raised serious questions in voters' minds about Clinton's character, undermining Goodman's claim and vindicating the news judgment of the *Star.* At the end of January 1992, the ABC/*Washington Post* poll found that 26 percent of respondents would not vote for a candidate who had committed adultery. Fifty-four percent said Clinton should withdraw from the race if it was shown that he had lied about the Flowers affair.

By week's end, the Clintons were in free fall, with everything they had worked for at risk. Even if Hillary had been able to deny or minimize such failings in the past, confronting his behavior was now unavoidable. It was also very public, and very humiliating. The proliferation of populist news outlets since 1988—from tabloid television to talk radio— meant that the power of even the establishment press to sit on or stifle the news would not be enough to quell the controversy.

The Clintons realized that the only way Bill could survive as a candidate was for Hillary to publicly declare her support. This conclusion was drawn from carefully parsed poll data showing that voters were much more likely to accept infidelity in a candidate's past if "the wife had been made aware of her husband's infidelity," as one *USA Today* poll put it. The *New York Times* paraphrased Clinton pollster Stan Greenberg's thinking at the time: "He said that as long as voters believe the candidate had not lied and that his marriage was 'real,' that they will not turn on him."

The Clintons would appear together to refute the allegations on CBS's

60 Minutes following the Super Bowl. In their campaign memoir, *All's Fair,* James Carville and Mary Matalin cite a memo by Carville prepping Clinton for the interview: "She [Hillary] is our ace in the hole. . . . She holds the ultimate trump card." In *Quest for the Presidency 1992, Newsweek's* book on the '92 campaign, Bruce Lindsey was quoted as saying the campaign would fold under the weight of the womanizing allegations only "when Hillary says it's too much."

The carefully calibrated *60 Minutes* script was designed to present a united marital front to the public, acknowledge past infidelity, and cut off further inquiry. But Clinton couldn't quite pull it off. He denied having had "a twelve-year affair" with Flowers, which seemed to leave open the possibility of a shorter one. Asked to categorically deny an affair, he answered artfully, "I've said that before and so has she." He generally acknowledged "wrongdoing" and "causing pain in my marriage," but his delivery was halting and uncertain. Correspondent Steve Kroft kept boring in for specifics: "You've said that your marriage has had problems. . . . What does that mean. . . . Does it mean adultery?"

Hillary sat silently beside Bill for much of the interview, her face taut as a drum, but she jumped in to rescue her husband when Kroft repeatedly tried to get Bill to admit directly to adultery. "There isn't a person watching this who would feel comfortable sitting on this couch detailing everything that ever went on in their life or their marriage," she said. "And I think it's real dangerous in this country if we don't have some zone of privacy for everybody. . . . We've gone further than anybody we know of and that's all we're going to say." She went on to declare forthrightly that if people weren't satisfied by what they were hearing, they didn't have to cast their ballots for the Clintons.

Kroft was left sputtering apologetically. "I couldn't agree with you more," the correspondent said. "And I think—and I agree with you that everyone wants to put this behind you." Kroft later told *Vanity Fair,* "She was in control. Hillary is tougher and more disciplined than Bill is."

"Hillary has always been willing to do what needed to be done, especially in the Flowers incident," said Rex Nelson. "He owes everything to Hillary. If she even hinted for a moment that something was wrong, he would have imploded." With her serene composure and steely determination to soldier on, Hillary held the campaign staff together as well. After the *60 Minutes* interview was taped, James Carville marveled at how Hillary and Yale Professor Robert Reich "ran a big policy-wonk discussion about job training, the state of worker skills, education, and income growth in America." After the session, she and Bill flew back to Little Rock to watch the broadcast with Chelsea.

Carville's anecdote in *All's Fair* suggests a view of Hillary as a cold and unfeeling political pro, who saw the *60 Minutes* interview as just another campaign detail, something to be endured for the sake of their political survival. Yet though the Flowers allegation (or something similar) was surely no surprise to Hillary, there is evidence that she privately found the revelations to be hurtful and embarrassing in the extreme. Her longtime friend Carolyn Huber, the office manager at the Rose Firm, has described a telephone conversation with Hillary at the time in which Hillary said, "It's hurting so bad, Carolyn." And she began carrying a small book of scripture with her when she traveled. Perhaps what the "policy-wonk" discussion suggested was an ability to rationalize or displace whatever personal pain she might be suffering, and the compromises she was making, for the greater good that she had always believed she and Bill could accomplish together.

Though it was the subject of endless fascination, no one in the campaign, not even the Clintons' closest friends, professed to fathom the true nature of their relationship. The signals were often conflicting. Press reports noted that the Clintons stopped sharing a joint "holding room" before Clinton went on stage to make speeches. A campaign memo advised the Clintons on how to look affectionate with one another. Yet during this same period, aides relied on Hillary to keep Bill's spirits up and advise him on how better to craft his speeches. The couple was seen on the campaign plane engaged in the sort of animated policy discussions that had always been an essential part of their connection. And there were glimpses of tender moments, too, when Bill seemed to be bucking up an exhausted or irritable wife with a considerate hug.

Though the Clinton staff considered the *60 Minutes* appearance a success, the mood shifted the next day when Flowers held a news conference in New York and played the incriminating tapes. On the tapes, Clinton shows a keen grasp of the difficulties reporters would face in getting stories into print about his personal life. He reassures himself, "[T]hey can't turn a story like this unless somebody said, 'Yeah, I did it with him.' " He instructs Flowers to deny that they ever talked about getting her a state job: "If they ever ask you if you've talked to me about it, you can say no." And he makes a self-pitying comparison of himself to Nebraska Senator Bob Kerrey: "[He's] got all the Gary Hart/Hollywood money and because he looks like a movie star, won the Medal of Honor and since he's single, nobody cares if he's screwing." (The Clinton campaign maintained that it had evidence that the tapes were doctored. The *Star* had them examined by Truth Verifications Laboratories, which concluded they had not been tampered with.)

Unfortunately for the Clintons, the *60 Minutes* interview had made the story legitimate news in the eyes of the establishment press. All three networks led with the Flowers press conference that night. Appearing on a previously scheduled CNN interview, which aired following the Flowers live press conference, Hillary froze when asked about the tapes.

By all accounts, she was furious. The tapes indicated among other things that the relationship with Flowers might have continued until as recently as 1991, well after the "come to Jesus" understanding of 1989. Hillary turned so ferociously on Bill's accusers that it struck some as displaced aggression.

Putting on her lawyer's cap, Hillary seized on the fact that shortly after the Little Rock station aired Flowers' name for the first time in 1990 in connection with the Larry Nichols suit, her attorney had contacted the station and threatened to sue for falsely naming her as a Clinton intimate. Flowers had also hurt her credibility by falsely claiming to have appeared as a guest on the television show *Hee Haw*. On the day of the Flowers press conference, Gail Sheehy of *Vanity Fair* was traveling with Hillary. Thinking out loud, Hillary told Sheehy, "If we'd been in front of a jury I'd say, 'Miss Flowers, isn't it true you were asked this by A.P. in June of 1990 and you said no? Weren't you asked by the Arkansas Democrat and you said no?' *I mean, I would crucify her.*"

Hillary had always seemed to interpret opposition to her causes and initiatives as little more than the despicable partisanship of an immoral enemy, be it Richard Nixon, Howard Phillips, Ronald Reagan, or the GOP in Arkansas. So she found it relatively easy now to make the issue the accusers and their motives—not without some justification, in this case by attributing the Flowers story to a Republican effort to derail everything she and Bill stood for in the campaign.

On the air with Sam Donaldson later in the week on *PrimeTime Live,* Hillary unveiled her new spin, calling the Flowers story "the daughter of

Willie Horton," instigated by the Republican National Committee, Larry Nichols, and Sheffield Nelson. She asserted, "Sheffield Nelson is a very bitter man because my husband beat him as he well should have, because he was a negative force in Arkansas politics. And he has now spent the last two years doing everything he can to try to get even and it's sort of a sad spectacle."

One could almost see Hillary's blood boil when Donaldson countered with the question of why, if there had been no affair, Bill had said to Flowers on the tapes, "Good-bye baby." Hillary replied: "I—I don't have any idea." She finally said, "Oh, that is not true. It just isn't true."

In the same interview, Hillary revealed to the public a personal side heretofore unseen. There was a certain pathos in the moment. When Donaldson asked her about her frame of mind when she decided against working for a "big city law firm" in order to move to Arkansas and marry Bill Clinton in 1975, Hillary explained: "I had to make a hard choice. But I also knew that I'd be real dishonest to myself if I didn't follow my heart and see where this relationship led, and take that leap of faith."

This was where that leap of faith had led: In late January 1992, Hillary stood alone before an audience of Washington glitterati and bore the public humiliation of a joke about Clinton's womanizing that she herself was in on. At a Democratic National Committee roast in Washington for party chairman Ron Brown, TV host Larry King began his monologue with, "It's ten o'clock, Hillary; where is Bill Clinton?" No doubt reluctantly bringing Chelsea into the fray as she had once before in a difficult Arkansas campaign, Hillary was teed up to respond, "Bill Clinton is with the other woman in his life, his daughter Chelsea." (The two were at a father-daughter dinner-dance at the Little Rock YWCA.)

She was also willing to undertake private missions to contain the political fallout. According to reporters Jack Germond and Jules Witcover in their book *Mad as Hell*, when Chicago Mayor Richard Daley expressed reservations about endorsing Clinton because of the Flowers story, Hillary offered to fly to Chicago and talk to Daley about it. "The proper and staunch Irish Catholic cringed from the notion of discussing such a subject with the man's wife," the reporters wrote.

Hillary had counseled against using womanizing allegations against John Paul Hammerschmidt in the 1974 campaign. Now, playing defense, she was willing to float an unsubstantiated rumor to *Vanity Fair* about an alleged affair between President Bush and a woman named Jennifer

Fitzgerald. True to her own code of political ethics, Hillary was counter-punching as hard as she could. The attack was not well received by the press, however, and she retracted the remark and apologized for it. Nevertheless, the Bush campaign had been put on notice that the Clintons were capable of fighting fire with fire.

As primary day in New Hampshire approached, Bill was angry and depressed about the focus on his personal character. After the Flowers story broke, ABC News had obtained a copy of a letter Clinton had written in December 1969 to Colonel Eugene J. Holmes, former head of the ROTC program at the University of Arkansas, who had helped Clinton get special treatment on draft deferments while he was a Rhodes Scholar. In the letter, which *Nightline* anchor Ted Koppel read out in its entirety on the evening broadcast, Clinton thanked Holmes for "saving me from the draft" and explained that he "opposed and despised" the war in Vietnam.

Faced with a serious image problem, Bill and Hillary turned to their friends Harry Thomason and Linda Bloodworth Thomason for help. Though known to the national media as a Hollywood figure, Thomason had roots in the same down-home soil as other Clinton cronies. Harry Thomason had grown up in the small town of Hampton, Arkansas, and was introduced to Bill in the early 1970s. He began his career making political commercials in his home state, made some low-budget films, and then started commuting from Little Rock to Hollywood, where his first major success in television was *The Fall Guy*, an action series starring Lee Majors. Linda, a Missouri native, was voted Miss Popularity in high school, attended the University of Missouri and then moved to California, where she soon tried her hand at writing for television in the mid-1970s. On a lark, she and a friend wrote a script for an episode of *M*A*S*H*, which won them an Emmy nomination.

Over the years, Harry had kept up with Bill, and the two couples became friends. When Roger Clinton needed a job after serving his drug sentence in 1985, the Thomasons hired him to work as a production assistant on their television show *Designing Women*. Hillary sat on the board of Claudia Company, a charity financed by Linda that sends Ozark women to college and counsels victims of domestic violence: Hillary also named the Thomasons' sitcom *Evening Shade* after a small Arkansas town.

It wasn't the first time the Thomasons were asked to help. In 1988, after Clinton delivered a disastrously ineffective nominating speech for Michael Dukakis at the Democratic National Convention, he was considered politically dead. Shortly thereafter, Linda had arranged for Clinton to appear on the *Tonight Show* with Johnny Carson, where he was an instant hit. Again, during the '92 campaign, Linda came up with the idea of showing off Clinton's talents in television venues like the *Arsenio Hall Show,* where Bill played the saxophone.

By the time the Thomasons were consulted in early February, Hillary's performance on *60 Minutes* had made her a star overnight and seemed to secure for her a more prominent position in the campaign. Though the circumstances were far from ideal, the crucial role she had played behind the scenes for so long in Bill's political career in Arkansas—the nature of the co-candidacy—was finally being openly recognized. Both Clintons felt free to acknowledge not only the extent of Bill's reliance on her but also her expectations of sharing power with him if elected. The power-couple idea, rejected by the voters of Arkansas a decade before, now became a critical part of the Clintons' glamour in elite circles. The appeal was not so much ideological or substantive as generational and stylistic. With their youth and energy, Bill and Hillary together held the promise of a new Camelot.

For New Hampshire, the Hollywood producers devised a thirty-minute paid spot in which the Clintons appeared together before a panel of ten undecided voters and answered questions on a broad range of subjects. The Thomasons knew it was the kind of intimate forum where Bill could be counted on to connect personally with the panelists as he flawlessly improvised his answers. Clinton's skill in the forum recalled his early days on the campaign trail in Arkansas, when the Cult of Bill was first taking root. The seductive skills that Hillary had spotted at Yale were on full display as Clinton seemed to convert each voter one by one.

Meeting Jerry Brown in a debate before the Illinois primary several weeks later, Clinton was the Democratic front-runner. Clinton won the primary, cinching the nomination. That night, taking the podium in her native Chicago, Hillary basked in a moment that was as much hers as Bill's. Carrying the event live, NBC's Tom Brokaw observed incredulously, "Not just an introduction, this is a speech by Mrs. Clinton." Speaking plainly in the plural voice of the co-candidacy, Hillary told the cheering throng: "We believe passionately in this country and we cannot stand by for one more year and watch what is happening to it!" Finally, she introduced Bill, whom she referred to as "the messenger," inadvertently revealing their respective roles in the political partnership. Bill is the messenger; Hillary is the author of the message.

Throughout the spring, the press saluted Hillary as a strong woman and equal partner. *Time* ran a piece entitled "Partner as Much as Wife." *Newsweek*'s Eleanor Clift enthused: "She represents a new generation of political wives; she's an accomplished professional with perhaps as much claim as her husband to a place in public life." The *Houston Chronicle* weighed in with "Hillary Clinton's Composure Carries Campaign Through Fire," and the *Chicago Tribune* echoed Susan Thomases' prophecy: "Hillary Clinton may be the candidate's top asset."

A *Time*/CNN poll asked respondents if Hillary "has what it takes to be President of the United States?" Bill began fielding questions about the possibility of appointing Hillary to a cabinet post. "I wouldn't rule it out," and, "She's the best I could find," he replied. Warming to the theme, he began answering questions about policy with the phrase, "Hillary and I...." Noting the role she had played as Arkansas' first lady, he announced that he would ask Hillary to study and recommend "solutions to problems" in such areas as education, health, and child care. Hillary wouldn't be quite "co-president" because "we have our differences of opinion and in the end, I have to decide," Clinton said.

In this series of comments, the Clintons were being admirably forthright about the nature of the co-candidacy. "If I get elected president," Clinton said in another speech, "it will be an unprecedented partnership, far more than Franklin Roosevelt and Eleanor. They were two great people, but on different tracks. If I get elected, we'll do things together." Clinton told the *New York Times* in 1992: "I'm not sure people aren't right when they say she is the one who ought to be running.... You can watch me watch her speak sometimes, and I've got the Nancy Reagan adoring look." Most famously, Bill announced a new campaign slogan: "Two for one" and "Buy one, get one free." Hillary quickly seconded the idea, commenting with a laugh, "If you vote for my husband, you get me. It's a two-for-one, blue-plate special."

The Clintons obviously thought the co-candidacy was a selling point, and with some segments of the populace it was. While she had never been wildly popular with the voters in Arkansas, Hillary was attracting a following on the national stage as a role model to a generation of women who were also balancing the demands of careers, modern marriages, and child rearing. To her fans, Hillary was an emblem of fundamental changes in male–female relationships that were natural, necessary, and good. On the campaign trail, crowds greeted her with signs declaring: "Hillary for First Lady"; "Hillary, Mrs. President"; "Elect Hillary"; "We Love You, Hillary."

In a series of speeches to friendly audiences, Hillary laid out her views on social policy and assured the faithful that she would be the guiding spirit of her husband's administration. Speaking to a group of Democratic women in New York, she said, "There are specific policies I want to work on. Everything from providing prenatal care to a family-leave act to sensible health-care policy. . . . I've got a whole big agenda that I think every woman in America needs to have, because we all need to be in this together."

Hillary recalled her Methodist roots in a speech at a Wisconsin church. Over a chorus of "amens," Hillary said, "This is not a campaign about my husband. It is not about me. It is not about any individual. We can no longer ignore what goes on around us. What we have to agree among ourselves is that we have to solve our problems." She also returned to Wellesley College, assuring the crowd in response to a question about why she wasn't running for president herself that she and Bill were "a team." She then spoke about her policy agenda: "It's time for us to call ourselves to a new type of politics. The solutions of the past are not adequate. . . . As good as our politics are and as strong as our economy is, we have to make some changes. . . . Every child born in this country deserves a chance to be born healthy, to be given good care, to attend a school that will give him or her the maximum opportunities to do that."

Appearing before an audience at the National Women's Political Caucus, where Betsey Wright had once worked as an organizer two decades before, Hillary exclaimed: "We're not going to be sucker punched as long as we make it clear we're not going to take it anymore!"

Hillary soon became what *U.S. News* called "a national Rorschach test" for views not only on the proper role of first ladies but of women in American society. "Hillary Clinton represents something at once extremely terrifying and extremely welcome, depending on which part of the 'American people' you happen to represent," wrote feminist Naomi Wolf. "She is the embodiment of the feminist future: a woman who combines feminist values with worldly power, in the form of her own sterling professional credentials, and with her influence on her husband. To working women and women struggling to combine family and professional identities, this is an inspiring role model and a vision of a union between gender idealism and real power, but to those anti-feminists who see in the triumph of feminism a doubling of competition in the workplace and doubling of male responsibility at home, she represents a waking nightmare."

Indeed, Hillary would soon find history repeating itself. Just as the Arkansas electorate had reacted negatively to her decision to keep her own name and pursue a career independent of Bill's, a sizeable segment of the public simply wasn't ready to accept a feminist first lady in a two-for-one political partnership with her husband.

Throughout the late winter and early spring Hillary's public ratings began to slip in inverse proportion to the accolades being heaped on her by the elite media and women's movement supporters. When an April Gallup Poll asked whether voters approved of Hillary taking a "major position" in the Clinton administration, 67 percent said no. But their concern seemed to go deeper than simply what role Hillary would play. More people rated Hillary unfavorably in the Gallup Poll than favorably. In a *Time*/CNN poll, among those who said their presidential vote would be affected by their views of Hillary Clinton, almost twice as many voters said they would vote against Clinton as for him based upon their opinion of Hillary.

The partnership struck many, unaware of the successful history of the Arkansas co-candidacy, as a peculiar and unprecedented symbiosis that was incomprehensible on the terms it was being offered. Nothing like a co-presidency had ever emerged on the national political scene before. There was also the contradiction of an articulate, outspoken liberal wife in an equal partnership with a candidate who was running on an avowedly centrist platform. Many others, of course, were simply threatened and offended by the sudden prominence of an assertive and strong-minded woman.

In the latter category fell Hillary's old nemesis Richard Nixon. Commenting on the Clintons' appearance as "co-candidates," Nixon said a strong wife could make a husband "look like a wimp." Hillary, Nixon continued, "pounds the piano so hard that Bill can't be heard." But the problem was not, as Nixon formulated it, that Hillary made Bill look weak; the real problem was that Bill was weak to begin with. The Eleanor-and-Franklin analogy would never suffice in the case of the Clintons because unlike Bill, FDR was a leader in his own right. One could imagine him as president without Eleanor. The same could never be said of Bill. "Two-for-one" wasn't just an offhand phrase: It was the reality of the Clintons' political partnership. Paired with a man like Bill, any strong, ambitious woman would inevitably appear to some to be grotesquely masculinized and power-mad.

Other objections to Hillary's high profile were based on more legitimate concerns. Historically in our democracy, there has been public suspicion of derived or imputed power, reflected in the passage of stringent anti-nepotism laws. Because no one had ever questioned the role Hillary played in heading up the education reform effort in Arkansas, the Clintons had underestimated this deep-seated public sentiment. In mid-March, former Nixon speechwriter William Safire published a *New York Times* column on "the Hillary problem." As one of six proposed "solutions," Safire advised: "Get more specific about what role Hillary would play in your administration. A pre-appointment would be presumptuous, but voters should know beforehand what sort of First Ladyship is in store."

Another reason Hillary's approval ratings were dropping had to do with lingering doubts about the manner in which she had first been introduced to the American public on the *60 Minutes* interview, where she was seen "spinning" her own marriage. For every viewer who was impressed and reassured by what they saw as Hillary's firm, even courageous, performance on *60 Minutes,* there was another who saw Hillary's decision to defend Bill's foibles and character flaws as a part of a Faustian bargain. In this view, the moral authority of the "two-for-one" concept as a trail-blazing stand on behalf of peer marriage was undermined by the suspicion that Clinton had been forced to accept the power-sharing arrangement in return for Hillary's agreement to stand by him. "She's only interested in being with a winner," a seventy-one-year-old retired housewife, Bernadine Elliott, told the *New York Times.* "And believe me, if he doesn't get elected, she's going to dump him. Mark my words."

As the spring of 1992 wore on, Hillary didn't help her standing in the polls with two unfortunate comments. Already on *60 Minutes,* she had made a sarcastic remark about the role she appeared to be playing for the cameras. "You know, I'm not sitting here as some little woman standing by my man like Tammy Wynette." After a storm of outraged protest on radio talk shows across the country, Hillary apologized to Wynette and her country music fans for the comment.

In late March at a campaign stop at Chicago's Busy Bee restaurant, Hillary was asked about charges Jerry Brown had made about her legal work on behalf of Jim McDougal's S&L. In a debate with Clinton the night before, Brown made the doubtful claim that Bill had "funneled money to his wife's firm," missing the more subtle question of whether Hillary had done anything to help Clinton friends and contributors for political rather than financial gain. When a questioner asked Brown about his father Pat Brown's law firm having done work for the state of California while Jerry Brown was governor, Brown answered with the defensive jibe: "Well, I don't control my father."

Clinton rose to the occasion just as he had in Arkansas in the row with Frank White in 1986, when he bested the Republican with a defense of his wife while simultaneously underscoring that it was her ethics, after all, that were in question. His chin jutting out indignantly, Clinton said, "Jerry comes in here with his family wealth and his $1,500 suit and makes a lying accusation about my wife. I never funneled any money to my wife's firm—never. You ought to be ashamed of yourself for jumping on my wife. You're not worth being on the same platform with my wife." Aides said they had never seen Clinton as energized as he was in this moment of faux chivalry.

Incensed that her ethics were being questioned and perhaps offended by Brown's implicit sexism, Hillary told reporters the next day, "My firm had done work for the bank, that's right, and I have done work for the bank not related to the state at all. All right?" She said, "I suppose I could have stayed home, baked cookies and had teas, but what I decided was to fulfill my profession, which I entered before my husband was in public life." Hillary further explained, "My gosh, you can't be a lawyer if you don't represent banks."

This appears to be the first time that Hillary had made an untrue statement on the public record; she had in fact represented Madison before the state. Now that she was under fire in a presidential primary, and with her life's work at stake, the truth would have opened the door to a host of questions about the Clintons' history that she wanted to avoid at all costs. (Bill, by contrast, had had a reputation for prevaricating for years in Arkansas, where the saying was that Clinton would rather climb a tree to tell a lie than stay on the ground and tell the truth.)

The cookie-baking remark reflected Hillary's understandable frustration with those who were stubbornly unprepared to accept a first lady who had been involved in law and business, with all of the questions, complications, and sometimes unattractive public perceptions that often characterize that line of work. The sarcasm in the response, however, only confirmed the irritation of some who believed that remarks like these exemplified the stigmatization of traditional sex roles by the elite culture of liberal professionals that Hillary represented.

In her involvement with groups like the Children's Defense Fund, the ABA, and Renaissance Weekend, Hillary's circle of associates had been strictly limited to people like herself; they were an inadequate proving ground for gauging the political and social fault lines of the national electorate. She appeared to have learned nothing from her experience in the late 1970s in Arkansas when the voters rejected Hillary Rodham. Thus when the inevitable backlash against her public image as a feminist occurred, she found that she was still out of touch with the sentiments of many average Americans. This may explain why she was unable to accept the reasonable aspects of the criticism and seemed incapable of responding to it gracefully.

Hillary's class conscious gaffes—revealing her, as some now saw it, as a liberal snob who couldn't be trusted—meant that a major retrenchment was called for. Realizing her image was hurting the campaign, Hillary underwent a thorough repackaging, reminiscent of that critical juncture in Arkansas politics in 1982 when she dropped the name "Rodham," drastically altered her physical appearance, and campaigned as a traditional wife and mother. As she had pandered earlier to the prejudices of the Arkansas electorate, she would once again retreat behind an "image," accept the advice of pollsters and political handlers, and revert to a traditional, even retrograde, model of a political wife.

The scripting of Hillary Clinton for a national audience was perhaps the final stage in her political seduction. In late April, campaign strategist James Carville and pollster Stanley Greenberg, who pushed Clinton to emphasize populist bread-and-butter issues with appeal to working-class Americans, composed a General Election Project memo, obtained by the *New York Times* after the November election, which interpreted poll and focus group concerns about Hillary. In the focus groups, people regarded her as " 'being in the race for herself,' and as 'going for the power,' and as a wife intent on 'running the show,' " the memo stated. Ironically for someone who had devoted so much time to children's causes, the *Times* reported, "the perception of her as unaffectionate and preoccupied with power and career 'allows George Bush (and probably Perot) to build up extraordinary advantages on family values.' "

The memo outlined ways to combat this impression, including Hillary appearing more traditional and feminine, "affectionate and maternal." According to the *Times*, "On a more intimate level, it included ideas for making the Clintons seem more warm and cuddly, like 'events where Bill and Hillary can go on dates with the American people.' Examples included arranging an event where 'Bill and Chelsea surprise Hillary on Mother's Day,' or 'joint appearances with her friends where Hillary can laugh, do her mimicry.' "

But first came a physical makeover: Around the time of the California primary in June, Linda Bloodworth Thomason and the actress Mary Steenburgen looked on while Christophe, the famed Beverly Hills hairdresser, lightened Hillary's hair. They also consulted with Cliff Chally, who did the clothes for *Designing Women,* for a more feminine wardrobe to replace Hillary's frumpy knit power suits.

Hillary also tried to reverse the perception that she would play a too-powerful role in a Clinton administration. At a speech at La Salle University in Pennsylvania she spoke of "being a full-time advocate for children's issues in the White House," and added that "the most important thing in my life right now is my daughter Chelsea." A week later in Washington, she said, "Work in the home is very important." Gone were the pronouns "we" and references to "Bill and I." There were no more hints that she might serve in the cabinet. Her husband, she assured voters, "has a real core of toughness"—perhaps the biggest whopper of the campaign.

In an interview with David Frost, she deftly downplayed Bill's earlier comments comparing them to Eleanor and Franklin as "very nice hyperbole." At Wellesley's commencement in June, she seemed to take a different tack than she had adopted on the campus earlier in the year, saying, "You may choose to be a corporate executive or a rocket scientist or you may stay home and raise your children. You can make any or all of these choices and they can be the work of your life." You can care for children, Hillary said, "by making policy or making cookies." She demonstrated that she could use a sewing machine at an International Ladies Garment Workers Union Convention. The same woman who had talked about her "big agenda" only a few weeks before was now "standing up for headbands in this campaign."

During the Democratic Convention in New York in July, an article on Hillary appeared in the *New York Times* Living Section, and included a cookie recipe that would later beat out Barbara Bush's in a *Family Circle* magazine bake-off contest. "My friends say my recipe is more Democratic because I use vegetable shortening instead of butter," she said with a straight face. "I am an old-fashioned patriot. I cry at the Fourth of July when kids put crepe paper on their bicycle wheels, so this is, like, just incredible—it's so extraordinary to me." The piece was accompanied by a photo of Hillary and Tipper Gore having tea and cookies at the Waldorf. At the convention, Hillary distributed thousands of cookies at various state conventions throughout the week and asked delegates to vote for her cookies in the *Family Circle* contest.

Hillary's abrupt turnaround did not escape notice in the press. "Hillary Clinton's campaign to get her husband of sixteen years elected has taken an unacknowledged mid-course change in emphasis, to put forward the kinder, gentler Hillary Clinton, to round off some of the sharper edges, to convince voters that she is not an ambitious, hectoring manipulator but one more working mom juggling through hectic days— a new American traditionalist, as down-home likable as she is intellectually admirable," wrote Patt Morrison in the *Los Angeles Times*. The *New York Times* noted Hillary's retreat from the outspoken campaigner she had been just weeks before: "[A]lthough Mrs. Clinton was originally seen as a formidable campaigner and hailed as a model new woman, able to balance her family life with a thriving law practice, by early summer she had retreated to the sidelines, appearing publicly only as a quiet presence at her husband's side."

Just as there had been a backlash against Hillary's authentic persona among conservative voters, there was now a backlash against the remade Hillary among her erstwhile feminist supporters. They had liked the real Hillary, as she appeared in the opening months of the campaign, and had high hopes for her as a path-breaking pioneer. Now, they felt sold out by Hillary's pandering to the right, as had many Arkansas liberals during her retooling of Bill's image in 1982. "Let Hillary Be Hillary," a dejected *New York Times* editorialist implored. Eleanor Clift wrote in *Newsweek:* "Today's Hillary is a burned-out buttoned-up automaton compared with the vibrant woman who strode purposefully onto the national scene last January. . . . You have the idea she's holding back."

To be sure, there was something about Hillary's over-the-top performance that rankled. Her traditionalist posturing seemed to shade into parody, leading some to wonder if she was really expressing contempt for the political process and even undermining feminist gains. But in fact, Hillary was behaving precisely like a modern politician. In an era of poll-driven politics, most politicians at Hillary's level go through such image-burnishing to win elections.

The implication of the *Times* editiorial—that Hillary was compelled to change her image by Clinton's political handlers—was clearly wrong. Hillary knew what she had to do to win. The problem for Hillary was that she was never viewed as just another politician. She was a symbol, even an icon, and as such she was expected to remain untarnished by the crass calculations and gimmickry that typically characterize American politics. Was the trademark plaid shirt of Republican presidential contender Lamar Alexander any different from Hillary's headband? What critics mistakenly interpreted as insincerity on her part was merely a political tactic. Instead of condemning her, Hillary's supporters might have applauded her ability to play the game so well.

Certainly, was hard to argue with success: The makeover sent Hillary's approval ratings through the roof and got her husband through the November election. Only later, after she abandoned the traditional model in the health care effort and her credibility was at stake in the Whitewater affair, did the patently phony image making, combined with the impression of deceit that some had already drawn from the *60 Minutes* performance, take its toll.

There was one final consequence of Hillary's verbal miscues and the confusion surrounding her abrupt image reversals: she was left vulnerable to being defined and demonized by the right. As *Chicago Tribune* columnist Mike Royko put it, "[T]he Republicans have found their new Willie Horton . . . [in Hillary Clinton]. I've heard right-wingers describe her as a Nazi, a pinko, a baby-snatcher, and a vicious, ambitious grasping man-hater."

Rather than intelligently setting forth their disagreements with Hillary's philosophy, the Republicans used crude caricatures of her actual views to frighten the electorate and play to its latent chauvinism. As the GOP convention opened in August, Republican National Committee chairman Rich Bond said, "Now, of course, advising Bill Clinton on every move is that champion of the family Hillary Clinton, who believes that kids should be able to sue their parents rather than helping them with the chores as they were asked to do. She has likened marriage and the family to slavery. She has referred to the family as a dependency relationship that deprives people of their rights."

"Elect me and you get two for the price of one, Mr. Clinton says of his lawyer-spouse," Pat Buchanan declared that evening. "And what does Hillary believe? Well, Hillary believes that twelve-year-olds should have the right to sue their parents, and Hillary has compared marriage and the family as institutions to slavery and life on an Indian reservation. Well, speak for yourself, Hillary! This, my friends, is radical feminism."

"Most women do not wish to be liberated from their essential natures as women," said Marilyn Quayle, the wife of the vice-presidential nominee, in her convention speech. Conservative activist Phyllis Schlafly listed two reasons to re-elect Bush: "One, if they don't like abortion, and two, if they don't like Hillary." Outside the convention hall, the Committee for Decent Family Values held a rally to "stomp out" Hillary. Even the reserved Barbara Bush piled on, saying the attacks were legitimate "if it's a self-proclaimed co-president."

The charge that Hillary was "anti-family" was a gross oversimplification. Hillary had never suggested that women wanted to be "liberated from their essential natures," nor did she want to give children the right to sue their parents over household chores. Her reference to marriage and slavery was a historically accurate comparison. Several classes of Americans, including slaves and women, were once "thought to be incapable of and undeserving of the right to care for themselves or make decisions on their own behalf," she had written.

Along with Marian Wright Edelman and others on the Christian left, Hillary believed that traditional moral values should be strengthened, not weakened. She differed with conservatives in that she sought to achieve her goals by enhancing the power of the state in child welfare and creating new "rights."

To anyone who knew Hillary, the anti-family charge was especially offensive. Even her sternest critics would have to concede that Hillary possesses an authentic commitment to children, demonstrated in her devoted mothering of Chelsea. As a lawyer at the Rose Firm, she often drove home in the middle of the day to take Chelsea to dance class, and during the presidential campaign, she was known to help Chelsea with her homework by fax. Campaign aides said that even on her most trying days, Hillary found time to ask them about their children, and she rarely passed a child on the campaign trail without stopping to say a few words to him or her.

In the end, the attacks could be read as a tribute to Hillary's role as the real ideological force to be reckoned with in the Clinton camp. The opposition correctly recognized her not only as a potential political liability for Bill but also as a real threat to conservatism.

While the campaign proceeded on one level before the public, there was also a vigorous shadow campaign overseen by Hillary. Having saved Bill publicly on *60 Minutes,* she was also fighting behind the scenes to keep the press from exposing the unseemly aspects of life back in Dogpatch with her husband.

The shadow campaign apparatus involved Hillary's lawyer friends— Susan Thomases, Harold Ickes, Vince Foster, and Webb Hubbell—as well as Betsey Wright and Hillary's best friend Diane Blair, who was assigned to combat womanizing stories as Wright's deputy in "the bunker," an office in a building adjacent to the campaign's main headquarters in downtown Little Rock. Bruce Lindsey, the loyal valet at Bill's side, performed a similar function. In this respect, anyway, the Clintons were indeed a second coming of Camelot: Not since the Kennedys had there been so many retainers on hand whose primary function appeared to be to keep a lid on all manner of personal scandals.

Hillary's own vulnerability arose only over the questionable tasks she undertook connected to the netherworld of Arkansas politics—seeking Beverly Bassett's approval for the Madison stock plan and the Castle Grande legal work. The McDougals, Jim Guy Tucker, and David Hale were all Bill's cronies, not Hillary's. She had met Bill's friend Dan Lasater exactly twice. The effort to turn out the black vote, fund raising, and patronage fell within Bill's domain, not Hillary's. She knew little of Clinton's ties to Tyson or other Arkoromans (with the exception of the commodities trading profits). It was Bill's womanizing that had turned their personal life into tabloid fodder.

But since theirs was a co-candidacy, all of Bill's sins were now Hillary's. At this point, it was impossible to separate the Clintons: she had as much of a stake in keeping things quiet as Bill did. "You can't imagine the number of dastardly deeds and undeeds that were conveyed to me on a daily basis," Betsey Wright would later say in congressional testimony. That many of the allegations streaming into Wright's bunker might be false didn't really matter; given Bill's personal history and character, Hillary and her team had to treat them all as potentially true.

After leaving her post as head of the Democratic Party in Arkansas, where she was under fire for failing to raise adequate funds, Wright become a guest lecturer at Harvard. On the night of his announcement for the presidency in October 1991, Clinton asked one of his trusted associates to contact Wright and ask her to join the campaign, but Wright refused. After the Flowers revelations, campaign chief of staff Eli Segal was dispatched to Boston, where he met with Wright and brokered a deal for her return to the Clinton fold. Wright's condition was direct access to the Clintons: she did not wish to report to the "white boys" around Clinton—James Carville, Paul Begala, and Stan Greenberg.

Sometimes known as "Major Betsey," Wright had a campaign style described in a *Time* profile as "abrasive and includ[ing] dervish-like activity, crying jags, yelling fits, and chain smoking." Running what she called, with an Orwellian flourish, a "truth squad," Wright monitored the comings and goings of reporters covering the campaign. As Rex Nelson recalled, "Betsey had graphs and charts during the campaign of where so-and-so had dinner and with whom, and she would track down the reporters and call them in their rooms—when they didn't even tell her they were here—and she'd say, 'I know you spoke to so-and-so, let me give you our side of that.' Women were called and told they'd make them look like whores if they came forward."

In a *Washington Post* article published in July 1992, Wright revealed that nineteen allegations from women who said they had affairs with Clinton surfaced in the few weeks following the convention, in addition to seven allegations previously known to the campaign. Referring to the allegations collectively as "bimbo eruptions," Wright claimed that cash offers from the tabloid press were responsible for fomenting the charges. "Since the convention, the gold-digger growth is enormous. There is a whole industry being spawned," Wright said. "The real heroes are the women— some of them low-income people—who have been offered six figures to lie and have said no . . . this is Scud missile on American politics."[2]

How vigorously the establishment press pursued the womanizing stories is not clear, but Wright wasn't one to take chances. As described in the *Washington Post,* Wright's operation sought to identify potential accusers in advance, collect information to discredit them, and then present the accusers with the information to intimidate them into staying quiet. Though some of the women Clinton had been involved with were Little Rock professionals—women who were often married with children and had no incentive to disrupt their lives by going public—many others were a good deal less established and had less to lose by talking. Yet these same women often had experiences in their past ranging from messy divorces to out-of-wedlock births, abortions, and even criminal records. This information was given to the press to induce reporters to spike their own stories. Even if they believed that the women were telling the truth, when confronted with derogatory information on the accusers, reporters would not get out front on a story for fear that their sources might be discredited. The cycle was difficult to break: Any woman who had slept with Bill and was willing to talk about it publicly was likely to be self-discrediting.

A $200-an-hour San Francisco attorney and private investigator named Jack Palladino, who was in business with his wife Sandra Sutherland, solicited this damaging material on potential accusers for Wright. Paid about $100,000 for his services to the Clinton campaign, Palladino was initially hired through the Denver law firm of James Lyons, who would soon do an internal investigation for the Clinton campaign on Whitewater that was used to throw the press off the trail. The use of a private investigator to do surveillance on—and attempt to intimidate—potential witnesses was an unprecedented scandal potentially far darker than the story of the ill-starred Whitewater investment. Yet with the sole exception of the *Washington Post* story in July, not one of the campaign reporters chose to write about the practice, even though many were quite familiar with it.

Operating out of a mansion in the city's bohemian Haight-Ashbury district, Palladino was one of an elite cadre of highly educated San Francisco spies who had apprenticed with the legendary Hal Lipset, a crusading liberal who made a name for himself in the 1950s doing trial investigations for the city's top criminal lawyers. When Palladino first got into the business in the 1960s, Lipset was the private investigator of choice for the radical movement. "[T]he cases they worked on became landmarks: the defense of Huey Newton, Angela Davis, Eldridge Cleaver, Bobby Seale, the Soledad Brothers, and Los Siete de la Raza. Even the Hell's Angels, when they needed detectives to help them beat drug charges, turned to the 'people's detectives,' " according to an article in

California Lawyer. "To their surprise, these scholarly iconoclasts found that private investigations could be an honorable alternative to academic or leftist journalism." Palladino and his wife and business partner Sandra Sutherland, an SDS organizer in the 1960s, were part of the same circle with which Hillary Rodham had been associated in the early 1970s. Lipset and Palladino were working for Black Panthers lawyer Charles Garry when Hillary went out to San Francisco to work as an intern for the law firm of Garry's associate, Robert Treuhaft. Garry had lived on the Yale campus while defending a cause that Hillary avidly supported as a Yale law student.[3]

In later years, Palladino, now donning open-necked silk shirts and gold chains, represented several clients who prepared him well for his work on the Clinton campaign: John DeLorean in his drug trial; S&L kingpin Charles Keating, Jr.; and a San Francisco developer accused of having sex with underage prostitutes. According to *California Lawyer,* Palladino's team of investigators descended on San Francisco's red-light district and befriended child prostitutes who were accusing the developer, and gathered damaging information on the minors in order to discredit them. "I needed somebody to go down and talk to the women who were the accusers," the developer's attorney, who hired Palladino, told the magazine. "They were the kind of witnesses that if you talked to them long enough, they'd give four or five different accounts of what happened. It was important to gain their confidence, and Jack's operatives did that."

Since her days of supporting the Black Panthers and opposing Richard Nixon, Hillary had been an advocate of take-no-prisoners tactics. Though it is not clear how much detail she knew about the operation, the hiring of Palladino suggested that with the White House in her sights, Hillary was willing to countenance intimidation of women to cover up Bill's peccadilloes. (Hillary, in fact, named the campaign's nerve center the "war room," according to Matalin and Carville's *All's Fair*).

Two lawyers close to Hillary, Thomases and Bernard Nussbaum, appear to have been at least peripherally involved in controlling the womanizing stories. One Clinton campaign aide told *Vanity Fair,* "Susan was the one Hillary cried with, debated divorce with. I also have a feeling that at some point, when one of these bimbettes threatened to come out and expose him for what he was, Hillary dispatched Susan as an out-of-town mean lawyer to threaten to ruin her life if she even thought about going

public." Hillary summoned Nussbaum to Little Rock to give legal advice
to Wright in connection with her damage control operation, according
to James Stewart's *Blood Sport*.

One case reported by the *Post* in 1992 involved Sally Miller Perdue, a
former Miss Arkansas, who claimed to have had an affair with Clinton in
1983. "Earlier this month," the *Post* reported,

> Palladino and his wife and partner, Sandra Sutherland, began calling
> former associates and estranged relatives of the woman seeking damag-
> ing comments about her credibility. One estranged relative, who dis-
> puted Perdue's story and made disparaging remarks about her
> character, said that Palladino "asked me if I would be willing to comment
> about Perdue to any reporters." The relative agreed, on a case-by-case
> basis, and since then the Clinton campaign has passed out his name as
> well as those of others to journalists making inquiries [about Perdue]'s
> allegations. The approach appears to have worked. Although Perdue
> later told her story to the nationally syndicated show hosted by Sally Jessy
> Raphael, no major news organization has reported the account.

Palladino sometimes used more intimidating tactics. Daniel Wattenberg reported in the *American Spectator* that Loren Kirk, a one-time roommate of Gennifer Flowers, who backed up part of Flowers's story publicly
in 1992, was personally visited by Palladino, who asked menacingly, "Do
you think Gennifer is the sort of person who would commit suicide?"
(Palladino declined to confirm or deny the story.)

By early fall, Wright and Palladino were not only tracking "bimbo
eruptions" but fighting a clandestine battle with Republican operatives
who were scouring every corner of the state in search of the silver bullet
that would stop Clinton's candidacy cold. The Bush campaign had little
interest in the kind of opposition research needed to unearth such allegations, but Arkansas Republican Sheffield Nelson, Clinton's Republican challenger for governor in 1990, was more than happy to spend his
own money in pursuing his vendetta against Clinton. Nelson hired his
own private investigators and began feeding leads to the press.

Nelson and his investigators spent a good deal of time in a comically
futile effort to substantiate rumors that Clinton had fathered an illegitimate child by a black prostitute. The story first started circulating shortly
after the Flowers revelations, when a local black activist, Robert "Say"
McIntosh, distributed leaflets from the back of his sweet potato pie truck-
restaurants showing photographs of a mulatto child named Danny

Williams. McIntosh claimed the boy was the son of Clinton and Bobbie Ann Williams, a Little Rock prostitute. "Bill Clinton has been with enough black women to cast a *Tarzan* movie. And he's got a little black son out there living in poverty," one leaflet said. In February 1992, Williams's sister sold the story to the supermarket tabloid the *Globe,* stoking the rumor mill to such an extent that, according to the Jack Germond and Jules Witcover campaign book, at a closed-door meeting of prominent Democrats in Chicago, Clinton was forced to exclaim: "Listen, I don't have a black baby."

Such mud-slinging must have only further determined Hillary's thinking about the dastardly nature of the opposition, the press, and perhaps the political process itself. "Rumors are a dime a dozen. I could stand out here and start ten of my own," she said in response to the black baby story. "They are titillating, but the fact that they get into the mainstream media just amazes me. Who would have thought something said by Say McIntosh would be taken seriously by anyone? It's pathetic. The press has spent more time following what Say McIntosh says than concentrating on the real issues."

McIntosh had put the story in circulation, but it was up to one of Nelson's investigators to eventually track down Bobbie Ann Williams. In September, as the presidential campaign heated up, the investigator said he took Williams to Dallas, where an affidavit was taped in which Williams claimed to have given birth to Clinton's child. Not surprisingly, when a polygraph was administered, Williams, an admitted prostitute and drug abuser, could not pass it and Nelson's investigator dropped the story.

Though the story came from a thoroughly discreditable source, it did illustrate a truth about the kind of sleazy tactics the Clintons were up against in the 1992 campaign and the mindset it must have engendered in those, none more so than Hillary, who were trying to fight back.

Alone among commentators, the liberal historian Garry Wills explained this phenomenon in two perceptive essays early in 1996, one in January in the *Washington Post* and another in April in the *New York Review of Books.* While Wills had written during the 1992 campaign that "Bill Clinton is not Gary Hart," he now conceded that Clinton is "presumably a philanderer." Wills argued that even if the sex stories themselves were not relevant to judging Clinton's fitness for office, living for years with Clinton's infidelity was the key to understanding much of Hillary's behavior. Thus the tabloid press had been onto something significant after all in its coverage of Bill's personal indiscretions.[4]

Reprising the argument that Bill's propensity to hide the truth might be the consequence of growing up in an alcoholic's home, Wills wrote in the *Washington Post:* "President Clinton's wife has no alcoholism in her background to explain a similar touchiness about the whole truth. But her book [*It Takes A Village*] shows a concern that is perhaps analogous to the alcoholic's secret. She has lived for a long time with the philanderer's secret. . . ." Apologizing for and covering up Clinton's womanizing all those years, Wills suggested, had instilled in Hillary a deep suspicion of the press and contempt for the democratic process itself.

"Given a spontaneous and imprudent husband, she seems to have leaned in the opposite direction, toward control, toward the suppression of spontaneity," Wills wrote in the *New York Review of Books*. "After all, she does not know, from day to day, what she may have to cope with. The novel *Primary Colors*, though lurid and over-done in most respects, does capture one aspect of the 1992 campaign. When allegations about Clinton—the draft, peace demonstrations, 'bimbos'—arose, those within the campaign were hampered by a lack of certitude about what he was capable of doing on impulse. If bimbos seemed to be out for profit—well, there was an Elvis veer in Clinton toward the trashy, 'a *nostalgie de les boobs.*' The campaigners only underwent this ordeal for months. Ms. Clinton lives with it. She must feel that she is walking through a minefield every day."

The aggressively defensive strategy Hillary used to contain the womanizing allegations would necessarily pervade campaign responses to every other scandal that was to follow, including Whitewater. With Garry Wills' concept of the "philanderer's secret" in mind, it is easy to see why Hillary could not accept the advice of aides who urged a policy of openness and full disclosure when it came to Whitewater. If the Clintons had nothing to hide, it was often said, why didn't they simply release all their documents and records and put the whole matter behind them? The answer was evident: Whitewater was a black hole. Hillary did not know where such a policy of openness would lead. Her years of consciously avoiding the facts would now paralyze her.

David Ifshin, the campaign's general counsel, was a veteran of Democratic campaigns who had helped then vice presidential candidate Geraldine Ferraro handle the controversy over her personal finances in 1984 by advocating a policy of full disclosure. Early in the Clinton campaign, Ifshin had a falling out with Hillary over the filing of financial disclosure forms that broadly illustrated her defensive posture regarding the Clintons' finances, and revealed a deep distrust of people in her own organization.

Within thirty days of declaring their candidacy, all candidates must file a form disclosing personal assets and liabilities. Ifshin said he forwarded the blank form to Bruce Lindsey in Little Rock, who passed it on to Bill, who passed it on to Hillary. There it sat, while the question of how to treat the Clintons' Whitewater investment was debated. According to the Clintons' accountant Yoly Redden, a decision was made, apparently by Hillary, to omit Whitewater from the statements. "We were told, it was our understanding that the Whitewater investment was worthless, they were not going to get anything out of it at this point in time," Redden later told the Senate Whitewater committee.

Ifshin, meanwhile, grew concerned as the thirty-day deadline for filing drew near. He called a Washington lawyer, James Hamilton, for advice. A legal ethics specialist, Hamilton had served on the Watergate committee with Hillary and remained close to her through the years. Hamilton told Ifshin that Hillary had called him the previous evening asking for his assistance in filling out the form. Given the minefields that she was trying to navigate, it is hardly surprising that Hillary sought help from an old friend rather than calling Ifshin, who had clashed with her friends Thomases and Ickes in previous Democratic campaigns. But cutting the campaign general counsel out of the loop was not a sound idea, and it bred suspicion of Hillary at campaign headquarters.

A few weeks after the conversation with Hamilton, Ifshin ran into Hillary at an annual Renaissance Weekend gathering and sought to smooth things over. According to Ifshin, when he approached her in the presence of several other people and asked if they could get together over the weekend for a chat, Hillary stiffly replied that it wouldn't be necessary, "if you'd just do the job you're supposed to do." Ifshin didn't know Hillary well, but her reputation for bluntly speaking her mind had preceded her. At the time he spoke with Hillary, Ifshin was walking along with his friend Susan Bayh, the wife of Democratic governor Evan Bayh of Indiana, who knew Hillary through the National Governors Association. "Don't worry," Ifshin said Susan Bayh told him. "You've just been Hillaryed."

It was an inauspicious beginning. Ifshin later learned that Hillary, in the rush to file the form before the deadline, had mailed it herself from Newark Airport in New Jersey without sending copies to the campaign. After an article appeared in the *New York Times* reporting on the Clintons' Whitewater investment, the campaign revised the form to reflect the Clintons' liability on a small mortgage loan on which they were guarantors.

The *Times* story was sparked by Sheffield Nelson, who met with Jim McDougal in Little Rock as the New Hampshire primary approached. Nelson himself had been involved in a speculative and ultimately failed real estate development project financed by Madison Guaranty Savings and Loan back in the early 1980s, but that didn't stop him from trying to muddy the waters for the Clintons. By this point, McDougal felt abandoned by the Clintons and was willing to grant interviews about his dealings with them. Nelson tape-recorded a conversation with McDougal about Whitewater in his law office in Little Rock's TCBY Tower. He then arranged for McDougal to talk to *New York Times* reporter Jeff Gerth, who had known Nelson for more than a decade, since the time Gerth reported on a financial scandal involving Nelson's enemies the Stephens brothers.

With the New Hampshire primary only days away, Gerth was now on the case. As a McGovern campaign worker in 1972, Gerth had investigated aspects of Watergate for the campaign shortly before Hillary Rodham had joined the House Watergate Committee under the direction of John Doar and Bernard Nussbaum. Like Hillary, Gerth was part of a generation of activists who took the zealous anti-Republican fixation of the Nixon period into their careers in politics and government, public interest advocacy, academia, and the media. Gerth joined the *Times* as a financial writer in the post-Watergate era, when investigative reporting had come into vogue at the elite journalistic outlets and everyone aspired to be the next Woodward or Bernstein. Both Gerth and Hillary and others like them had helped usher in a hyper ethics-conscious political and journalistic culture that could not have been more at odds with the nepotistic world of business and politics in Arkansas. The story of the Clinton campaign and the subsequent Clinton administration would, to a great extent, be the story of Hillary's efforts to breach that divide.

Watergate unleashed a wave of reforms mandated by the Democratic-controlled Congress, which fostered the growth of an elaborate public ethics industry in the capital—Watergate babies serving on congressional oversight committees, as independent "inspectors general" in the executive branch departments, and in Ralph Nader–type watchdog organizations. These entities, in turn, kept the new breed of investigative reporters in business. Public figures were now required to fill out disclosure forms laying bare their private finances. Congressional finance laws were passed with the intent of curbing big money in politics. Gift bans were enacted. Executive branch officials spent thousands of hours responding to congressional fact-finding expeditions. Even the appearance of a conflict of interest could be criminal.

Watergate also led directly to the establishment of a permanent independent counsel mechanism, on the theory that the Justice Department, headed by an attorney general appointed by the president, could not be trusted to investigate the executive branch impartially. The mere whiff of a scandal was enough to trigger the appointment of an independent counsel, often accompanied by a Watergate-style congressional inquisition running simultaneously. The practices of withholding information from Congress or violating congressional intent in the interpretation of a statute, became crimes. Senate confirmation hearings became tribunals where ethics charges were used as proxy issues to defeat political opponents.

A more open and accountable process was achieved, some corruption was weeded out of the system, and some bad apples didn't get elected or confirmed to high office. On the other side of the ledger, reputations were ruined, innocent people were bankrupted by legal fees, the time devoted by public servants to policy was substantially reduced, "gotcha" journalism based on arcane technicalities became the rule, and an atmosphere of cynicism and suspicion pervaded the political culture.

For many years conservatives tried to temper these liberal reforms. Their objections were sometimes based on principle, as when they questioned the constitutionality of the independent counsel statute, and sometimes based on the practical reality that Republicans controlling the executive branch were being targeted mercilessly by a Democrat-controlled Congress. One need only recall the long list of Republican officials shot down—Richard Allen, Michael Deaver, Ray Donovan, Anne Burford, Ed Meese, Caspar Weinberger—to say nothing of the Iran-Contra casualties, to appreciate the Republican claim of abuses in the system. This, of course, was precisely why efforts to slow down the scandal machine fell on deaf ears: The Democratic Congress and the liberal media were not about to give up new and devastatingly effective weapons of political combat against the Republicans.

Beginning in the '92 campaign, the Clintons—he would be the first Democrat to hold the White House since many of the liberal reforms were passed—were ground down by this ethics machinery. Not surprisingly, now that the guns were aimed in the other direction, conservative complaints about prosecutorial excesses were rarely voiced. Indeed Republicans in Congress and the conservative press and lobby groups avidly played their part in turning up the heat on the Clintons. But zealous liberal reporters like Jeff Gerth, working for liberal newspapers like the *New York Times,* really made Whitewater a national scandal. The editorial pages of the *New York Times* and the *Washington Post* had far more influence on the evening news coverage than did Rush Limbaugh and the *American Spectator.*

Hillary was especially targeted. As Whitewater became a gripping piece of political theater, Hillary's image and reputation were gradually worn down and the same liberal establishment of which she was still a charter member turned against her with a vengeance. Because Hillary was at one with this elite culture, she would be held accountable for her own lapses in judgment—and for Bill's more egregious ones as well. Bill, by contrast, was held to the standard of the Arkansas lumpenproletariat from which he had sprung and thus remained virtually unscathed by the revelations. The unforgiving tone of the media criticism from forty-something liberal reporters and columnists toward Hillary reflected a personal disappointment in her that they evidently did not feel toward Bill.

Jeff Gerth's first Whitewater story appeared on March 8, 1992, in the Sunday edition of the *New York Times,* on the eve of the critical New York primary. The Gerth article detailed the history of the Whitewater land deal and raised the question of whether the McDougals' failed S&L had subsidized the real estate venture. Gerth also reported on questionable tax deductions taken by the Clintons related to the Whitewater investment. In some years, the Clintons deducted principal as interest and took some deductions on their personal returns that may have been the company's. (Evidence produced by the Senate Whitewater Committee showed that shortly after the Gerth article appeared, Hillary discussed one of the tax problems with Loretta Lynch, a campaign lawyer working for Susan Thomases, and the Clintons' accountant, Yoly Redden. Redden testified that she discussed with Hillary in 1992 whether certain deductions were improperly "double-counted" on the Clintons' 1986 and 1987 tax returns. The Clintons never acknowledged or corrected the error until late 1995, however.)

Gerth found out little about the S&L's dealings with Hillary at the Rose Firm, a testament, perhaps, to the effectiveness of Hillary's damage-control operation. The appearance of a conflict of interest in Hillary's law practice was just the kind of allegation that the *New York Times,* too skittish to cover the Flowers imbroglio or investigate Bill's relationship with Dan Lasater, would have loved to seize on.

Heading up Hillary's Whitewater damage-control operation was Susan Thomases, known as "Hillary's Enforcer." Though she was officially the campaign scheduler, Thomases' relationship with Hillary gave her wide latitude to butt into any area she saw fit. Thomases terrorized the senior Clinton campaign staff, including campaign manager David Wilhelm. At the end of each day, when Thomases called Wilhelm, he put her on a speaker phone with several other aides present. "She would come on and say 'this is the stupidest fucking campaign I've ever seen,' " said one senior official. The abuse got so intolerable, the official said, that Wilhelm threatened to quit the campaign and several top officials were prepared to go with him. "We had to go to Hillary and tell her to pull Susan back," the official said.

Thomases' defenders believed that she, like Hillary, was a victim of unfair stereotyping by a macho political culture. The campaign "white boys," for instance, called Thomases "Tootsie" behind her back. "If she [Thomases] knocked heads, she didn't knock enough of them," Betsey Wright told the *Washington Post.* "If there were bruised feelings, they deserved to be bruised. . . . There was such a sexist strain in that campaign, the men in the campaign were so unbelievably rude and awful the way they treated people. But, my God, if somebody like Susan gets strained and under pressure and knocks heads [they'll say] it's some kind of 'woman thing'—some kind of 'temperament problem,' a 'hormone thing.' "

Thomases seemed especially intent on deflecting Gerth's inquiries about Hillary's representation of Madison Guaranty. As he investigated the Clintons' links to the McDougals, Gerth filed requests with the Arkansas Securities Department seeking information about the state's regulation of Madison. Charles Handley, second in command at the Arkansas Securities Department, testified that a day after the request was filed, Loretta Lynch, an aide of Thomases', showed up seeking the same files.

At the Rose Firm, on the day of Lynch's inquiry, Vincent Foster collected Hillary's billing records for the Madison account. Foster focused on a particular point of vulnerability: He underscored in red ink the line in the billing records that documented Hillary's 1985 telephone conversation with Bassett about the preferred stock deal. Thomases and Webb Hubbell, meanwhile, appeared to discuss how to downplay Hillary's role in bringing the Madison account to the firm by playing up the role of Rick Massey, the associate who was involved in bringing the client in. Thomases' notes of a telephone conversation with Hubbell show that Hubbell told her "Rick will say" he brought the client in, while leaving Hillary out of it.

Hubbell also examined Hillary's records, which appeared to include records relating to Bill's extramarital affairs. According to a 1996 report in *Newsweek*, "[A]t the darkened law firm, Hubbell emerged from the shadows and handed them [two campaign aides] two or three boxes of documents. . . . Inside the box was a jumble of letters and receipts. The aides began pawing through them. *Newsweek* has learned that when one staffer pulled out American Express receipts for room charges at Little Rock's Excelsior Hotel, signed by Bill Clinton, the others laughed nervously and prayed that the bills didn't signify what they were all thinking. Then the staffer found receipts, also signed by the governor, for purchases from Victoria's Secret." (The Arkansas troopers had told of Bill sending them to Victoria's Secret to buy gifts for his girlfriends.)

Thomases, meanwhile, stonewalled Gerth for weeks about Hillary's billing records, telling him that Rose's managing partner William Kennedy would not release them. In retrospect, it is easy to see what was at stake in keeping the records hidden. As Foster's notations showed, Hillary had sought approval from a state official appointed by her husband for a plan that might have kept a corrupt S&L in business. Moreover, the owner of the S&L was her business partner in a real estate deal.

Even assuming that Hillary knew nothing of McDougal's shady practices at the time, there was still an appearance of impropriety. And by now, of course, McDougal had been exposed as an accused felon in a 1990 Little Rock trial. At a minimum, Hillary would have been quite concerned with how her actions in Arkansas jibed with her image on the national scene. What would Marian Wright Edelman think if she found out Hillary had represented a trailer-park developer who was an accused S&L felon?

Hillary's link to the fraudulent transaction at Castle Grande was kept hidden until it was revealed in Rose Firm billing records that surfaced in 1996. Webb Hubbell, her partner and the point person on press inquiries at Rose, may have known about the fraudulent aspects of the deal all along. If, as the Republican majority on the Senate Whitewater committee argued, Hillary knew that her work product was being used to advance a sham-purchaser scheme, she would have wanted to hide the records at all costs. But even if she did not know at the time, as seems likely, she was still in political jeopardy if the role was disclosed now. Questions would be raised about her competence as an attorney in drafting an option for Seth Ward without investigating its purpose. At the least, some would suspect that she had smelled a fishy deal, consciously avoided getting the facts, and gone along with it anyway.[4]

When Thomases read Gerth's story in the Sunday *New York Times,* she felt vindicated, according to *Blood Sport.* She thought the story was impossible to follow, and she was further relieved when it produced few follow-up accounts, even from the *Times* itself. Within the Clinton campaign, however, open warfare broke out over whether to call in an outside lawyer to investigate the Whitewater investment independently. Having just barely survived the Flowers bombshell and the initial Gerth investigation by brazening it out, Hillary's forces opposed the outside audit that Clinton officials in Washington, led by Ifshin, were arguing for. Eli Segal, a longtime FOB and the campaign's chief of staff, flew to Little Rock and met with Thomases to press for an investigation.

Segal later told Ifshin that when he arrived in Little Rock, Thomases told him she was "in charge" of Whitewater. Segal asked Thomases if she intended to cut out of the loop the campaign's lawyers, who were pushing for an independent investigator and full disclosure of all documents to the press. Thomases exploded: "David Ifshin is the enemy. I'm handling it. And if you don't like it, you can get your ass back on a plane to Boston or wherever you came from. We don't need you!"

Hillary eventually turned to a trusted insider, the Denver lawyer James Lyons, to handle the investigation. Known as a show-boating cowboy, Lyons had met Clinton in 1977 when Clinton was attorney general and the two worked together on a case. He used to brag that he could fly into Little Rock on behalf of clients and meet with anyone he wished. Lyons was deemed trustworthy on account of his connection to Vincent Foster, with whom he sometimes stayed when he was in Little Rock.

The Lyons report on Whitewater, drafts of which were faxed to Hillary, Loretta Lynch, and Jim Hamilton as it was being prepared, concluded that the Clintons were passive investors in a money-losing partnership. Due to an apparent accounting error, however, the losses to the Clintons were overstated by about 30 percent. Two copies of the report were prepared: a summary omitting several details that was released to the press and a confidential complete report that went only to the Clintons. The report appeased the press, already favorably skewed toward the Clintons and unable to follow the arcane details of the story anyway. Hillary's strategy of playing hide the ball with the Lyons report and counting on the liberal bias of the press to protect the favored baby-boomer power couple worked brilliantly.

The Clintons' liberal critics in the press later argued that if a policy of openness and full disclosure had been followed from Day One, the entire Whitewater scandal would have been avoided. As the subsequent convictions of the McDougals and Jim Guy Tucker on twenty-four separate felony counts in 1996 showed, this line of argument wrongly assumed that the Clintons had nothing to fear from disclosure. If any of the evidence that trial produced—such as the fact that money went from David Hale's fraudulent loan operation into the Clintons' real estate partnership—had been known by voters in 1992, there is no telling how the election might have been affected. If Eli Segal and David Ifshin had run the show—divulging the Clintons' tax returns from the late 1970s showing the $100,000 cattle futures commodities profits, or releasing Rose Firm billing records revealing Hillary's link to the Castle Grande project—it is quite possible that the ensuing media frenzy, justifiably or not, could have kept Bill Clinton out of the White House.

On November 3, Bill Clinton was elected president with 43 percent of the vote. Hillary's long march to the White House was now complete.

The co-candidacy, born of Bill's despair and depression following the 1980 defeat, had been a phenomenal success. The Clintons were an awesome political team, complementing one another's talents perfectly. With her education plan, Hillary had given Bill the political identity as the "education governor" that he used to get re-elected three times and that served him as a springboard to the presidency. She had cut some corners in her legal practice to boost the political partnership. She had changed her name, her hairstyle, and even her public persona for political gain. She went on national television to defend Bill against charges of infidelity and then assembled one of the most effective political damage-control operations in the history of American politics to make sure there were no further embarrassments. She ably navigated the "minefield" that Garry Wills had written of, keeping the press and the GOP at bay and sealing a Clinton victory.

But Hillary had not only been on the march; she had been on a mission as well. She was now poised to enact the initiatives for social change to which she had been committed since her days in Park Ridge assimilating the Reverend Don Jones's Methodist social gospel. Saul Alinsky would have been proud, too: Hillary had not only adopted his goal of radical political change for noble ends but also his tactical rules of secrecy, angle-playing, and manipulation of the process to advance the cause. She had also proven Alinsky wrong in one respect: If you put your mind to it, you could achieve power *within* the system, making the government an instrument of moral progress.

Hillary prepared to join her husband and Al and Tipper Gore on the steps of the Old State House in downtown Little Rock to celebrate their victory. As the Clintons' car pulled up, Bill the messenger jumped out to soak up the adulation of the crowd. Hillary lagged behind, collecting a sheaf of papers. When she emerged a few moments later, she turned to a reporter and mumbled, "Bill's speech."

11

Rodham Rides Again

Two weeks after the November 1992 election, ABC's *Nightline* aired a show on the role that Hillary Clinton could be expected to play in the new administration. Though the two-for-one deal had been put in cold storage several months before, *Nightline*'s focus on Hillary showed that the partnership was understood by a small circle of political insiders and media people to have been revived. The Clintons still believed in it, they knew it had worked for them in the past, and they were apparently intent on setting a historical precedent with it.

On the broadcast, *Newsweek*'s Eleanor Clift, who had followed the Clintons closely since she first named Bill as a rising star in the Democratic firmament in a 1990 column, said, "I think when Hillary Clinton leaves office in four years or eight years, that she would like to have a record of accomplishments on her résumé as well. . . ." In an indication of how official Washington viewed the partnership, host Ted Koppel interjected, tersely: "[You] had an interesting choice of words there . . . you said when she 'leaves office.' To the best of my knowledge, she hasn't been elected to any office."

With discussion on the Sunday morning chat shows focusing on

Hillary being named Attorney General and serious consideration being given within the Clinton transition team to making her domestic policy adviser, Clift realized something that Koppel—and the American people, perhaps—did not: Hillary might not have been elected, but she would have a major hand in governing the country. "The expectation among friends and aides is that she will act as an unofficial chief of staff," Clift and fellow reporter Mark Miller announced in *Newsweek* shortly after the election. "[She] will find a way to oversee everything. . . . Hillary Clinton is Bill's Daytimer, the gentle lash who keeps him focused, who doesn't mind making decisions and refereeing disputes when Clinton would rather stall." Refereeing disputes between contending factions, of course, was really a fundamental part of governing.

To their credit, the Clintons and their aides were forthright about their intentions. "She knows more about this stuff than most of us do," Clinton said, explaining Hillary's unexpected attendance at his first working dinner in Little Rock with the Democratic congressional leadership. At an economic summit held in Little Rock that December, Bill was flanked by Hillary, briefing book in tow, on one side, and by Marian Wright Edelman on the other. When asked if Hillary would attend cabinet meetings, a Clinton aide said: "Cabinet meetings would be a step down for her." *U.S. News & World Report* quoted an administration official as saying, "Of course she's in the loop. She is the loop."[1]

To say that the Clinton partnership had a honeymoon with the media would be an understatement. The Clinton inaugural, *Newsweek* editorialized, would be "the most important inaugural of our lifetime." Columnist Joe Klein wrote, "Democrats, baby boomers, 'new idea' types, all were hoping that their moment had finally come, that it was time to reclaim the idealism of the Kennedy years." After a White House dinner for the winners of the National Medal of the Arts, singer Carly Simon gushed: "It is reminiscent of the Kennedy administration, and to see that respect given again can do a lot for the esteem of artists and morale. I will be producing better albums." During a two-hour national town meeting with the new president on CBS, anchor Dan Rather remarked that he would soon be teaming up on the evening news with Connie Chung. "If we can be one-hundredth as great as you and Hillary Rodham Clinton have been together in the White House, we'd take it right now and walk away a winner."

The dispatches of Clift and her colleague at *Time*, Margaret Carlson, were the most important signals of how the press—especially accomplished women reporters, who identified with Hillary—viewed the new first lady. Clift and Carlson, two savvy professional women who had both fought their way to the top of a highly competitive, male-dominated profession, admired Hillary's intelligence, hard work, and ability to more than hold her own with men, including her husband. They also shared her feminist ideals. Not unreasonably, they defended the two-for-one deal on the grounds that Hillary had earned her place, but also that she would be a breath of fresh air after a long run of official hostesses who exercised their power furtively.

In one typical pre-inaugural dispatch, Carlson wrote: "Perhaps a First Lady who consults lawbooks rather than astrologers doesn't look so frightening after all. And perhaps Bill Clinton, rather than seeming weak by comparison with his wife, has proved that it takes a solid, secure man to marry a strong woman." Carlson later told the *Washington Post*, "As much as we try to think otherwise, when you're covering someone like yourself, and your position in life is insecure, she's your mascot. Something inside you roots for her. You're rooting for your team. I try to get that bias out, but for many of us it's there."

Of course, Carlson was right about Hillary, but she was wrong about Bill. Bill's reliance on his wife was not a testament to his strength, but rather a reflection of his fundamental weakness. Bill Clinton would be perhaps the weakest chief executive since Warren Harding. Left to his own devices, he might have floundered, just as he did during his first term as Arkansas governor. Even Clinton's friends were the first to concede that his desire for acceptance and approval undermined his ability to make decisions and stick with them. While Clinton, a political organizer who had risen to the presidency, had the ambition to be president, he didn't seem to have the convictions to carry it off. He appeared uninterested in exercising the powers of his office. Even Ronald Reagan, an ex-actor who had been widely derided as a great pretender, possessed a firm core that Clinton lacked.

Thus it was not only out of desire, but out of necessity that Hillary assumed the role she did. Hillary was not a scheming interloper, calculating how to wrest power from her husband, nor was she a fifth column of influence—a "social Lady Macbeth" as columnist Cal Thomas put it. Since she had been in large measure responsible for Bill's political success, it was only natural that she would play a pivotal role in the new administration and that her ideological agenda would shape it significantly. At this point in the history of the co-candidacy, any other arrangement was unthinkable. When Hillary said during the campaign, "If you vote for him, you get me," she wasn't kidding.

Hillary was, therefore, not only the most powerful first lady but also the most powerful unelected official in history, surpassing even legendary presidential aides like Woodrow Wilson's confidant Colonel House and FDR advisor Harry Hopkins. She orchestrated the first two years of the administration. The truth of the matter was captured in a famous remark by Chelsea Clinton, who advised a nurse at her school who wanted to talk to Hillary before administering an aspirin: "Call my dad; my mom's too busy."

Hillary's own words on this point are telling. During a public meeting in Texas where she made an appearance to promote the administration's health care plan, Hillary was asked what it was like to be governing. "It's been exhilarating, frustrating, eye-opening," she replied before catching herself and adding, "I'm also, just to keep the record straight, not really governing either." In an interview with the *Los Angeles Times* three years later, Hillary compared herself with two former first ladies who exercised exceptional influence. "My goodness, Mrs. Wilson ran the country when her husband had his stroke. Mrs. Taft used to go in and tell Cabinet officers and Supreme Court justices what they should do." But even these two important women did not assume official authority in the government. Eleanor Roosevelt, the first lady to whom Hillary most frequently compared herself, assumed a high public profile with her charitable and philanthropic work. When she briefly held a post in civil defense at the Defense Department, she was heavily criticized and quit in six months.

Hillary was named to spearhead the administration's major domestic initiative: health care reform. With spiraling health care costs contributing to the federal deficit, the entire budget was hostage to health care. She appointed and vetoed cabinet officers, and named the top White House lawyers, who vetted all political and judicial appointments and held sway over the government's vast regulatory authority. Aside from environmental policy, the purview of Vice President Al Gore, and foreign affairs, which was turned over to veterans of the Carter administration, there was precious little for Bill to do except what he did best: Continue to campaign for office. While Bill remained the inexhaustible candidate, Hillary and those accountable to her controlled budget priorities, the legal and social service departments, presidential personnel, judicial selection, and the White House counsel's office. In sum, she ran a good-sized chunk of the government.

Hillary, it would soon be clear, was the one with the strong political destiny to fulfill. Hillary's ascension signaled a coming of age of the East Coast left-liberal, Watergate-era cadres of lawyers, policy wonks, academics, and political activists. She would recruit these people to provide the new administration with both its ideological edge and technocratic style. The new administration's purpose, she declared, was nothing less than a "remaking of the American way of politics, government, indeed, life . . . I have a burning desire to do what I can."

Hillary's longtime goal of institutionalizing the left and directing social change from inside the government was now within reach. All of the policies and programs she had fought for at the Children's Defense Fund and the Legal Services Corporation and the American Bar Association— more welfare benefits, federal day care, family leave, outcomes-based education, increased spending on child immunization—could be guaranteed with new federal mandates and controls. Gender equity and multiculturalism would be the order of the day—not only in the law, education, and cultural programs, but in a "gender-neutral" military, and mandated in quotas governing every other facet of government policy, from defense and agriculture contracting to communications licensing. Most dramatically, she would seek to bring one-seventh of the U.S. economy under government control in a bid to solidify the gains of FDR's New Deal with a new health care entitlement. The law could be used as a political tool as well: Whatever rights could not be enhanced through executive branch programs and the new legislation would simply be achieved by fiat through a sweeping takeover of the federal courts by a new generation of activist judges in the tradition of William O. Douglas.

Early comments made by some of Hillary's strongest backers raised the question of what Hillary's ultimate ambitions might be. Now that the two-for-one had been endorsed at the ballot box, would Hillary try to move beyond the confines of the political partnership, which required her to exercise power through her marriage to Bill, and into her own sphere? The question Ted Koppel didn't ask was: Why would Hillary be building a résumé, as Clift had indicated, unless she viewed the first lady's position as a stepping stone to something even greater?

When Hillary was named to head the health care reform effort in early 1993, Margaret Carlson wrote: "If Hillary Clinton is able to untangle the health care mess, she will be seen as such a miracle worker that she may become the leading candidate for president in 2000." On a *McLaughlin Group* appearance, Eleanor Clift seconded the nomination: "If you want to see someone with the qualities to be president, it's Hillary." (Clift's comment was an interesting reprise of the 1990 view of some Arkansans that Hillary would have made an excellent governor.)

In her piece published in the *New Yorker* in the spring of 1994, Connie Bruck reported that Betsey Wright, the longtime Clinton operative who had first recognized Hillary's political potential when they met in the Texas McGovern campaign in 1972, discussed the idea of Hillary succeeding Bill in the White House. "Some friends have suggested that her goal now may well be to become president herself," Bruck wrote of Hillary. "Betsey Wright told me last December, 'There are a great many people talking very seriously about her succeeding him. Their staff will say, 'We have to do it this way and that way, and then we'll be here at least twelve years.' And it's not just the staff. Friends, Democrats, people out across the country think it is a very viable plan of action." Veteran Washington reporter Elizabeth Drew wrote in *On the Edge* of the efforts by Hillary's majordomo Susan Thomases to position her for a run for the White House. "Susan gets into everything, protecting Hillary Clinton," one White House source told Drew. "She's her campaign manager for President of the United States, and I'm not kidding. Susan believes that somewhere down the road Hillary will be the first woman candidate for President of the United States. She's positioning her. Not that anybody thinks it's a bad idea—it's just a little early."[2]

There was nothing self-evidently wrong with Hillary's exercising unprecedented power or even setting her sights on succeeding her husband in office. The partnership had propelled the Clintons into the White House. Why change a good thing? the Clintons must have thought. Yet their presumption that America would be comfortable with Hillary exercising power as an unelected official proved woefully wrong.

The job of first lady has always been a delicate balancing act. Hillary had an even tougher time as a "transitional" first lady—the first in a new generation of modern career women to occupy the White House. "Every first lady who has used her position in this way [to influence public policy] has been ridiculed or vilified as being deviant from women's proper role or feared as emasculating," Smithsonian curator Edith Mayo told the *Washington Post*. "The furor over Hillary Clinton is but the latest chapter in a theme that runs throughout First Lady history. It is much less about Hillary herself than it is about America's deep-seated ambivalence, even hostility, toward power in the hands of women."

Yet it is hard to imagine there would have been vociferous objections to Hillary's exercise of power if she had taken a job as a cabinet officer in, say, Mario Cuomo's administration. Part of the opposition to her role was based on the view that granting political power to a first lady, who could not be removed from office, was undemocratic. When Rosalynn Carter sat in on cabinet meetings and Nancy Reagan engineered the firing of chief of staff Don Regan, public controversies ensued. *New York Times* columnist A. M. Rosenthal was one of the few to elucidate this theme early in the Clinton administration, commenting in March 1994 that "in concept, the First Ladyship is an affront to American democracy . . . In practice, it skews the administration of government, evades anti-nepotism law and avoids the responsibility that should go with authority. . . . It is the only political post in the country that demands the essential qualification of being married to a particular man at a particular time in his life."

There was another early warning sign about Hillary's role that stood in sharp contrast to the encomiums from Eleanor Clift and Margaret Carlson. Writing in *Newsweek* before Clinton was even inaugurated, former *Washington Post* reporter Sally Quinn penned a brilliantly prophetic column headlined "Beware of Washington." Before long, Hillary would break every one of Quinn's rules for surviving in the capital city, where public and press scrutiny was far higher and where the exercise of power, the only commodity in the capital, was more finely parsed than any other place on earth.

Hillary Clinton and Sally Quinn were perhaps destined to clash. "Quinn, 54, came to prominence penning acid features for the *Post* Style section in the 1970s," *Washingtonian* magazine reported in a profile in 1996. "She rocketed up the social ladder by marrying [Ben] Bradlee in 1978, when he was the *Post*'s powerful executive editor. She quit the paper and wrote two novels, but her real work has been fashioning herself as both the arbiter and chronicler of Washington society. Thus, you can find her many evenings dining at the most exclusive tables and rubbing elbows at every important gala."

Under her honey-colored hair and contact lenses, Hillary, in contrast to Quinn, was a plain, unpretentious working mom raised in the mid-western frugality of Hugh Rodham. She had neither the glamour of Nancy Reagan nor the aristocratic touch of Barbara Bush. Most evenings Hillary was content to stay home in the White House residence having dinner with Chelsea and reading briefing papers while leaving the so-cializing to Bill. While understandable and in some ways admirable, Hillary's failure to use her role as first hostess to political advantage would redound to her detriment. Georgetown society was appalled by her failure to schedule a state dinner until 18 months into the adminis-tration. And much of the country still wanted a first lady who fretted over china patterns. Yet, "Mrs. Wonk Goes to Washington" was how the *Los Angeles Times* had aptly announced Hillary's arrival in town. Sometimes code-named "Woodstock" by the Secret Service, Hillary's idea of a good time was listening to Earth, Wind and Fire records in the White House residence on Saturday mornings. As for Quinn, some Washington gos-sips said she was threatened by Hillary and feared being upstaged by the younger, more substantive Yale-educated lawyer.

Whatever Sally Quinn's motives, no one writing about Hillary came closer to predicting—and perhaps even contributing to—the pitfalls she would soon meet in the capital. Quinn began her column with a dig at Hillary's personal presentation at a recent Washington dinner party— "Hillary Clinton appeared in a pale blue suit with a blue satin highnecked blouse, her hair on top of her head in a mass of blond curls—very glam-orous, very Krystle in *Dynasty*, very un-Hillary."

She then described how to survive the "complicated" and "unchari-table" city, raising a delicate subject that Clift and Carlson preferred to overlook: For all of Hillary's talents, she was wielding political power be-cause of her marriage. This made her an uneasy feminist symbol, a would-be pioneer trapped in an anachronistic reality: "Hillary Clinton was not elected president," wrote Quinn. "At a Washington dinner recently she was heard to talk about the budget. She was impressive and knowledge-able. But her conversation was peppered with 'we': 'We got our first look at the budget.' Those who've known Hillary for years say that she has al-ways used 'we,' that the Clintons have always operated as a team. But Lit-tle Rock is not Washington. 'We' is the kiss of death in Washington."

Obviously unaware of how much Bill needed Hillary on site, Quinn also advised Hillary to get a job outside the White House, pursuing her interests in child welfare, health, and education independently. "To say she should just be First Lady and operate through her husband is sexist, demeaning and insulting. To have her own job would broaden her choices, not narrow them," she wrote. If she was unwilling or unable to restrain herself, Quinn advised Hillary to resort to deception: "If Hillary Clinton is actually running the country, only Bill Clinton should know about it."

In the most prescient passage, Quinn warned Hillary not to become a scapegoat. "As in any family where one member is silently elected to act out the problems of the rest, so Washington plays out the same scenario. Washington wants to like and respect the president. It's not just him; it's the job. So when things start going wrong, they look for others to blame," she observed.

"The president takes the blame as a last resort. A smart president will appoint at least one person close to him who is actively disagreeable and unpopular so he can play the good cop/bad cop routine. John Ehrlichman and H. R. Haldeman, Zbigniew Brzezinski, James Watt, Donald Regan and John Sununu all come to mind. If the president doesn't do this, and sometimes even if he does, then the wife has to play the scapegoat. . . . Shrew, harridan, bitch are all words that are easy to pin on a First Lady who appears to be wielding power when things go wrong. And things always go wrong."[3]

Hillary began breaking Quinn's rules during the transition, which was ostensibly run from Washington by Democratic lawyers Warren Christopher and Vernon Jordan. Their role amounted to creating the appearance of a transition process by floating names of prominent Democrats who had little chance of being chosen. The real power was with Hillary and Susan Thomases in Little Rock. Operating for years in the southern capital, the supremely confident Hillary had never really needed to broaden her circle or alter her decision-making process, which resembled a very narrow pyramid. She also saw no need to reach out to the political opposition in making appointments in the government or even to bring in Democrats who had opposed Clinton, like Senators Bob Kerrey or Paul Tsongas. "She spent her life thinking she knew what it was all about and she gets into the big leagues and she had no communication with other people, the kind of people you need to get yourself straightened out," said David Ifshin. "Her attitude was typical of the baby boomers. 'I'm going to do it my way, and if the world doesn't like it, fuck the world.'" (Hillary didn't even take advice on the little things. Her aides begged her not to wear a floppy blue velour hat on inaugural day, but the stubborn first lady insisted. Sure enough, the Associated Press panned the look, headlining its story, "Oh No, it's Hillary's Chapeau").

Democratic insiders soon figured out that Hillary was the wheelhorse in the inner councils of the transition. When Clinton was considering naming his Democratic Leadership Council colleague Dave McCurdy, the former Oklahoma representative, as secretary of defense, Speaker Tom Foley opposed him because McCurdy had challenged his leadership of the House the prior year. McCurdy believed that Foley had gotten word to Hillary that he opposed the nomination, and Clinton named Congressman Les Aspin instead.

Susan Thomases decided not to go into the administration, preferring to exercise her vast power from the outside. Thomases may have sensed that she could accomplish more from behind the scenes rather than by taking a public post, where she would likely become a lightning rod for criticism as Hillary's alter ego. She had the best of both worlds: unparalleled access to the highest levels of power, plus the lucrative salary she continued to rake in practicing law and now lobbying at Willkie, Farr & Gallagher, which gave her an office in Washington in recognition of her clout with the Clintons. Thomases held a rare unrestricted White House pass. Outside the private elevators going up to the family residence, a photo of Thomases was posted with instructions that White House security was not to stop her for any reason. She soon acquired the name "the midnight caller," as she issued orders to White House staff by telephone from her Park Avenue apartment in New York at all hours of the night. A particular challenge for the staff was determining where Hillary stopped and Thomases started; Thomases' propensity to speak in Hillary's name would later spell trouble for the first lady.

Thomases was the kind of empire builder who made a career of getting people jobs. She played the role of top ideological cop similar to that of Reagan White House aide Lyn Nofziger, who made sure the true Reaganites were placed in key posts. She installed loyalists in virtually all of the key West Wing offices, including two of the most important—congressional affairs and the advance and scheduling operation, two nerve centers. For the legislative shop, she chose Howard Paster, a veteran lobbyist closely allied with the most liberal elements in leadership of the U.S. House. Longtime Democratic operative Marcia Hale went to scheduling and advance. Ricki Seidman became a deputy communications director. A former private investigator and former director of Norman Lear's People for the American Way, as an aide to Senator Ted Kennedy Seidman had played a key role in bringing Anita Hill forward with her sexual harassment allegations against Clarence Thomas.

Though Bill had been elected as a moderate New Democrat on promises to "end welfare as we know it," enact a middle-class tax cut, and cut the size of government, once the election was over, that agenda and the advisers who advocated it were suddenly nowhere to be found. With the exception of the North American Free Trade Agreement, which had been negotiated by the Bush administration, the DLC-oriented agenda dissolved and a much more liberal one replaced it: health care reform, gays in the military, abortion rights, Robert Reich's proposals to deny tax benefits to "socially irresponsible" businesses, and safe sex lessons from Surgeon General Joycelyn Elders.

The centrist Democrats of the Democratic Leadership Council, who had believed Bill to be their ally, held prominent but powerless posts in the transition and were completely shut out of top jobs in the administration. By the time the dust settled, all of the prominent moderates—from former Congressman Steve Solarz to Jimmy Carter policy adviser Stuart Eizenstat and DLCers Al From, Will Marshall, and Dave McCurdy—had been excluded. Former representative Tom Downey of New York, who had been sharply criticized by Marian Wright Edelman in the late 1980s over his stance on welfare reform, was crossed off the cabinet list. Veteran Democratic operative Tom Donilon, who clashed with Thomases during the campaign, was unable to get a White House job. David Ifshin, fired as the general counsel of the Clinton campaign after clashing with Thomases and Harold Ickes (who, according to Ifshin, had physically attacked him during a confrontation in New York) could not even get named ambassador to Indonesia.

The Clinton White House staff was divided into three issues clusters. Foreign policy was the domain of former Carter administration national security aide Anthony Lake; economic policy was under Robert Rubin, a Wall Street investment banker; and social policy was run by domestic policy adviser Carol Rasco, a former staffer in the Arkansas Health Department under Joycelyn Elders. Al From, William Galston, and Bruce Reed of the DLC had all been touted for the domestic policy post, but Rasco was named instead. She had worked at the Little Rock children's advocacy project that Hillary helped found and was widely seen as a stalking horse for the first lady.

With no one to advance their interests, many of the DLCers concluded that Clinton had joined their movement only to position himself against New York governor Mario Cuomo, whom the Clintons had expected to be the main competitor in an eventual national race. As a member of the DLC as well, Vice President Al Gore might have been expected to fill the role of interlocutor, but going up against Hillary and Thomases wasn't a fair fight. When one news account during the transition said that Gore, who was a friend of former New York congressman Tom Downey's, was at the table as appointments were being made, he felt compelled to deny it. Thomases had already shown Gore who was boss during an infamous altercation in the presidential campaign, when Gore suggested in a conference call with Thomases and other aides that a Clinton cross-country bus tour end in St. Louis. "Susan said, 'That's the stupidest fucking idea I've ever heard,' " *Vanity Fair* quoted one participant in the conference call as saying. "There was just total sputter. We were all sitting stunned on various telephones. It was really incredible."

DLC surrogates in the media, meanwhile, warned of "creeping Rodhamism," in the words of *New Republic* columnist Mickey Kaus. Kaus attacked Hillary's mentor Marian Wright Edelman and the Children's Defense Fund as promoting outdated, failed policies in a cover story for the magazine in early 1993. Kaus' attack, however, was misplaced. He tended to see a struggle among contending factions within the administration for Bill's "soul"—when in fact he had no soul, politically speaking, and there wasn't any struggle. Kaus' real problem was with Clinton.

Bill had no agenda but Rodhamism, and unlike past presidents he had no "people," in the sense of Hillary's ideological cadres, to place in high positions. If further proof was needed that Hillary and Dick Morris had conceived the idea of recreating Bill Clinton in 1982 as a centrist to win elections it could be found in the vanquishing of the DLC forces ostensibly allied with Bill. Once the Clintons took power, much of the care that had been taken to position him as a centrist candidate in tune with public opinion was now overtaken by Hillary's long-suppressed ideological imperatives. Hewing for ten long years to Alinsky's doctrine of "policy after power," Hillary was now firmly in the saddle.

Though she had always mixed her politics with pragmatism, Hillary's core beliefs and convictions had not changed since the 1960s. Thus it was only natural that she was the person to whom members of the liberal activist groups which comprise much of the base of the modern Democratic Party looked as their ally and protector in the jockeying for power and position that takes place in every presidential transition. In a letter of support sent to her soon after Clinton was elected, Rick Best, executive director of the National Lawyer's Guild, which had been founded in the 1930s as an adjunct of the American Communist Party, wrote: "I thought I better not correspond during the campaign. It was a major effort to make sure that the NLG did not publicly endorse you . . . The effect of your victory is wonderful . . . Congratulations and thank you from the bottom of my heart . . ." Hillary, who had supported the work of the NLG at the Legal Services Corporation and the New World Foundation, responded in a letter dated March 4, 1993, which Best reprinted in the group's publication "Guild Notes," under an introduction that hailed the response as "the first letter from the White House since FDR wished us well in 1944."

The Clinton White House claimed to embrace "diversity" in its appointments, but the diversity it referred to was not ideological. The quota system was employed not only to appoint people of the desired gender and race, but to favor only those who were politically correct. Under the guise of diversity, Hillary eliminated contending power centers and imposed a remarkable degree of ideological uniformity throughout the government. In the vast social services area, she picked the equivalent of the secretary of state, NSC adviser, and secretary of defense. Named to head the chief domestic department of government was Health and Human Services Secretary Donna Shalala, who chaired the Children's Defense Fund Board after Hillary stepped down during the '92 campaign. She had also been chairman of the Committee to Save *Roe* and was dubbed the "high priestess of political correctness" by *New Republic* columnist Morton Kondracke because she had advocated limits on so-called hate speech as chancellor of the University of Wisconsin. A five-foot-tall dynamo known as "Boom-Boom" for her blunt, take-charge style, Shalala publicly thanked not Bill but Hillary when she was named to

HHS. Marian Wright Edelman's husband Peter was named counselor to Shalala. Other Children's Defense Fund officials hired at HHS included policy director Olivia Golden, who headed the department's section on children, youth, and families, which runs Head Start and other children's programs on a $7 billion budget.

Another CDF connection came through Sheldon Hackney, named to head the National Endowment for the Humanities (NEH). Hackney's wife Lucy had served on the CDF board with Hillary. Like Shalala, Hackney had been criticized by civil libertarians for his enforcement of a hate speech code as president of the University of Pennsylvania. As NEH director, Hackney began a multi-million-dollar program called "A National Conversation on American Pluralism and Democracy." The *Chicago Sun-Times* columnist Dennis Byrne wrote in August 1995, "The big winner is the American Library Association, which gloms onto $383,000 for 100 conversations in 20 states on people's views of work in an examination of American values. . . . It is the idea that government has to provide the 'settings,' 'structures,' 'formats,' and 'agendas,' as well as huge servings of advice, guidance and direction, to get us to channel our discussions in the right directions. It is elitism masquerading as populism."

Complaints about the transition process were registered by many white male Democrats who had spent more than a decade in the wilderness, waiting for a chance to work in a Democratic administration, only to be aced out by quotas once their party took power. During the transition, an ad hoc women's group trooped to Little Rock to protest the paucity of women appointees to top jobs, bypassing Warren Christopher and Vernon Jordan in Washington. At the time, former Vice President Walter Mondale was under serious consideration as the new ambassador to the United Nations. Suddenly, Madeleine Albright, who had been an assistant to the national security adviser in the Carter administration, was named. Mondale suggested in a published interview that he had been passed over because he was a white male: "when I was giving all of those speeches about affirmative action, I didn't mean me," he said.

In staffing her own office, Hillary practiced what she preached. Her chief of staff, Maggie Williams, a former press aide at the Children's Defense Fund, headed a virtually all-female staff of eighteen known as "Hillaryland." Williams viewed herself as on a bureaucratic par with White House chief of staff Mack McLarty, sometimes complaining if she wasn't invited to the same high-level meetings. Melanne Verveer of People for the American Way was named Hillary's deputy chief of staff. Verveer's husband Phillip worked with Thomases at Willkie Farr & Gallagher. Another deputy, Evelyn Lieberman, came from the staff of Senator Joseph Biden of Delaware, where she had fought the Robert Bork and Clarence Thomas Supreme Court nominations. The one male on staff fit Hillary's ideological profile: Neel Lattimore had been on the staffs of the United Food and Commercial Workers Union and the Government Accountability Project, an arm of the Institute for Policy Studies.

Though Hillary could be a demanding boss, she was also a genuinely warm and caring person. Her personal staff was among the most loyal to serve in any White House and very few of her aides left their jobs during the first term. In this respect, the individual characters of Bill and Hillary were something of a reversal of their respective public images. Though Hillary was often depicted as a "screamer," as *New York Times* columnist Maureen Dowd once put it, it was Bill who had an ugly, abusive streak, which he often vented at underlings like George Stephanopoulos. (In Arkansas, Clinton had once slapped Betsey Wright and come to blows with Dick Morris, who later named Clinton "The Monster" because of his explosive temper.)

Hillary's zealousness, however, could result in political embarrassment. One of Hillary's earliest intended appointments was shot down by moderate Democrats exerting pressure from outside the transition, because none of the moderates had the clout to face her down in internal battles. A friend of Hillary's, Johnetta Cole, president of Spelman College in Atlanta and an Afro-American Studies professor, was named to head the Clinton transition team in charge of education, arts, and the humanities. In a 1991 profile in the *Atlanta Journal and Constitution,* Cole said, "I have many heroes and sheroes," among them Spelman alumna Marian Wright Edelman. Just before election day in 1992, Hillary appeared at Spelman College's "Sister Chapel" and was introduced as "the first sister of Arkansas, soon to be the first sister of the United States." Hillary referred to Cole as "sister president."

Cole, untempered by the social gospel themes of the Christian left, was on the left-wing fringe of the Democratic party. While Cole was clearly much more radical than Hillary, Hillary's promotion of her for Secretary of Education showed that she was comfortable placing a hard-core radical in a very sensitive and important post. After Cole's name was floated, an article in *The Forward,* a Jewish weekly newspaper, revealed Cole's ties to Marxist groups, including membership in a committee connected to Cuba's intelligence forces and to the World Peace Council, a Soviet front organization that was also vehemently anti-Israel. Cole was also revealed to be a member of the Grenada Friendship Society, a support group for the Communist regime in that country. When A. M. Rosenthal of the *New York Times* labeled Cole a "propagandist for dictatorships," the pending nomination was dead in the water. The episode revealed that Hillary's assessment of national politics was tin-eared; she did not seem to understand that people she admired for their commitment to "progressive" causes would be viewed by mainstream America as anti-American left-wing ideologues.

The Cole defeat was a rare setback for Hillary and her forces, who controlled most of the top White House jobs.

The chief of staff and the White House counsel are the two most important jobs in any administration. Hillary and Thomases reportedly backed Mack McLarty, a childhood friend of Clinton's and the former chief executive of Arkla, as the chief of staff; in that role he was expected to do little more than be the gatekeeper to the Oval Office and manage the paper flow. Mickey Kantor, who had served with Hillary on the Legal Services Corporation board in the late 1970s, appeared to be in the running for the chief of staff post; he was named United States Trade Representative. His exclusion from the inner circle—known as the Murder on the Orient Express—was done quickly and quietly. Only later did it emerge that he had run afoul of Thomases during the campaign. (Harold Ickes, who was very active in the transition, did not join the White House staff for more than a year while his law firm's alleged ties to organized crime were investigated in New York.)

Because Mack McLarty was utterly devoid of an ideological agenda, the White House counsel's influence was even greater. The counsel's office was one area where Hillary appeared to set aside her penchant for quota appointments: All the power was concentrated in the hands of white men who were beholden to her. There would be four White House counsels in as many years; the reason for the revolving door appeared to be that Hillary was the *de facto* counsel. Through her control of the counsel's office, which functions as the president's in-house law firm, Hillary had a chokehold on the entire government. Because of its function of legal review, every important piece of paper—every statement of administration policy and proposed legislation; every bill and executive order and proclamation that the president would sign; all testimony by executive branch officials; every presidential speech—flows through the counsel's office. On questions of law, it usually has the last word. On all policy questions, from gays in the military to the administration's review of affirmative action policies, the White House counsel has a seat at the table. To the extent that all public policy issues involve legal issues, the counsel's office can weigh in on virtually anything. At the very least, the counsel was able to operate as a policy checkpoint for Hillary, allowing her to monitor every issue working its way through the bureaucracy to the president's desk.

The White House counsel's office is charged as well with giving ethics advice to White House officials, making sure financial disclosure statements are properly filed, and reviewing critical background checks in issuing security clearances. In the post-Watergate era of partisan ethics warfare, these functions have made it the single most sensitive office in the White House, the place where presidencies—from Carter's Billygate to Reagan's Iran-Contra to Bush's Iraqgate—have increasingly come to break down. By the end of the first Clinton term, the counsel's office would be the scene of every mishap and scandal the White House suffered, from the early flaps over gays in the military and the failure to properly vet nominees, to the search of Vincent Foster's office following his suicide, to the firings of the White House travel office workers, to the possibly illegal requisition by the White House of confidential FBI files and IRS records.

No matter how much Hillary wanted to proceed with a positive agenda for the future, she was still in charge of damage control. Thus the counsel's office, under Hillary's influence, would become the successor to Betsey Wright's campaign bunker. Wary of the minefields all around her, uncertain of the full history and activities of her husband and his associates, and deeply wounded by press intrusiveness during the campaign, Hillary must have felt she had little choice in staffing the counsel's office but to look for loyalists who could be counted on to protect her and her husband from public exposure. The disastrous decision to run a damage control operation inside the White House was later attributed in the media to baby-boomer bumbling, Arkansas ineptitude, or Nixonian paranoia. But Hillary acted with simple prudence and foresight, knowing exactly what choices she faced: Either risk political suicide or bring the aggressively defensive operation of the campaign into the West Wing. For Hillary, the stakes were higher now than they were in the campaign: Her husband's presidency, the precedent of the two-for-one partnership, the massive overhaul of the nation's health care system, the carefully placed network of Children's Defense Fund operatives, and perhaps even her own political future all rested on her ability to keep the lid on possible scandals as effectively as she and her surrogates had done on the road to the White House.

Hillary knew there were going to be problems figuring out the tax status of the tangled Whitewater investment when it came time to file financial disclosure forms and 1992 taxes in the spring of 1993. The Clintons' personal tax records from the 1970s documenting the $100,000 commodities profits had been shielded from public view for more than a decade. And there was the disturbing tip Hillary had gotten from Betsey Wright in the closing weeks of the presidential campaign: Wright was hearing rumors that the Kansas City office of the Resolution Trust Corporation, the federal agency charged with cleaning up savings and loan failures from the 1980s, had sent a criminal referral to the U.S. attorney in Little Rock in an investigation of an S&L with ties to the Clintons.

No less important for Hillary would be navigating the morass of Washington ethics rules that could easily ensnare the uninitiated. In contemporary Washington, even a trivial oversight could produce front-page headlines alleging ethics violations. The Clintons, moreover, set themselves up for a fall by self-righteously contending that they were better, smarter, more ethical, and more caring than anyone else. Clinton, for instance, had announced that his would be the most ethical administration in the history of the republic. As the Clintons would soon find out, excessive moralism of this sort often meets with swift punishment.

In the years following Watergate, an entire generation of political operatives and lawyers had learned that openness and full disclosure were the only effective ways of diffusing political scandal. Though she was said to have kept a copy of *How to Impeach a President* on her bookshelf at the Rose Law Firm, Hillary was understandably reluctant to apply these lessons to her own situation. So she went in the other direction, perhaps deciding simply to go Nixon one better in battening down the hatches. It seems fair to suggest, in retrospect, that the lesson Hillary drew from her Watergate experience was that stretching and manipulating legal procedures could produce victory on the political battlefield. Stonewalling, artful dodging, the benefit of a press corps that shared her politics, and a little luck might do the trick.

The top lawyers in the counsel's office, who had no experience as Washington insiders, could not be counted on to give sound political as well as legal advice. Representing a president was different from representing a private company or an accused mobster. Relying on niggling distinctions and legal technicalities, playing with the law intellectually, while perhaps correct legally, inevitably looks defensive and deceptive in the political arena.

But among the top White House lawyers there was a deeper problem than lack of political skills. Representing the president meant dealing substantively with a mind-numbing array of legal requirements and procedures—the Public Records Act, to name just one example—that did require scrupulous attention to detail. Too often, the tendency in the Clinton counsel's office was either to not treat these requirements and procedures with the proper seriousness, or else to try to get over and around them by brazening it out. By any measure, this was bad lawyering. At worst, it suggested that the Clinton White House viewed itself as above the law.

One of Hillary's first appointments was her close friend and colleague Vincent Foster as deputy White House counsel. Having just announced his candidacy for the presidency of the Arkansas Bar Association, Foster was not eager to come to Washington. But now that Hillary had reached the pinnacle, how could he refuse her request? Foster, after all, shared Hillary's ideals. A liberal Democrat, he embraced Hillary's mission of legal services activism and social reform through the courts. His diary, kept after the election, showed that he had discussed with Hillary how to overhaul the American health care system as well as her intention of playing a major policy role in the new administration.

But Hillary would need Foster for other reasons as well: He was one of the few people who knew as much about the Clintons' past in Arkansas as she did. While on the public payroll, Foster also assumed the role of the Clintons' personal lawyer, handling their taxes, financial disclosure forms, and arrangements for putting their holdings in a blind trust. Performing this private work for the Clintons was a contravention of federal ethics laws. White House lawyers were not hired to work on the personal business of the first family but rather to function as lawyers for the president in his official capacity. Foster, nonetheless, was tasked with delving into Whitewater.

As deputy counsel, Foster also acted as White House liaison to the Justice Department. In the wake of the Watergate scandal, all White House contacts with Justice were required to go through the counsel's office. The deputy counsel was traditionally the designated point of contact. So it was probably no coincidence that, in an unusual move, Hillary put her closest friend in the world into this deputy's slot before even the counsel himself had been chosen.

For the top job, Hillary turned to Bernard Nussbaum, the New York lawyer who had supervised her work on the Watergate Committee and kept in touch with her ever since, contributing to Bill's campaigns for governor and sometimes sending legal work her way. Nussbaum ran the litigation section at the New York firm of Wachtell, Lipton, Rosen & Katz, where he made millions specializing in corporate mergers and acquisitions law. In choosing Nussbaum, who described himself in a *Washington Post* profile as "slightly" more liberal than Clinton, Hillary forsook a key qualification for the job—Washington political connections and finesse—choosing instead a trusted loyalist whose pugnacious corporate litigating style won him few friends in the capital. But this was precisely what Hillary thought she needed to keep official Washington—the press corps and congressional investigators—at bay. Nussbaum's experience with bare-knuckle tactics and intimidation of opponents in the Watergate Committee could not have been better training for the task at hand.

Foster and Nussbaum were joined at the White House by Rose managing partner William Kennedy, who had helped Hillary, Foster, and Webb Hubbell take control of the firm from Joe Giroir in the late 1980s. Unlike Foster, Kennedy very much wanted a White House position, but his relationship with Hillary had never been close. After the inauguration, Kennedy called Foster constantly, pressuring his former partner to find him a position, according to someone close to Kennedy. Foster was so overwhelmed by the volume of work facing him that he relented and offered Kennedy a job working for him. Ironically, Kennedy's clumsy maneuverings in the travel office firings would play a central role in Travelgate, the apparent catalyst for Foster's suicide.

The preference for loyalty over skill and competence was most glaringly seen in Foster's appointment of Kennedy—a strong-willed loyalist, but also a Washington neophyte with a mediocre intellect whose office was the scene of many multi-car pileups. Names of possible administration nominees leaked out before vetting was complete, resulting in terrible embarrassments for several prospective officeholders. Kennedy was responsible as well for a huge backlog of security passes for the thousand-member White House staff, about a third of whom still had only a temporary security pass fourteen months into the administration—even though the clearance process normally took only a few months. Of the one thousand employees, hundreds had blotches on their records—alcoholism, tax problems and even a few drug convictions—and consequently paperwork and clearance decisions bottlenecked. Kennedy dealt with the problems found in the background checks by the FBI or Secret Service by sitting on hundreds of applications, thereby jeopardizing the security of the White House. Working directly under Kennedy was Craig Livingstone, who had worked for Susan Thomases in the campaign advance operation. The former bar bouncer became a central figure in the 1996 Filegate scandal and Hillary was blamed for hiring him, a charge she denied.

Hillary's friends also held strategic posts in federal agencies with broad investigative powers. To head the Federal Deposit Insurance Corporation (FDIC), the White House turned to Renaissance Weekender and friend of Hillary Ricki Tigert. The FDIC would soon be investigating the Rose Firm's work for Madison Guaranty to determine whether the firm had any liability in connection with Madison's collapse. Another longtime ally of Hillary, Margaret Richardson, who had raised money for Clinton and advised Hillary on women's issues during the campaign, was named director of the Internal Revenue Service. Her husband John was a friend of Vince Foster's. With all these people in place, Hillary had erected an early warning system, freeing her to pursue her political goals.

Though Bill's longtime confidant Bruce Lindsey was named to head the White House personnel office, Hillary put in her own person, former Wellesley roommate Jan Piercy, as Lindsey's deputy, with special responsibility for recruiting "diverse" job candidates. (Piercy's husband Glenn was named chief of staff for the general counsel of the Commerce Department.) The struggle for diversity, sometimes called "Hillary's legacy" in administration councils, was achieved through 1970s-style quotas. The informal governmentwide goal—even in the career ranks, where appointments couldn't be undone—was a two-to-one ratio of women and minorities to white males. New race- and sex-based hiring quotas were instituted at the Department of Defense, the FBI, the State Department, and even local police departments nationwide. Federal air traffic controllers were issued "diversity handbooks" and women firefighters were mandated at the U.S. Forest Service.

An emblematic "diversity" pick was Regina Montoya, a Hispanic lawyer who had gone to Wellesley and Harvard. Montoya had served briefly with Hillary on the Wellesley board and once brought her to speak to a civic group in Dallas, where she lived. Montoya's husband, a Rhodes Scholar, had gone to Yale, where Robert Reich had been his thesis adviser. The couple raised money for Clinton in Texas in 1992. "Hillary was a legend. She was considered by all of us to be a role model," Montoya said. A few weeks after the election, Montoya got a call from Susan Thomases—whom she did not know—telling her that if she was interested in a position at the White House, she should fly to Austin to meet chief of staff McLarty. Montoya was later offered the important post of assistant to the president for intergovernmental affairs, which put her in charge of White House relations with all state and local governments across the country. Though she was bright, articulate, and earnest, Montoya didn't know much about political operations, and she lasted less than a year in the job.

When Montoya left, another Hispanic was quickly named as a deputy in the political affairs office, apparently to keep a racial balance. One black person in the White House was constantly fielding calls from presidential aides saying, "I need a black for such-and-such." After deciding to leave the administration, she was taken aback when queried, regarding recommendations for a replacement, " 'Do you have anyone black?' I was recommending two white men as the most qualified to replace me. They eventually put a black guy in there."

Though much of the quota system was implemented out of public view, the ill effects of the approach could be seen in the nomination for U.S. attorney general. Hillary's insistence that a woman be appointed to the post led to an early impression of gross incompetence when a series of trial balloons were cast aloft only to be embarrassingly burst. D.C. Circuit Judge Patricia Wald—who had been a researcher with Hillary on the book *All Our Children* at Yale—declined the job after reportedly refusing to approve Hillary's choices for second-tier Justice Department appointments. A friend of Susan Thomases, Connecticut lawyer Zoe Baird, was up next.

Before the nomination was proposed, the White House had known that Baird had not paid Social Security taxes on a nanny who was an illegal alien. When the problem was disclosed, conservative talk show hosts had a field day talking about the $500,000-a-year liberal corporate lawyer who wouldn't pay her nanny's Social Security. Baird soon withdrew. Next, Thomases' classmate at Connecticut College, Kimba Wood, was considered, but she was never nominated due to similar nanny-tax concerns. Though Hillary told the Associated Press she had not interviewed candidates for any jobs other than her own staff, it was later reported that Wood's interview with Hillary lasted twice as long as the one with Bill.

By the time Janet Reno was named attorney general, she was the fourth publicly known choice for the job. Reno had been introduced to Hillary when a Clinton campaign aide from Florida set up a meeting between the two during the campaign. The aide had heard through the grapevine that if Clinton was elected Hillary would appoint the first woman attorney general in history. According to the *Miami Herald*, Reno enjoyed the support of Marian Wright Edelman, who was familiar with her work in juvenile justice programs. Reno was also acquainted with Hugh Rodham, Hillary's brother, who had settled in Florida as a public defender. But her record as a prosecutor in Miami and Dade County, Florida, was less than sterling. "She has a losing record in the highest-profile cases. Her office has been accused of lacking investigative zeal, often letting cases languish for years," the *Houston Chronicle* noted. (Reno's runners-up were said to have been Nebraska Judge Lindsey Miller-Lerman, a classmate of Hillary's at Wellesley, and Brooksley Born, who had served with Hillary on the ABA's Commission on the Status of Women.)

Reno won respect outside the Beltway early on when she took responsibility for the deadly confrontation between federal agents and members of a religious cult at Waco, Texas, though she later conceded she had given the order based on a "misunderstanding" of ongoing child abuse inside the Branch Davidian compound, essentially an admission of incompetence. Reno had little presence in Washington, as her habit of reading the *Miami Herald* rather than the *Washington Post* showed. Never part of the Clinton inner circle, she preoccupied herself with promoting Hillary's social issues—dead-beat dads, hate crimes, gun control, children's rights, and domestic violence. She also authorized the use of the RICO statutes to prosecute pro-life protesters for blocking abortion clinics.

Two weeks into her appointment Reno came under fire for dismissing all of the U.S. attorneys nationwide. While an eventual replacement is standard practice, the timing suggested that it had been dictated by the White House for political reasons. All ninety-three U.S. attorneys were to be replaced by personnel handpicked by Hillary's appointees. It was a brash act no administration had ever undertaken so early in its tenure, suggesting an unprecedented level of partisanship and distrust of anyone who had ever served the United States under a Republican administration. Some also suspected that the firing of the U.S. attorneys was a means of creating cover for the replacement of the Little Rock U.S. attorney with Paula Casey, a former law student of Bill's who had worked as a volunteer in his races for governor and president. She was named just as a decision was pending on whether to act on the criminal referral from the RTC targeting associates of Madison Guaranty, including the McDougals, for prosecution. The *New York Times* editorialized that the mass firings "puts a premium on political control before she [Janet Reno] has established her own independence of White House politics, or even fielded her own top management. . . . When Ms. Reno says that dismissing all the U.S. attorneys was a 'joint decision' with the White House, she hardly reassures voters that she will be free of White House political manipulation. She needs to make it clear that she, not Mr. Hubbell, is running the department."

Webster Hubbell was the fourth member of the Rose Firm to join the Clinton administration. He went not to the White House but to the Justice Department. Like Foster, Hubbell was chosen before his nominal superior was named. Insisting that he be called "Judge" even though he had served on the bench in a temporary post for a short time, Hubbell was one person both Bill and Hillary appeared to trust implicitly and probably wanted as attorney general. But after John Mitchell's tenure in the Nixon administration, Washington looked askance at close political cronies of the president becoming attorneys general. Hubbell was placed in a deputy slot but he effectively ran the department anyway.

The original plan was that Hubbell would be the counsellor to the Attorney General—the White House's eyes and ears at Justice. This would have spared him Senate confirmation, which Hubbell may have feared because of the ethical cancer in his background: His overbilling of the Rose Firm and some of its clients would end in Hubbell's pleading guilty to mail fraud and tax evasion in December 1994. Hubbell was persuaded to become associate attorney general, ostensibly the department's number-three position, and he was easily confirmed before the overbilling matter surfaced. He took over a suite of offices next to the attorney general's—grand quarters usually reserved for the head of the Office of Legal Counsel.

Early in the administration questions surfaced about possible political direction from the highest levels of Justice into prosecutorial decisions in the corruption trial of Democratic Representative Harold Ford in Memphis, Tennessee. When Ford drew a jury that he argued was racially biased against him, he called Clinton to complain. Hubbell arranged for the Congressional Black Caucus to meet with Stuart Gerson, a Bush Justice Department holdover who was named acting U.S. attorney general until a Clinton appointee could take office. Hubbell also personally met with Ford's lawyer. When Gerson asked that the jury be dismissed, the U.S. attorney resigned and the trial judge protested. Gerson soon reversed himself.

Philip B. Heymann was named deputy attorney general and was put in charge of Justice's criminal division. As a veteran of the criminal division under President Carter, and a Harvard professor who prided himself on a squeaky clean reputation, Heymann lent an air of rectitude to the department that initially defused concerns about Rose Firm cronyism. Relations between the deputy and the associate attorney general have historically been tense, as they normally compete for power and access to the White House. Each administration divides the responsibilities differently, and one or the other appointee is often out of favor with the powers that be. In the Clinton administration, the plan was that the criminal side of the department was to report to Heymann and the other departments to Hubbell.

There was never really any contest between Heymann and Hubbell, as Hubbell immediately outflanked Heymann as the point of contact for the White House, even on criminal justice policy matters. Hubbell had regular meetings on Justice Department matters with Nussbaum to which Heymann was not invited; Hubbell also spoke almost daily with Foster. During his unhappy eighteen-month tenure, Heymann was so removed from the inner circle that he never met either Bill or Hillary Clinton outside of a large social setting.

In an interview on *Court TV* after he resigned in early 1994, Heymann stated the administration was making a "relatively serious mistake" by using Hubbell as the liaison to the White House. "It is no way to run a department," he said, adding that the relationship between Justice and White House should not be on "an informal, old-friend basis." Heymann's complaint might be dismissed as the sour grapes of a bureaucratic also-ran, but he was right that the close relations between Hubbell and the White House had the potential to compromise the institutional integrity traditionally associated with the department.

Yet another early imbroglio suggested that Hillary was willing to use the Justice Department to achieve political ends. During the Bush administration, House Energy and Commerce Committee chairman John Dingell had charged that the environmental division of Justice was lax in prosecuting environmental crimes, overruling local prosecutors to let polluters off the hook. Dingell launched an investigation, but the Bush Justice Department refused to make career attorneys available to be interviewed or disclose documents about their internal decision-making processes. When Janet Reno took office, she permitted the interviews, disclosed the documents, and handed the issue off to Hubbell, who appointed an internal committee to examine Dingell's charges and report to Congress, giving Dingell more ammunition to pursue his investigation.

The chief of the environmental division eventually resigned in protest. "There was a wave of euphoria [among career lawyers] when they [the Clinton appointees] arrived, but you would be amazed at the speed with which that dissipated. Congress has no right to look into the way prosecutorial decisions are made," said one environmental division lawyer. "I wrote internal memos on what was wrong with Dingell's investigation to Reno and Hubbell. Those documents got subpoenaed by Dingell. When they gave them over, the result was that no career person would ever trust [the Clinton appointees] again. The White House counsel, i.e., Hillary, really made the decision and Justice didn't go to bat," the lawyer said. He believed that the issue was hostage to Hillary's health care initiative, in which Dingell was a key player.

With the exception of the head of the civil division, who was Al Gore's brother-in-law, Justice's key divisions under Hubbell and Heymann were headed by women or minorities who shared Hillary's expansive rights-based view of the law. A typical choice was Anne Bingaman, the assistant attorney general for the antitrust division, who had met Hillary when she worked as a fund-raiser for the Children's Defense Fund. The wife of New Mexico senator Jeff Bingaman, her "main political interest had been the adoption of laws to protect women's rights, and she notes that she wrote one of the only books about the Equal Rights Amendment," a *New York Times* profile noted. Bingaman had also served as general counsel to Planned Parenthood of New Mexico. "Her hero is Thurman Arnold [the Yale Law School professor], who, in the late 1930s, embarked on an antitrust crusade in a vain attempt to revive Franklin Roosevelt's then-moribund New Deal," *Forbes* magazine wrote of Bingaman, who reversed the *laissez-faire* approach to enforcement of the anti-trust laws of prior Republican administrations and scrutinized corporate mergers more closely. Yale Law School professor Drew Days was named Solicitor General. He advocated a legal standard on gender equivalent to that on race, making it almost impossible for any classification based on gender to be upheld by the courts, and he filed a controversial Supreme Court brief arguing for the narrowing of child pornography laws. Vince Foster's sister, Sheila Anthony, the wife of a former Arkansas congressman, was named the department's top legislative strategist.

Judicial selection is one of the most important responsibilities of any president. The Justice Department's chief judge-picker for the mid- and lower-level federal courts was Boston lawyer Eleanor Acheson, a close friend of Hillary's at Wellesley. Breaking with precedent, the administration cut out the department's Office of Legal Counsel from participating in judicial selection, centralizing control in Acheson's Office of Policy Development. All told, through 1996 the Clinton administration appointed about a quarter of the federal judiciary. The general thrust of the opinions of these Clinton judges was one of liberal activism, including an expansive view of the rights of criminal defendants even in drug cases, endless death-row appeals, and defending race- and gender-based quotas. Liberal interest groups with political stakes in the outcome of such cases influenced the selection process, and Acheson made a major effort to appoint more women and minorities to the bench. Some of the appointed judges were members of the gender-bias movement in the law that Hillary had been intimately involved in at the ABA.

Hillary wanted even tighter control over the Supreme Court and top federal judgeships. Rather than relying on Justice to review and recommend potential Supreme Court nominations, as was the procedure in the Reagan and Bush years, the White House put together a "secret" team of seventy-five lawyers who scrutinized potential nominees' writings and judicial decisions. The team was headed by Washington lawyer James Hamilton, Hillary's friend from the House Watergate Committee. With Whitewater damage controller Jim Lyons, Hamilton had been the legal adviser to the Clinton transition. The highly unusual process—forgoing the seasoning and the institutional memory of the Justice Department—raised eyebrows in Washington legal circles and the legal press, but drew little notice otherwise. "Who are Clinton's Vetters and Why the Big Secret?" the *Legal Times* asked. The publication noted that the administration's failure to divulge the names of the judge screeners created the appearance of undue influence.

When a Supreme Court vacancy opened up in the spring of 1993, résumés and recommendation letters marked for Hillary's attention were faxed directly to the White House usher's office facsimile line. Hillary also participated in meetings in which the choice was deliberated. The first nominee to the high court was Ruth Bader Ginsburg, widely regarded as the Thurgood Marshall of equal rights for women. As an advocate with the ACLU's Women's Rights Project, Ginsburg won several landmark gender discrimination cases and had become the first woman law professor at Columbia shortly before Susan Thomases attended the school in the mid-1970s. Though she has said she had nothing to do with the appointment, Thomases was once Ginsburg's research assistant.

Ideological uniformity was also highly valued in the selection of appellate judges. Among the most controversial were Judge Martha Doughtrey of the Sixth Circuit, who had not voted to uphold one death sentence during her two-and-a-half-year tenure as a state Supreme Court justice in Tennessee; H. Lee Sarokin of the Third Circuit, who opposed all pretrial detention of criminal defendants; and Rosemary Barkett of the Eleventh Circuit, who struck down parental consent laws on abortion and used the justification of "emotional deprivation during childhood" as grounds for sparing convicted murderers from the death penalty.

Two of Justice's picks for U.S. attorney jobs engendered significant controversy as well. Janet Napolitano, named as U.S. attorney for Arizona, was a former legal services lawyer who represented Anita Hill during the Clarence Thomas Supreme Court confirmation. Napolitano was accused by ABC's *20/20* of having thwarted an undercover law enforcement operation to catch child molesters and child pornographers because she believed the sting unfairly targeted gay men. (Napolitano denied it.) The U.S. attorney in San Diego, Alan Bersin, a friend of Hillary's from Yale Law School, came under fire for determining that there is not a sufficient basis to prosecute border officials who have been accused by whistle-blowers of collaborating with Mexican drug traffickers.

The nomination of University of Pennsylvania professor Lani Guinier as head of the civil rights division of the Justice Department was in keeping with this philosophic orientation. Guinier was a classmate of Bill and Hillary's from Yale as well. As in the Johnetta Coles case, the nomination was defeated by moderate Democrats outside the administration who saw it as yet another betrayal of Clinton's moderate campaign stance. In an editorial headlined "Withdraw Guinier," *The New Republic* charged: "[Guinier] is a firm believer in the racial analysis of an irreducible, racial 'us' and 'them' in American society . . . her intellectual response to racial polarization is to polarize it further; to assume that racism is so endemic that electoral gerrymandering has to be supplemented with legislative gerrymandering; to hold that a color-blind equality of opportunity has to give way to a race-saturated equality of outcome."

In a book she later wrote on the controversy, Guinier told an anecdote to suggest that Hillary withdrew her support once Guinier's nomination engendered intense political opposition. As Guinier related the story, she ran into Hillary one day in the West Wing at the height of the controversy, and Hillary "breezed by me with a casual 'Hi, kiddo.'" Guinier continued: "When somebody tried to tell her that we were in the White House to strategize on my nomination, she turned slightly and said 'Oh.' She turned, full circle this time, and, to no one in particular, announced, 'I'm 30 minutes late to a lunch.'"[4] Some interpreted the anecdote to mean that Hillary was unprincipled, throwing Guinier off the sleigh at the first sign of trouble. What it really showed was that Hillary valued the political cause over personal loyalty: Guinier's less controversial successor, Deval Patrick, nonetheless followed many of the same policies Guinier might have been expected to impose.

A small but telling example of how Hillary's control of Justice's personnel process translated into policy could be seen in the Office of Legal Counsel. The OLC, which provides the attorney general—and often the president—with opinions on constitutional and statutory interpretation, was headed by Walter Dellinger of Duke University, a liberal scholar who had been active in the campaign against the confirmation of Robert Bork to the Supreme Court. One of Dellinger's key deputies, Dawn Johnsen, had been the general counsel of the National Abortion Rights Action League. The issue of Hillary's influence arose over the question of whether Clinton would sign an international convention on children's political, economic, and civil rights that had been unanimously adopted by the General Assembly of the United Nations in 1989 and ratified by more than 170 countries. True to Hillary's agenda on child welfare, the treaty created "international standards" governing adoption, sexual abuse, child labor, health care, and education and guaranteed an "adequate" standard of living for all children, encompassing "physical, mental, spiritual, moral and social development."

Conservative Christian activists attacked the treaty and tied its ideas, implicitly, to Hillary's views on children's rights. *Arizona Republic* columnist Kathleen Parker wrote that a

careful reading of the 21-page international treaty suggests a dangerous erosion of parental rights. . . . Children have the right to decide who constitutes acceptable company regardless of what Mom and Dad say? Children have the right to enjoy any media, including, say, electronic pornography, despite parental protestations? Children have the right to join a religious cult that contradicts their parents' beliefs? Given recent courtroom dramas in which children have challenged their parents' authority, even divorcing them in some cases, one can easily envision children suing parents who challenge these "rights." Although the treaty makes numerous seemingly perfunctory references to parental rights, the higher authority in cases of parental dispute could conceivably fall to the state. In the hierarchy of the treaty, parents are reduced to instruments of propagation. The state does the real parenting.[5]

Though defenders of the treaty said that it would be enforceable only under existing federal and state laws, some OLC lawyers in the Justice Department were wary of the United States being bound by a treaty that set standards for matters such as education and adoption, which are primarily the responsibility of states, not the federal government. "If the treaty became the law of the land, it would be ignoring our own Constitution," said one person who served in the department. "We received memos from Marian Wright Edelman pushing it. Non-government entities will often comment on treaties, but it was made explicit that Hillary Clinton really wanted it and we can't object on constitutional grounds." Hillary announced Clinton's decision to sign the treaty in February 1995. (It has yet to be ratified by the Senate.)

In addition to controlling the White House counsel's office, Hillary or her aides oversaw the appointment of general counsels of the various departments outside of the Justice Department as well. These lawyers review the policies and regulations of the agencies and have virtual veto power over them; they may use legal rationales as proxies for policy objections. Most of the general counsels were liberal women—Jamie Gorelick at the Pentagon, Jean Hanson at Treasury, and Judith Winston, of the Women's Legal Defense Fund, at the Department of Education.

What was unusual about Hillary's role in the personnel area was the extent of her network, which seemed both wider and more ideologically cohesive than Bill's. Hillary's cronies from the Carter Legal Services Corporation—including Steven Engelberg, F. William McCalpin, and Hulett "Bucky" Askew—either advised the Clinton transition or went back into high-level posts at the LSC. Kris Olson, a Wellesley and Yale classmate, was named U.S. attorney in Oregon. William Wilson, Jr., the "dimestore lawyer" with whom Hillary had practiced in Little Rock in the late 1970s, and who had represented Roger Clinton on drug charges, was named a federal judge. Martin Slate, a friend of Hillary's from Yale, was named to head the Pension Benefit Guaranty Corporation. Political science professor Diane Blair, Hillary's best friend, was named to a prestigious seat on the board of the Corporation for Public Broadcasting. Hillary's close friend Brooke Shearer headed a White House internship program. Shearer was the wife of top State Department official Strobe Talbott, Clinton's Oxford roommate who was *Time*'s diplomatic correspondent during the 1980s. Talbott had used his column to defend Clinton against draft-dodging charges during the '92 campaign. Brooke Shearer was also the sister of Derek Shearer, an economist, former Santa Monica city planning commissioner, and former anti-war activist, whom Clinton appointed ambassador to Finland.

Unfortunately for Hillary, the cultural divisions that had emerged in the Clinton campaign between her friends Susan Thomases and Harold Ickes and Bill's handlers were institutionalized during the transition. The FOBs who came into the White House stood in stark contrast to "Hillary's people." Though there was a general perception in the press that Hillary had brought an unsavory element into the White House—"all these Little Rock people are her people," columnist Morton Kondracke had said on the *McLaughlin Group*—it was really Bill who was responsible for bringing to Washington a gang of "Smart-Assed white boys," as columnist Maureen Dowd called them. While the FOHs tended to be serious policy people like Donna Shalala and Peter Edelman, the FOBs included aides de camp like chief of staff Mack McLarty; personnel chief Bruce Lindsey; White House administration director David Watkins; Dan Lasater protégé Patsy Thomasson; and part-time Clinton hanger-on Harry Thomason, the TV producer.

In addition to heading the personnel office, Bruce Lindsey performed the damage control function for Clinton that had been Betsey Wright's responsibility during the campaign. Though Hillary and her coterie had gotten deeply involved in containing Whitewater, she was not known to involve herself directly in managing the womanizing stories. Wright, whose personal style was considered too unpredictable for the White House, had not been asked to join the administration, though she continued to do freelance damage control from the outside. She became a lobbyist with a company run by Anne Wexler. Wexler had met Clinton in the 1970 Senate campaign of her husband Joseph Duffey, whom Clinton named director of the United States Information Agency.

According to a September 1994 *Washington Post* account, six months earlier, Lindsey had contacted a former flight attendant on the Clinton campaign plane, Christy Zercher, to see if she had been approached by reporters sniffing for allegations of sexual impropriety. In the spring of 1994, the *Post* was researching Paula Jones's sexual harassment claims. Multiple instances of alleged harassment might constitute a pattern, perhaps lending credence to Jones's charges. Zercher apparently had told the *Post* of Clinton's overtures to her on the campaign plane. "Did you say anything to anybody? What did they want to know? Did they want to know if Clinton was flirting on the plane?" Zercher quoted Lindsey as having asked her in the spring of 1994. Lindsey urged her to "say all positive things," the *Post* reported. (One of the other campaign plane flight attendants, Deborah Schiff, was hired as a personal assistant to Clinton in the White House.)

David Watkins, director of administration at the White House, was also a pal of Clinton's from Little Rock. He held a senior position in the 1992 campaign and, in what would prove to be a pattern of alleged misconduct, he was accused of sexually harassment by a campaign worker, who said Watkins made sexually suggestive comments to her as well as one sexual advance. Kathlyn Graves, a partner in Bruce Lindsey's Little Rock law firm, served as the escrow agent for a $37,500 payment by the Clinton presidential campaign to settle the complaint. (Graves would later defend Bill Clinton in the Paula Jones harassment case.)

Named as Watkins's top deputy was Patsy Thomasson, an Arkansas Democratic party operative and longtime aide to FOB Dan Lasater. When Lasater and his partner George Locke were jailed on drug-related charges in the late 1980s, Lasater gave Thomasson power of attorney over his business and personal affairs. In connection with the investigation of Lasater, an employee of Lasater's, Michael Drake, told the Arkansas state police that in 1984, Thomasson and Lasater "flew in Dan's jet—to allegedly buy a cattle ranch" in Belize. Drake and some other skeptics have questioned whether this was the only purpose of the trip. Among other duties, Thomasson was charged with overseeing the White House drug testing program; she was among those staffers who faced delays in getting a permanent security pass.

TV producer Harry Thomason (no relation to Patsy), a veteran FOB who had helped pull Bill's campaign together after the Gennifer Flowers revelations, was co-director of the inaugural. He and his wife Linda had choreographed the 1992 Clinton nomination, bringing down the house with their film, "The Man from Hope." In planning the inauguration, Thomason was assisted by future Filegate figure Craig Livingstone and sitcom star Markie Post, a Hollywood friend who had traveled extensively with Clinton during the 1992 campaign. "[W]herever the president went, she [Post] would be at his side," *People* quoted a Clinton campaign aide as saying. Post was named executive producer of the inaugural events for children. On the night after the inauguration, Thomason and Post celebrated with Bill in the White House residence past 2 A.M. In the following weeks, Thomason, sometimes accompanied by Post or Hollywood character actress Bobbie Ferguson (whose son Jay R. Ferguson starred in *Evening Shade*), worked in the White House on several projects, one of which, the shake-up of the White House travel office, would end in political disaster for the Clintons.

Many of the FOBs, like Lindsey and Walkins, didn't care much for Hillary. Others showed her outright disrespect. Marsha Scott, who referred to herself as Bill's "hippie girlfriend" from the time they dated in the 1960s when they both worked for Senator Fulbright, was the unofficial social director of the Arkansas set, organizing weekly get-togethers for the gang. She was given a job in the White House as director of correspondence. Late one night, Scott showed up at the residence, apparently a bit tipsy, with Webb Hubbell's two daughters in tow, demanding a tour. When told Bill wasn't in and Hillary had gone to bed, Scott insisted that the usher on duty phone up and get her access. Hillary was awakened, but there was no tour for Scott that night. Another FOB, Robyn Dickey, came to the White House with the Clintons from the Arkansas governor's mansion, where she had been the administrator. The residence staff nicknamed her "Thumbs" because one of her jobs was to give Clinton back rubs. Dickey often told the joke that Kentucky Fried Chicken had a new special in honor of Hillary—two large thighs, two small breasts, and a left wing.

If Hillary thought that by moving to Washington, DC she had escaped Arkansas' alien culture and the trials of life with Bill Clinton, she would quickly be disabused of that notion. Even on Inauguration Day, perhaps the most memorable and important day of her life, the moment was severely strained, if not spoiled, by an ingrained pattern of marital discord that was always on the verge of public exposure. That morning, there was an embarrassing delay at Blair House, where the Clintons were staying. The Clintons kept the Bushes waiting at the White House for twenty-seven minutes before arriving for coffee and then rushing off for the constitutionally mandated noon swearing in on the steps of the Capitol. "In the morning, at Blair House across the street from the White House, the TV cameras captured Clinton on the front stairs, looking impatient, apparently waiting for his wife Hillary. He stopped, looked up toward the door and said some word the microphones didn't catch. After he yelled again, she came scurrying down, rushing past him," *USA Today* reported. The newspaper headlined the piece: "Many a 'wow,' and hugs all around."

But it wasn't exactly all hugs at Blair House, according to a park police officer who was standing in close proximity to the Clintons that morning, witnessed the scene, and overheard Bill as he came out of Blair House, saying "That fucking bitch!" When Hillary came charging out after him, she was saying, "You stupid motherfucker!"

The scene was reminiscent of the accounts the Arkansas troopers had given of volatile married life in the governor's mansion. In a nightmarish replay of Hillary's experience in Arkansas, the story was widely repeated by a security staff which normally could be counted on to keep the confidences of the first family. Hillary once again would have to contend with a hostile security and residence staff which constantly traded derogatory stories about the Clintons' marriage and their personal habits.

The most infamous example of this came in the opening weeks of the administration, when it was reported in the *Chicago Sun-Times*, and then in *Newsweek*, that Hillary had thrown a lamp in the White House residence during a heated argument with Bill. The items were sourced to the Secret Service, which subsequently confirmed to this author that after Hillary threw the lamp, she seemed mortified when she realized she had been observed by a security officer. Shortly thereafter, Secret Service agents were permanently moved out of parts of the residence. The clear message from the first family to the staff was not to speak outside the White House about the Clintons' private life. Though she did not concede that Hillary actually threw the lamp, Maggie Williams later told Congressional investigators that Hillary had felt "compromised" by the breach of security. In April 1993, *Newsweek* reported that the first family was tired of the Secret Service talking to reporters and quoted a Treasury department official as saying that a new agency would be found to guard the Clintons if the tongue-wagging didn't stop.

From day one, the Clintons had been uncomfortable with the agents on the White House detail. Clinton had specifically complained that the agents didn't seem to like him. Hillary also sensed their hostility, and she was concerned about its impact on Chelsea. She made inquiries about replacing them with the agents who had guarded the Clintons during the campaign and the transition and took the matter up with Vince Foster and David Watkins, but no change was made.

Part of the problem stemmed from a cultural and political clash between the first couple—the first children of the 1960s to occupy the White House—and the career civil servants and security officers who worked for them there, recalling the reaction Hillary had received from the state troopers when she first moved into the governor's mansion in 1978. The early Clinton policy initiatives—gays in the military and executive orders expanding abortion rights, not to mention the elevation of the first lady to a policy-making role—were not popular with the many Republicans and even the traditionalist Democrats who served on the permanent staff.

Many on this staff also disapproved of the Clintons' lifestyle: meals on the run; Hillary flopping around in sweat pants; off-color language from both the president and his wife; the first couple sleeping in separate bedrooms. There were endless comparisons with the beloved Bushes—particularly Barbara, who had a patrician's touch for putting the servants at ease. When the Bushes had friends to the White House for dinner, they calculated to the penny the cost of the personal meals (only official entertainment is billed to the taxpayer). The Clintons weren't always so fastidious. The White House ushers were scandalized when Dorothy Rodham used a government car and driver to take her to a discount fabric outlet. In another example that runs contrary to their public image, the staff generally liked Hillary better than Bill, who, while supposedly the more "likeable" of the pair, was seen as thoughtless, unmannered, and unpresidential.

This undercurrent of personal disapproval was later taken public by FBI agent Gary Aldrich, who had been assigned to both the Bush and Clinton White Houses before retiring in 1995 and publishing a best-selling exposé on the Clintons, *Unlimited Access*. Like the troopers before him, Aldrich violated the discretion and respect for the office of the presidency—and the FBI itself—traditionally associated with such sensitive postings. After Clinton won election, Aldrich told people in the Bush White House that he hated the Clintons and intended to collect information for a book about them. While in his White House posting, he also fed sensitive information to Republicans on Capitol Hill who were investigating the White House staff. Among Aldrich's more outlandish claims was that Hillary had instituted a policy whereby the White House staff was instructed never to look at her. "When 'Queen Hillary' walks down the hall, you're not supposed to look at her. You're actually supposed to go into an office if there is one nearby. She doesn't want staff 'seeing' her."

His most sensational allegation was the report that Clinton, hiding under a blanket in the back seat of Bruce Lindsey's car, slipped his Secret Service detail and was whisked off to the Marriott Hotel in downtown Washington to meet women. Though it was nothing more than idle gossip, the full-scale White House damage control effort against the Aldrich book indicated the extreme sensitivity with which it regarded even unsubstantiated allegations of Clinton's womanizing. The overreaction suggested an awareness on the part of the Clintons' staff that such stories obtain a certain level of currency due to Clinton's reputation and his own behavior—particularly his enjoyment as president of opportunities to entertain attractive female celebrities like Barbra Streisand, Sharon Stone, Markie Post, and Eleanor Mondale, daughter of the former vice president and a television talk show host. (According to the Secret Service, it is almost impossible for a president to slip his detail. If he wanted to meet someone, the person would simply be brought into the White House or the president would travel to a hotel accompanied by security.)

It was little wonder, then, that once the Clintons' topsy-turvy private life came under intense scrutiny by hundreds of White House residence and security staff, Hillary would redouble her efforts to construct the "zone of privacy" that she had invoked in Arkansas to keep the press at bay. Though Hillary's near-obsession with privacy and staff loyalty would strike many as Nixonian paranoia, she had real cause for worry, as the lamp leak and, later, the Aldrich book demonstrated. The story-telling showed that some members of the staff did not exactly wish them well and that they were vulnerable to exposure. Only the White House press corps was able to fend off one of Hillary's protective maneuvers: When she suggested that they be moved out of their prime digs in the West Wing, an open revolt caused the White House to retreat. Others—including an usher Hillary fired who had a Bush/Quayle bumper sticker on his car and had maintained contact with former first lady Barbara

Bush, and seven workers in the White House travel office—weren't so lucky.

If nothing else, Hillary's ability to place her friends and associates in positions of influence in the new administration was a testament to the extraordinary energy with which she had pursued her networking contacts in the left-liberal establishment over the previous decade. First ladies have always played some role in guiding or advising their husbands in staffing the White House, and have sometimes adopted special policies or causes as their own. Never before had a first lady exercised direct influence over political appointments across the executive branch, nor had her predecessors seen fit to clear out career staffers seen as potentially disloyal. But then, no presidential spouse before Hillary had been so vital to the policy direction and political survival of her husband.

Ironically, while Hillary appears to have regarded the transition process and the creation of the damage control apparatus as merely the threshold of a much grander phase of activity—really, the culmination of her lifelong drive to grasp the levers of power in order to fulfill the promise of the New Deal and the Great Society—the successful placement of "Hillary's people" throughout the government would be the high-water mark of her public career. Her power would never be greater than in the very early days of the administration. Clearly, she did not appreciate the dangerous ambiguity inherent in her mold-breaking role as a nonelected government official—an ambiguity that would soon return to haunt her in the ill-fated health care initiative. Nor could she foresee that the great leap forward for women represented by her arrival in the White House would be undone by the backlash to follow.

12

Charge of the Light Brigade

The well-publicized failure of Hillary Clinton's health care reform initiative is one of the most spectacular shipwrecks in recent American history. Various explanations have been offered for the embarrassing debacle: the bewildering complexity of the plan and the sweeping scope of its prescriptions; the surprising strength of opposition from Republicans and special interest lobbies; the stunning disarray of the advisory process run by Ira Magaziner; and most damaging of all, sheer political ineptitude on Hillary's part. All of these explanations are plausible and even true to some extent. Where they fall short is in assuming that Hillary was somehow overtaken by events beyond her control, or that she simply lacked the experience and skill to carry it off. In fact, a careful reconstruction of events suggests that Hillary was the architect of her own defeat.[1]

Hillary's involvement with health care began early in the 1992 campaign, when Nebraska Senator Bob Kerrey was campaigning on national health insurance and faulting Clinton for having no health care plan. Not unexpectedly, Bill called in Hillary to help. Together with campaign aides Bruce Reed and longtime friend Ira Magaziner, who had given a seminar on health care at the Renaissance Weekend a few weeks before,

Hillary produced an eleven-page plan that promised health care for all. The plan, refined a bit in the Clinton-Gore campaign manifesto, "Putting People First," was later modified to include "managed competition," the perfect catchphrase for a candidate campaigning as a New Democrat.

While the plan relied on government controls, the campaign recognized the need to package it to appeal to moderate voters and thus establish Bill as the most conservative Democrat in the race. The strategy succeeded—so well, in fact, that after the dust had settled and the election was over, the Clintons realized that their narrow victory had rested on their promise to "do something" about health care and welfare reform. Welfare, it was quickly decided, would be left for the second half of their first term. Health care reform thus became the centerpiece of the new administration's domestic policy agenda.

Five days after his inauguration, Bill named Hillary to head a task force charged with drafting a bill within one hundred days to reform the health care system. "When I launched our nation on this journey to reform the health care system, I knew we needed a talented navigator, someone with a rigorous mind, a steady compass, a caring heart. Luckily for me and for our nation, I didn't have to look very far," Bill told a joint session of Congress later in the year. In this and other statements, Bill evoked an unalloyed warmth and enthusiasm for the choice, making it the occasion for the sort of public acknowledgment of Hillary's gifts that had undoubtedly been part of his seductive charm for her since their days at Yale. Inadvertently revealing his naïve expectation that the appointment would at last end the need for them to downplay the long-standing co-candidacy, Bill had also said of the choice: "I am grateful that Hillary has agreed to chair this task force, and not only because it means she'll be sharing some of the heat I expect to generate."

In a confessional moment at a 1996 press conference, Clinton conceded that he had been wrong to relinquish these responsibilities to his wife. "I may have asked her to do more than anybody should ever have been asked to do when I asked her to undertake the health care effort," he said. But having Hillary sort out the most complex challenges facing him had become a well-established habit. As she had shown in the educational reform effort in the mid-1980s, Hillary had a keen analytical intellect that allowed her to take in large amounts of complicated material and boil it down to its essence. She was a skillful and engaging public speaker and an impassioned advocate for causes in which she believed. She had shown herself willing to make difficult decisions and to disappoint supporters when necessary to achieve political victory. And she had an ability to present controversial initiatives in the language of traditional values.

There should be no doubt of the high purpose and sense of historical mission that Hillary brought to the enterprise. The role of health care czar was one she had been rehearsing for all her life. Following Social Security in the New Deal and LBJ's War on Poverty, government-run health care was to be the third sweeping liberal reform of the twentieth century, creating a new entitlement and thereby cementing the Democratic lock on the political system which began with Franklin Delano Roosevelt's first social security bill. As Donna Shalala put it, health care was the "last great social policy of this century. . . . the last piece, the country focusing on improving the quality of life for its people at the turn of the century." The legacy of universal health care would be the capstone of Hillary's political résumé, conceivably putting her in line, as Margaret Carlson had suggested in *Time,* to succeed her own husband as president in the year 2000.

As Hillary seemed to view it, more than health care itself was at stake. Health care reform was but one aspect of her larger mission to reform the society and even improve human nature. "This is one of the moments in history when we talk about national service and health care that we will not be helping ourselves, but we will truly be building the kind of community that we will be proud and grateful to live in," she said in one speech. In another she expounded on her view of American society as flawed and essentially uncaring: "This is what I hope—that in a few years we will not only have a streamlined, more efficient system . . . but we'll feel better about ourselves . . . [because] we'll all be part of a community of caring again."

In another address, Hillary suggested that the health care mission was a means not only of bettering society but of finding her own core of personal meaning:

> As students, we debated passionately what responsibility each individual has for the larger society, and just what the college's Latin motto—"Not to be ministered unto, but to minister"—actually meant. The most eloquent explanation I have found of what I believe now and what I argued then is from Vaclav Havel, the playwright and first freely elected president of Czechoslovakia. In a letter from prison to his wife Olga, he wrote: "Everything meaningful in life is distinguished by a certain transcen-

dence of human existence—beyond the limits of mere 'self-care' toward other people, toward society, toward the world. . . . Only by looking outward, by caring for things that, in terms of pure survival, you needn't bother with at all . . . and by throwing yourself over and over again into the tumult of the world, with the intention of making your voice count— only thus will you really become a person."

Health care also presented Hillary with the opportunity to leave her mark as a trailblazer among first ladies, as she became the first presidential spouse in American history to take a line-authority government job. As a result, she came up against everything from old-fashioned views of a woman's "place" to the Kafkaesque anti-nepotism and other procedural constraints put in place after Robert F. Kennedy's unprecedented service in his brother's administration.

From the beginning, the public was uncertain about the arrangement. An NBC/ *Wall Street Journal* poll in December 1992 found that 59 percent opposed Hillary having an official position in the Clinton administration and 32 percent favored it. Nonetheless, with a few exceptions—*New Republic* faulted Hillary for being a "false feminist" and decried the nepotism involved—the mainstream press was willing to overlook these inherent danger signs because journalists liked the idea of a first lady getting involved in policy as an equal partner and they frankly favored a government-run health care system.

Dismissing any concerns as out of touch with the progressive spirit of the moment, a *New York Times* editorialist wrote in January 1993: "Her more formal role is less a radical break than a logical evolution of earlier developments in a society where women are seen as partners and co-workers, not simply homemakers. . . . The argument that she was not elected is only half-true, since she was clearly as much a running mate as Al Gore. Did anyone doubt that she would play a policy role? Need anyone really mind?"

Columnist Morton Kondracke likewise endorsed the move on the *McLaughlin Group:* "She is precisely the right person for it. When she comes up with the program that she devises, Clinton will believe in it. . . . Old-fashioned people think that first ladies are supposed to be little wifey. Clinton and Hillary have broken the mold and Godspeed to them. I think it's great."

The goodwill of the media—which could have only emboldened Hillary— was best captured by CNN's Larry King, who described an interview with Hillary in his column in *USA Today* on October 4, 1993: "I saw a Hillary Clinton that I'd never seen before. She was funny, charming, sexy—yes, gang, sexy. We are both Scorpios, which tells you a lot. . . . Meanwhile, she has earned the respect of everyone (except the wackos) with her handling of the health care issue. Indeed, she has gotten everyone (except the wackos) to agree that we need health care for everyone. This is a very formidable lady, ladies and gentlemen."

Indeed, with the exception of Sally Quinn, who had recommended that Hillary find a job outside the White House, reservations about Hillary's role were expressed *sotto voce*. In their book on the Clinton health care effort, *The System,* veteran *Washington Post* reporters David Broder and Haynes Johnson wrote, "At the time, people in Washington widely suspected that Clinton had promised his wife the generalship in return for her support when he faced accusations of infidelity during his presidential race. We were never able to substantiate those rumors." Ever since the Flowers story first broke, rumors circulated among those close to the campaign that Hillary and Bill had fashioned a "Treaty of Georgetown"—an explicit or implicit deal giving Hillary a sphere of influence in exchange for her standing by Clinton amid the controversy. While those who had known the Clintons in Arkansas discounted such talk— surely she needed no deal or pact to secure her influence—the persistent rumors undermined her position and moral authority.

In approaching the assignment, Hillary's strategic model seems to have been the successful conduct of her education reform initiative. There, abetted by Dick Morris, she had seized upon an issue identified with moderate conservatives and presented a coercive scheme in the guise of centrist technocratic reform. She set up a bogus advisory committee and staged an elaborate public consultation process to validate a preconceived initiative. She gave the appearance of working very much within the established political process, building consensus and seeking votes, while short-circuiting debate within her own advisory group. She also discovered the usefulness of identifying an enemy and demonizing it to galvanize public support.

Thus, the idea that the failure of health care reform was largely due to Hillary's political inexperience cannot be sustained. She understood the importance of the reforms not only to average Americans—who she believed had given her and Bill a clear mandate to enact them—but to Bill's re-election prospects in 1996. The fact that these two purposes were apparently fused in her mind may explain why she concluded that the reforms were too important to be left to chance, or to an open political process. Therefore she once again relied upon a Trojan Horse technique. Unfortunately for Hillary, the same tendencies and characteristics that had worked for her in Arkansas, and appeared there as strengths, when tested now in a truly partisan political environment, would reveal not just surprisingly poor judgment on her part but character flaws of a particularly dangerous and self-destructive sort.

In the first flush of the hundred-day effort, Hillary framed the outline of the Clinton plan and talked to members of Congress, lobbyists, interest groups, and the public, in an effort to create momentum and rally support. She made dozens of courtesy calls on Capitol Hill, testified before committees in both houses of Congress, and went on a nationwide speaking tour reminiscent of her effort to sell Arkansans on her education plan. As part of a massive public relations blitz, Hillary went to Capitol Hill to introduce her plan to Congress that fall: "I'm here as a mother, a wife, a daughter, a sister and a woman," she began. In marathon sessions before five key House and Senate committees, the first lady demonstrated her command of the subject. Why was it necessary for employers to pick up the tab? someone asked. Employer mandates are practical, said Hillary, since "nine out of ten people who now have health insurance get it through their jobs." Could the plan's financing survive a "reality check?" asked another member. Yes, "there are considerable and substantial savings in the system," Hillary replied. "No previous first lady occupied center stage so aggressively or disarmed her critics more effectively," the *New York Times* said. "I think in the very near future," Ways and Means Chairman Dan Rostenkowski said, "the president will be known as your husband. 'Who's that fellow? That's Hillary's husband.' "

"It's hard to follow that answer, that was so brilliant a response," said Christopher Dodd, the Connecticut Democrat, before asking a question at one hearing. "As a nation, and as a people, we're blessed to have you leading this effort," said Representative John Lewis, a Georgia Democrat. Representative John La Falce of New York said, "I probably shouldn't say it, but she is so smart and I like her so much that I feel like squeezing her."

After meeting with individual legislators, Hillary always sent a letter the next day—and often an autographed photo—thanking them for their input. At hearings, she would ask them about family members by name and never missed an opportunity to compliment a specific piece of legislation they had worked on. One of Hillary's first private meetings was with Senator Dave Durenberger of Minnesota, a moderate Republican who had spent years developing expertise on the health care system. His vote would be crucial for the Clinton plan in the Senate. Durenberger was impressed by Hillary's preparation, which included a knowing reference to his home state. "When I called Mrs. Clinton at the end of February, she said she'd love to get together," Durenberger recalled. Displaying her intelligence, wit, and even a touch of flirtatiousness, "She said, 'Your place or mine?' When I went down to the White House, she mentioned an author from Minnesota she'd read [John Hassler]. She had picked up one of his books at the airport in Cincinnati and started reading them all." (Obscure nationally but popular in his home state of Minnesota where his novels are set, Hassler's stories revolve around tensions between tradition and more modern ideas about the church.)

Hillary's successful performances turned on political savvy and carefully planned attention to detail. But while Hillary's poise and charm worked wonders on congressional egos, her calculated efforts also raised some suspicions. "She impressed the finance committee, it was such a new event and glamorous in those circumstances," said former GOP Senator Malcolm Wallop of Wyoming. "But it was very unserious—it was all for the cameras. I suddenly realized I didn't have my make-up on. No one asked tough questions at all."

It would soon be clear that no amount of skilled politicking could paper over the deep divisions over the product Hillary was trying to sell and the way she was selling it. The public and many Republicans were ready to address serious problems in the health care system, from rising costs to the portability of benefits. But rather than talking about how the Clinton plan would make health care more affordable and reliable for the middle class, or help the elderly afford prescription drugs, Hillary presented the plan in the language of a welfare advocate. The hard truth was that extending full and free benefits to the uninsured and unemployed struck many as another budget-draining government giveaway. Hillary also did not seem to appreciate the public's deep distrust of the idea that government could make the system better by getting more involved.

In its design, the Clinton plan reflected who Hillary was and where she had come from. Hillary Rodham had gone into politics to improve people's lives by extending what she saw as the beneficent potential of government. She made no bones about her distrust of the free market system, or her lack of confidence in the prudent rationality of average Americans. She simply did not believe that a largely unfettered private sector could provide adequate health care at affordable prices. "We know that we have the finest doctors and researchers and scientists and hospitals and nurses in the world," she said in a speech before employees of the National Institutes of Health in February 1994. "But we also have the stupidest financing system for health care in the world, and the stupidity of that system threatens the quality of all that you do and are engaged in doing to try to improve the health of both individuals and a nation."

Hillary was especially troubled by the seeming imperfectibility of the market. When she gave speeches in support of her reform plan, she sometimes told the story of how she had realized something was deeply wrong when she sat down with a legal pad and tried to describe the current American health care system. It got so complicated and confusing she couldn't do it and gave up. As many in the business community saw it, Hillary conveyed an attitude that bordered on contempt for the private sector. When she was challenged on what might be done to ease the burden on small business of paying for employees' health care in one public appearance, Hillary responded, "I can't go out and save every undercapitalized entrepreneur in America."

To Hillary and her allies, central planning meant eliminating inequalities in the system, providing for the disadvantaged, and sharing the costs of health care equally among all Americans. But to critics, the plan's state-run "alliances," mandatory membership in health maintenance organizations, caps on insurance premiums, and annual limits on overall health care spending meant more government, fewer services, and less choice. The plan was loaded with politically appointed government boards and oversight agencies, designed to enforce corporate and individual compliance with federal standards, which specified in intricate detail the kind of health care services that could be provided, to whom, under what circumstances, and at what prices. Employers would pay for the bulk of the coverage, establishing a new middle-class entitlement, while government covered the uninsured. Most everyone would be required to join state-run or regional health "alliances," government-controlled middlemen who would contract with various health plans, collect and negotiate insurance premiums, and oversee the allocation of benefits. A National Drug Price Advisory Board would decide whether drug prices were "fair." Confidential medical records would be centralized and accessed through special identification numbers placed on government issued health security cards.[2]

Dennis Hastert, a Republican from Illinois who chaired the GOP's House task force on health care, began meeting in February with Clinton administration officials as part of an effort to craft a bipartisan approach to reform. One evening in June 1993, a group of Republican congressmen, including Hastert, met with Hillary at the Alexandria home of Republican Representative John Kasich of Ohio. One of Hastert's ideas under discussion that night would have allowed employers the option of establishing medical savings accounts for their employees as an alternative to a government-managed system. Under Hastert's plan, employers would put the money they were willing to spend subsidizing employees' health care into tax-deferred accounts. Employees would be encouraged to buy high-deductible catastrophic care policies and pay for rudimentary services with the remainder of the money. At the end of the year, the unused funds could be rolled over tax-free into the next year and, like an IRA, be withdrawn at retirement. Hastert and other advocates believed that as people shopped around for insurance and spent their own money to purchase care, costs would be controlled and competition enhanced. But critics said the accounts would benefit healthier people, who would spend less than what employers contributed, and hurt the poor, who might pay higher premiums as healthier and wealthier people formed their own insurance purchasing pools.

Hastert soon concluded that there was little common ground on which to negotiate with the administration. "I guess the straw on the camel's back was a meeting that I had one evening with Mrs. Clinton," Hastert recalled.

> I mentioned . . . to the first lady about medical savings accounts and just right away she said, "We can't do that." And I said, "Well, why?" And she said, "Well there's two reasons." And I said, "Well, what are they?" [And she said] "The first reason is with the medical savings account, people have to act on their own and make their own decisions about health care. And they have to make sure that they get the inoculations and the preventative care that they need, and we just think that people will skip too much because in a medical savings account if you don't spend it, you get

to keep it or you can . . . accumulate it in a health care account. We just think people will be too focused on saving money and they won't get the care for their children and themselves that they need. We think the government, by saying 'You have to make this schedule. You have to have your kids in for inoculations here, you have to do a prescreening here, you have to do this'—the government will make better decisions than the people will make, and people will be healthier because of it." I said, "Well, part of that's an education process. People have to understand that [if] they behave a certain way, they're going to save money, [with the] preventive medicine issue—you get the prescreenings, if you can inoculate your kids you save money on it. I mean, they're not sick. You save money." She said, "No. We just can't trust the American people to make those types of choices. . . . Government has to make those choices for people."

I said, "Okay, we just disagree there. But what's the second reason?" And she said, "Well, the second reason is, with a medical savings account, savings are [like] an IRA. They go in as actually money saved and all that money will go into IRAs which goes to the private sector." And she said, "We can't afford to have that money go to the private sector. The money has to go to the federal government because the federal government will spend that money better than the private sector will spend it." And so [I thought] holy mackerel. I can't argue these issues, these are philosophical issues.

Hillary's pro forma outreach to the Republicans was short-lived. The opportunity for a truly bipartisan approach to health care reform was squandered early on at a time when many moderate Republicans, including senators John Danforth of Missouri, John Chafee of Rhode Island, and even minority leader Bob Dole had signaled a commitment to universal coverage and a readiness to work with the White House. "We're going to start down the road together," Dole had said. Had Hillary not been so dismissive or mistrustful of the Republicans, many would have supported a middle-ground bill giving her most of what she wanted. "Dole had formed a task force under [John] Chafee before the Clinton bill got started," said Senator Paul Coverdell, Republican of Georgia. "They were Washington-wonking it. [Senator Phil] Gramm came out of one of their meetings and turned to me and said, 'Good grief. We've got to do something.' " Hillary's stance left the moderates with little ground to stand on, and conservatives like Gramm soon came to dominate the debate on the Republican side of the aisle. After meeting with Hillary,

Dennis Hastert reported back to the GOP minority in the House that there was no basis for cooperation with the administration, and he soon began drafting a Republican alternative.

It should be no surprise that Hillary's visits to Capitol Hill left Republicans feeling perplexed. She seemed interested neither in their votes, nor in their input. Rather than reflecting her political clumsiness, however, what the Hastert incident seems to illustrate is Hillary's extraordinary confidence in her mandate. She and her staff had already counted the votes and they apparently believed that with Republicans in the minority they simply were not needed to win. Such tough political calculations are made all the time in the legislative process. Hillary, however, did not seem to appreciate the dangers of tearing down an entire health care system—something that affects every American—without some degree of consensus and bipartisanship. The view of Hillary as uninterested, and perhaps even insincere, in her solicitation of the opinions of Republicans and conservative Democrats was reminiscent of her unwillingness in Arkansas to entertain criticism of her education reform proposals. The difference was that while there was broad consensus in Arkansas that the school system was badly in need of sweeping reform, many Americans believed that the health care system, whatever its faults, was still the best in the world and that therefore only incremental reform was needed.

Surprisingly, even some top officials in the Clinton White House appeared to believe that Hillary's "outreach" was merely tactical. In early 1993, Hillary made an overture to one senior Democratic senator, David Boren, a moderate from Oklahoma, in an effort to gain not only his support but also his help in bringing others aboard, including moderate Republicans like Chafee. "Before the meeting, I was warned by senior people in the White House that she didn't really want a centrist approach and not to allow myself to get used by her," Boren said. " 'Don't get yourself used,' I was told. I had explicit warnings not to front for her."

Hillary's confidence also illuminates another unexplained feature of her approach: her mystifying reliance on a circle of advisers whose ideas were far out of the mainstream. Curiously, the ideology of Hillary's top advisers was not a subject of interest to the press: CNN's health correspondent, Jeff Levine, for example, referred to central-planning advocate Ira Magaziner as a "free marketeer," and most other reporters hewed to the administration's spin that the Clinton plan was a moderate market-based approach to reform. On closer examination, however, it is clear that the press missed the story.

Like Hillary, Ira Magaziner, a senior White House adviser overseeing the health care task force, had an appetite for the big and bold. The gangly, frizzy-haired New Englander, described by one colleague as "a cross between Ichabod Crane and Svengali," was the quintessential Washington outsider. "I'm not interested in chip shots," he told the *Washington Post Magazine*. "I want to do stuff that, if it is successful, will make a big difference. A lot of people in politics win a lot of battles but never win a war." According to one participant, upon opening the first health care working group meeting Magaziner declared: "It's now show time. It's going to happen this year, there is going to be comprehensive legislation submitted, and there's going to be the full force of the presidency behind it."[3]

Magaziner first met Bill Clinton at Oxford, where he led antiwar demonstrations along with actress Vanessa Redgrave at nearby U.S. military bases. But it was Hillary and Magaziner who were the true kindred spirits. In high school, the young student activist led a boycott against saluting the flag, and at Brown University he spearheaded efforts to eliminate required courses and grades. During graduation ceremonies, valedictorian Magaziner got his class to stand up and turn their backs on an honorary degree recipient—National Security Adviser Henry Kissinger. "Realities exist, but they're not real to me," he confessed in his commencement address. He was mentioned in the same *Life* article on student speakers that featured Hillary at Wellesley; Magaziner's future wife graduated from Wellesley a couple of years after Hillary.

Magaziner gained something of a reputation in the 1970s and 1980s as a guru for the so-called "Atari Democrats," who advocated a European-style industrial policy of government investment and central planning. He advised Michael Dukakis, Gary Hart, and Richard Gephardt, among others, and co-wrote a book with Robert Reich, *Minding America's Business* (1982), that contended U.S. industry is hurt when the government clings to a "laissez-faire approach that is both naïve and dangerous."

In the early 1970s, Magaziner and his classmates from Oxford and Brown had set out to take over the industrial, shoemaking city of Brockton, Massachusetts, and transform it into a "social democracy." They sponsored rent strikes and food coops and fought local developers. After the failure of several factories, Magaziner and his young band of reformers abandoned the city. A decade later, he pushed a plan to create state-subsidized "greenhouses" in Rhode Island that would foster new enterprises in robotics, photovoltaics, medical technology, and computers to replace declining manufacturing industries with about $250 million in new taxes. The entire economics department at Brown University panned the plan. "Ira's economic ideas were primitive, just off the wall," economics professor George H. Borts told the *New York Times*. When the greenhouse plan was presented to the electorate, the scheme was defeated by a four-to-one margin.

In the 1980s, he commanded $600 an hour from corporate giants who saw his innovative management principles as the magical solution to their companies' lagging productivity. Though he eventually sold the consulting business he had built for a reported $6 million, Magaziner's actual record was checkered at best. Working for General Electric's refrigerator unit, he recommended that the company switch the type of compressor it used, which ended up costing GE more than $300 million when the compressors Magaziner recommended had to be replaced because of design flaws. He told an already financially ailing Wang Laboratories to stop building computers and try imaging software instead. Wang followed his advice and went bankrupt soon after.

Hillary knew Magaziner through Renaissance Weekend circles and also through her work in the early 1990s with the National Center on Education and the Economy, a nonprofit, state-subsidized policy foundation in New York. In 1990, the center released a report entitled "America's Choice: High Skills or Low Wages," prepared under the direction of Magaziner. The report advocated state-funded education for all Americans for four years beyond high school, and the establishment of a nationwide network of federal and state employment and training boards to "organize and oversee the new school-to-work transition programs and training systems" for those who sought an alternative to college education. It also sought to introduce nationalized health care through the nation's schools. The Rose Law Firm was paid more than $100,000 for Hillary's work to promote the new programs and work on their implementation. The recommendations of the center were consistent with the technocratic liberalism of Hillary's education standards and outcome-based education programs in Arkansas, designed to make schools and students conform to a narrow set of state-mandated learning goals. (Goals 2000, the Clinton administration's education plan, also emphasizes outcome-based education.)

Shortly after Clinton was elected, Marc Tucker, the director of the National Center on Education and the Economy, wrote to Hillary addressing the issue of "what you and Bill should do now about education, training, and labor market policy." In the introduction to a section of the letter entitled "Vision," Tucker wrote, "Radical changes in attitudes, values, and beliefs are required to move any combination of these agendas." He went on to suggest a quasi-socialist scheme whereby government, schools, and big business would be compelled to work together to produce and certify "world class" workers.

Another influential adviser of Hillary's was Vicente Navarro, who openly espouses Marxist views and is an advocate of socialized medicine. A health policy professor at Johns Hopkins University, Navarro has devoted his career to promoting government-controlled medicine. "The private sector is dangerous to our health," Navarro once wrote. In a 1992 article "Has Socialism Failed?" Navarro contended, "contrary to what is widely claimed today, the socialist experience (in both its Leninist and its social democratic traditions) has been, more frequently than not, more efficient in responding to human needs than the capitalist experience." In 1988, Navarro joined Harold Ickes in the Reverend Jesse Jackson's presidential campaign as an adviser to help craft a comprehensive national health insurance scheme.[4]

Navarro was a leading advocate of a "single-payer" health care model, such as the one in place in Canada, where the government is the sole provider of medical services. This approach, which relies on taxes to pay for "free" medical care for all, was backed by key Democratic constituencies, such as labor unions, and was championed in Congress by Senators Jay Rockefeller, Bob Kerrey, and Paul Wellstone and Congressman Pete Stark.

According to internal White House memos Navarro co-chaired a health care group exploring a single-payer plan, which gave him significant access to Hillary. (The documents were later released in a bitterly contested lawsuit over the legality of the health care task force operations.) Navarro told Hillary that without a liberal base, her plan would be a flop. In the September 1993 issue of the *Nation*, Navarro opined, "The Clinton administration is well aware that health care reform cannot occur without the support of the single-payer constituencies, which include some of the key grass-roots sectors of the Democratic Party. Hillary Clinton has repeatedly said as much."

Navarro appeared to confirm Hillary's belief that proposals to rely on the market to achieve reform should be rejected not only in principle but also as bad politics. "It will be assembly-line capitalism for the masses and their health care givers, with the elites continuing to enjoy free choice and fee-per-service medicine," he wrote in the *Nation* in late 1993. "I told Mrs. Clinton that if she and the president went ahead with that [managed competition] plan that it would be defeated, and that her husband would lose his reelection," Navarro told the *Capitol Times* newspaper in December 1994.

Navarro's participation in the task force came over the strong objections of some top White House staff advisers, including health care aide Walter Zelman, a former Common Cause official who made a name for himself in California by designing a health care plan for the state that combined competition with price controls. In a March 1993 memo to Ira Magaziner, Zelman warned that Navarro had been asked specifically by Hillary to become involved in health care "governance" issues. "[A] number of individuals involved in our effort have vigorous objections to Navarro's involvement," Zelman wrote. "Apparently, he is a real left-winger [and] has extreme distaste for the approach we are pursuing. He wants to be involved to the greatest extent possible in a role, he explained to me, that gives him the greatest opportunity to influence our process. . . ."

Like Ira Magaziner and Vicente Navarro, Hillary's third recruit, Luanne Nyberg, leaned toward technocratic socialism. Nyberg was a career left-wing activist in Minnesota, where she staged protest drives on behalf of various causes, including expanded state health care benefits. After being fired from a job at a Minneapolis print shop for trying to form a union, she founded a group to demand "rights" for people on Minnesota's welfare rolls. She successfully spearheaded a bill requiring the state to provide basic health care for uninsured pregnant workers and for children under eight. She then joined a state representative in expanding the program to the rest of Minnesota's uninsured. The program costs reached nearly $1 billion a year, bankrolled by state residents paying higher insurance premiums. Nyberg's main connection with Hillary came as founder of the Minnesota chapter of the Children's Defense

Fund in 1985. As a friend of Hillary's Chief of Staff Maggie Williams, Nyberg had a temporary assignment in Hillary's office in the summer of 1994, when crucial decisions on health care strategy were being made.[5]

Associates said that while Hillary and Magaziner privately favored the single-payer plan, they understood that it would be politically impossible to pass a Canadian-style plan under that name in the United States. The strategy they therefore chose was a classic exercise in cooptation. Early in the year, Hillary and Magaziner met with representatives from the Jackson Hole Group—academics and industry professionals who had coined the phrase "managed competition," which was used to distinguish the original Clinton plan from the single-payer version advocated by Bob Kerrey. But if the architects of managed competition thought that their ideas would be adopted by the task force, they were soon disappointed. Alain Enthoven, a Stanford University economics professor and board member of the group, said, "I resent the fact that they dressed up the single-payer plan in the language of 'managed competition' à la the Jackson Hole group. It discredited us. They were borrowing our rhetoric. It was really deceptive and misleading."

In their meeting, Enthoven and his associates laid out their idea: health maintenance organizations (HMOs) would compete for patients and large insurance purchasers would then bargain with the HMOs for reasonable prices. "I made the point that the market was working, and that it was not necessary to have price controls," said Dr. Paul Ellwood, president of the Jackson Hole Group. "And I can remember very distinctly Mrs. Clinton saying to me, 'You're wrong about that.' There was that kind of up-front assumption, at least on her part, that the market wasn't working. . . . They flat out denied what I had said, and not 'they'—her—she."

Hillary and Magaziner had originally considered slapping across-the-board price controls on virtually every sector of the health care industry. She saw this as both ideologically sound and pragmatic: She believed that government control over the marketplace was the only way to achieve results before Clinton ran for re-election in 1996. In her meeting with the Jackson Hole Group, Hillary said little during the presentation, but when she finally spoke up, Enthoven recalled her saying: "Yeah, that's all very well, but my husband wants to get re-elected . . . so we'll have to put the whole thing under price controls." (Consistent with the Trojan Horse strategy, formal price controls were dropped from the plan, replaced by government controls through the back door: The health alliances would cap insurance premiums).

Enthoven conceded that Hillary was correct that market reforms were harder to predict than government mandates, but he believed her bias toward the single-payer plan was a sign that she simply did not comprehend the recent lessons of history. "Let's take some steps backwards. Take the blinders off," he said. "We've had a century-long struggle between socialism and capitalism and guess what? Capitalism won."

Members of the Jackson Hole Group were soon banished from the inner councils and left to "hang around the halls" of the Old Executive Office Building during working group meetings, according to one group member. "Mrs. Clinton thought they owned the Democratic Party and to get their plan through they thought they had to purge all the dissidents, but what they did was end up taking shots at the moderates—their crucial mistake," Alain Enthoven said.

Meanwhile, White House aide Walter Zelman fretted that the administration's insistence on disguising the plan as moderate "managed competition" was causing confusion among putative allies on the left. "They [liberals] believe our direction is somehow fundamentally different from the 'single-payer' approach they favor. It is not. . . . Perhaps we have done too good a job about selling managed competition," Zelman wrote in an internal memo. Representative Pete Stark, for example, favored a more straightforward single-payer plan. After Clinton's election, a jubilant Stark—an important would-be ally who chaired a key House Ways and Means subcommittee—canceled a vacation with his new wife, hoping for an invitation from the White House to meet on a universal health care plan. The phone never rang, and Stark became a critic of the administration from the left. "What I have trouble with is a program which suggests to me we can save money, broaden access, and provide better medical care and I can't figure out what it costs [or] who it hurts," Stark said. "It's somewhat akin to [televangelist] Pat Robertson: If we just pray the right prayer to the right god, all our cares will go away."

Hillary clearly understood the advantages of making a rhetorical concession to the right, masking the fact that substantively the plan was quite close to the single-payer approach. "As a political document . . . it was brilliant," said Tom Scully, a former lobbyist with the Federation of American Health Systems who was hired by a group of hospitals to try to kill the health insurance purchasing cooperatives or HIPCs. "The liberal Democrats could look at the caps and the global budgets and the HIPCs and think the plan was headed towards single-payer. But if market people looked at it, they saw competition. It was cagily written to make everyone see what they wanted to see. Their problem was, legislatively, they never moved to the middle. So politically it was brilliant. Substantively, it was massive overregulation and big-government disaster."

The blackballing of the Jackson Hole Group also showed that Hillary needed firm control over the advisory process itself if the final plan was to follow her preconceived one. Like the use of "managed competition," a figleaf for a highly centralized approach, hundreds of advisers were brought in to create the appearance that contrasting views were being solicited and the best minds in America were being consulted. This was primarily intended to cloak the plan in the armor of intellectual respectability. The participating organizations were also given the illusion that they were actually being consulted, thereby neutralizing their potential opposition.

In an effort that ended up costing more than $13 million, Magaziner set up a five-hundred-member working group comprising hundreds of federal workers, Capitol Hill staffers, academics, and private sector consultants. He then constructed an elaborate "tollgate" process to monitor the fifteen "cluster groups" and forty smaller committees which were conducting in-depth studies of virtually every issue associated with health care, ranging from cost control and long-term care and mental health issues to medical ethics and anti-trust regulations. As one working group member put it, "he wanted to invite the world in"—everybody, that is, but Republicans and certain business and doctors' groups, all of whom were pointedly excluded. (While the health care working group was made up of over five hundred members, the official twelve-member health care task force, chaired by Hillary, was made up of cabinet members and top aides to the president.)[6]

But it soon became clear even to those who were included that their participation was largely illusory. Just as she had done with education reform in Arkansas, Hillary made up the plan before the health advisers ever met. "One of the popular games we played was to sit around and try to figure out why we were there," said Tom Pyle, a highly regarded health care expert who originally led one of the important working groups. Hillary appeared to mistrust even members of her own team who might

raise questions about the approach to reform. One government employee who was assigned to the working group said, "I don't know how
the decisions were being made. I can tell you flat out I was told, 'We want
to talk about this, but we don't want to hear from you feds about it.' "

"Ira Magaziner approached this like he was Zeus preparing to give
birth to Athena out of the side of his head," said another working group
member. "He used these five hundred people as his personal tutorial to
make him an expert in health care policy which he'd had little involvement with before. At the end of the tutorial, he would, as the genius that
he holds himself out to be, conceive a grand interrelated, internally consistent health care reform policy that he would give birth to, and all of
Washington would just accept it."

While plausible enough from the perspective of a bewildered participant, this seems not to have been Magaziner's intention at all. Rather
than synthesizing the great outpouring of material generated by the
process, the broad outlines of Magaziner's plan were already written.
Some participants sensed as much. "It was very difficult to know if their
interest in our feedback was real. I had a nagging sense that they had
written the whole thing before we got there," one health care working
group member said. A higher-ranking group member confirmed these
suspicions: "There was no even-handed review of alternative policy options. Ira Magaziner drafted a work plan which I read the day before I
started work, which laid out, chapter by chapter, exactly what was going
to be done. . . . Not only was managed competition assumed, it was assumed that price controls would be required. That was part of the original, day-one work plan. It was worked out before the five hundred
people got there. Now Ira Magaziner was listening to these working
groups for sort of tactical implementation kinds of ideas. But the basic
broad parameters were set in place."

In the same vein, Hillary seemed less concerned with hearing all
points of view than she was with the racial and gender composition of
those contributing them. "There were constant attempts to rebalance
the working groups racially," Tom Pyle said. "People were added to the
working groups based on their gender and color. We were told to add
people to groups. It was embarrassing because it was demeaning to the
people involved. At one point a White House aide said: 'Hillary wants to
see more black faces.' We were always shuffling people around to bring
someone into a role as a group head who didn't feel comfortable in that

role. With this constant movement in the groups, we couldn't get anything done." Memos released by the White House also reflected this concern. One working group member reported that the group studying
health care ethics included "a Protestant minister, a Jesuit, . . . a
Rabbi, . . . four African-Americans, one of whom is also a woman. . . . We
also contacted a woman who teaches medical ethics and is herself un-
sighted." (One of Hillary's less noticed proposals was to nationalize all
U.S. medical schools to achieve a more desirable racial and gender mix
among doctors.)

In conducting his tutorials, Magaziner insisted on a captive audience.
In a comic effort to meet the hundred-day deadline imposed by President Clinton, he made group members sit in discussion groups literally
around the clock. "Ira Magaziner would wear the same clothes the whole
session," Andrea Bempong, a working group member, recalled. "Every
day he had the same outfit on. And we thought unless he had two or
three of the same shirts—we didn't know what he was doing. We guessed
he was staying up all day and all night." Ultimately, the person most in
need of health care seemed to be Magaziner himself. "He was constantly
getting sick," said another member of the working group. "He was going
around the clock. The two months I was working on it he must have had
three separate colds or flus. He was sick almost the entire time. Cough-
ing in front of everyone."

As Magaziner pushed toward a deadline he would never meet, it became clear that the plan was sealed off from any and all internal criticism. The view among many even in the Clinton administration who were
serving on the working groups was that the plan was simply too ambitious and expensive. Not even the White House's own economists believed the resources matched the goals. "None of the [administration]
economists supported the Clinton health care plan," said one senior
Treasury Department official.

Yet nobody appears to have told Hillary—who may have seemed om-
nipotent by virtue of her marriage to the president—that she was on a
collision course with fiscal reality. "I was in some meeting with Rubin
[Robert Rubin, chairman of the National Economic Council] and he
didn't speak up. He never really weighed in," said a health care lobbyist
who had substantial access to the White House. "I think he was afraid of
her. All those guys were afraid. It was fairly obvious that a lot of those

guys there were intimidated by her—the top ten to twenty people in the White House. A lot of them knew it [the plan] was ridiculous."

Originally, the goal had been universal care with modest benefits. But Hillary wanted a more generous plan: The government simply had to take a more aggressive role in ensuring proper care. By including more benefits, the administration was hoping to satisfy the multitude of interest groups scrambling to be included in the plan as well. Strategically, the White House knew that a big benefits package would give them bargaining chips in dealing with Congress. The catch was that the larger the benefits package became, the more regulations were needed to control how they would be administered, and the more costly still the plan would become. Said the Treasury official: "She [Hillary] went around the country finding out what people's gripes were, and each time she came back with one more load of what needed to be included. Things like long-term care, mental health, dental care, and substance abuse. She just came back and kept saying 'We have to include this, we have to include that . . .' She would end up listening to people's problems all over the country and being the sympathetic person she is she said, 'These are their problems and they need to be addressed.' By the end it was full-scale cradle-to-grave medical services for everyone. There had to be some cost consideration. Those were the things giving people over here in Treasury severe gas pains. We saw the price would be so high it was not economically viable."

Finally, it was left to Laura Tyson, chairman of the Council of Economic Advisors and one of the few senior women working in the area, to raise critical questions about the plan's financing. In a memo summarizing an April 1, 1993 meeting where Tyson and administration aides struggled to figure out how to pay for all the benefits Hillary wanted in the package, a Treasury Department economist wrote, "We sat around the table making guesstimates of the savings to be realized. It was an appropriate exercise for April Fool's Day."

Though Hillary's working group members often felt as if their contributions were unimportant to the development of the plan, she nonetheless mandated that they operate under strict secrecy rules. While confidentiality is important in any such undertaking, Hillary went to such extraordinary lengths that the effort was self-defeating. As the plan was drafted, no copies could be made of any materials. In some cases, not even pencils and paper were allowed into rooms where someone might take notes, and room monitors kept track of who looked at what. "They [the task force] would take documents away from us and look for leaks. They didn't trust us. You'd think you were in the FBI," said Mary Jo O'Brien, Minnesota's former health commissioner and a working group member. ". . . They made lots of attempts at security. You couldn't take your documents with you. You had to keep the stuff there. The funny thing was, these were not new ideas. I expected it would be stuff that could be patented, but there was nothing new, just discussions of policy. It was handled very poorly. It became a military operation."

Of course, Hillary may have thought it necessary to keep even the names of the five hundred working group participants secret to ensure that they were not harassed by influence-seeking lobbyists and meddlesome journalists. As she and her husband had moved more into the national spotlight and everything from the couple's finances to Bill's personal peccadilloes were subject to exposure, Hillary's incipient distrust of the press had intensified, ironically becoming more Nixonian. The close scrutiny of the press irritated Hillary, who had previously operated only in the narrow confines of the legal services community and in one-party Arkansas, never developing an appreciation for openness in democratic politics. This coercive approach had functioned very well up to the time she moved into the White House, and she was not about to reverse course now.

The decision to operate in secrecy, then, was not a blunder but a calculation. Now that the administration was planning to push through legislation that would not only be damaging to certain special interests but also too complex and too intrusive to sell to the average voter, secrecy might be the only prudent tactic. Thus, while many have concluded that Hillary, in her naïveté, simply didn't expect strong political opposition, the opposite view seems much more plausible. Hillary needed to protect a plan she must have known was far too progressive to be put through the normal political process. She wanted to move the ball farther than she could within the rules of the system, so she employed means that were questionable in a democracy. Once the ends were in place and health care was available for all, the public would see its wisdom over time.

Given the press's near-hysteria about the alleged health care "crisis" in the spring of 1993, and the uncertain position of GOP moderates, if the administration had submitted a bill, hatched in secret, to the Democrat-controlled Congress by April, it might have passed, if narrowly, in a few weeks. This appeared to be the strategy pushed on Hillary by the congressional Democratic leadership, which believed that a plan could be passed without a single Republican vote. Hillary accepted the advice: She was already predisposed to stiffing the GOP and aware of the mistakes another southern governor, Jimmy Carter, had made in going his own way and alienating the Democrats on the Hill. "They [the administration] had a fifty-vote strategy in the Senate and they believed they would not need a cloture vote [sixty votes to cut off debate and move to a vote] on this legislation," said Lawrence O'Donnell, former staff director of Democratic senator Daniel Patrick Moynihan's Finance Committee. O'Donnell, a critical player who met frequently with top White House officials, including Hillary, continued, "This notion was held at the highest levels. . . . They thought Republicans would not stand in the way of the bill. It was a delusion. They believed [their plan] was a 'noble good' and believed the Senate would be afraid to stand in the way and would be punished for it by their constituents. They didn't believe they had to deal with any Republicans at any point in time. By the time they realized they had to deal with any Republicans, it was too late."

The alternative strategy would have been to run an inclusive process for about a year, persuading various segments of the health care industry as well as many Republicans to support a modified Clinton bill. Instead, Hillary took the worst elements from each approach. She antagonized much of the profit sector and the GOP and frightened the public by running a military-style operation. Yet she let the one-hundred-day deadline become hostage to Magaziner's three-ring circus and it wasn't until a year and a half later that Congress finally took legislative action. This gave interest groups from all sides and the Republican opposition plenty of time to organize against Hillary's "secret" plan.

The secrecy issue also put Hillary in the cross-hairs of the Washington press corps, which, despite its ideological affinity with the plan, always reacted badly when denied information. Hillary had never liked the press in Arkansas, and her insistence on secrecy in the health care matter got her relations with the Washington press off to a rocky start from which she never really recovered. Despite the administration's preoccupation with security, throughout the spring of 1993 officials were treated almost daily to stories by *New York Times* reporter Robert Pear detailing one aspect of the plan or another. The *Times,* the *Washington Post,* and the *Wall Street Journal* all published lists of names of likely working group members in an effort to determine what interests they might be beholden to; this forced the White House to release an official list grudingly in late March of 1993. (The Reporters Committee for Freedom of the Press, a journalism watchdog group, was among a bipartisan group of members of Congress and interest groups that filed briefs in a 1993 suit which fought the secrecy of the working group.)

Meanwhile, the Association of American Physicians and Surgeons (AAPS), a fifty-year-old organization of about three thousand doctors dedicated to preserving private medical practice, was up in arms—its members had been excluded from the working groups and the organization couldn't even find out the names of those who were serving on it. These doctors stood to lose substantial income if the Clinton plan was passed.

Dr. Jane Orient, the AAPS's executive director, became a leading general in the war against the Clinton plan. A specialist in internal medicine at the University of Arizona, Orient was outraged by Hillary's claim that secrecy was necessary to protect the process from special interests, because she knew that many of the nation's largest health care providers, some of which had well-developed ties to Hillary dating back to her political work in Arkansas, were strongly represented on the task force, and could perhaps even obtain trade secrets or proprietary information through secret channels. Most of the health professionals advising Hillary's task force supported organized medicine—a single-payer system or at least a requirement that people join health maintenance organizations—a goal Orient and AAPS members thoroughly opposed.

Most prominent among these health care interests was the Robert Wood Johnson Foundation, a nonprofit organization and a major stockholder of Johnson & Johnson Inc., the international pharmaceutical and medical supply company. The company serves as the exclusive contractor of medical supplies to several major nations with single-payer plans like Canada's and would have benefited substantially from a deal with a government-operated health care system. Johnson & Johnson was represented in Washington by the Wexler Group, a lobbying company headed by Clinton associate Anne Wexler, who hired Betsey Wright as a lobbyist. Though Clinton had pledged to end the practice of high-priced influence peddling in the capital, Wright was able to lobby Hillary personally on behalf of one of her clients, the American Dietetic Association. The nutritionists wanted to be sure their services were covered in the Clinton plan—and they were.[7]

Internal White House memos released during litigation with Jane Orient's AAPS showed that Steve Schroeder, president of the RWJ Foundation, was asked to recommend working group appointees, even though he was not named on official lists of participants. Schroeder had been part of the Clinton transition team, heading a group on labor policy. Organizations affiliated with Robert Wood Johnson, such as the Alpha Center, a research group that received 70 percent of its funding from the foundation, were intimately involved with the Clinton working group committees. Six RWJ fellows served on the working groups. Of the more than two hundred computer disks containing internal e-mail messages on health care that were later released by the White House for public inspection, eight disks labeled "R. W. Johnson" were indexed by the National Archives as blank.

The foundation had a long history of involvement with government-sponsored health plans: It funded the task force—on which left-wing activist Luanne Nyberg sat—that expanded Minnesota's health care program to a universal coverage plan. Thomas Gore II, the vice president's cousin, was a foundation vice president in 1993, when the organization spent about $690,000 for a series of four public forums in which Hillary discussed health care and participants offered recommendations regarding "the design and potential impact" of the administration's program.

Thus Hillary encouraged the involvement of "special interests" when they shared her goals. Though her actions in this respect were like those of any skilled politician who has learned to reward friends, the Clintons had set themselves up for criticism and charges of hypocrisy by employing moralistic rhetoric about ending the Washington lobbyists' revolving door that they claimed had been characteristic of previous administrations. It was in the effort to conceal these ties that Hillary took extreme measures.

The RWJ Foundation's involvement in health care in Arkansas began when Bill put Hillary in charge of the state's effort to reform health care in rural areas during his first term in the late 1970s. The foundation had helped fund the Office of Rural Health, created largely under Hillary's direction as part of the Arkansas Department of Health, and was helping states like Arkansas procure federal funding for rural health projects. It would later be a boon to Hillary's health projects—and by the early

1990s, Arkansas was receiving millions in RWJ Foundation grants. Another beneficiary of the foundation's largesse was Joycelyn Elders' Arkansas Department of Health, which received Foundation grants totaling $1.2 million in 1993 alone. Another $133,000 grant from RWJ came to Elders through the University of Arkansas Medical School. Foundation director Thomas Chapman, who signed that check, was named to the Clinton transition team and was a member of the health care working group in Arkansas. Elders received grant money as well from the Kaiser Family Foundation, which also would advise Hillary's working group. A philanthropy with ties to the Kaiser Permanente managed-care hospitals, in 1991 the Kaiser Foundation gave a three-year, $400,000 grant to the Arkansas Department of Health. The year before, the same group gave Elders a $50,000 grant for the Arkansas Initiative, to promote community health. Kaiser was also a Children's Defense Fund benefactor.

In what appears to have been an attempt to shield these favored interests from public exposure, Hillary handed Orient and her allies a lethal weapon. On the heels of the establishment of the task force, AAPS immediately filed a request under the Freedom of Information Act for the names of working group members and materials about task force operations. Stonewalled by the White House, the doctors' group took its case to Republican allies on Capitol Hill. When William Clinger, then the ranking Republican on the House Government Operations Committee, requested information on task force operations from the White House, he was told by Bernard Nussbaum, "You're in the minority, I don't have to give you these documents, and I won't give you these documents," according to Clinger.

Nussbaum's bluster notwithstanding, the law required that if the working group of five hundred or so members was to be considered a presidential advisory committee—nongovernment employees who represent outside groups and interests and function collectively in advising the president—it would be subject both to the FOIA and to a federal law passed by high-minded government reformers during the Watergate era. Called the Federal Advisory Committee Act, or FACA, the law was intended to prevent outside interest groups from unduly influencing presidential committees by opening up the advisory process to public scrutiny. It requires that the meetings of presidential advisory bodies be conducted in public and that all documents be subject to public access. Orient suspected that Hillary's working group—a crazy quilt of federal workers, private sector workers on leave from their outside jobs, part-time consultants and academics still working in the private sector, health care lobbyists, and volunteers—was filled with nongovernment employees and was therefore a classic case where FACA would apply.[8]

Orient and her lawyers, backed by Republican opponents of the Clinton plan, reasoned that there was at least one nongovernment employee who they knew for sure sat on the task force—Hillary herself. They could use Hillary's status to argue that the task force was operating illegally, thereby prying the process open and forcing disclosure of the names of other members of the group.

In the years since Watergate, the Republicans had discovered that they could turn the tables on the Democrats by waging political warfare over alleged violations of the panoply of ethics laws passed by liberals in the 1970s. The National Legal and Policy Center, run by conservative activist Peter Flaherty, was one outfit that had sprung up to uncover allegations of ethical wrongdoing by Democrats in the same manner that dozens of liberal-oriented organizations had investigated Republicans during the Reagan-Bush years. Together with the National Legal and Policy Center and a group calling itself the American Council for Health Care Reform that had close ties to a conservative marketing firm, the AAPS filed suit, arguing that because Hillary was not a government employee all future task force meetings should be open to the public and the press. The suit also sought the names of all participants and access to the group's working papers, as required by the FACA.

Apparently regarding it as a partisan attack on the Clinton plan, the press barely covered the lawsuit. The *Washington Post*'s David Broder, for example, told one of Orient's lawyers, Genevieve Young, that the lawsuit "isn't a story," according to Young. But the motives of the protagonists aside, the lawsuit was perhaps the most important and untold story of the first Clinton term. By focusing attention on Hillary's role as head of the task force, it made the first lady a lightning rod for public criticism and became a vehicle through which the plan itself would be attacked and ultimately killed. The mishandling of the suit would also play a major part in the unraveling of the White House counsel's office and place tremendous pressure on Vince Foster, possibly contributing to his subsequent suicide.

Legally, Hillary was between a rock and a hard place. If Hillary was not a government employee, the task force she headed would have to be open to the public under the FACA. Were she to argue that she was a federal employee, in which case the meetings could remain closed, Hillary might then be violating the federal antinepotism law.

As Nussbaum's comments to Clinger suggested, the White House had no intention of complying with the laws that would open up the task force to public scrutiny. But rather than seeking a legislative exception to make Hillary a federal employee outright, White House lawyers argued that Hillary was the "functional equivalent" of a federal employee, allowing her to keep her position as head of the task force, maintain its secrecy, and remain exempt from ethics rules and financial disclosure requirements that bound other federal workers. Getting around the law in this fashion seemed the perfect solution, or so the White House thought.

The legal strategy soon came a cropper. In early March, U.S. District Judge Royce Lamberth ruled that the formal twelve-member task force had to be opened to the public due to the presence of the first lady, who, despite the White House argument, did not qualify "as an employee or even a quasi-employee of the federal government. . . ." Lamberth did give the White House a victory in a second section of the ruling that said the FACA did not apply to the regular, day-to-day meetings of the much larger working group, which could therefore continue to meet in secret so long as Hillary did not attend. That part of the decision rested on a sworn declaration from Ira Magaziner drafted by attorneys in the White House counsel's office that the working group members were all government employees. "The judge really gave a stamp of approval to the work that's already gone on and is planned to go on," Hillary said in response to the ruling. "It's very clear that the working groups are not covered by the law and we're going to comply with the law."

Behind the scenes, however, Hillary wasn't sanguine about being singled out as the reason the twelve-member task force meetings had to be open to the public. So rather than accepting the decision, which allowed her to keep the larger working groups secret, the White House decided to appeal the portion of Lamberth's decision that said Hillary was not a federal employee. The plaintiffs, in turn, filed a cross appeal of the portion of Lamberth's decision that allowed the working groups to stay secret. Ultimately, it was the White House's decision to appeal that prolonged the legal process, exhausted much time, energy and political capital, and eventually derailed the entire reform effort.

To Hillary and her allies, the plaintiffs in the lawsuit were interested merely in protecting their own narrow interests, frustrating the "noble good" of health reform, and publicly humiliating Hillary. The anxious first lady, in particular, saw the lawsuit as an attack on her personally and on what she was trying to accomplish for the country. Therefore, giving any ground to the opposition, even if it made the most sense legally, was out of the question. "Nussbaum complained that this [lawsuit] was a political stunt," said Kent Masterson Brown, the lead attorney for the three plaintiffs, and a nationally recognized litigator in constitutional and administrative health care issues. "He thought it was a battle over Hillary's head, so they conspired to protect her role. You could really feel it. That's what was going on. It was an ego battle. It was based on egomania to maintain her role, even to her demise. It wasn't the White House counsel doing it, it was Hillary."

Hillary, of course, was substantially correct in her view that the lawsuit was a political tactic designed to stall health care reform. But once the legal process had begun, the suit could not be dismissed as a partisan gimmick, as Hillary and her lawyers (and the press) seemed quick to do. Lacking experience in fighting Washington ethics wars, Hillary and her legal Dobermans thought they could brazen out the challenge instead of coming to grips with the substantive points raised by the lawsuit and crafting a sound legal position of their own. Once a decision was rendered, they dug their heels in deeper, trying to find new ways to massage and manipulate legal technicalities. "This [lawsuit] was a serious problem," said one government official who asked not to be identified. "I don't think they understood the gravity of it. They were not calloused, they just didn't understand. The White House counsel didn't understand his job. They regarded themselves as the president's lawyer when really they're the lawyer for the presidency. They were in fact in contradiction of [FACA]. The counsel should have told them straight out, instead of coming on like a Johnny Cochran and saying, 'I'll get you off.' "

In retrospect, it was becoming plain that Hillary's decision to staff the counsel's office exclusively with trusted loyalists who had no Washington experience had serious drawbacks. It seems especially tragic in retrospect that Hillary should have charged her close Rose Law Firm intimate Vince Foster with responsibility for the legal affairs of the health care task force.

Foster was even less able than Nussbaum, Hillary's former boss on the Watergate committee, to render the kind of cool, independent legal analysis that was needed. His close emotional bond with Hillary may have led him instead simply to follow the wishes of his client, who had turned to him, as she had done so many times before, to help her through a difficult situation. There seemed to be no one on hand in the counsel's office willing to tell Hillary she was making a mistake.

Suits of the type that Orient filed are pursued all the time by public interest groups seeking access to government information. Ordinarily, the matter would simply be handled by the appropriate division of the Justice Department. The close management of the health care task force litigation by the White House counsel's office was in part necessary because the first lady was at issue, but also because Foster was increasingly worried about the legal advice rendered when the working group was first established. Perhaps Foster could see that the legal arguments devised to shield Hillary and the task force from the law's reach were starting to come apart at the seams.

To find out how good a lawyer he was up against, Foster called Terry McBrayer to get the scoop on the legal background of Kent Masterson Brown, the plaintiff's lead attorney. McBrayer, a former Kentucky gubernatorial candidate who served as the state's Democratic party chairman, knew Brown from local legal circles. Information about Brown later turned up in a dossier detailing Brown's entire legal background, which was found among White House records released to the National Archives. One document referred to Brown as "extremely conservative, a Reagan Republican" and "mortified that Clinton won."

With the case now pending in the appeals court in May, the pressure on Foster went up another notch when it appeared that task force records had been destroyed. Though the task force had disbanded at the one-hundred-day mark without completing its work, federal law still required the administration to save all of its records and documents, including correspondence. On June 14, the *Washington Times* reported that an employee in the New Executive Office Building in the White House complex had been seen the week before shredding boxes of letters relating to health care. The *Times* later reported that the same General Services Administration worker "said he dumped several boxes of health care letters into the paper shredder" and that there were "two carts of mail hand-labeled 'Office of the First Lady' which workers said were destined for the shredder." While the White House denied the story, the AAPS rushed to court to get an order from Lamberth to protect the papers.

The day before Lamberth was to rule on protecting the papers, Brown submitted evidence that the White House had "continually evaded—even flatly disobeyed" Lamberth's previous ruling requiring fourteen-day advance notice of task force meetings, as the Federal Advisory Committee Act required. Foster, who was responsible for the filings, had consistently submitted them too late to the *Federal Register,* which meant that no one ever had any notice of the "public" meetings. Had Foster been so overwhelmed by the demands on his time and out of his depth on the order's requirements that he neglected to make timely filings? Or had Hillary, determined to defy the judge's orders, instructed Foster to "forget" to file them? When Lamberth realized the White House had not only defeated the purpose of his order, but might have also ordered the shredding of documents, he was outraged. He roared from the bench that he wanted the name of the person who would be held in contempt if documents were destroyed. That person could well have been Foster.

Though the Justice Department was the government's counsel in the case, strategy appeared to be coming from the White House. Since Hillary was the client, a certain amount of White House direction was to be expected, but heavy-handed micromanagement threatened to compromise Justice's institutional integrity. Moreover, by excluding lawyers who were more independent from and less protective of her, Hillary ensured that the legal advice she received was colored by personal and political loyalties.

Associate White House counsel Steven Neuwirth, a protégé of Bernard Nussbaum's at his New York law firm who was known around the White House as Hillary's "hey boy," was a constant presence in the courtroom. "If something went wrong, he'd slink down or storm out," said Kent Masterson Brown. "In terms of the court [proceedings], he was an inconsequential player. [But] Neuwirth showed visible anger at the court for blocking the further destruction of records. It left me with the growing impression that the White House counsel was dictating Justice's moves. The client was counseling the lawyer. You wondered 'How can Justice get

this case so messed up?' They didn't. Someone else was dictating the circumstances and they were just going along."

"All the way through [the lawsuit] they expressed to the court and to
me they were having difficulty obtaining from the White House information relevant to the case," said Brown. "Clearly, they were having difficulty with the White House being candid with them." After the
Washington Times story about the shredding of health care related documents appeared, Brown told of being approached by Jeffrey Gutman,
Justice's chief lawyer in the case, who asked him what he knew about the
alleged incident since the White House wouldn't tell him anything.

What happened next was a vivid illustration of the maxim "Be careful
what you wish for—you might get it." On June 22, a federal appeals court
in Washington agreed with the White House that, for purposes of the
FACA, Hillary was a de facto federal employee after all. This meant that
the task force meetings could remain closed—no more advance notices,
no more public forums. But the court also overruled the portion of Judge
Lamberth's ruling stating that the five-hundred-member working group
was not subject to FACA. The appeals panel said that it wasn't sure what
the working group's status was under the law, so it sent the case back to
Lamberth for further investigation of whether the group was comprised
of government or nongovernment employees.

In January 1993, to avoid all these legal pitfalls, Foster and Neuwirth
had recommended classifying all working group members as temporary
government employees. But the advice had not been followed across the
board. Whether it was arrogance or ineptitude, no one had seen to it
that all of the nongovernment workers were converted to temporary federal workers, which would have forced them to sever outside ties and
publicly disclose their financial interests. In March, however, Ira Magaziner assured the court that all members were in fact government employees in a sworn declaration drafted by the counsel's office. Now,
questions would be raised about the illegal task force and the veracity of
Magaziner's declaration.

Warning bells had been sounded. Atul Gawande was a twenty-six-year-
old "whiz kid" health policy expert who had joined the Clinton staff
after working on Capitol Hill for Democratic Representative Jim Cooper
on health care. After the working group's first meeting in January,
Gawande was so distressed over what he characterized as Magaziner's refusal to heed legal and ethical concerns that he warned him in a memo

of the danger of private-sector persons having high-profile positions on the task force.

Because they were not converted into temporary government workers and made to sever their private interests, many working-group members could therefore face criminal liability for violating conflict-of-interest statutes by making policy in an area where they had a financial stake. Tom Pyle was a health care consultant and a director and stockholder at several companies in the industry while working full-time as a White House "cluster group" leader. He wasn't sure whether he was considered a federal employee under the law. "I verbalized my conflict repeatedly to them. I said, 'I have what I think may be a conflict,' " Pyle said. The day before he began work at the White House, Magaziner "said he didn't bother about that stuff and someone else would call me," Pyle recalled. "When no one did, I got the name of the guy to talk to about conflicts. 'Send me your résumé,' he said. I told him I didn't think sending him my résumé would be enough to solve the conflict problem. , , , For the next two weeks, Magaziner's people repeatedly told me it was no problem. You could tell they didn't know what they were talking about. It was like airline people who say the plane should be here any minute." Pyle finally consulted a private attorney, who set up a meeting for Pyle and Beth Nolan, Nussbaum's deputy for ethics issues. "When I went to see Beth, she said I could have criminal liability!"

Pyle was soon demoted from cluster group leader to consultant. The move was leaked to the *New York Times* by an unknown insider, making Pyle the first working group member publicly identified. Since Pyle was one of the few avowed free marketeers involved in the development of the Clinton plan at a high level and had ties to the blackballed Jackson Hole Group, it was not unreasonable to think that he was singled out by bureaucratic enemies to take him out of the process. "They treated me the same way they treated Lani Guinier. They screwed up processing it . . . and you're made to look like a crook on the front page of the *New York Times*," Pyle said.

Because the appeals court decision allowed the plaintiffs' discovery on the composition of the task force, the White House frantically tried to shift the working group members into the federal worker category. But it was too late: The plaintiffs were able to produce thirty-seven pounds of evidence documenting hundreds of people—over 350 outsiders and special interest representatives—who were participating in the secret working group illegally because they were not government employees.

The White House next tried various legal somersaults—arguing that the working groups hadn't really advised the president directly and were thus exempt from the FACA—but the court didn't buy it. "We now know, from records produced in this litigation, that numerous individuals who were never federal employees did much more than just attend working group meetings on an intermittent basis," said Judge Lamberth, "and we now know that some of these individuals even had supervisory or decision-making roles." Among these were representatives from large HMO operators like United Health Care Corp., Blue Cross/Blue Shield, the Robert Wood Johnson Foundation, and Telesis, Magaziner's former consulting firm.

Close observers of the process saw the appeals court decision and the subsequent move by the physicians' group to bring perjury charges against Magaziner as the point of no return for the health care reform effort. "Once Ira became a defendant in that suit, it was really all over," said Senator Wallop. Judge Lamberth called Magaziner's sworn statement about all working group members being government employees "misleading, at best," and said that a decision on a perjury charge would turn on whether he had been "intentionally untruthful."

Attorney General Janet Reno declined to appoint a special counsel to investigate Magaziner's alleged perjury, as Republicans had urged. Several months later, the U.S. attorney in Washington, a Clinton appointee to whom the matter had been referred by Judge Lamberth, decided not to prosecute. In a memo to Judge Lamberth, the U.S. attorney noted that, although portions of Magaziner's affidavit were confusing and imprecise, they could not be proven true or false, thus precluding any finding that the affadavit was intentionally false. The U.S. attorney later clarified his position to Judge Lamberth and stated that the court had felt misled due to "a combination of oversights, tactical misjudgments, and aggressive—perhaps, in hindsight, overly so—advocacy in the context of hard-fought civil litigation." The lawsuit was eventually mooted in September 1994, on the eve of the day of reckoning—scheduled testimony by Hillary before Judge Lamberth on the composition of the working groups. The White House agreed to turn over all of the documents sought by the doctors' group about its inner workings, ending the need for the suit to continue—but by that time its goal had been accomplished: Health care was dead.

Any concern Foster may have had about the task force lawsuit could only have been exacerbated by another legal quagmire that directly endangered Hillary. If Hillary was a de facto federal employee under the FACA, as the White House had argued and the appellate court agreed in June, she might be covered by conflict-of-interest laws prohibiting her from acting in a policy area where she had a financial interest.

In glossing over the "details" of public ethics in her zeal to bring about health care reform, Hillary would once again suffer a self-inflicted wound. While heading the task force, Hillary owned an interest, through a limited partnership, in several health care stocks, exposing her to potential liability under the 1978 Ethics in Government Act, which makes it a crime for government employees to knowingly influence any policy that might have a "direct and predictable" effect on their financial interests. A "willful" violation could lead to five years' imprisonment and fines of up to $50,000. The original law, enacted by President Carter, also established the Office of Government Ethics, which oversees and upholds conflict-of-interest rules affecting executive branch officers and employees.

The Clintons' 1992 financial disclosure report, released in May 1993, showed a net worth of about $863,000. Their largest investment, nearly $100,000, was a stake Hillary held in a special growth fund which held more than $1 million in health stocks and which, at least during 1992, sold pharmaceutical stocks short. The fund, called ValuePartners, was run by Smith Capital Management, Inc. of Little Rock. (Investors who sell short are speculating on a sudden drop in price, and borrowing shares they do not hold with the intention of repurchasing them later at a lower price to replace the borrowed shares.)

As teachers had been the "enemy" in the education reform drive in Arkansas, the pharmaceutical and insurance industries played the role of the black hats in the health care effort. Shortly after the health care task force went to work, both Clintons began publicly singling out pharmaceutical firms for allegedly charging exorbitant prices and defrauding consumers. Magaziner told an insurance company lobbyist that the administration's pollsters had also thought that portraying pharmaceutical companies, doctors, and insurers as "enemies" would help sell the plan. "The pharmaceutical industry is spending $1 billion more each year on advertising and lobbying than it does on developing new or better drugs," Bill Clinton said during a speech at a Virginia health clinic in February. "Meanwhile, its profits are rising at four times the rate of the average *Fortune* 500 company. Compared to other countries, our prices are shocking." The President added, "We cannot have profit at the expense of children." Hillary also spoke of the drug industry's "record profits." In one speech she said, "Talk to your friends and neighbors about what you see every day in terms of price gouging, cost shifting, unconscionable profiteering. Explain how you see the system that is being gamed and ripped off because it has no real discipline, no budget, no controls. . . ."

As concern mounted on Wall Street that price controls on medicines would be central to the administration's reform plan, pharmaceutical firm stock prices plummeted over 27 percent, relative to the rest of the stock market, between January 1, 1993 and September 9, 1993, according to a study conducted by the Chicago-based Catalyst Institute. (The issue of the Clintons' financial holdings aside, the rhetoric of the speeches was criticized as irresponsible for draining half of the equity out of the pharmaceutical industry and driving down the value of biotech stocks. The sources of new capital for the biotech industry began to dry up, hurting research and development of new drugs.)

During the time that Hillary was head of the health care task force, the ValuePartners fund maintained at least one short position in biotech while holding long positions on other health-related stocks such as HMOs. Thus there was little question but that she might have financially benefited from the changes in the health care system she was proposing. The amount of money involved was not insignificant. When William Smith signed Hillary's shares in ValuePartners holdings over to the company managing the blind trust in July 1993, the investment was valued at $150,000.

But the darker implications of some of Hillary's critics—that she may have excoriated the drug companies for financial advantage or shifted around her investments based on her inside knowledge of the health plan—are unfounded. For one thing, ValuePartners did not even sell pharmaceutical stocks short in 1993—a fact lost in much of the negative media coverage. Hillary, moreover, was a limited partner in ValuePartners and had no control over its investment decisions.

For purposes of the ethics laws, though, it didn't matter if money had been made or lost, or whether Hillary had any control over the fund. If Hillary knew what types of stocks were in her fund at the time she was making policy and therefore had the ability to affect those stocks, she was arguably in violation of the law. At the very least, it would create an appearance of impropriety. (Similar controversies had dogged other federal officials, including Reagan attorney general Ed Meese and Bush secretary of state James Baker, though no violation of law was found in either case.)

After the court decision came down conferring de facto federal employee status on Hillary, Foster worried that she could be criminally prosecuted because he had failed to get the Clintons to place their holdings in a blind trust or, at a minimum, instruct Hillary to divest herself of ValuePartners before assuming the health care post. Had the Clintons put their financial holdings into a blind trust, Hillary would have been in the clear, because once a trustee is selected, he or she has complete control over the fund, and may not communicate with the government official who is the beneficiary except to send periodic reports documenting the trust's overall loss or gain. All three of Clinton's predecessors—Carter, Reagan, and Bush—had arranged for such trusts prior to taking the oath of office.

Working in his capacity as private lawyer for the Clintons—albeit on the public payroll—Foster struggled for months to put the Clintons' financial portfolio in order and establish the blind trust. It appears as if he knew of the potential time bomb from the very beginning. In early 1993, Foster reviewed a year-end report sent to the Clintons by William Smith, the ValuePartners manager, which listed several health care stocks Hillary held, including those sold short. Smith later told Congressional investigators that White House aides had called him with special requests for more information on the fund's portfolio listings early in 1993.

Foster committed suicide before establishing the Clinton blind trust. Ricki Seidman, a White House aide who was involved in anticipating press interest in the Clintons' finances, told the special prosecutor investigating Foster's death that she had had discussions with Foster about the ValuePartners investment. Seidman, an old Washington hand, said Foster had behaved like a "guppy plopped into a goldfish bowl" as he described his frustrations in not being able to steer the Clintons free of the ethics morass and the Washington culture of "gotcha" journalism. According to the special prosecutor's report, Foster also approached associate White House counsel Beth Nolan, the ethics specialist on staff, and solicited her opinion on whether Hillary would be subject to the conflict-of-interest laws.

The confusion stemmed from the fact that Hillary was both claiming to be a federal employee and claiming to be exempt from the conflict-of-interest laws that govern federal employees. The president and vice president have traditionally been considered exempt from the law, and Justice Department opinions dating from the early 1970s have argued that first ladies are exempt because they are not government employees. The White House based its claim on a 1985 opinion from the Department of Justice designed to clarify a question about Nancy Reagan's status. The opinion affirmed that first ladies are not subject to the conflict laws, but the reasoning was based on the fact that the first lady was not "an officer or employee of the United States." Because the White House had argued that Hillary was a *de facto* federal employee for purposes of FACA, it invited the question of Hillary's conflict-of-interest status.

Since the AAPS suit did not deal with this matter, it is not possible to say whether the White House argument would have held up in court. In a footnote to the June 22 appellate court ruling on the health care task force, Judge Laurence Silberman wrote: "We do not need to consider whether Mrs. Clinton's presence on the Task Force violates . . . any conflict of interest statutes." But in a concurring opinion, Judge James Buckley telegraphed his view that the laws would apply to Hillary: "To put it another way, could Congress have intended that Mrs. Clinton alone of the twelve members of the Task Force and 340 members of the working group, would be entirely exempt from the reach of ethics laws? . . . I think not."

If Hillary was subject to the law at all, the question of whether she violated it would have turned on whether Hillary knew the details of ValuePartners holdings. Though Foster knew of Hillary's holdings early on, the evidence suggests that Hillary herself may not have known. ValuePartners manager William Smith told reporters and GOP investigators that he stopped sending the Clintons regular reports on the fund in March 1992 during the campaign, in effect setting up a blind trust for the Clintons without being asked to do so. He also said he had not spoken to Hillary since August 1992 and did not discuss specific investments with her at that time. The investments of the fund, including several short positions in health care stocks, were detailed in the December 31, 1992 report from Smith that was attached to the Clintons' financial disclosure form, filed in May 1993. The form was signed by Bill, not Hillary, so she might not have been held legally responsible for the information disclosed in it.

Yet Republican members of Congress found the idea that Hillary was unaware of her own investments hard to believe, and they requested an investigation of the matter in early 1994 by the Office of Government Ethics. The agency found no grounds to allege a violation of law by Hillary and noted that appearances of a conflict of interest do not necessarily have merit once examined. Reasonable legal arguments could be made to support both Hillary's position and that of her Republican critics, who contended that the OGE analysis itself was flawed.

Even if it was not a legal violation, Hillary's situation fit the layman's concept of a conflict of interest. At a minimum it was clear that bad lawyering by Vince Foster had put Hillary in a position where her credibility and integrity would be attacked. Legal hair-splitting might be good enough in corporate litigation or criminal defense work, but the first lady of the United States had to be not only legally defended but beyond reproach in the court of public opinion. Even if the White House counsel was correct about the technical requirements of the law, as a political matter, Hillary and Foster should have known better than to have her holding any health care stocks while she was making health care policy.

The twin issues of the legality of the health care task force and short-selling of health care stock were the first signs that the culture clash between Arkansas and Washington was exacting a toll on the Clintons, who had not been held to a high standard of public accountability in Little Rock. In one interview as first lady, a frustrated Hillary said that the ethical standards to which she and her husband were being held in Washington were "just absurd." Secure as she was in her view of her own moral rectitude, Hillary likely found it impossible to believe that anyone could seriously accuse her of trying to profit personally from her historic mission to bring better health care to all Americans.

Foster's fears that Hillary would be embarrassed by the public revelation of her stock holdings were in fact borne out when the Clintons released their disclosure forms that May. "Investment Fund for Hillary Clinton Sold Short Several Health-Care Stocks," read a May 21 *Wall Street Journal* headline. A *Tampa Tribune* editorial cartoon showed a wife exclaimng to her husband, "Blind trust! Isn't that the same thing we did when we voted for him?" Conservative columnists Robert Novak and Tony Snow joined in with sharp questions. In the July issue of *Money* magazine, released a few short weeks before Foster's suicide, managing editor Frank Lalli charged: "Largely lost during President Clinton's recent Bad Hair Week, buried under the headlines about travel-office cronyism, manipulation of the FBI and the $200 haircut itself, was the disturbing disclosure that he and Hillary had not yet put their investments, worth nearly $1 million, in a blind trust. The President and the First Lady are working on it, a press aide told *Money*. That's not good enough. The damage to the public trust has already been done."

Lalli went on to quote Charles Lewis, director of the Center for Public Integrity, a self-appointed ethics "watchdog group." Lewis was a former producer for *60 Minutes* and a major source for Beltway journalists looking to zap politicians allegedly beholden to special interests in the business world. His public criticism of Hillary was an early sign that liberal reformers took a dim view of her apparent attitude that she did not have to meet the standards to which other public officials were held. Lewis noted that while Hillary may not have had an actual conflict of interest, her health care holdings created the appearance of impropriety. Hillary's investment failed "the red-face test—you know, do you want to see this on the front page of some newspaper? . . . If you are going to be involved with policy, especially something as explosive as health policy, you've got to put yourself beyond the pale entirely," added Lewis.

It was later discovered that in his White House office, Foster had kept a copy of a June 18, 1993 *USA Today* article on Hillary's ValuePartners investment. After reporting on the potential conflict of interest, the article noted erroneously that the Clintons' investments "are now held in a blind trust." Foster circled the places in the article where the trust was mentioned and sent copies to Hillary's chief of staff, Maggie Williams, and to her press secretary, Lisa Caputo. Foster appended a handwritten note: "The assets are not yet in a blind trust. The document has been approved but is not signed yet, pending working out of the details." Foster then called Smith, the ValuePartners manager, to complain about his having talked to the press.

Hillary and Foster were coming under heightened scrutiny from the other end of the political spectrum as well. The *Wall Street Journal* editorial page focused not so much on Hillary as on the heretofore invisible Vince Foster. In a series of related editorials, the first of which appeared on June 17, 1993, and was headlined "Who Is Vincent Foster?" the *Journal* criticized the White House for destroying task force documents, and advocated that Foster take responsibility for the preservation of task force records. "Will a task force bearing the First Lady's name blithely ignore a district court order even as its appeal is being heard by the D.C. Circuit? . . . Who ensures that this administration follows the law, or explains why not? A good question. While Constitutional law may not have been the big part of the Rose firm's practice, it seems to us that a good man for the job would be Deputy Counsel Foster." A week later, a second *WSJ* editorial facetiously congratulated Foster on the appellate court ruling which said Hillary was a federal employe and the health care meetings could therefore stay secret. In "Vincent Foster's Victory," the editors wrote, "With one mighty sweep he has struck a blow for separation of powers, executive authority, critics of the litigation explosion, and we dare say, even for the formulators of the Reagan White House's off-the-books Iran-Contra operation."

For Hillary, the reform of America's health care system had been the apotheosis of the co-candidacy and the greatest opportunity and challenge of her life. By now, however, it appears to be the case that Hillary's own misjudgments and aversion to compromise, the inherent grandiosity of her plan, and her apparent belief that noble ends could trump the procedural niceties of the post-Watergate ethical regime had doomed it to defeat, even though it would be more than a year before Congress put the last nail in its coffin.

One of the lasting lessons of the health care debacle may have been that neither Bill nor Hillary is able to succeed without the other. In Arkansas, she had master politicians Dick Morris—and Bill himself—at her side. In Washington, she replaced Morris with Ira Magaziner and Bill receded into the background. Had Bill been more directly involved, his innate tendency to compromise—a weakness in isolation, but a strength in the context of the co-candidacy—would likely have tempered Hillary's zeal and made it possible to sell the plan politically.

Despite Hillary's manifest abilities and talents, which were amply acknowledged by all who encountered her, her actions in the health care battle starkly revealed her limitations as a politician. By mid-1994, as polls showed Americans opposing the plan by wide margins, Hillary soldiered on, refusing to seek a compromise with Congress and deciding to take the issue of universal health care into the 1994 election. The results were catastrophic for her party, which lost control of Congress for the first time in forty years.

If anything, then, Hillary should be faulted not for clumsiness or cynicism, as some allege, but for a too-great consistency with principle which clouded her tactical judgment. Her principles, of course, which demanded a massive government-sponsored managerial approach to social change, were precisely the root of the problem. Americans have wisely tended to reject such schemes, perhaps understanding that our system of government cannot be used for social engineering without the risk of its being coopted by the various factions and interests that make up American politics. On some level, no doubt, Hillary knew this as well, which may have led her to adopt the Trojan Horse strategy in the first place.

One can only speculate on the effect of this defeat—the first real personal reversal she had known—on Hillary herself, but it must have been a crushing blow to her sense of self-worth. Or it would have been for anyone prepared to take responsibility for these failings. Hillary, however, seemed to ascribe the defeat not to her own flaws or errors, but to a fatally flawed system, manned by corrupt politicians and sinister conservatives and dominated by corporate special interests.

Others saw her failure for what it was, and her political standing suffered greatly for it. Not to be underestimated in the subsequent turn against Hillary on the part of the liberal press was her failure to deliver on her promise to pass health care legislation. It was particularly embarrassing to the many women who had embraced Hillary as an inspiring role model and were now reading—and writing—disparaging accounts of her performance. Even Eleanor Clift wrote in the *Washington Post* in late 1994, making an unfavorable comparison with Nancy Reagan: "The key to a first lady's effectiveness is not whether people like you, but whether you help the president. By that measure, Nancy was a success. Indeed, it can be argued that she had more positive impact on substantive issues than Barbara Bush or Hillary Rodham Clinton." Diminishing Hillary, perhaps as a way of expiating their own disappointment and failed hopes, would be an increasingly common journalistic theme as Hillary moved on to face her biggest hurdles yet.

13

The Revenge of the Ozarks

If Vincent Foster was already seriously worried about the political and legal issues surrounding the pending health care legal case, his troubles would soon deepen with the firing of the White House travel office employees. As events unfolded, Foster's White House office would be the fatal point at which two speeding trains would intersect: Bill's legacy of cronyism and favor-trading, and Hillary's increasingly aggressive efforts to thwart politically damaging disclosures. While the effort was intended to protect the "zone of privacy" so that Hillary could pursue her historic mission unhampered by outbreaks of scandal, her hand-picked lawyers in the White House counsel's office seemed to cause more problems than they solved. When Hillary stepped in to take control once again, her ill-considered actions turned her from Bill's greatest asset into his greatest liability.

More than any other single action, her role in the firing of seven career workers in the White House travel office would prove to be Hillary's undoing, triggering the suicide of her closest friend and adviser and placing her actions at the center of several federal investigations, including

that of the Whitewater independent counsel Kenneth Starr, who is probing, among other matters, the White House effort to conceal Hillary's
role in the affair, as well as possible obstruction by Hillary herself. These
inquiries have made public thousands of pages of documents that make
it possible to piece the story together.[1]

Travelgate, as it was soon dubbed in the press, easily fits the now-fa-
miliar pattern of the Clinton scandals and the co-candidacy. Like Whitewater, its roots can be found in long-standing political and business ties
between Bill Clinton and his Arkansas cronies. Once again Hillary
stepped in at a crucial moment and then tried to defuse the political fallout, and as a consequence she, rather than Bill, got caught in the cross
hairs.

During the 1992 campaign, Hillary had been central to the presentation of the Clintons as progressive baby boomers who possessed a keen
sense of public ethics, while all the time she was working to keep a lid on
the seamy side of their Arkansas past. Now, having reached the highest
levels of power, having placed her liberal foot soldiers in strategic places
throughout the government, and having launched a historic effort to
bring Americans universal health care, she was about to discover that
while she could take Bill out of Arkansas, she couldn't take Arkansas out
of Bill.

The trouble started when Bill authorized Harry Thomason to set up
shop in the White House after working on the inaugural. Thomason got
a temporary White House pass, and was given a desk and telephone in
the East Wing of the White House. According to documents later released by Congress, Thomason and the actresses Markie Post and Bobbie Ferguson (who accompanied Thomason to the White House as his
assistants) worked on a plan, known as the "White House project" to
shape Clinton's image. Among their suggestions was to use the "best and
brightest" Hollywood directors to "get the most appealing visuals from
our events." A new presidential seal was commissioned, to show "an image of the new generation of leadership." A "bible" was to be prepared
noting Clinton's "intellectual and stylistic preferences" so they could be
worked into official events. Another proposal was the staging at the
White House of a sixty-fifth birthday party for Mickey Mouse. (White
House notes produced to Congress showed that George Stephanopoulos, Mack McLarty, and Clinton personally had approved the White
House project.)

Though Thomason is seen as a glitzy Hollywood figure, he also had his finger in an array of small business enterprises. In addition to the "White House project," Thomason sought government business for a company he partly owned, a Cincinnati-based aviation consulting firm called TRM. The company had chartered "Air Elvis," the airplane that transported Clinton and his aides during the presidential race. TRM's president and a co-owner was Darnell Martens. On January 29, 1993 Martens wrote a memo to Thomason suggesting that TRM be hired by the government as a paid consultant for a variety of projects: to consult on the White House travel office operation; to perform a review of all nonmilitary government aircraft to determine possible savings; and to advise the White House in picking the new Federal Aviation Administration director. Martens also advised Thomason to change the name of the company to Harry Thomason and Associates, in order to "capitalize on 'Thomason' name recognition." Martens estimated the cost of the audit alone at half a million dollars.

Clinton had made a campaign pledge to reduce the size of the White House staff and cut administrative costs. Thus in a cabinet meeting on February 10 Clinton was pleased to announce that "staff" had told him there were major savings to be had in a review of the government's civilian air fleet. On February 11, Martens again wrote Thomason, asking him to "put me in front of the right person at the White House." Five days later, Thomason was an overnight White House guest. The next morning, a copy of the original Martens memo, stamped "The President Has Seen," was forwarded to McLarty and David Watkins, White House administration director, for "action." Clinton had hand-written on the memo: "These guys are sharp."

During this period, a related project was brewing: the takeover of the White House travel office, which arranged charters for the White House press corps traveling with the president. A plan to essentially privatize the functions of the office had been drafted in late January by another group of Clinton cronies with their eyes on a piece of the business.

The scheme involved World Wide Travel, a Little Rock travel agency that had booked all the travel for the Clinton campaign. The agency was originally owned by the Worthen Bank, in which the powerful Stephens family held a major interest. In 1979, Worthen was forced to sell the agency when the Federal Reserve Board ruled that banks had to divest themselves of their travel services; Stephens arranged for it to be bought by its manager, Betta Carney. In the mid-1970s, Watkins, who ran the Worthen-owned Advertising Associates, Inc., and did the ads for Clinton's campaigns, became a major client of Carney's and vice versa. Watkins and Carney also forged relationships with Mack McLarty, who had been chief executive of the Stephens-owned Arkla Gas Company in the early 1980s.

The White House charter business alone was worth $40,000 a day, and private brokers would stand to make substantial commissions. Carney had already made over $1 million as the Clinton presidential campaign's travel agent in a contract arranged by Watkins. According to a 1992 report in *Travel Weekly*, World Wide did the Clinton campaign a big favor: It allowed them to defer paying part of their travel debt, enabling them to wait until federal matching funds started pouring in. The agency also adopted an unusual billing policy for journalists. Typically, when members of the press fly on a candidate's chartered aircraft, the campaign is charged for the cost and bills the journalists later. World Wide required journalists to pay the campaign in advance, generating desperately needed cash to pump into advertising in crucial primary races, such as those in Michigan and Illinois; the money would otherwise have been only a ledger entry in accounts receivable for weeks. Watkins told *Travel Weekly* that, were it not for World Wide Travel, Clinton might not have won the Democratic nomination.

When the White House later fired seven travel office workers, it would claim that financial misconduct by the travel office workers had prompted their dismissal. It is evident, however, that Clinton's Little Rock supporters had designs on the operation from day one. Two weeks after the election, Steven Davison, director of customer services for World Wide, told *Arkansas Business* in a little-noticed article that World Wide was studying the possibilities of opening an office in Washington, D.C., to handle travel plans for Clinton's staff when he became president.

Shortly after Clinton's election, Watkins met with representatives from World Wide Travel, including Catherine Cornelius, who had been the liaison between the campaign and World Wide Travel, to discuss plans to privatize the White House travel operation. Cornelius, then 25, subsequently went to work in the White House as an aide to Watkins. In a January 26, 1993 memo, Cornelius proposed that she and Clarissa Cerda, who had supervised the campaign's early-billing operation, could perform the functions of the White House travel office in conjunction with World Wide. The arrangement would both save money and help meet the president's commitment to reducing the White House staff by 25 percent, Cornelius argued. Almost immediately after the inauguration, the White House travel office began receiving phone calls for Cornelius. She happened to be Bill Clinton's distant cousin, though this was not generally known at the White House.

FOB Harry Thomason, who had an interest in presidential travel that dovetailed with World Wide's, moved the plan forward. Thomason arranged for Martens to call the longtime director of the office, Billy Dale, to inquire about the business. Martens would later tell White House aides preparing an internal report on the matter that he had been inquiring about opportunities not for TRM but for his girlfriend, Penny Sample, who owned a company called Air Advantage, a charter airplane broker used by World Wide during the Clinton campaign. In any case, the call with Dale did not go well: both TRM and Air Advantage were charter brokers, not charter operators, and the White House already had a charter broker—the travel office itself. So it was no surprise that Dale told Martens there was "no chance" the White House could fit a charter broker into its current operations.

The travel office was staffed by six government workers and overseen by Dale, a White House veteran of thirty-one years. The workers did not enjoy the protections of the career civil service; they held their jobs only at the pleasure of the president. Most of the seven employees had served in the office well over a decade, however, working for both Democrats and Republicans without incident.

Following the call, Martens wrote a memo (later forwarded to the White House) which questioned the management of the travel office by contending that it was awarding the lucrative contract for press travel on a noncompetitive basis to a "Republican operated" charter airline that had a "decidedly anti-Clinton philosophy." Martens maintained that the airline in question should be replaced. Thomason soon alerted Clinton himself and David Watkins. Watkins told investigators from the Justice Department that he had received a call from Thomason in early April in which Thomason told him that the travel office employees were "crooks" and should be fired. Watkins, of course, had already reviewed a proposal to replace the travel office workers with World Wide Travel. Watkins summoned Catherine Cornelius to his office. When she arrived he opened a brown leather-bound notebook and read to her a quote, referring to the travel office employees: "Those guys are a bunch of crooks. They have been on the take for years." Watkins did not identify the source of the statement at the time, but Cornelius told investigators that she later learned it was Thomason. Craig Livingstone, who had worked with Thomason on the inaugural, tipped off White House associate counsel Bill Kennedy to the alleged malfeasance. (The rumors of Republican influence and kickbacks were never proven, and an executive of the airline has filed suit against Harry Thomason for libel and slander. The slander claims have been dismissed as time-barred and the libel claim is proceeding. Thomason denies any wrongdoing.)

Dale was vulnerable to the rumor-mongering because he used slipshod accounting methods and kept poor records. The press corps was often billed for trips by estimate, with no subsequent confirmation of competitive pricing. And Dale kept in his private accounts large amounts of cash collected from media organizations, which he withdrew as needed to cover incidental expenses for press trips. No media organization was known to have complained about this long-standing practice, however. On the contrary, reporters liked Dale and his coworkers and many later vouched for his integrity.

Cornelius was soon reassigned to the travel office, a move that was mutually agreeable. As it turned out, Watkins and his deputy Patsy Thomasson had little use for the young woman. Thomasson had openly referred to her as "useless." Cornelius, meanwhile, was complaining about Watkins. She told House investigators in a deposition that she found working for Watkins "very demeaning." She continued, ". . . the office was hostile towards women. . . . I don't know if it was sexually hostile. I never felt sexually threatened by David Watkins. I think he touches people and pulls their hair and does stuff like that that was inappropriate, but I personally never felt like I was being sexually threatened by him. . . ." (Watkins denies any misconduct.)

Cornelius had taken her concerns to Susan Thomases, whom she knew from the campaign's scheduling operation. Thomases advised Cornelius to speak with Vincent Foster about the Watkins issue and her transfer was subsequently arranged with Watkins. Watkins suggested that Cornelius let him know if she observed anything untoward in the travel office. That is, Cornelius was moved to an office to closely observe employees whom she was already on record as wanting to replace. Soon enough, Cornelius was surreptitiously copying financial records from the office and taking them home.

Once Thomason communicated the problems in the travel office to Hillary, evidence suggests that she quickly brought the issue to a head in her usual forthright and businesslike manner. Though he had initially mentioned the problem in the travel office to Bill Clinton directly, Thomason must have known that Hillary, who had made it her business to oversee the operations side of the White House, was the person of action. Hillary would now fall victim to the dynamic of the co-candidacy, recalling the division of labor they had struck years ago. As Hillary's chief of staff Maggie Williams later told the *New Yorker* in explaining Hillary's role, "Clinton doesn't have a Haldeman." Her remark recalled the admonitions of Sally Quinn at the outset of the administration; she had warned that if Clinton didn't bring in someone like Haldeman to play the bad cop, the task might fall to Hillary. That scenario, in which Hillary would then be stigmatized and scapegoated for doing her job, was about to play out.

Just as with Whitewater, Bill distanced himself from the brewing scandal by leaving the details to Hillary. Though he escaped responsibility for the firings, the record shows that he was not only fully informed of the decision before it was taken but played a role in effecting it. Janet Green, an aide to David Watkins, told Billy Dale two days before the dismissal, "Billy, I am going to tell you something and if you ever repeat it, I will deny it. There is one person and only one person responsible for what has taken place with your office and he occupies the Oval Office," according to Dale's later congressional testimony.

Subsequent events made it clear that Hillary had become involved. On May 10, Thomason arrived at his White House office and had a reminder on his calendar to "call Hillary." In preparation for the call, he began to collect information, checking in with Watkins about the travel office, and asking Martens to fax a copy of his memo about the supposed Republican ties of the airline to him at the White House. Before leaving the White House that day, according to his calendar, Thomason called McLarty, Watkins, and Cornelius to set up a White House meeting for the following morning. He also wrote himself a note: "Call Susan Thomases at home after 9:30 P.M."

The next morning, Thomason received a message to call Craig Livingstone, who had worked in Thomases' advance operation during the 1992 campaign: "Come over while Susan is here." Thomason and Thomases met later that afternoon. Thomason also met separately at the White House that day with Harold Ickes, another Hillary adviser, who was not yet a member of the staff. Thomases was said to consider herself to be an expert on presidential travel because of her scheduling job in the campaign. Once Thomases became involved in the effort to fire the workers, the die was cast.

Thomason met with Clinton in the Oval Office the following morning. At midday, he met with Hillary, who told him to "stay ahead" of the problem and agreed with the image consultant that rooting out corruption in the travel office and implementing a new money-saving system would make a "good story." This would not be the last time that Hillary misjudged the reaction of the White House press corps. Apparently, she did not stop to think that it would be a "good story" only if the evidence bore out the corruption charges. Furthermore, the press would lean toward the travel office workers, whom reporters knew and liked. Hillary did not see that the far better press story would be how Clinton's friends, who stood to benefit, were behind the firings.

Thomason then went to Watkins, telling him that he had "bumped into" Hillary and that "she's ready to fire them all that day." Whether Thomason was brashly overstating Hillary's position to get Watkins' attention is not clear. Watkins' own position is somewhat ambiguous as well. Though he later sought to portray himself as simply following Hillary's orders to fire the staffers in a "soul-cleansing memo" released by the White House in January 1996, he seemed to play an active role in circulating damaging rumors about the workers and moving the process forward. Knowing that Hillary favored action, Watkins took the matter to Vince Foster, the person closest to her in the White House. Watkins told Foster of Cornelius's suspicions about the "lavish lifestyles" of the travel office seven (one had a modest vacation home and a $6000 pontoon boat), and her discovery of a number of unaccounted-for checks made out to cash, and he repeated the rumor about kickbacks. Later in the day, Watkins took Cornelius to meet with Foster and Kennedy. In that meeting, Cornelius added to the earlier indictment of the travel office workers. She told the lawyers they used "sexist and racist language," a charge which, had it reached Hillary at any stage, would have only strengthened her resolve to solve the situation. After the meeting, and before anything had been done to substantiate Cornelius's claims, Watkins instructed her to call his friend Betta Carney in Little Rock and tell her to prepare to send staffers to Washington to take over the travel operation.

Foster, however, wasn't impressed with the Watkins-Cornelius presentation; he knew no action could be taken without harder evidence and he asked Watkins if his office had the ability to undertake an audit. When Watkins told him no, Bill Kennedy suggested that he consult with the person he had been dealing with at the FBI in processing White House security clearances. (The FBI had the capacity to conduct a fraud audit.)

Inexperienced in Washington procedure, neither Foster nor Kennedy seemed aware of post-Watergate protocol concerning White House contacts with the Department of Justice (of which the FBI is a part) on pending investigations. The general principle set forth by the Carter administration, and reaffirmed subsequently, is that White House contacts with law enforcement agencies on civil or criminal investigations should go through the White House counsel's office first, and should only then proceed to the highest levels of the Justice Department. The decision to contact the FBI at the working level would later be seen as an improper attempt by the White House to politicize the agency and use it to cast criminal suspicion on a group of blameless government employees. Kennedy in particular seemed to give these implications no thought; as one senior official later put it, "For all he knew, Kennedy could have been calling in the CIA."

According to a later account by FBI agents, Kennedy came on like gangbusters, telling them that interest in an investigation of the travel office was directed at "the highest levels" (a possible reference to Hillary) and threatening to contact Internal Revenue Service auditors if the bureau would not do White House bidding and respond—within fifteen minutes! Kennedy has said he was only seeking guidance from the FBI on how to handle the problem and not pressuring the agency to investigate. (Indeed, soon after the firings the IRS was knocking on the airline's door. In mid-June Bill Kennedy met IRS Director and FOH Peggy Richardson at a Washington party and later told aides that the IRS "is on top of it.")

On May 13, Foster met twice with Hillary. Notes Foster took of the meeting showed "HRC generally appeared less than satisfied with timeliness of decision-making, i.e., cloture." It is not known what else was said.

Did Foster tell Hillary that little evidence of wrongdoing had been established to justify the firings? If he did, did she nonetheless insist on plunging ahead anyway? Or did Foster keep his worries that the process was spinning out of control to himself, leaving Hillary with the impression that there were in fact serious problems that warranted the workers' dismissal? Did he mention the FBI to her?

In any case, Foster, seeking an evidentiary basis for further action, commissioned an accounting audit. Conveniently, an auditor, Larry Herman of the accounting firm KPMG Peat Marwick, was already in residence in Vice President Gore's office, examining ways of saving money by reducing bureaucracy. Herman was called in to do a quick audit over the weekend. (Because it could not examine all pertinent documents, Peat Marwick noted that its work did not constitute an audit, examination or review in accordance with standard accounting procedures.)

During the audit, Foster asked Watkins to call Hillary directly to inform her of the preliminary findings. This suggests that there may have been friction between the two in the May 13 meeting. According to the GAO investigation of the matter, Watkins incited Hillary further, telling her the fiscal mismanagement was worse than had been thought. Watkins's notes of the phone conversation show that Hillary told him, "Harry says his people can run things better; save money, etc. And besides we need those people out—We need our people in. We need the slots." (Hillary denies saying this.) According to Watkins, Hillary also told him she had been advised not to keep on holdovers from the previous administrations. "She stated action needed to be taken immediately to be certain those not friendly to the administration were removed and replaced with trustworthy individuals," Watkins told Justice Department investigators. This last point was telling, and it fit with something Thomason's attorneys later suggested to White House counsel. Counsel office notes show that Thomason remembered telling Watkins that the travel office employees should be replaced because they were disloyal and that Hillary shared that view. This raises the question of just what Hillary's motives were in pressing the travel office issue.

If the absence of hard evidence was a red flag to a careful lawyer like Vincent Foster, one might expect Hillary to have waited for the results of an independent audit before urging action. As her experience in Arkansas had revealed, however, Hillary was caught in the web of cronyism. She had been willing, for example, to represent Jim McDougal before a state regulator appointed by her husband. And she seems to have avoided knowledge about certain aspects of Madison and her involvement in Whitewater. Thus it is possible that Hillary asked few questions and simply saw the travel office business as payback to a travel agency that had helped Bill win election, and to the Thomasons (to whom, after all, she was much closer than she had ever been to the McDougals). In this view, whatever other considerations she may have had simply reinforced or justified what was at bottom a self-interested motive.

On the other hand, Hillary has rarely, if ever, acted from such base and trivial motives. Higher political goals were surely at work. As her comments about "saving money" showed, one goal was probably fulfilling Clinton's pledge to downsize the White House staff. Hillary was likely encouraged to act as well by the stories she was hearing about corruption in the travel office, which she may have accepted at face value. At this juncture, under fire for her role in the health care task force, and facing a severe political test with the Lani Guinier nomination, the White House could ill afford another scandal. Hillary may have felt that clearing out an allegedly corrupt travel office was the only responsible course. Imagine the headlines if the press had discovered wrongdoing in the White House before the Clintons had taken any positive action to ferret it out.

In Hillary's mind, the charges of financial corruption appeared to be joined with the fear that the travel office employees and the charter company were politically untrustworthy. After the Secret Service leaked the lamp-throwing story, Hillary must have been particularly inclined to root out those who were not allies. According to the Watkins memo, he acted swiftly on Hillary's concerns because he did not relish a rerun of the Secret Service incident earlier in the year, when Hillary had wanted action and became upset when she got no response. Thus one can rather easily understand Hillary's eagerness to replace any and all staffers from previous White Houses with the Clintons' own people as a protective impulse rather than as a ruthless and arbitrary attack by a latter-day Marie Antoinette.

The Peat Marwick audit of the travel office conducted the weekend before the firings found poorly documented records and $18,000 in unaccounted-for funds. Though the auditors uncovered no evidence to support any other allegations, they did conclude that the dismissal of the head of the office was warranted.

On Sunday evening, Mack McLarty brought the news to Bill and Hillary at a private dinner in the residence. McLarty's handwritten notes of that day reflected "HRC pressure." Later that night, Foster had a meeting with Clinton. The next morning, McLarty briefed Watkins on the audit and told him "this is a hot topic around here." According to the memo written by Watkins, McLarty also told him the issue was on Hillary's "radar screen" and "immediate action must be taken." McLarty, however, told investigators he did not remember Hillary specifically recommending that the workers be fired. "I don't recall her saying anything of that nature to me, and I just simply don't believe she did," McLarty said. "I think that really what she was saying was, 'let's make a decision.' "

Indeed, it may have been Susan Thomases, speaking in Hillary's name, who gave the final order to McLarty. Invoking Hillary in this way was a common bureaucratic power play for Thomases, and it was bound to result in disaster eventually. The notes of White House aide Lorraine Voles, disclosed to Congressional investigators, said that Thomases went to Watkins and McLarty "but they wouldn't fire." According to these notes, Thomases then said to McLarty, "Hillary wants these people fired."

On Monday, Watkins sent a memo to McLarty outlining a plan to fire the travel office workers. Catherine Cornelius would head the new White House office and World Wide Travel and Penny Sample's Air Advantage would handle business from the outside. Watkins copied the memo to Hillary prominently across the top of the title page. He also faxed the memo to Bruce Lindsey, who was traveling with Clinton in California. Lindsey briefed Clinton, who was already familiar with Thomason's proposal, about the plan to replace the workers. Thus, while Hillary may have been motivated to act by higher ends, Bill likely considered the travel office shake-up a reward to his Arkansas cronies.

On the instruction of chief-of-staff McLarty, the firings were carried out by Watkins on Wednesday morning, May 19. Watkins' contemporaneous notes show that while he favored the plan to "privatize" the travel operation in principle, he questioned why events had to move so quickly. One possibility is that on that Wednesday morning the White House was about to become embroiled in a major controversy over Clinton getting a $200 haircut on his plane on Tuesday night in Los Angeles, which required grounding Air Force One for nearly an hour and shutting down two runways. The image flew in the face of Clinton's populist election theme. Since Thomason and Hillary had already thought of the travel office cleanup as a "good story," the White House may have thought of using it to deflect attention from a bad one.

The wholesale firings went well beyond addressing the concerns in the Peat Marwick audit. Five of the seven workers did not even handle money in the office. According to the workers, when Watkins convened the employees that morning and told them they had two hours to clean out their desks, he said he had decided a "surgical" procedure would be more effective than a discriminating consideration of the evidence.

Almost immediately, the action backfired. Earlier in the morning, Watkins had given White House press secretary Dee Dee Myers written talking points on the travel office firings. In an apparent effort to bolster the White House position and make the allegations seem credible, Watkins included in the talking points the White House contacts with the FBI. Though Watkins may not have realized the significance of implicating the employees in a criminal probe, when Foster saw the talking points he panicked and told him to remove any mention of the FBI. However, Watkins could not find Myers before she took a press call and disclosed the FBI contacts. The disclosure of these contacts violated long-standing FBI policy against confirming or denying the existence of an investigation—a policy designed to protect the innocent. The disclosure also raised the question of whether the White House had used political pressure to gin up a criminal probe.

But the White House had a second problem. Though there had been contacts between the White House and the FBI, the bureau had not yet opened an investigation. In full damage-control mode, the White House then pressured the FBI into confirming that a probe was in fact under way. John Collingwood, the chief spokesman for the FBI, was summoned to a White House meeting convened by George Stephanopoulos and attended by Bernard Nussbaum, Foster, and Kennedy. Given his experience in the Watergate inquiry, Nussbaum, of all people, should have been particularly wary of White House contacts with the FBI. The White House soon released a statement from the FBI saying that it had "sufficient information . . . to determine that additional criminal investigation is warranted." The FBI later claimed that the statement was not intended for public release. The travel office workers were now publicly smeared as the targets of an FBI investigation.

White House actions aroused so much suspicion in the press that the original goal of replacing the travel office employees with the Arkansas gang had to be quickly abandoned. Catherine Cornelius, who, to make matters worse, was quickly identified as Clinton's cousin in the press, never really took control of the office. At Watkins' instruction, World Wide had moved into the White House the day of the firings, but the agency's representatives were tossed out two days later.

Within a few days after the firings, the White House was backpedaling furiously. McLarty announced that five of the seven employees hadn't really been fired after all, but rather placed on administrative leave, and he said he would undertake an internal investigation of the matter (even though his own conduct was partly at issue). The internal review quickly concluded that the charges against the five were baseless and they were rehired by other government agencies. The assistant director of the office filed for retirement.

Billy Dale was indicted for embezzlement in December of 1994. Facing enormous legal costs in fighting what his Republican defenders called a political show trial, Dale offered to plead to charges against him by returning $69,000 to the government that he kept in his private account and admitting to a count of inadvertent wrongdoing that would expressly specify that he did not use any government funds for personal reasons. The government rejected the deal and Dale stood trial. He won acquittal after a jury deliberation of less than two hours.

The White House had every right to fire the travel office workers without cause. The idea to privatize the operation might have even been a good one, provided that the business was competitively bid. But the real motives behind the firings were unattractive, and so, it seems, a cause was invented. The audit and the contacts with the FBI appeared to be an effort to find evidence for a decision that had already been made. Now that the decision was a political disaster, no one wanted to own up to it.

David Watkins tried to deny and cover up his own role: According to Cornelius' deposition testimony, the day after the firings, Watkins saw Catherine Cornelius and Clarissa Cerda outside of Dee Dee Myers' office. "You never saw me read the memo. . . . You guys did this on your own, right?" Watkins said. A May 21 calendar note of Harry Thomason's said: "DW saying he never read any of Catherine's memos, and they are getting ready to come after him." Separately, Cornelius claimed Patsy Thomasson pressured her to resign. Brian Foucart, another aide to Watkins, said in a House deposition that Watkins had told him to tell Cornelius to resign.

Clinton, though he had been briefed by Bruce Lindsey on the firings before they occurred, said in a public statement, "I had nothing to do with any decision, except to save the taxpayers and the press money. . . . There's nothing going on here. We really were just trying to save everybody money." The fact that Clinton knew and approved of the firings was omitted from Mack McLarty's internal White House review of the firings, as was the fact that Clinton had pushed forward Thomason's pitch for government business auditing the use of all non-military aircraft.

Unfortunately for Hillary, the White House did not do as good a job in covering up her role. As her later denials of involvement would make clear, Hillary was intent on minimizing her role in the affair. In response to various inquiries, Hillary issued carefully worded statements that she "had no role in the decision to terminate the employees"; that she "did not know the origin of the decision"; and that she did not "direct that any action be taken by anyone with regard to the travel office. . . ." The veracity of these statements was challenged directly in the Watkins "soul cleansing memo," which had been sought for months by three separate investigative bodies before it surfaced in the files of Patsy Thomasson in early 1996. In that memo, Watkins claimed that Hillary was the motivating force behind the firing of the travel office workers.

McLarty had assigned the unenviable task of drafting the internal White House review to John Podesta, a longtime Democratic operative who had first met Bill Clinton during the Joseph Duffey Senate race in Connecticut in 1970. In the initial round of interviewing, it appears that the White House investigators steered clear of probing into Hillary's role and no one volunteered any information about it. The first version of events given to the White House investigators by Foster—who likely knew more about Hillary's role than anyone—left her completely out of the chain of events. During his interview, Foster, who referred to Hillary as "the client," said, "I assume many of the conversations I had were privi-

leged." After failing to mention Hillary, Foster was asked whether anyone else was "involved" and he responded: "I think that's all I should say
about that." In a notebook he began to keep on the travel office firings,
Foster made a notation for that day: "thereby defend HRC role whatever
is, was in fact or might have been misperceived to be. . . ." Podesta, however, began to pick up signs that Hillary had played some role. He interviewed Foster a second time in an effort to elicit more information,
but he was unsuccessful.

Clearly Podesta and an aide, Todd Stern, were under enormous pressure to airbrush Hillary out of the report. A handwritten note from Todd
Stern, later turned over to congressional investigators, said: "The problem is that if we do any kind of report & fail to address these Qs, press
jumps on you wanting to know answers; while if you give answers that
aren't fully honest (e.g., nothing re Hillary) you risk hugely compounding the problem by getting caught in half-truths. You run risk of
turning this into 'cover-up.' We need to think seriously about whether
or not it won't be better to come clean. In sense of saying, even to point
of conceding, that HRC . . . had some interest."

The question of why Hillary felt the urgent need to conceal her involvement can only be answered by examining her continuing struggle
to preserve her public image and moral authority as first lady. As an unelected official, she could not afford to be unpopular—least of all in the
midst of completing her historic mission to bring health care coverage
to all Americans.

Hillary had further concerns: How could a woman who personified
the self-image of an entire post-Watergate generation—a generation that
felt uniquely fit to bring the highest moral and ethical standards into
government—be seen as having anything at all to do with a process that
misused the FBI, the focus of a torrent of press criticism? (Foster, in fact,
may have told Hillary of the FBI contacts in the May 13 briefing.) Hillary,
after all, had worked on the Watergate inquiry, which ushered in a wave
of reforms designed to ensure a more accountable government with
higher ethical standards. One of the articles of impeachment drawn up
against President Nixon by Nussbaum and Hillary had charged that he
"misused the Federal Bureau of Investigation, the Secret Service, and

other executive personnel," by ordering "investigations for purposes unrelated to national security, the enforcement of laws or any other lawful function of his office."

By this point, Hillary was also aware of the public's deep ambivalence about the extent of her influence in White House operations. From a public-relations standpoint, Hillary may have been trying to follow Sally Quinn's advice: If a first lady is running the White House, nobody ought to know about it but her husband.

Once the Watkins memo surfaced in January 1996, the press's censure of Hillary vindicated her fear that if word had gotten out sooner about her involvement, she would have been harshly criticized. "The confidential memo written by David Watkins about the travel office gives the maternal image a Joan Crawford twist, portraying the first lady as a scary 'Mommie Dearest,' " Maureen Dowd wrote in the *New York Times.* "Mr. Watkins said he realized there was a more humane way to handle the situation than firing seven people, sicking the FBI on them, leaking it to the press, and pretty much ruining their lives," Dowd continued. "An associate of the first lady through all this confirms Mr. Watkins' portrait: 'She's a good screamer. She can cut someone to ribbons and make them feel like an idiot. It was a lot easier to do what she wanted.' "

Caricatures of Hillary as "Mommie Dearest" were possible because Hillary's dislike and distrust of the press and her own personal reticence led her to give very few interviews in which journalists—and therefore the public—could see a real person. She rarely played the role of official hostess to the Washington establishment. "I don't get out a lot in Washington and I didn't get out a lot in Little Rock, because when I have time that is not spent on my work and my public activities I want to be with my family," Hillary told the *New Yorker* in 1996. "I think that's one of the reasons people say, 'Well, who is she? We don't know her.' I don't get out as much as many people do because these years of child rearing go by so fast—I mean, Chelsea's going to be gone. I can go to dinner parties from now to kingdom come when she's in college and when she's grown up."

Ironically, at this time her staff had been working for weeks to arrange the first major profile of Hillary as first lady in a prestige journalistic venue. The article, "Saint Hillary," written by staff reporter Michael Kelly, was the cover story of the *New York Times Sunday Magazine* on May 23, a few days after the travel office staff was fired. Based on exclusive interviews, the Kelly piece described her accurately and in a generally favorable light as the modern-day heir of the religiously inspired social-gospel tradition in American politics, with such precursors as Harriet Beecher Stowe, Jane Addams, Carrie Nation, and Dorothy Day. Kelly quoted Hillary denouncing "the ethos of selfishness and greed" of the Reagan years, calling instead for a new "politics of meaning" which actually was not new at all but was perfectly consistent with Hillary's brand of Christian leftism. In a speech the month before the article appeared, delivered shortly after Hillary's father died, she had declared: ". . . we have to summon up what we believe is morally and ethically and spiritually correct, and do the best we can with God's guidance . . ." Invoking Christ's commandment to "love thy neighbor as thyself," Hillary encouraged all Americans to pay more attention to those who make society run but whose contributions are often overlooked. "You know, I'm going to start thanking the woman who cleans the restroom in the building that I work in. . . . I want to start seeing her as a human being." With statements like these on the record, Hillary could hardly afford to be seen as the malevolent force behind the purging of career employees in the White House travel office. Whatever her intention in the first place—rooting out corruption? protecting her family from "disloyal" aides?—the firings were now seen as a crooked scheme to enrich Clinton friends and relatives by ruining the lives of seven innocent people.[2]

While the Kelly piece took political observers by surprise with its unveiling of the religious basis of Hillary's political activism, the impulse had been there all along. Kelly even quoted the Reverend Don Jones to this effect: "There is nothing wrong with wielding power in the pursuit of policies that will add to the human good. I think Hillary knows this. She is very much the sort of Christian who understands that the use of power to achieve social good is legitimate." While his portrait was respectful, at the same time Kelly signaled his discomfort with the absolutist tendencies he saw in this philosophy. The secular liberal elite was comfortable with Hillary's image as the lawyer and children's rights advocate, but not with her spiritual side. He dismissively described Hillary's political theology as tinged with "New Age mysticism" and concluded, "Returning to moral judgment as a basis for governmental policy must inevitably mean curtailing what have come to be regarded as sacrosanct rights and admitting to a limit to tolerance. And that will bring the politics of meaning hard against the meaning of politics." These words would prove to be prophetic, not only of Hillary's experience in government, but of the unexpected turn against her on the part of liberal journalists and intellectuals who cringed at the idea of invoking a religious justification for progressive policies and dismissed the search for "meaning" as a sign that Hillary was uncentered.

Under these circumstances, it is easy to see why the White House review, released July 2, downplayed Hillary's role in the firings. But even the glancing mention of Hillary was enough to put Republicans and the press onto the trail. The headlines of mid-July were filled with GOP demands for congressional hearings and the appointment of a special counsel. Hillary, Nussbaum, Foster, Kennedy, Watkins, Patsy Thomasson, Harry Thomason, and Darnell Martens—as well as senior officials in the FBI and Justice Department—all stood to be drawn into any investigation. (Hillary, unlike the president, could be compelled to give Congressional testimony.)

Vince Foster was particularly worn down by the pressure. He had always done everything right. He was number one in his law school graduating class, and he had a winning litigation record and a sterling reputation for integrity in Arkansas. Foster "had never suffered a defeat," his Rose partner John Phillip Carroll later told the FBI. But in a few short months, he had made the biggest mistakes of his life.

Back in Arkansas, Foster had been remembered for occasionally being withdrawn from colleagues and friends. "But people didn't take it personally. They would say 'He's the same way with his wife and kids,' " former Rose lawyer B. Michael Bennett said. Former colleagues said that in one particularly black period, Foster didn't talk to his own secretary for weeks, preferring to communicate in writing. Little Rock journalist Carol Griffee said it was well-known among mental health workers in the city that Foster was a depressive. Such emotional instability would only have been heightened in Washington.

When Loraine Cline, Foster's former Rose Firm secretary, had lunch with him in the White House in late May, she asked him, "Are you having fun yet?" And he responded: "Well, it's an experience. We have one 'gate' after another." On the night of Zoë Baird's withdrawal as a nominee for attorney general, Foster had what was described as an anxiety attack; he was unable to sleep and sweating profusely. He was also under intense public criticism for his role in the health care task-force litigation. His office had crafted the legal argument whereby Hillary became a senior government official, a claim endorsed by the second-highest court in the land. This was a terrible error because Hillary was holding an investment portfolio containing health care stocks.

In late May, Foster began to compile a notebook reviewing the travel office firings. He gave special attention to the question of whether Harry Thomason, who had been working at the White House while seeking government business, had violated federal conflict-of-interest laws. But his biggest worry appeared to be the White House contacts with the FBI. Though Kennedy denied it, the FBI agents were saying that Kennedy had pressured them and had referred to "the highest levels" in demanding action. As Kennedy's superior, Foster felt responsible for the contacts, and he may have worried that he had told Kennedy too much about the interest of the Clintons, especially Hillary, in resolving the matter. What if Kennedy had, in fact, mentioned "the highest levels" to the FBI, thus pointing the finger in Hillary's direction?

When the White House travel office review was released July 2 and David Watkins and Kennedy received official reprimands, Foster became angry that he had been spared. Linda Tripp, Nussbaum's secretary, told investigators that Foster had wanted to take the "fall" and was overheard to say to Nussbaum, "This is *my* blame. "Let *me* take it." "Foster was concerned that the White House report would lead to unwarranted investigations of well-intentioned actions. He felt responsible for Kennedy's situation because he had assigned Kennedy to the matter. He was heard to raise his voice uncharacteristically in insisting that Nussbaum allow Foster to take the blame instead of Kennedy," according to the report of Robert Fiske, the first Whitewater independent counsel.

Foster tried to find a lawyer. He seemed to worry that he would be a witness, if not a target, in any investigation and should therefore no longer serve as the Clintons' lawyer. He talked to Jim Lyons, the Denver lawyer who had written the Whitewater report in the 1992 campaign, about hiring outside attorneys for the Clintons to advise them on the travel office case. In mid-July, Foster placed an urgent call to Lyons, asking him to come to Washington because political pressure for a travel office investigation "was escalating." Foster told Lyons that "private-sector attorneys should be handling many of the matters they [White House counsel] were handling, both for ethical and workload reasons," according to the Fiske report on Foster's suicide. Foster also discussed retaining outside counsel for the Clintons with Susan Thomases and James

Hamilton, the Washington lawyer who had worked with Hillary on the Whitewater inquiry.

In addition to the Republicans, the press was stirring up trouble for Hillary. On July 9, one of Mack McLarty's deputies, former Senate aide Ricki Seidman, left McLarty a message: "Heads up—Possible *NY Times* negative editorial re Hillary/Travel. Maggie and Podesta trying to stop." On July 11, the *New York Times* ran an editorial focusing on Hillary and excoriating the White House for the FBI contacts, headlined "A Stealthy, Evasive Confession." "When the White House was getting ready to fire all seven employees of its travel office, why was notice sent to Hillary Rodham Clinton and not her husband the President?" the editorial began. (The *Times*, of course, was wrong in saying that Hillary had been notified about the firings and Bill had not. That editorial was a prime example of how the press was harder on Hillary, the zealous Watergate reformer, than on Bill, who was able to skirt accountability.)

On July 14, Senate minority leader Bob Dole called for a special counsel to investigate "this sorry episode of mistakes, misstatements, and downright wrongdoing." On July 20, the day of Foster's suicide, Democrats on the House Judiciary Committee quashed a Republican attempt to force the president to furnish documents concerning potential misuse of the FBI in the travel office investigation. But the House Republican Policy Committee adopted a statement calling for a special counsel on Travelgate: "Who authorized or directed a presidential counsel to summon FBI agents to the White House to seek an investigation of the travel office? Who authorized him to threaten the FBI with transferring the investigation to the IRS unless agents took prompt action? In other words, how high up did this shocking politicization of law enforcement reach? Why was Hillary Clinton, and not the president, briefed on decisions involving the travel office?"

On this last point, of course, the Republicans were as wrong as the *New York Times* had been, but they must have viewed Hillary as an inviting political target. Hillary's role in the travel office firings was going to be a major issue in subsequent investigations by the General Accounting Office and the Justice Department, if not by a special counsel. Foster knew better than anyone what that role had been, and he was undoubtedly going to be compelled to describe it under oath—perhaps even revealing that he had told Bill Kennedy of Hillary's concerns—leading Kennedy to mention "the highest levels" to the FBI. Foster may also have told Hillary of Kennedy's contacts with the FBI. The White House was already on record as minimizing Hillary's role, and Foster appears to have dodged John Podesta in his interviews for the management review. At some point he would have faced two equally unacceptable choices: lie or give up Hillary.

Foster took his life on July 20 at Fort Marcy Park outside Washington. No satisfactory explanation has yet been offered for this tragic act. Because he was a seasoned corporate litigator, the theory that Foster simply folded under the pressure of his White House job or criticism from the *Wall Street Journal* editorial page seems wholly inadequate. His bouts of depression before coming to Washington likely predisposed him to suicide. (Shortly before his death, Foster told his sister Sheila Anthony that he was fighting depression; she recommended that he see a psychiatrist. Instead, he called his doctor in Little Rock for antidepressant medication.) Depression may have shaded into desperation when Foster saw exactly what was in fact coming: a series of revelations that resulted in the appointment of a special counsel on Travelgate, with Hillary testifying before a federal grand jury.[3]

Perhaps Foster felt guilty about his complicity in Bill Kennedy's call to the FBI, and even worse, about having told Hillary of the improper contacts. His failure to protect her must have weighed heavily on him. Hillary, moreover, may have made Foster feel even worse by expressing irritation at the way he had handled matters—subjecting her to personal embarrassment in connection with the health care task force, Value-Partners, and now the travel office. According to a 1996 article in the *New Yorker* on the travel office scandal, Hillary was known to vent her frustrations at Foster when things went wrong. "If she was mad at anyone— it didn't matter who it was—Vince got it," one Clinton associate was quoted as saying. There was a hint that their relationship had been ruptured in Hillary's later comment that she had not spoken with Foster for about three weeks before his death—an unusually long period for such close friends.

Hillary's judgment in placing Foster in such a sensitive post in the first place, and her self-protective unwillingness to acknowledge her role in the firings, must be severely questioned. Hillary had chosen a man of unquestioned personal integrity for the task of maintaining in the White House a damage-control operation that was really an extension of the one set up during the 1992 campaign. This operation collapsed in Foster's office: a man of more elastic ethics, understanding Hillary's needs, might have done whatever was necessary in the name of damage control. Foster, by all accounts, was simply incapable of such behavior.

On the day Foster died, Hillary had stopped in Arkansas to make a speech on her way back from a trip to Hawaii. When she was notified that Foster's body had been found she, Chelsea, and her staff were at her mother Dorothy Rodham's condominium in Little Rock. It was close to 10:00 P.M. when Mack McLarty telephoned with the news. Bill was a guest on *Larry King Live* at the time, though nobody in the Rodham home was watching. Describing her reaction in a deposition, Hillary's press secretary Lisa Caputo said Hillary appeared so devastated by McLarty's call that Caputo assumed the president was dead.

Though she appears never to have called Foster's widow Lisa, Hillary made a series of phone calls later that evening. The first was to chief of staff Maggie Williams. Williams had worked with Foster for only six months but had grown closer to him than perhaps anyone else on the White House staff. They worked together on the health care task force, and presumably on the many personal legal tasks Foster was performing for the Clintons as well. Williams went immediately to Foster's office at the White House, arriving before law enforcement investigators examined the scene. There she found Patsy Thomasson, David Watkins's deputy, already searching for a note. Williams later told friends that she had gone to the White House that evening not on Hillary's instructions but out of concern that a suicide note personally embarrassing to the first lady might have been left behind there.

Like many people close to the Clintons, Williams must have heard rumors about the relationship between Foster and Hillary. In early 1996, *Newsweek* reported that some Clintonites believed Foster had a "crush" on her. In late 1995, a report in the *Washington Post* on the contents of a diary Foster had left behind also suggested that Foster and Hillary may have had more than a professional relationship. "It was months after Foster's death that officials revealed he had kept a sporadic journal, and Foster family lawyers tried unsuccessfully to keep police investigators from examining it," the *Post* reported. "Most of the journal's few entries focused on Hillary Clinton. A Park Police supervisor told the FBI that after the 1992 election Foster's journal said Hillary Clinton was happy because she would have a big role in the administration and that 'he was happy because Hillary was happy,' the supervisor said." Whether the rumors were true or false, Hillary's staff had to act as though they were true.

Hillary's second call that evening was to Harry Thomason in California. Before arriving in Arkansas en route from Hawaii, Hillary had stopped off in California for a few days, staying at the Thomason home. Thomason said in a deposition that Hillary had expressed her utter dismay that Vince "did it," suggesting that Hillary and the Thomasons may have previously discussed the state of Foster's mental health and even the possibility of suicide. Indeed, in the days before the suicide, the Clinton inner circle seemed to know that something was deeply wrong with Vince. During the week before his death, Foster had a private dinner with Susan Thomases. Webb Hubbell swam and played tennis that weekend on Maryland's Eastern Shore with Foster and his wife. On Monday, the day before the suicide, Marsha Scott, the White House correspondence director and Clinton's ex-girlfriend from the 1960s, had met privately with Foster in his White House office. She told investigators she thought Foster had "come to a decision." And Clinton himself called Foster the night before his death, ostensibly inviting Foster to join Bruce Lindsey and Webb Hubbell at the White House residence to watch a movie. (Foster declined.) Some in the Clinton inner circle speculated that Bill had said something to Foster, perhaps suggesting that he had to hang tough, that may have tipped Foster over the edge. Officially, however, everyone involved had memory lapses, telling investigators they didn't have a clue about why Foster killed himself. Clinton hurriedly announced that "[W]hat happened was a mystery about something inside of him." Susan Thomases told the FBI she had no idea what might have motivated Foster to take his life and mentioned only a lunch with Foster attended by several people, not a dinner. Describing the weekend in Maryland in a later deposition, Hubbell sat nervously twisting the ring on his finger and denied speaking with Foster about the travel office, "even though you may find that hard to believe."

According to friends, Hillary went to ground emotionally in the ensuing weeks and months, although she was able to hold herself together well enough to ensure that the investigation into Foster's death was carefully controlled. The rash and improper actions of the next few days, particularly the removal of documents from Foster's office to a closet in the

White House residence where they could be screened by Hillary before being turned over to the Clintons' private lawyer, would later precipitate the appointment of a special counsel to investigate Whitewater. These actions were not, as some have suggested, simply the result of confusion or poor judgment on the part of panicky aides. As the Senate Whitewater Committee concluded, the author of the problem, and its consequences, was Hillary herself.

Echoing the carefully worded denials she had issued in the Travelgate case, Hillary has said that she did not "direct" anyone to "interfere" with any investigation of Foster's death. Calling her denials "lawyerly word games," the Senate Whitewater committee concluded: "Although this statement may be technically correct, that Mrs. Clinton did not 'direct' anyone to 'interfere' with investigations, the evidence established that she communicated concerns about the handling of documents in Mr. Foster's office. Those concerns were passed on, in Mrs. Clinton's name and by someone known to have her authority [Thomases] to White House officials. Here, as in Travelgate, that is enough. The invocation of Mrs. Clinton's interest in the matter commands a clear message: 'Immediate action must be taken.' And the action taken, denying investigators access to documents in Mr. Foster's office, had the effect of interfering with the investigation."

In post-Watergate Washington, it has often been observed, the cover-up is often worse than the crime. But the corollary to the rule is that the political payoff has to be worth the risk. In this respect, it must be said, Hillary's operation was effective, at least in the short term. Only Hillary knows if the great suspicion aroused in the press and the public over the handling of Foster's papers was worth it.

Whether or not documents were removed from Foster's office will probably never be known. Secret Service agent Henry O'Neill testified that he saw Williams remove a handful of file folders from Foster's office that night. (Williams passed two lie detector tests backing up her denial that she removed any papers). Another Secret Service agent, Bruce Abbott, testified that the next morning he saw Craig Livingstone carrying a brown "leather or vinyl type briefcase, opening at the top, much in the fashion of a litigator's bag or lawyer's briefcase." The agent said he also saw Livingstone leaving the White House with an unknown person "carrying one or perhaps two boxes with what appeared to be, looked to me to be loose-leaf binders." (Livingstone denies that he took any documents from Foster's office.) Also that morning, according to testimony by park police office Peter Markland, members of the White House counsel's office monitored park police interviews of White House staffers "to report back to Mr. Nussbaum what was being said in the interviews."

Throughout the day on July 21st, White House officials held off a review of the documents in Foster's office until Nussbaum reached agreement with deputy attorney general Philip Heymann on how the review would be conducted. A spot check of the office, of course, had already been conducted by Thomasson and Williams the night before, after which Williams reported back to Hillary and Susan Thomases.

Although he claims only to have been exercising his duties as an attorney to review documents for privilege, Nussbaum appears to have been concerned with documents relating to two issues: Whitewater and especially Travelgate—the latter scandal already under investigation by the Justice Department. On the morning of July 21st, Webb Hubbell had told Nussbaum, "[You] ought to think about staying out" of the investigation of Foster's death because of questions surrounding Travelgate. But Nussbaum charged ahead anyway.

Why the need for a controlled search? There were simply too many vulnerabilities to allow a proper search. By the time of Foster's death, it was known at the highest levels of the Clinton administration that the federal Resolution Trust Corporation, in charge of S&L clean-up, had sent a criminal referral mentioning the Clintons to the Justice Department for possible prosecution, raising the prospect of criminal or civil liability for the Clintons in connection with the now-defunct Madison Guaranty S&L. The referral contained charges on which the McDougals and Jim Guy Tucker were convicted in May 1996. Though the Clintons were not implicated in the case, Bill was called to testify as a witness for the McDougals, and the convictions proved a major political embarrassment.

Hillary had first heard word of the Madison Guaranty investigation from Betsey Wright in the fall of 1992. In March 1993, Roger Altman, deputy Treasury secretary and acting head of the Resolution Trust Corporation, was briefed on the referral. That day, Altman faxed a copy of Jeff Gerth's March 1992 *New York Times* article on Whitewater to Nussbaum at the White House. Nussbaum, who in private practice had recently represented a law firm sued by the RTC over a failed S&L, would have immediately recognized Hillary's potential exposure. (Altman denied any recollection of having sent such a fax; Nussbaum denied receiving it.) In addition, Small Business Administration chief Erskine Bowles, a Renaissance Weekend friend of the Clintons, was briefed in May by lower level SBA officers about the agency's investigation of alleged fraudulent loans by David Hale's Capital Management Services. Bowles then filled in Mack McLarty. Though there is no evidence Foster knew about it, an FBI search warrant for Hale's Little Rock office was approved on the day of his suicide.

When the search of Foster's office finally commenced on July 22nd, Nussbaum clashed over procedures with two Justice Department lawyers, Roger Adams and David Margolis (who knew Madison was under investigation). According to Deputy Attorney General Philip Heymann, the day before, Nussbaum had agreed to a process for review that included Justice Department lawyers examining the documents. Nussbaum, perhaps initially unaware of just how sensitive the documents in Foster's office might be, suddenly went back on the deal. (Nussbaum and his associates denied the existence of any agreement.)

That morning had begun at dawn with a round of telephone calls between Thomases and Hillary, still in Little Rock; Thomases and Nussbaum; and Thomases and Hillary once again. Nussbaum testified that Thomases told him "people" were concerned about giving investigators "unfettered access" to Foster's office. Nussbaum then told his aide Stephen Neuwirth that Hillary herself was concerned about controlling access to Foster's office, according to testimony by Neuwirth.

Nussbaum now insisted on examining the documents himself, providing only a very general description of them, as Justice Department lawyers, Park Police investigators, and lawyers for the Foster family stood idly by. He justified his actions as protecting attorney–client and executive privilege regarding the documents. A Park Police report described the process: "There was some conversation between Nussbaum and Margolis as to what constituted privileged communication. Nussbaum carried his interpretation of what was considered privileged to the extreme; one example was when he picked up a xeroxed copy of a newspaper article and declared that it was privileged communication even though it had been in the newspapers."

During the Watergate inquiry, Nussbaum and Hillary had done legal research to rebut President Nixon's claims of executive privilege. Now Nussbaum was trying to assert the same privilege—not against Congress, as Nixon had done, but against another department of the executive. At one point Margolis confronted Nussbaum, telling him this was wrong. "I think it was at that point," Margolis later testified, "when I also said to him, 'You know if this were IBM that we were talking about, I would have a subpoena duces tecum returnable forthwith with these documents. But I recognize this is not IBM.' And he made the facetious comment about, if this were IBM rather than the White House counsel's office, a smart lawyer would have removed the documents before the subpoena ever got there."

When the Justice Department lawyers complained to Philip Heymann about the procedure instituted by Nussbaum, Heymann phoned Nussbaum and reiterated Margolis's warning. Nussbaum told Heymann he would call him back, but he went ahead and conducted the search his own way. That evening, according to Heymann's testimony, he called Nussbaum from his home and angrily accused him of using the Justice Department to make a sham search appear legitimate. "I told him that I couldn't imagine why he would have treated me that way. How could he have told me that he was going to call back before he made any decision on how the search would be done then not call back?" Heymann later testified. He then told Nussbaum: "You misused us," and asked, "Bernie, are you hiding something?"

"[N]o, Phil, I promise you we're not hiding something," Nussbaum responded.

Among the files that Bernard Nussbaum had failed to tell anyone about as he was sifting through documents in Foster's office, the White House conceded many months later, was a file labeled "WHITEWATER DEVELOPMENT, Personal and Confidential VWF." Since December 1992, when the Clintons had sold their remaining interest in Whitewater to Jim McDougal for $1,000, Foster had been trying to figure out how to report the transaction on the Clintons' 1992 tax return. (The transaction had been arranged by Jim Blair, who loaned McDougal the money for the purchase.) The core of the problem was that during the campaign the Clintons had understated the extent to which they had actually been shielded from substantial Whitewater losses by the McDougals, ostensibly their 50–50 partners. Foster had feared that claiming a loss on Whitewater in their 1992 returns could trigger an IRS audit and open up to renewed scrutiny the Lyons report, which had quelled the controversy in March 1992 with figures overstating the Clintons' losses.

(Clinton later said that a $20,744 check counted as a Whitewater payment was actually a loan to his mother that he had forgotten he made.)

Claiming a loss, Foster wrote in his notes, would be "a can of worms you shouldn't open." He was also concerned with the "propriety of some of the deductions" the Clintons had taken with respect to Whitewater. In the Clintons' 1984 and 1985 tax returns, Foster wrote, they took personal interest deductions "for debt that should be corp[orate]." If these documents got out, the Clintons could easily have faced front-page headlines about not paying their taxes, or worse.

Furthermore, as the Senate Whitewater investigation revealed, a notebook Foster had kept on the travel office—which recorded Hillary's role—was removed from Foster's briefcase and concealed by Nussbaum. Although travel office documents had been under subpoena by special counsel Fiske since January 1994, the notebook was held by the White House for a year after Foster's death. The Justice Department, which was conducting an investigation of the FBI's role in Travelgate, did not learn of the notebook until two years after Foster's death, when the White House made it public. At that time, Michael Shaheen, director of the Office of Professional Responsibility at Justice, wrote in an internal memo that he was "stunned" to learn of the notebook, which was "obviously relevant" to his investigation. Evidence also suggests that an index of the documents in Foster's office was altered or destroyed to remove references to Whitewater.

The note in Foster's briefcase may well have been found several days before the counsel's office claimed it had been discovered. (The note could be interpreted as referring to Travelgate in five of nine lines, though not once to Whitewater.) Several people testified they had seen scraps of paper in Foster's briefcase some days before the note was "discovered" on July 26 by Nussbaum's aide Neuwirth. Deborah Gorham, Foster's secretary, says that she told Nussbaum on the day after Foster's death that Foster had "placed shredded remnants of personal documents" in his briefcase. Michael Spafford, one of the lawyers for the Foster family who was present during the July 22nd search of Foster's office, testified that he overheard Nussbaum and Clifford Sloan, a Nussbaum deputy, talking about "scraps in the bottom of the briefcase." Detective Markland of the Park Police accused Nussbaum of flatly lying to him: He "physically picked up the briefcase at one point [on July 22nd] and tilted it and I saw it come off the floor and tilt, and then he put it down and said it was empty." (Several other witnesses confirmed that Nussbaum handled the bag; Nussbaum testified that he did not recall doing it.) When the note was finally found on July 26th by Neuwirth, Park Police Major Hines said that "[O]ur oldest, blindest detective would have found the note [on July 22nd]."

If Nussbaum were in fact to have found the note on July 22nd, he might have pieced it together on his own and pondered what to do with it before returning it to the briefcase, where it was discovered by Neuwirth on July 26. In any event, when Neuwirth took the note to Nussbaum that day, Nussbaum alerted Hillary and Susan Thomases. The note was not turned over to authorities investigating Foster's death for another thirty hours. The delay suggests there was some thought of not turning over the note at all. Bill Kennedy, for one, told an associate that if he had found the note, he would have eaten it. (The brash Kennedy also had the temerity to ask Hillary for Foster's job on the day of his funeral. He didn't get the promotion.)

In August 1996, when the White House released thousands of pages of documents that had been withheld from congressional investigators under a claim of privilege, the cause of the delay in turning over the note was revealed. A memo written by a White House counsel's office lawyer quotes Mack McLarty, who was traveling with Clinton in Chicago on the 26th, as saying Hillary insisted "the president should not be told" of the note until it was decided whether or not to turn the note over to the Justice Department. Counsel's office attorneys furiously researched legal issues surrounding the note, including assertions of privilege. (The memo identifying Hillary's role was of a conversation White House lawyer Miriam Nemetz had with a lawyer for former White House aide David Gergen, who was also traveling with the president and McLarty. Nussbaum contradicted the memo when it surfaced, saying that Hillary had not expressed a view about how the note should be handled: "It was my decision to delay, from day one, producing the note, so that the President and Lisa Foster could have an opportunity to view it first." Neither the president nor Lisa Foster, however, were told of the note that day.)

The note was turned over to the Justice Department thirty hours later, on the evening of the 27th, following meetings in the White House residence between Hillary and Thomases, whom Hillary had summoned from New York. Congressional investigators believe that a leak from inside the White House to the press of the note's existence may have forced its release. When the Justice Department launched an investigation of the delay, neither McLarty nor Gergen told investigators of Hillary's order that the president not be informed of the note.

According to FBI reports of interviews of Nussbaum and other officials present in a meeting in the counsel's suite on the 26th when the note was reviewed—a meeting which Hillary walked into, realized that the note was being pieced together, and then quickly left—no one mentioned that Hillary had seen the note before it was turned over. The notes of a July 28th staff meeting by deputy White House chief of staff Bill Burton listed "HRC" with an arrow pointing to an adjacent letter "n"—a suggestion that there may have been discussion of not revealing to the authorities that Hillary had seen the note. (Burton later tetified that he did not know what his own notes meant.) This was part of a consistent pattern present throughout subsequent investigations. Despite the existence of evidence supporting meetings or other contacts with Hillary during this period, people consistently erased such contacts from their memories or descriptions of events.

Whether or not the defensive tactics of Hillary and her White House protectors amounted to criminal obstruction of the investigation into Foster's death has been under examination by the Whitewater special counsel. There can be no question, however, that their conduct was a serious infringement of the public trust. White House lawyers are supposed to protect the interests of the presidency, not act like mob lawyers, asserting tenuous legal claims to deflect legitimate inquiries. The Senate Whitewater committee concluded that "[T]hese numerous instances of White House interference with several ongoing law enforcement investigations amounted to far more than just aggressive lawyering or political naïveté . . . [but rather] a highly improper pattern of deliberate misconduct."

It was not only Republicans, of course, who took a highly critical view of the conduct. As one high-level Justice Department official in the Clinton administration put it: "The question wasn't whether or not Bernie was too aggressive. The question was whether Bernie knew the Constitution." Hillary and her coterie would also be hoist on their own petard by her erstwhile allies in the liberal press. As news of the search of Foster's office filtered out in early August 1993, the *New York Times* was the first to raise the specter of a special counsel investigation into the events surrounding Foster's death: "... [I]deally, an independent counsel wholly free from executive branch control needs to be appointed. First, there must be a thorough reinvestigation of the White House travel office and the attempt in the spring to shift its function to Clinton campaign supporters. ... A special prosecutor-style inquiry is also needed into how the White House handled Mr. Foster's death. ... critical evidence was carelessly handled or out of sight long enough to raise suspicions about the integrity or competence of those involved."

Throughout the fall of 1993, the White House damage control operation was on full alert: top administration officials monitored the progress of the Resolution Trust Corporation investigation of Madison Guaranty, which in October produced nine new criminal referrals in which the Clintons were named as possible witnesses to civil or criminal wrongdoing at the S&L. Issues under investigation included whether funds from Madison were illegally diverted to the Whitewater investment or to Clinton campaigns, as well as possible civil liability for Hillary in connection with her legal work for Madison.

Even if there was no obstruction of any investigation, independent investigative agencies of the government appear to have been compromised. In what the Whitewater Committee concluded was a clear violation of RTC procedures, Jean Hanson, the general counsel of the Treasury (the agency that oversees the RTC) gave Bernard Nussbaum advance word of the referrals in late September—providing the White House with information that would not have been available to ordinary citizens. The referral named Arkansas governor Jim Guy Tucker as a target; two days later, Tucker met with Clinton at the White House. Little Rock federal prosecutor and longtime FOB Paula Casey, who reported to Webb Hubbell in Washington, declined to prosecute the RTC's first criminal referral on Madison Guaranty and rejected the subsequent referrals three weeks after Tucker visited the White House. Casey also refused to discuss a plea arrangement with David Hale, who was offering information to prosecutors implicating Bill Clinton in the solicitation of a fraudulent loan from Capital Management, the SBA-backed company set up to help the disadvantaged. After Casey later recused herself, the referrals were reinstated and eventually resulted in the convictions of the McDougals and Jim Guy Tucker on 24 felony counts.

April Breslaw of the RTC, who was in frequent telephone contact with Webb Hubbell during this period, told Jean Lewis, the lead RTC investigator in the case and author of the referrals, that the "head people would like to be able to say Whitewater did not cause a loss to Madison." Jean Lewis was subsequently transferred off the case. (Breslaw denies that she ever said that anyone in Washington wanted any particular outcome or that she discussed the RTC investigations with Hubbell.)

The White House counsel's office, meanwhile, continued to be misused to assist the Clintons' private defense effort on Whitewater. Political work for the president may fall into a gray area, but beyond a certain point political fixing and spin control is not the work of the nation. Nevertheless, it was typical of the Clinton crowd, accustomed as they were to the insider dealing and concentrated power of imperial Arkansas, to fail to make the crucial distinction between their personal business and the official business of the United States. Notes taken by Bill Kennedy of a November 5 meeting between counsel office lawyers and the Clintons' private lawyers outlined the defensive tactics under discussion:

> "Try to find out what's going on in Investigation"

> "Vacuum Rose Law files WWDC docs-subpoena

> *Documents → never know go out quietly"

In December, two bombshells hit the White House within two days. First, the Arkansas troopers' charges of Bill's philandering and his alleged offer of federal jobs to two of the troopers in an effort to keep the lid on the Troopergate story were aired in the *American Spectator* and the *Los Angeles Times*. In response, the White House virtually closed up shop, canceling its regular daily press briefing two days in a row. All three networks canceled interviews with Hillary planned for December 23rd because of White House ground rules that she could not be asked about Troopergate. By week's end, when the story showed no signs of abating, Hillary had to bear the indignity, during Christmas week, of cleaning up after Bill one more time. She came out swinging, calling the troopers' story "trash for cash," and a "political vendetta." (James Stewart would later report in *Blood Sport* that Betsey Wright had told White House counselor David Gergen that, as far as she could tell, the troopers were telling the truth.)

The day after the Troopergate story appeared, the *Washington Times* disclosed that papers had been removed from the office of Vincent Foster after his death and stashed in the White House residence for several days before being handed off to the Clintons' private attorneys. Following the carefully orchestrated search of Foster's office with Justice Department and Park Police officials present, Bernard Nussbaum and Maggie Williams had apparently undertaken a second secret search a few hours later. In congressional testimony, White House aide Tom Castleton said that Williams asked him to take files from Foster's office to the residence, where the Clintons could review them to see if they contained items of a personal nature before they went to Williams & Connolly (the Clintons' law firm). (Maggie Williams did not recall saying this.) The delay in turning over the documents to private counsel raised suspicions that the documents had been tampered with.

The combined impact of these disclosures along with David Hale's offer in the fall of 1993 to turn over state's evidence, led to GOP demands for a special counsel. Skittish about the troopers' story, the media began picking through Whitewater with a fine-tooth comb, sometimes exaggerating trivial matters. Writing in the *New York Review of Books*, Garry Wills drew the connection: "[T]he media had felt uncomfortable and constrained when reporting allegations, with some evidentiary backing, of Clinton's philandering: people doubted whether this was a matter for publication or extended discussion. Financial charges, on the other hand, were clearly relevant to public integrity, and even the wildest claims could be indulged with abandon."

As a follow-up to a conversation they had at the Renaissance Weekend at year's end, Jim Hamilton, the lawyer who worked with Hillary on the Watergate committee and was retained by the Foster family after Foster's suicide, wrote a letter to Clinton with "ideas on management of the Whitewater and trooper matters." In a moment of supreme irony, the ex-Watergate lawyer advised Clinton on how to stonewall: "Investigations, like other significant matters, must be carefully managed. . . . The White House should say as little and produce as few documents as possible to the press. . . . The White House should not forget that attorney–client and executive privileges are legitimate doctrines in proper contexts. . . . Bernie initially acted properly in protecting the contents of Vince's files. . . . If politically possible, Janet Reno should stick to her guns in not appointing an independent counsel for Whitewater. . . . Because you will continue to receive reporter questions about these matters . . . I expect that 'no further comment' often will suffice."

Two weeks before the appointment of a special counsel in January, Harold Ickes joined the White House staff and immediately formed a Whitewater response team. One of the new RTC criminal referrals discussed the question of whether improper influence had been brought to bear on Beverly Bassett to get Madison's preferred stock deal approved. In the margin of a *New York Times* editorial mentioning Bassett in late December, Bill Clinton wrote that Bassett had "held up" during the campaign and wondered if she could "keep it up." According to notes of a January 7, 1994, White House meeting, aides discussed sending emissaries to Arkansas to meet with Bassett to "make sure her story is OK." In the meeting, Harold Ickes exclaimed: "[Beverly] Bassett is so fucking important! If we fuck this up, we're done!"

In White House deliberations in early January, top officials argued about the appointment of a special counsel. A White House document marked "Confidential: Second Draft, Summary of Arguments Re: Whitewater," dated January 10, 1994, listed reasons against appointment of a special counsel, including that a special counsel investigation "may result in focus on friends and associates of the president, begin to squeeze them and may make some subject to indictment." Notes of a January 7 White House meeting showed that Nussbaum, who had consulted with Betsey Wright on damage control during the campaign, predicted: "Indictments will be Betsey Wright."

"Sadly, the Whitewater affair is exploding into a press frenzy," deputy Treasury secretary Roger Altman wrote in his diary on January 3, 1994. "It's mostly a testimony to the press mania and the crazed world of Washington." Two days later he wrote: "This Whitewater situation is one big mess. Administration perceived as stonewalling; 'There must be something to hide.' Big issue is independent prosecutor. Lots of speculation that HRC is the one who handled this in Arkansas. . . . White House seems engulfed in this and is mishandling it; for the president's lawyer to persuade DOJ to issue a subpoena for the documents so they won't be subject to FOIA looks very weak."

In internal deliberations on the appointment of a special counsel, Hillary dug in her heels. The attorney general had the authority to make the appointment; the question was whether the president should take the lead in calling for one. In the January 7 meeting, White House officials discussed how to get Hillary to reverse her position. Everyone seemed to realize that Hillary was calling the shots. Her "adamant opposition" was listed as the major obstacle to the appointment. At first, Ickes suggested that Secretary of State Warren Christopher or private attorney Robert Barnett be brought in to talk to Hillary, but he ultimately concluded it would be "impossible" to get her to change her mind. The notes reflect that everyone in the meeting agreed that not even Clinton could get Hillary to change her position.

In early 1994, Altman, as a friend of the Clintons' and a political appointee, was under media pressure to recuse himself as acting head of the RTC for Madison Guaranty matters. He was also feeling White House pressure to stay in the position. Altman sat on Hillary's health care task force during this period as well. His notes show that Maggie Williams told him, "On Whitewater, HRC was paralyzed by it." If the Whitewater problem was not defused, Williams warned Altman, there would be no health care reform. Altman noted that Williams told him: "HRC 'doesn't want [an independent counsel] poking into 20 years of public life in Arkansas.'"

Hillary's fears were soon validated: once the counsel began his investigation (Fiske was named, later to be replaced by Kenneth Starr), and a parallel inquiry on Whitewater was launched by Congress, the Clinton administration ground to a halt. The discipline and commitment Hillary brought to the White House policy agenda in 1993 was now directed to containing the fallout from Whitewater, which soon became an all-purpose term for Clinton political scandal.

In March 1994, Jeff Gerth of the *New York Times,* tipped off by Jim McDougal, broke the story of the commodities futures trading profits Hillary had earned in the late 1970s. Though commodities regulations were loose at that time and no laws were likely broken, Hillary was clearly embarrassed by the revelation, first claiming that she had made the trades herself after studying the *Wall Street Journal,* then conceding that Jim Blair had placed the trades for her. The liberal press seemed particularly chagrined by the revelation that the Clintons, who had campaigned for office denouncing the "decade of greed," had made some easy money through a lawyer who had clients with business before the state. While both Clintons had signed tax returns reflecting the trading profits, and Clinton was governor at the time, Hillary was blamed. William Safire described the deal as a "bribe," *U.S. News and World Report* characterized Hillary as a "greedy yuppie," and *Spy* put Hillary on its cover—complete with male genitalia peeking out from under her skirt.

Under fire in mid-April, Hillary held an unprecedented press conference in the White House state dining room, where, clad in a pale pink sweater, she deftly fended off dozens of hostile inquiries about her involvement in Whitewater and the commodities trades. She answered each question with technical precision: Did she get special treatment on the trades? "There's really no evidence of that," she said. At another point she responded, "I had absolutely no reason to believe I got any special treatment." But when asked if she should not have kept closer tabs on how the Whitewater mortgage was being paid during the time the Mc-Dougals were financing it, the lawyer's mask slipped: "Well, shoulda, coulda, woulda, we didn't." Hillary's dismissive, even contemptuous, responses to legitimate queries did nothing to boost her credibility with the media, which began to pile on rather indiscriminately, questioning the veracity of everything Hillary had ever said and the propriety of her every action for the next two years.

Columnist Molly Ivins chided Hillary for deducting as a charitable contribution on the family taxes Bill's used undershorts, though it was actually Bill who kept a handwritten ledger listing his underwear as a gift to the Salvation Army. *Esquire* questioned Hillary's statement that in 1947 Dorothy Rodham had named her after Sir Edmund Hillary, the New Zealand mountaineer who was the first man to reach the summit of Mount Everest in 1953. No one considered whether Dorothy had simply told her daughter an apocryphal story. Republicans charged that Hillary improperly used military aircraft on her book tour, though Barbara Bush had done the same thing without censure. NBC News reported that the book was written by an unacknowledged ghostwriter, though the White House had reams of handwritten notes showing that she had written it herself.

Just when it seemed that things couldn't get worse, only three weeks after the special counsel was appointed in 1994, Jim McDougal—heavily medicated and suffering from manic depression and acute memory loss—emerged after two years from his trailer, appearing on ABC's *Night-*

line for an exclusive interview in which he assured anchor Ted Koppel that Bill Clinton had never done anything unethical. When asked if he could give the same assurances about Hillary, McDougal paused, then said: "I don't know Mrs. Clinton well enough to give that broad a guarantee." McDougal and his wife Susan were suddenly given immense credence by the liberal press at Hillary's expense, as when Susan appeared on a later *Nightline* broadcast to contradict a sworn statement Hillary had made about the McDougals' Castle Grande project. Hillary told Resolution Trust Corporation investigators that she did not recall doing work on Castle Grande. When confronted with billing records showing that she *did* work on Castle Grande, Hillary explained that the project was known within the Rose Firm as Industrial Development Company, or IDC, the entity which had sold the Castle Grande property to a subsidiary of Madison Guaranty. Though Rose firm billing records showed the project was in fact billed as "IDC," corroborating Hillary's account, Susan McDougal appeared on *Nightline* to aver that Castle Grande and IDC were "one and the same." Viewers were left with the strong impression that Hillary had lied.

Beverly Bassett, the former Arkansas securities regulator who approved the preferred stock deal for McDougal's sleazy S&L, also slammed Hillary. She told the *Los Angeles Times,* "I don't know why she (Hillary) hasn't been more open. The people left behind in Arkansas are bearing the brunt of this."

Hillary saw it differently, of course. "Before I moved to Little Rock, I had a spent a lifetime dealing with David Kendall-type people," she said, referring to her soft-spoken Yale-educated Whitewater lawyer. "I thought it would be nice to deal with the colorful people of Arkansas for a change. Well, all those colorful people keep coming back to haunt me."

Throughout the spring, top White House aides spent untold hours (while on the public payroll) undertaking political damage control efforts. The counsel's office, which had been carefully organized to shield the Clintons from exposure, was in shambles. Vince Foster, of course, was dead, a blow from which the White House, and Hillary personally, never really seemed to recover. Bernard Nussbaum resigned amid criticism of his handling of the Foster office search and for allegedly pressuring Roger Altman not to recuse himself from all matters regarding Madison Guaranty. William Kennedy also resigned, following revelations that he had failed to pay social security taxes on a nanny's wages. The final Rose Firm recruit, Webb Hubbell, went to jail for bilking his Rose clients.

In May, the *Washington Post* published the results of a three-month investigation triggered by an Arkansas state trooper who had identified a woman named "Paula" as someone he had taken to Bill Clinton's room at the Excelsior Hotel in Little Rock in 1991. Jones denied the implication that she had consensual sex with Clinton and sued. Clinton hired high-priced Washington lawyer Robert Bennett to defend him, and set up a legal defense fund to finance it. Bennett argued that Clinton should be immune from civil lawsuits while serving as president. Though a federal district court rejected the unprecedented argument, the lengthy appeals process guaranteed that the suit would not be decided until after the 1996 election. Notably, Hillary, who had worked on issues of gender bias and sexual harassment for two decades, did not rise to Clinton's defense this time around.

Hillary herself seemed to attribute the collapse of the health care initiative that summer to the return of Whitewater and the assorted personal scandals dogging her husband. "We thought we had a real window," she told David Broder and Haynes Johnson for their book *The System*. "I said to Bill after NAFTA passed [in the fall of 1993] and his ratings were so high, 'Well, I wonder what's in their arsenal now.' We soon found out. We had Troopergate. We had Whitewater as an issue, and in the immortal words of Rush Limbaugh, 'Whitewater's about health care.' We had to deal with this whole onslaught. We were under siege again."

Hillary certainly acted as if she were under siege, raising the question of whether the partisan attacks from Republicans on the Whitewater front had made her even more resistant to compromise on health care than she had been previously. Rush Limbaugh and the *American Spectator* were simply not going to prevent all Americans from having adequate heath care!

With the effort to pass the Clinton plan stalled in Congress in June of 1994, Clinton suggested publicly that he was willing to settle for a compromise bill providing for less than universal coverage. But he issued a feeble recantation of the offer the next day. "Everyone understood that to be Mrs. Clinton," said Lawrence O'Donnell, the former aide to Senator Moynihan on the Senate Finance Committee. "The next day, Mrs.

Clinton was assuring her troops that wouldn't happen." "Some kind of moderate bill could have passed but it was clear to a lot of us that it wasn't going to happen because of her," said a private sector health care expert who spoke regularly with Hillary during this period. "Once she said, 'I'd rather have no bill at all and I'd rather run on the issue than just have some compromise.' Some people said that she didn't mean it, but I know she did because I looked her in the eyes when she said it. She said, 'This is not the process as usual.' She was a real ideologue on the issue."

Hillary appeared to suffer from the mistaken impression that poll results showing an overwhelming number of Americans rejecting her approach to health care reform were a reflection of misunderstanding, miscommunication, and sheer ignorance rather than of a fundamental disagreement over the proper role of government. A senior democratic senator who had spoken with Hillary about her strategy recalled: "Her view was 'take it into the election.' She really believed the people were on her side. Taking Hillary's health care plan into the election wasn't a winner."

Hillary's prominent role in the first two years of the Clinton administration undoubtedly contributed to poll results showing that most voters found Clinton too liberal. The number of people calling themselves Republicans nationwide had increased dramatically on Hillary's watch. When the results of the 1994 elections were in, the Democrats had lost control of both houses of Congress and the GOP even took control of fifteen more state legislatures across the country.

After the Republicans won control of Congress, special Whitewater committees were established in the Senate and the House chaired by Republicans Alfonse D'Amato of New York and Jim Leach of Iowa to re-examine ground that the Democrat-controlled committees had investigated only cursorily. Meanwhile, Pennsylvania Republican William Clinger launched a one-man crusade to expose the Travelgate fiasco. Dozens of new staffers—many as zealously ideological as young Hillary once was in the pursuit of Nixon—were hired to ferret out wrongdoing by the Clintons.

Hillary accordingly redoubled her efforts to short-circuit the investigations. After Nussbaum resigned, two seasoned Washington players— lawyer Lloyd Cutler and Judge Abner Mikva—were brought in as consecutive White House counsels to bring the aura of independence and rectitude to the office. But a shadow counsel's office of Clinton loyalists was also set up. Los Angeles lawyer Mark Fabiani became special counsel for Whitewater, reporting to Harold Ickes directly. And Bruce Lindsey—whose own conduct was under scrutiny by independent-counsel and congressional investigations—took Vince Foster's post after the first replacement, Joel Klein, clashed with Hillary over the handling of Whitewater documents. In the next two years, White House lawyers stonewalled the Republican investigators and shielded documents from public disclosure, asserting various claims of privilege. The assertions of executive privilege for political protection exceeded the similar claims of the Nixon White House that young Hillary had once condemned.

The counsel's office carefully scripted the Democrats on the congressional committees before televised Whitewater hearings were convened. During a House committee deposition, one White House lawyer defended the scriptings by favorably citing the practice of the Nixon White House, which "submitted the proposed questions for John Dean" during the Watergate hearings. The counsel's office also systematically debriefed the attorneys representing various administration witnesses after the witnesses were deposed by congressional investigators—apparently to explain any inconsistencies in the various stories of Clinton insiders.

On Travelgate, a damage control operation was put in place to protect Hillary. One New York lawyer, Natalie Williams, was hired as an assistant White House counsel to monitor the question of Hillary's role in the firings as it was being investigated by a House committee and the independent counsel. Documents released by the White House to Congress under a contempt citation showed that when certain material was withheld under the claim of privilege, the titles of the documents were misrepresented on the so-called "privilege log" provided by the White House to Congress. One document actually titled "HRC Travel Office Chronology" was listed as "Chronological Analysis of Travel Office Events." Another one titled "HRC Role" was renamed "Draft Chart Analysis and Comparison of Various Travel Office Investigations."

As the investigations proceeded, numerous Clinton aides and associates were forced to hire high-priced Washington lawyers and spent much of their time preparing to give testimony in court and before Congressional committees, distracting them from the business of government. Roger Altman and Jean Hanson resigned under fire. A succession of adminstration witnesses contradicted under oath their own written notes and diaries, and one even claimed she couldn't recognize her own voice on a tape. Bernard Nussbaum testified that he couldn't remember key events more than seventy times.

In dramatic testimony, Hillary's trusted confidantes, Susan Thomases and Maggie Williams, repeatedly swore that they could not recall anything about key telephone conversations and meetings surrounding the search of Vince Foster's White House office and the discovery and handling of the note he left behind, raising questions about possible obstruction of justice.

Williams, meanwhile, held private "Maggie summits" with a close circle of friends in which she openly speculated that Hillary might be indicted. She discussed her desire to leave the White House staff and take a job in Minnesota, but like many aides, she was stuck between a rock and a hard place. If she remained a federal employee, her legal fees—which now ran to over a quarter of a million dollars—might be reimbursed by the taxpayer.

Thomases appeared to split off from the White House altogether by the spring of 1996, bringing in a team of top-notch white-collar criminal defense lawyers and adopting a legal strategy designed to save her own skin. "I have my lawyers and Hillary has hers," a friend of Thomases quoted her as saying.

In January 1996, the lid was blown off the effort to hide Hillary's role in the travel office firings. The "soul-cleansing" memo (actually a draft that was never sent) written by David Watkins after the firings in 1993 was finally disgorged by the White House and turned over to the relevant investigative bodies. In the memo, Watkins said that Hillary had personally directed the effort to fire the travel office workers; there would have been "hell to pay" if he had "failed to take swift and decisive action in conformity with the First Lady's wishes." For her part, Hillary held to her unsworn statement to the GAO that she "had no role in the decision to terminate the [travel office] workers," and "did not direct that any action be taken with regard to the travel office. . . ."

Republicans hailed Watkins as a truth-teller and the memo was widely portrayed by the press as proving that Hillary was a liar. Indeed, the memo prompted *New York Times* columnist William Safire to publish his famous column branding Hillary a "congenital liar." As the charge led evening newscasts, Clinton came to Hillary's defense by threatening to punch the columnist in the nose. Clinton appeared subtly delighted to defend Hillary's honor à la Harry Truman while deflecting attention from his own Whitewater woes—including his complicity in the decision to fire the workers.

Ignored by the press were Watkins' serious credibility problems. Watkins himself admitted that he initially misled White House and congressional investigators about Hillary's role. His memo, he wrote, was the "first attempt to be sure the record is straight, something I have not done in previous conversations with investigators—where I have been as protective and vague as possible." About three weeks before being forced to resign in May 1994 for using a presidential helicopter to travel to a nearby golf course, Watkins sent Hillary a handwritten note that seemed to contradict much of what he told the GAO and also what he had written in the 1993 memo: "The GAO erred in stating that I said you urged me to replace members of the travel office with 'our people' . . ." In sworn congressional testimony following the 1996 release of the draft memo, Watkins backed off the claim that Hillary had told him to fire the travel office workers. Both Hillary's and Watkins' roles in the travel office firings are under scrutiny by the independent counsel.

Even allowing for the possibility that Watkins' memo exaggerated Hillary's role in an effort to blame the boss for a disastrous decision, on the evidence available (including the notes of Watkins, McLarty, and Foster), it is difficult to defend Hillary's statements as correct, except in a very technical sense. The evidence, however, does not justify Safire's characterization of Hillary as a "congenital liar"—a classic political smear. (Any legal implications to Hillary from Travelgate are unclear. Although she may be vulnerable on issues of obstruction or the contempt of Congress statute, the Supreme Court has ruled that unsworn statements made in court or to Congress are not covered by the criminal statute prohibiting false statements. Whether her statements to the GAO would be considered statements to Congress or an independent agency—to which giving unsworn false statements could be a crime—is not settled.)

Within a few days of the release of the Watkins memo, a copy of Hillary's Rose Firm billing records documenting her work for Madison Guaranty was discovered in the White House office of Carolyn Huber, a close aide to the first lady and former administrator of the Rose Firm. Huber testifed that she had picked up the records in the White House book room in the Clinton's residence next to Hillary's office in early August 1995 and, not realizing what they were, carried them to her White House office to file. Not until January 1996 during an office move did Huber find the records, examine them more closely, and realize they were copies of Hillary's billing records that had been under subpoena in the Whitewater investigation since early 1994.

The copies were apparently the only complete set of the billing records still in existence. The Rose Firm no longer had copies; the last person known to have had a copy was Vince Foster, who reviewed the records in February 1992 during the presidential campaign and presumably took them with him to the White House. The discovery of the records in the White House residence posed for Hillary perhaps the most significant legal exposure. If she knew about the records and intentionally failed to produce them in order to obstruct the Senate committee investigation, she could well be criminally liable.

In the Senate Whitewater report, the Republicans concluded that Hillary, whose fingerprints were found on the records, likely hid them from investigators to conceal the extent of her role in representing Madison Guaranty. During the period that the records were missing, investigators from the RTC were trying to determine if Hillary had any civil liability in connection with her legal work for the failed savings and loan. Republicans argued that Hillary had a motive to hide the records because they contradicted statements she made to investigators about the work. Hillary characterized her work for Madison as "minimal" and claimed she did not believe she knew anything about the Castle Grande parcels and projects. The records showed that Hillary billed Madison for a total of 60 hours of work over fifteen months, including about 30 hours' work on Castle Grande. They also showed the phone call to Beverly Bassett not previously known to the public. When asked to answer under oath to "any knowledge" she had about the disappearance or discovery of the records, Hillary gave a curiously incomplete response that she did not know how Huber had found the records.

But the motive question remains less settled than the Republicans claim. Hillary said she recalled the Castle Grande transactions as "IDC"—the entity which sold the property to Madison—and the bills reflect that designation. The definition of "minimal" work is, of course, subjective. Hillary had told RTC investigators of the phone call with Beverly Bassett months before the bills were discovered.

In fairness to Hillary, an alternative scenario of how the billing records may have been discovered, suggested by the Democrats on the Whitewater committee, cannot be ruled out. White House counsel's office secretary Linda Tripp testified that Carolyn Huber frequently entered Foster's White House office (while he was still alive) and exited carrying out piles of papers for filing. It is possible that Huber removed the records herself before July 1993, left them in the book room, moved them to her office, and then closely examined them only when they reappeared in 1996—all without Hillary's knowledge.

Still, Hillary, more than anyone, had reason to keep the records hidden. Even if she had been truthful with the investigators, she likely would have wanted to avoid the potential fallout of public disclosure of her ties to Madison. Public reputations have been ruined by less.

In May 1996, the McDougals and Jim Guy Tucker were convicted on mutliple counts of conspiracy and mail fraud in the looting of Madison Guaranty, including the Castle Grande transactions. Soon after the trial, McDougal began cooperating with prosecutors in an effort to reduce his sentence. In an interview with the Asssociated Press, McDougal suggested that Hubbell may have actually done the legal work on Castle Grande for which Hillary billed Madison. If true, this would explain why she may have known so little about Castle Grande, as she claimed, but it could open up a range of new questions about her billing practices at Rose.

Nevertheless, Hillary's strategy of running out the clock on Whitewater appeared to be working. By early fall 1996, the gears of the independent counsel were turning slowly and Clinton was headed toward re-election. But the costs to Hillary of this strategy were high. As the Clinton in charge of damage control, it was likely Hillary—not Bill—who would be caught in any obstruction of justice charge. William Safire noted that the ultimate meaning of "two-for-one" might well be that one pays for the crimes of two.

This much was certain: At a minimum, Hillary's long struggle to maintain her personal credibility and reputation, especially in the eyes of her admirers, had probably been lost. One lawyer working for the independent counsel recalled going to the White House to take Hillary's deposition one weekend in 1995. The attorneys had chuckled to themselves when the tense session was interrupted by an aide to Clinton, who had come into the room to retrieve Clinton's golf clubs. After the deposition, remarking on Hillary's careful hedging under oath, one of the liberal Democratic lawyers working in the special counsel's office turned to his conservative Republican colleague and said: "I lost a lot of respect today for Hillary." There could be no surer sign of just how thoroughly—and in what form—the "colorful characters" of the Ozarks had exacted their revenge.

EPILOGUE

Revolutions come in many forms, and revolutionaries fail in different ways. Hillary Rodham Clinton is a revolutionary—though of a type that is not easily recognized by most Americans. She is a "soft" revolutionary—or "establishment" radical—of the kind that thrives today in the social democracies of Western Europe and Scandinavia, and it is safe to say that if Hillary could have her way, she would establish here exactly the sort of cradle-to-grave nanny state that exists in Denmark and Sweden.

Hillary is neither a Marxist sympathizing firebrand like Johnetta Cole, nor a secular P.C. liberal like Donna Shalala. Rather, like her mentor Marian Wright Edelman, she has always stood somewhat apart from the cultural left. While she clearly recognized the political advantages of emphasizing conservative cultural themes—both in the education campaign in Arkansas, in the post-1994 re-positioning of Clinton as a centrist conservative on "values" issues, and even in her book *It Takes a Village*—this was not, as it may have seemed, a cynical political tactic. Hillary's politics have long been colored by the religious moralism of the Christian left. What distinguishes Hillary from both New Democrats and many conservatives is her unwavering desire to impose this moral vision through government control. The legacy she thus carries with her from the 1960s is not the moral relativism of Abbie Hoffman but the self-assured, dry-cleaned moralism of the Reverend William Sloane Coffin. Three decades later, school uniforms, curfews, and the V-Chip—all key elements of Clinton's post-1994 posture—are proposals taken right out of *It Takes a Village*.

Why, then, has there been so much confusion about the true nature of Hillary's politics? Hillary has been nothing if not up-front about what she stands for, but the mainstream press has been unreliable in reporting on her real views and also in explaining the extent to which Hillary is the ideological engine driving the co-candidacy. Most national political reporters—members of the same Baby Boomer generation that came of age in the 1960s and cut their teeth in the Watergate period—share Hillary's beliefs and prejudices about the role of government in American society and persist in glamorizing the Clinton partnership as a progressive and enlightened pairing of equals. Clinton biographer David Maraniss of the *Washington Post*—who was clearly seduced by Clinton's charms during the 1992 campaign, as were so many of his colleagues—is perhaps the foremost example of the type, insisting on seeing "complexities" in Bill's politics where there are none. This serves to take the spotlight off Hillary. (Tellingly, it took a work of fiction—*Primary Colors*, written anonymously by former Clinton enthusiast Joe Klein of *Newsweek*—to cut through the mythology and produce an apparently accurate portrait of the Clintons' relationship.)

Wittingly or not, these reporters have been a key element in a long-term strategy of the left to coopt centrist liberalism, beginning with the McGovern nomination in 1972—Bill and Hillary's first campaign. To the extent that Hillary is herself a Trojan Horse in this effort—and not, as she sometimes appears to be, Helen of Troy—it is in the interest of liberal reporters and editors to leave her politics hazy and ill-defined and the extent of her influence unacknowledged. That is why most of the mainstream press barely noted the purging of the New Democrats by Hillary's forces in the 1992 Clinton transition and effectively disinformed the public about the true aims of Hillary's health care initiative—letting fig leaves like "managed competition" obscure what amounted to a socialized government takeover of the private health care system.

Hillary had the ill fortune to take power at a moment in history when much of the public had turned against the panacea of big government as a way of solving social problems. In retrospect, Americans should be grateful that Hillary and her ideological cohort have so far failed to realize their "visionary" ends. In the case of health care, Hillary failed because her plan was too radical, both substantively and in its pace and scope. Her efforts to end-run the democratic process exposed her disdain for real compromise with opponents she saw as morally corrupt, and she adopted a Hillary-knows-best philosophy in implementing her ideals that ultimately trumped her well-honed pragmatic instincts.

Hillary also failed because she doesn't seem to have learned from her experience: The failure of her bureaucratic education reform inspired no second thoughts. Indeed, the basic assumptions of 1960s-style Great Society social and political activism remain with Hillary today, unexamined even after the devastating losses to the Democratic party in the 1994 elections—as clear a sign as any of what the public will accept and of the basic conservatism of ordinary people that Hillary still can't seem to appreciate. Thus, in a speech shortly after the election, Hillary compared the Republicans to the nostalgic and reactionary Hebrews who tried to stop the exodus to the Promised Land and urged a return to Egypt.

Significantly also, Hillary has failed because she never really accepted the simple truth that legal and ethical strictures and standards of accountability exist not just to protect us from the ambitions of the wicked but from the hubris of the good. Hillary's antinomian fallacy—traced to its roots in the loose, untethered teachings of the liberal Methodist activists and the view of Saul Alinsky that the system is inherently corrupt—is as consistent a theme as any in Hillary's life, and it has reaped the most serious political and legal consequences. Whether in violating the charter of the Legal Services Corporation to defend the agency against Ronald Reagan; telephoning a regulator appointed by her husband on behalf of a client who was a political supporter and business partner; imprudently destroying documents at the Rose Firm; thwarting public access to the health care task force; holding onto her health care investments while she designed the overhaul of the system; impeding the Justice Department's "unfettered access" to Vince Foster's office; or concealing her role in Travelgate—Hillary gradually put Alinsky's end-justifies-the-means philosophy into practice. Indeed, one must finally ask whether Hillary really believes that the profound moral vision that inheres in our system of divided government has any value apart from the perceived morality of a particular political agenda.

Yet this complex philosophical and political seduction—by the idol of big government, compounded by the experience of exercising unfettered political power in the service of moral ends—does not seem able to explain the air of fatalism that has hung over so much of Hillary's life. For that, we must look to her marriage and political partnership with Bill Clinton—"the greatest seducer who ever lived," as David Watkins had called him—extremely talented, intellectually facile, an unparalleled campaigner, organizer, and silver-tongued orator, but also a wayward child, requiring continual emotional support and moral supervision.

From the beginning, as was evident to all their friends, Bill and Hillary uniquely complemented one another—recall Yale Professor Guido Calabresi's analogy to a "hot bath" and a "cold shower." Bill was warm, open and gregarious, though he was seen in her circle as a social upstart and political pretender. Although sharing the political ideas and aspirations that were fashionable among their generation, he did not really have the pristine vision of a good society anchored in profound moral conviction that Hillary did—nor did he ever claim to. He therefore looked to Hillary and listened to her carefully. Established at Yale, this erotic/intellectual bond was tested in Fayetteville, solidified in the depths of Bill's defeat in 1980, and institutionalized after 1989 in the full-fledged co-candidacy. Hillary's ability to put his political career back on course and then rocket him onto the national stage via education reform conferred on her, in his eyes, almost supernatural powers. Hillary became Bill's everything—including, as he has said, his "moral compass."

What Bill has gained from the partnership is painfully obvious. Yet the question remains: Why was an outstanding and to all appearances remarkably independent young woman like Hillary susceptible to Bill Clinton in the first place? Every time Hillary appeared on the verge of independent accomplishment, Bill seemed to drag her down and ruin everything. In 1974, Hillary moved from the Watergate committee to Arkansas; in the early 1980s, she sacrificed her legal career and changed her name to salvage his political career; in the '92 campaign, she was introduced to the American public on *60 Minutes*. Finally, while pursuing the health care initiative, she was paralyzed by Whitewater. Why, then, did she choose not only to "stand by her man" but to recommit herself to Bill and the co-candidacy at several crucial points in his career? (Hillary's erstwhile supporters in the ranks of upper-class professional women seem especially irrated by this seeming contradiction. The *New York Times'* Maureen Dowd, for instance, refers derisively to Hillary as "the-stander-by-her-man.")

Clearly, the answer must lie in the hidden psychological realm of Hillary's innermost needs and weaknesses, a subject about which observers can only speculate. But it does seem clear that despite her success as a student leader at Wellesley and Yale and her other youthful accomplishments, there seems to have remained a kind of empty place or well of insecurity in Hillary. As a young girl, she felt clumsy and unattractive. In her drive to excel, she may have been overcompensating for the fact that boys regarded her as a friend or den mother rather than a date. On some level, she also may have been trying to win her father's approval—if not his love, at least his admiration. Bill provided everything that Hugh Rodham did not: approval, admiration, public praise, and a feeling of being wanted by a popular and desirable man. At the same time, she may have been perversely drawn to the rejection implied by Bill's philandering. But perhaps all that can be said for sure is that Hillary's need to be needed in a thoroughgoing way must have played a part in drawing her to Bill and keeping her by his side.

The co-candidacy, then, may best be understood not as a cold political bargain but as a kind of co-dependency. Bill and Hillary not only complemented one another in a remarkable way: over time they came to seem eerily necessary to one another, as though neither can really exist or succeed on their own. Rather than two-for-one, the truth is more like two-*as*-one. Thus did the co-candidacy contain the seeds of its own demise. For when a fundamentally weak person like Bill relies on a "moral compass" that itself becomes askew, the results can be tragic. In placing so much responsibility on Hillary's shoulders, Bill relied on someone who believed she was simply too good to do wrong.

Hillary may stand convicted of intellectual rigidity, elitism, moral vanity, and poor judgment. But these are not high crimes or even misdemeanors. Viewing her actions in light of the rough-and-tumble nature of American politics, one must finally ask: Has Hillary really done anything more egregious than that which most political figures do as a matter of course?

At this juncture, the Whitewater scandal has raised serious questions about the Clintons' public ethics and character. But as yet no crimes have been alleged against them, much less proven. Americans may well make the informed judgment not to re-elect a candidate whose close friends and business associates are in jail. If so, though both Clintons will suffer the consequences, the roots of the problem can be traced not to Hillary, but to the Ozark mob into which she had the misfortune to marry, ultimately allowing herself to be compromised by it.

Be that as it may, many of the attacks on Hillary by Republicans and the press arise not from her having done anything wrong but simply from her attempt to pursue a legal career in an incestuous state governed by her husband. As more professional women (such as Elizabeth Dole) begin playing the additional role of political wife, we can expect tough questions about the way they have managed their careers and finances to become a normal part of our political discourse. As to some of Hillary's evasiveness and lawyerly nit-picking—recall her shifting answers on the commodities trades—it might simply be said that politicians shade the truth all the time.

Politics at the level Hillary has played it is a dirty business. If Hillary skates by with her image makeovers and artful dodging of politically inspired attacks, why should she be judged so much more harshly than anyone else in similar circumstances? What about President Bush's suspicious Iran-Contra notes, belatedly discovered after the 1992 election, when they had been sought since 1987 by the independent counsel? Or the stock deal that earned Senator Alfonse D'Amato $37,000 in one day and violated the rules of his brokerage firm, run by campaign contributors?

Whitewater may have never really registered with a citizenry that has grown inured to two decades of the politics of personal destruction in Washington. It is an environment where allegation gets mixed with fact and serious wrongdoing is confused with trivial oversight. Sloppy mistakes are magnified well beyond their real importance. Guilt by association becomes the standard. Personal defects are dragged into the public arena. In the effort not only to defeat the opposition but to destroy it, the sense of balance, proportion, and fundamental fairness is lost. Perhaps now that the prosecutorial politics unleashed in Watergate by Hillary and her colleagues (and institutionalized in their fight against Reaganism) has come full circle, a truce of sorts can be declared after the scandal runs its course. The independent-counsel law, for example, might be done away with in an effort to scale back the rampant and overgrown ethics machinery.

Until then, Hillary's status as first lady should not exempt her from being held accountable for her actions and pursued to the full extent of the law. As she once said of Nixon, even moral or historical imperatives cannot place one above the law. We do not yet know how far Hillary was willing to go in her defensive maneuvers—but we do know she was armed with sophisticated rationalizations to justify whatever she thought needed to be done. Should Hillary be prosecuted for protecting the political co-candidacy from exposure, some may say that she deserves her fate for the choices she made. But one might also say that in a larger moral sense, for Hillary to be put in the dock while Bill goes golfing would be a miscarriage of justice. For in the end, no matter what transpires in the legal process, the view of the Clintons described by Arkansas journalist John Robert Starr will likely stand: "The difference between Hillary and Bill is that deep down Hillary is a good person."

Why have so few people seemed to recognize this? It goes without saying that Hillary herself has invited the many exaggerated and unfair attacks on her character: Her image is not that of Al D'Amato, George Bush, or even Bill Clinton, but of "Saint Hillary," and as we know, people enjoy nothing more than the humiliating fall of those who set themselves up as moral exemplars. But the treatment of Hillary by the press and her opponents must be seen as well for what it says about American society itself.

For one thing, it is clear that the societal expectations laid on Hillary—as wife, mother, professional woman, official hostess, and political partner—were exorbitant, and would have been enough to overwhelm and demoralize any woman—even Hillary. No other first lady in history has had an entire generation identify so personally with her, and it is a particular irony of Hillary's story that the women of her own generation, particularly in the media, have been not only her strongest supporters but also her worst enemies. Their expectations of what she could accomplish as first lady were not only unrealistic but inconsistent with the nature of the office itself, and ultimately seemed to rest on what these women may or may not have accomplished in their own lives. A whole generation of women is trying to square the demands of an independent career with those of wife and mother, and they are finding the challenge surprisingly painful and difficult. Hillary has in this context become a symbol of that struggle. If Hillary succeeds in her effort to "have it all," then so can other women—at the very least, she vindicates their efforts and assuages their guilt for the sacrifices they are forced to make. When she fails, however, Hillary calls the whole enterprise into doubt and earns the wrath of those who see themselves reflected in her image. What else but self-disgust can explain the vitriol spewed at Hillary by ostensible feminists like Maureen Dowd?

On the other side of the ledger, one cannot underestimate the persistent power of sexism and misogyny in this society, which may explain the excesses of many of her other critics. In a facetious column in which he argued that "we've been too tough on President Clinton," Wesley Pruden of the *Washington Times* wrote, "He did Gennifer Flowers and Paula Jones, all right, but the devil in Miss Hillary made him do that too . . . Maybe Hillary's long-suffering husband deserves not censure but a night out."

At the Democratic Convention in 1996, Hillary returned to her home town of Chicago to see her husband become the first Democrat renominated for the presidency since FDR who actually appeared headed for a second term. In no small measure, the achievement was as much hers as his.

When she entered the convention hall to deliver her first speech ever on prime time television, Hillary was the same as she had always been, but also somehow different—Hillary without illusions. In the portions of her speech dealing with policy and politics, Hillary—after consistently ducking the limelight since the 1994 Congressional election—may have surprised some by the unapologetic way in which she laid out her agenda to expand government in a second Clinton term. She openly defended her controversial concept that "it takes a village to raise a child" and described in detail a variety of new federal programs and government mandates on business in the areas of child and family policy. She even included an in-your-face reference to her role as health care czar and promised to continue working toward the goal of universal health care.

Those who disagree with her views would find ample cause in Hillary's speech to vote against her husband out of a well-founded fear that Hillary Rodham may ride yet again. Yet even her opponents had reason to be proud and inspired that night. For in her quiet dignity and confident strength they could see the best of what her generation had to offer in terms of social commitment, idealism, and energetic public service.

Looming in the background, of course, was Clinton's signing of a Republican welfare bill ending the federal entitlement that Hillary and the Children's Defense Fund had long defended as essential to the social safety net. Marian Wright Edelman had called Clinton's signing of the bill "a moment of shame," and though Hillary has listed ways the bill could be improved, one had to wonder whether she did not feel that the strategy of moving to the center had perhaps been taken too far. (In an interview with CNN, the best thing Hillary could say about the welfare bill was that it would not go into effect for another year.)

In a replay of Clinton's 1982 move to the center after a devastating defeat at the polls with Hillary's support, Dick Morris had been brought back into the Clinton fold after the '94 debacle and began to refashion Clinton as a centrist conservative while distancing him from his first two years in office. Hillary meanwhile went under cover, writing a fluffy syndicated column and working on her book about child-rearing while staying out of the policy loop—at least so far as anyone knew. The strategy had worked in 1982, and it was working now as well, with Clinton in a double-digit lead in the opinion polls. But unlike in Arkansas the move to the center was not simply rhetorical. It was having profound policy consequences that Hillary may not have been able to abide, creating deep fissures between the old-style liberals in Hillary's camp (such as Donna Shalala, Harold Ickes, and Maggie Williams) and Morris, who had convinced Clinton that moving to the right was the only way for him to be re-elected. (In another twist of fate, on the day of Clinton's acceptance of his party's renomination, Morris resigned the campaign in a call-girl scandal that resurrected the issue of Clinton's own character defects. Hillary was said to have been especially furious that Morris had shown the call-girl an advance copy of her convention speech. One wonders what she thought of the later revelation by the call-girl that Clinton and Morris conspired in a plan to blame the Whitewater scandal on her.)

As Hillary moved on to the more personal parts of her speech, paying tribute to Bill and to their marriage, some viewers may have cringed. It was the same reaction many (especially feminist supporters) had to her initial appearance on *60 Minutes*; to her bringing out a tray of Christmas cookies after the Troopergate story; to one of her syndicated columns in which she wrote of a romantic midnight swim with Bill; and to her floating the idea of having another child just as the 1996 election kicked off. For such people, Hillary's determination to stick with the marriage appears as nothing but cynicism and hypocrisy and thus can never be forgiven. In giving short shrift to Hillary's sense of responsibility and commitment, these critics also implicitly blame Hillary for Bill's shortcomings. Others, perhaps a majority, likely see the Clintons' flawed marriage as no different from their own relationships. These people remain tolerant of the Clintons because they see in them the warts and blemishes that everybody has. We try to do good, yet we fail; we are all imperfect and need help; we all rely on spouses or lovers—this is only unsettling in politics. Perhaps this is why the tactic of making the Clintons' character flaws a political issue, while perfectly legitimate, has so often seemed to fail. In today's culture, where everyone is blameless and there is no such thing as shame, instead of bringing opprobrium on the Clintons, attacks on their character only serve to make them seem more human and approachable.

When Hillary looked down at Bill from the viewing stand as he accepted renomination in Chicago, one could see that the gawky Yale den mother was still seduced by the talented boy from the Arkansas backwoods. In this regard, it might be said that Hillary was just like many voters. Polls show that the overwhelming majority of Americans would rather have their child grow up to be like Bob Dole; yet most of those same respondents still prefer Clinton for president. Because she clearly still believes in Bill's basic altruism—his desire, as former Clinton aide Rudy Moore once put it, to "help people" however he can—Hillary stays with Bill in spite of his defects—just as millions of voters do.

The highlight of the evening came when Hillary spoke of her daughter Chelsea and the television cameras panned to a view of a poised young woman who had, quietly and out of the public eye, come of age during the difficult four years in the White House. In this moment, one saw the side of Hillary too rarely on public display—Hillary in her role as a successful mother. Whatever trouble she would face in the future, much of it her own making, that was something no one could take away from her.

September 9, 1996
New York City

NOTES

Note to the Footnotes

For each chapter of this book, my researchers and I conducted dozens of interviews. Because many sources were reluctant to be quoted even indirectly about Hillary Rodham Clinton, much of the material has been used as background in explaining Hillary's character and actions. Where quotations are used, unless otherwise noted, the quotes come from interviews conducted for this book.

In addition to original research, much of this book is based on a careful distillation and analysis of the written record, including the many books and articles written about the Clintons cited below, as well as documents and records produced by the White House in the course of several congressional investigations. The following notes are intended to be a general guide to the reader of these published sources.

Chapter 1

1. The incidental facts of Hillary's early life and her career at Wellesley College are drawn from Connie Bruck, "Hillary the Pol," *The New Yorker,* May 30, 1994; Michael Kelly, "Saint Hillary," *New York Times,* May 23, 1993; Charles Kenney, "Hillary: The Wellesley Years," *Boston Globe,* January 12, 1993; Norman King, *The Woman in the White House: The Remarkable Story of Hillary Rodham Clinton* (New York: Birch Lane Press, 1996); Rex Nelson, *The Hillary Factor* (New York: Gallen Publishing Group, 1993); Donnie Radcliffe *Hillary Rodham Clinton: A First Lady for Our Time* (New York: Warner Books, 1993); Gail Sheehy, "What Hillary Wants," *Vanity Fair,* May 1992; Martha Sherrill, "The Education of Hillary Clinton," *Washington Post,* January 11, 1993; Judith Warner, *Hillary Clinton; The Inside Story* (New

Notes

York: Penguin Books, 1993); and interviews. Unless otherwise noted, quotations are from interviews conducted by the author or researcher George Neumayr.

2. Hillary's quotations about her childhood are drawn from the several media appearances she made in early 1996 in connection with the promotion of her book, *It Takes a Village and Other Lessons Children Teach Us* (New York: Simon & Schuster, 1996).

3. Paul Johnson, *A History of Christianity* (New York: Atheneum, 1979), pp. 368–369; see also *The Encyclopedia of Religion*, Vol. 15 (New York: Macmillan, 1987), and Jean Caffey Lyles, "Hillary Clinton: Wesley's Theology Fits Her Life," United Methodist News Service, September 16, 1992.

4. For more on the student movement, see Mari Jo Buhle, Paul Buhle, and Dan Georgakas, eds., *Encyclopedia of the American Left* (Urbana, IL: University of Illinois Press, 1992), and John Hersey, *Letter to the Alumni* (New York: Alfred A. Knopf, 1970).

5. Saul Alinsky, *Rules for Radicals* (New York: Random House, 1971), p. 148; Sanford D. Horwitt, *Let Them Call Me Rebel* (New York: Random House, 1989), and Saul Alinsky, *Reveille for Radicals* (Chicago: University of Chicago Press, 1946).

Chapter 2

1. Works consulted on Hillary's years at Yale Law School include Norman King, *The Woman in the White House;* David Maraniss, *First in His Class: A Biography of Bill Clinton* (New York: Simon & Schuster, 1995); Rex Nelson, *The Hillary Factor;* Donnie Radcliffe, *Hillary Rodham Clinton: A First Lady for Our Time;* Martha Sherrill, "The Education of Hillary Clinton"; and Judith Warner, *Hillary Clinton: The Inside Story.* For more on Yale's legal realism school, see Robert H. Bork, *The Tempting of America: The Political Seduction of the Law* (New York: The Free Press, 1990); William W. Fisher, Morton J. Horwitz, and Thomas Reed, eds., *American Legal Realism* (New York: Oxford University Press, 1993); Michael S. Green, "Legal Realism, Lex Fori and the Choice-of-Law Revolution," *Yale Law Journal,* 104, no. 4 (January 1995); Chris Goodrich, *Anarchy and Elegance: Confessions of a Journalist at Yale Law School* (New York: Little, Brown, 1996); John Hersey, *Letter to the Alumni;* Gary Minda, *Postmodern Legal Movements, Law and Jurisprudence at Century's End* (New York: New York University Press, 1995); and John Henry Schlegel, *American Legal Realism and Empirical Social Science* (Chapel Hill, NC: University of North Carolina Press, 1995). Interviews for this chapter were conducted by the author or researcher George Neumayr.

2. See, e.g., James Boyle, ed., *Critical Legal Studies* (New York: New York University Press, 1992); Allan C. Hutchinson, ed., *Critical Legal Studies* (NJ:

Rowman & Littlefield, 1989); and Mark Kelman, *A Guide to Critical Legal Studies* (Cambridge: Harvard University Press, 1987). Hillary's history at the *Yale Review* is discussed in Daniel Wattenberg, "The Lady Macbeth of Little Rock," *American Spectator* (August 1992).

3. The portrait of the Yale protests is drawn significantly from Hersey, *Letter to the Alumni*. See also Peter Collier and David Horowitz, *Destructive Generation: Second Thoughts About the Sixties* (New York: Summit Books, 1989), and Jessica Mitford, *A Fine Old Conflict* (New York: Alfred A. Knopf, 1977).

4. Radcliffe, *Hillary Rodham Clinton*, p. 8.

5. Michael Medved, "When Bill Met Hillary," *Sunday Times* (London), August 21, 1994, p. 17.

Chapter 3

1. The story of the 1974 campaign is told in *First in His Class* by David Maraniss, who quotes the Frays as authoritative sources, and in Meredith Oakley, *On the Make: The Rise of Bill Clinton* (Washington, DC: Regnery Publishing, 1994).

2. Watergate history is drawn from Richard Ben-Veniste and George Frampton, *Stonewall: The Real Story of the Watergate Prosecution* (New York: Simon & Schuster, 1977); Jimmy Breslin, *How the Good Guys Finally Won* (New York: Viking Press, 1975); Elizabeth Drew, *Washington Journal: The Events of 1973–1974* (New York: Random House, 1975); Sam Ervin, *The Whole Truth: The Watergate Conspiracy* (New York: Random House, 1980); James Hamilton, *The Power to Probe: A Study of Congressional Investigations* (New York: Random House, 1976); Maraniss, *First in His Class;* and Bob Woodward and Carl Bernstein, *The Final Days* (New York: Simon & Schuster, 1976). In addition, the following Senate documents were consulted: Report of the Committee on the Judiciary, U.S. House of Representatives, "Impeachment of Richard M. Nixon," House Report 93-095, 93rd Congress, 1st sess., 1973; Committee on the Judiciary, U.S. House of Representatives, "Selected Materials on Impeachment," Committee Print, 93rd Congress, 1st sess., 1973; Committee on the Judiciary, U.S. House of Representatives, "Selected Materials on Impeachment Procedures," Committee Print, 93rd Congress, 2nd sess., 1974.

3. Jerry Zeifman, *Without Honor: The Impeachment of President Nixon and the Crimes of Camelot* (New York: Thunder's Mouth Press, 1996), p. 123.

4. Leonard Garment, "The Guns of Watergate," *Commentary* (April 1987).

5. Rex Nelson, *The Hillary Factor*, p. 189.

6. Oakley, *On the Make*, p. 21.

7. Virginia Kelley, *Leading with My Heart* (New York: Simon & Schuster, 1994), p. 151.

Chapter 4

1. In addition to supplementary interviews, the facts of Clinton's early political rise are drawn from Meredith Oakley's *On the Make* and contemporaneous press accounts in the *Arkansas Gazette* and the *Arkansas Democrat.* Also consulted were David Maraniss, *First in His Class,* and Charles F. Allen and Jonathan Portis, *The Comeback Kid: The Life and Career of Bill Clinton* (New York: Birch Lane Press, 1992). Hillary's early role is described in Connie Bruck, "Hillary the Pol"; Michael Kelly, "Saint Hillary"; Charles Kenney, "Hillary: The Wellesley Years," *Boston Globe,* January 12, 1993; Norman King, *The Woman in the White House;* Rex Nelson, *The Hillary Factor;* Donnie Radcliffe, *Hillary Rodham Clinton: A First Lady for Our Time;* Martha Sherrill, "The Education of Hillary Clinton"; and Judith Warner, *Hillary Clinton: The Inside Story.*
2. See Sara Fritz, "Clinton Ties to Tyson Scion Still Drawing Critics' Fire," *Los Angeles Times,* June 12, 1994. See also: Michael Kelly, "The President's Past," *New York Times,* July 31, 1994, and Jeff Gerth, "Top Arkansas Lawyer Helped Hillary Clinton Turn Big Profit," *New York Times,* March 18, 1994.
3. David Osborne, *Laboratories of Democracy* (Boston: Harvard Business School Press, 1990), p. 90.
4. The Rose Firm is described in John M. Broder and James Risen, "The Rose Firm Proudly Sent Four Partners to the Clinton Administration— And It's Faced Disaster Ever Since," *Los Angeles Times,* April 3, 1994; Bruck, "Hillary the Pol"; L. J. Davis, "The Name of Rose: An Arkansas Thriller," *New Republic,* April 4, 1994; Audry Duff, "Is a Rose a Rose?" *American Lawyer* (July–August 1992); Maraniss, *First in His Class;* Nelson, *The Hillary Factor;* Oakley, *On the Make;* Michael Putzel, "Hillary Clinton Set to Begin High-Stakes Balancing Act;" *Boston Globe,* January 19, 1993; Radcliffe, *Hillary Rodham Clinton,* James B. Stewart, *Blood Sport: The President and His Adversaries* (New York: Simon & Schuster, 1996); and Thomas G. Watts, "The Law Firm Riding Out Furor on Whitewater," *Dallas Morning News,* April 17, 1994. Interviews about Hillary's career at the firm were conducted by the author or reporter Matt Labash.

Chapter 5

1. Examples of litigation undertaken by local LSC boards appear in *Legal Services Corporation: The Robber Barons of the Poor* (Washington, DC: Washington Legal Foundation, 1985); LeaAnne Bernstein, "Permanent Guerrilla Government: Legal Services Corporation," in *Steering the Elephant,* edited by Robert Rector and Michael Sanera (New York: Universe Books, 1987); John C. Boland, "Unholy Alliance," *Barron's,* June 2, 1980; Warren Brookes, "Scandal Brewing in LSC Under Carter," *Boston Herald,* Sep-

tember 11, 1983; and Donald Lambro, *Fat City: How Washington Wastes Your Taxes* (South Bend: Regnery Gateway Inc., 1980).

2. See Rael Jean Isaac, "Bringing Down the System Through 'Training'—The LSC Manuals and Training Materials," in *Robber Barons of the Poor,* pp. 93–110.

3. LSC's political lobbying and organizing violations and its survival efforts are detailed in *Robber Barons of the Poor;* Tom Diaz, "Probe Sought of Legal Services Campaign Activity in California," *Washington Times,* October 21, 1983; editorial, "Illegal Services," *Wall Street Journal,* September 29, 1983; William Kucewicz, "A Little Larceny in Legal Services," *Wall Street Journal,* August 19, 1983. See also U.S. Senate Committee on Labor and Human Resources, Oversight of the Legal Services Corporation, 1983; and opinion letters from Milton J. Socolar, U.S. Comptroller General, to U.S. Representative F. James Sensenbrenner, May 1, 1981, and September 19, 1983.

4. For details on the New World Foundation, see Daniel Wattenberg, "The Lady Macbeth of Little Rock," *American Spectator* (August 1992).

5. Material on the Children's Defense Fund, the children's rights movement, and Hillary Clinton's writings on the subject comes from Jean Bethke Elshtain, "It Takes a Village and Other Lessons Children Teach Us," *New Republic,* March 4, 1996; Patricia A. Vardin and Ilene N. Brody, eds., *Children's Rights: Contemporary Perspectives* (New York: Teachers College Press, 1979); Mickey Kaus, "The Godmother: What's Wrong with Marian Wright Edelman, Children's Defense Fund Founder," *New Republic,* February 15, 1993; Pat Lewis, "Marian Edelman's Equality Crusade," *Washington Star,* March 18, 1979; Hillary Rodham, "Children Under the Law," *Harvard Educational Review* (November 1973); Hillary Rodham, "Children's Policies: Abandonment and Neglect," *Yale Law Journal* (June 1977); and Hillary Rodham, review of Kenneth Keniston's *All Our Children: The American Family Under Pressure* in *Public Welfare* (Winter 1978).

6. Christopher Lasch, "Hillary Clinton, Child Saver," *Harper's* (October 1992), p. 80.

7. Editorial, "Judicial Intimidation," *Wall Street Journal,* May 1, 1996, p. A14.

Chapter 6

1. In addition to interviews and contemporaneous news reports, the history of the 1980 governor's race is drawn principally from Meredith Oakley, *On the Make,* and is also covered in Charles F. Allen and Jonathan Portis, *The Comeback Kid,* quote at p. 71; Connie Bruck, "Hillary the Pol"; David Maraniss, *First in His Class;* Rex Nelson, *The Hillary Factor;* Donnie Radcliffe, *A First Lady for Our Time;* and Judith Warner, *Hillary Clinton: The Inside Story.*

2. Ernest Dumas, comp., *The Clintons of Arkansas: An Introduction by Those Who Know Them Best* (Fayetteville, AR: University of Arkansas Press, 1993), p. 90.
3. For more on the black vote, see John Brummett, "Getting Out the Black Vote," *Arkansas Democrat-Gazette,* May 9, 1995; Joan I. Duffy, "Counsel Probes '90 Clinton Vote Drive," *Commercial Appeal,* May 29, 1995; Paul Fick, *The Dysfunctional President: Inside the Mind of Bill Clinton,* which contains an interview with Bert Dickey (New York: Birch Lane Press, 1994), p. 144; Oakley, *On the Make;* Edward T. Pound and David Bowermaster, "New Twists in the Whitewater Inquiry," *Washington Post,* February 6, 1995; Marilyn W. Thompson and Howard Schneider, "Clinton Campaign Aide Angers Black Clergy," *Washington Post,* February 16, 1995; and Daniel Wattenberg, "Cash Voting," *American Spectator* (December 1994).
4. Dumas, comp., *The Clintons of Arkansas,* pp. 92–93.
5. Bruck, "Hillary the Pol," p. 64.

Chapter 7

1. Articles and books which discuss Hillary Clinton's role in Arkansas' education reform initiative include Charles F. Allen and Jonathan Portis, *The Comeback Kid: The Life and Career of Bill Clinton* (New York: Birch Lane Press, 1992); Arkansas Board of Education, *Standards for Accreditation,* February 1984; Diane Blair, *Arkansas Politics & Government: Do the People Rule?* (Lincoln: University of Nebraska Press, 1988); Connie Bruck, "Hillary the Pol," *New Yorker;* Paul Greenberg, *No Surprises: Two Decades of Clinton-Watching* (McLean, Virginia: Brassey's Inc., 1996); Lloyd Grove, "Hillary Clinton, Trying to Have it All," *Washington Post,* March 10, 1992; Blant Hurt, "Mrs. Clinton's Czarist Past," *Wall Street Journal,* March 19, 1993; David Maraniss, *First in His Class;* Robert Marquand, "Arkansas Governor and His Spouse Both Put Education First," *Christian Science Monitor,* August 25, 1986; Rex Nelson, *The Hillary Factor;* Meredith Oakley, *On the Make;* Roy Reed, "I Just Went to School in Arkansas," *The Clintons of Arkansas: An Introduction by Those Who Know Them Best,* Ernest Dumas, ed. (Fayetteville: University of Arkansas Press, 1993); Paul Root, "Lessons from the Student," *The Clintons of Arkansas;* Thomas Sowell, " 'Billary' Continues to Push Frightening, Radical Ideology," *Arizona Republic,* March 29, 1993; John Robert Starr, *Yellow Dogs and Dark Horses,* (Little Rock: August House, 1987); Dennis A. Williams, "Can the Schools Be Saved?" *Newsweek,* May 9, 1983, p. 50.
2. Winthrop Rockefeller Foundation, *Fulfilling the Promises of Freedom: A Three Year Study of School Reform in Arkansas,* December 1988.
3. Unless otherwise noted in the text, quotes are from interviews conducted by John Meroney, George Neumayr and this author. Hillary Clinton's

quotes are compiled from local press accounts of the education reform effort and copies of her speeches.

Chapter 8

1. See American Survey, "Wifewater," *Economist,* January 13, 1996, p. 31; L. J. Davis, "The Name of Rose: An Arkansas Thriller," *New Republic,* April 4, 1994, p. 14; Al Hunt, "The Other Vision Problem," *Wall Street Journal,* March 14, 1996, p. 19; Doug Ireland, "Hot Water: Whitewater Investigations," *The Nation,* February 19, 1996, p. 5; Charles Peters, "Tilting at Windmills," *Washington Monthly,* April 1996, p. 7; William Powers, "Time, Engaging in 'Blood Sport'," *Washington Post,* March 12, 1996, p. D7; and James Stewart, *Blood Sport.* Interviews were conducted by the author and Matt Labash.
2. Accounts of the 1986 campaign can be found in *On the Make;* Rex Nelson, *The Hillary Factor;* Donnie Radcliffe, *A First Lady for Our Time;* Judith Warner, *Hillary Clinton: The Inside Story.*
3. Information on Hillary's career at Rose is drawn from Audrey Duff, "Is a Rose a Rose?" *American Lawyer,* July/August 1992, p. 68; Daniel Klaidman, "Hillary's Real Legal Problem," *Newsweek,* March 11, 1996; and Stewart, *Blood Sport.* Information on the Clintons' finances can be found in Charles R. Babcock and Sharon LaFraniere, "The Clintons' Finances: A Reflection of Their State's Power Structure," *Washington Post,* July 21, 1992, p. A7; Kevin McCoy, " 'Not a Yuppie': A Look at the Clintons' Income Through the Years," *Newsday,* April 3, 1994, p. 4.
4. See David Maraniss, *First in His Class,* p. 429.
5. Interpretations of Hillary's dealings with Madison have been offered in Gene Lyons, "Fool for Scandal: How the *Times* Got Whitewater Wrong," *Harper's,* October 1994, p. 55; David Maraniss and Susan Schmidt, "Hillary Clinton and the Whitewater Controversy: A Close-Up," *Washington Post,* June 2, 1996, p. 1; James Stewart, *Blood Sport;* Stuart Taylor, "The Hillary Scandals: How Much Beef?" *Legal Times,* January 16, 1996, p. 45; Garry Wills, "The Clinton Scandals," *New York Review of Books,* April 18, 1996; also see the final report of the Special Committee to Investigate Whitewater Development Corporation and Related Matters, U.S. Senate, 104th Congress, 2nd Session, June 17, 1996, and Robert L. Bartley, ed., *Whitewater, From the Editorial Pages of the* Wall Street Journal (New York: Dow Jones & Company, Inc., 1994).
6. Maureen Dowd, "On Washington; A Cautionary Fable," *New York Times,* February 13, 1994, section 6, p. 24; Tony Snow, "The Amnesia Defense," *Arkansas Democrat-Gazette,* May 1, 1994, p. 4J.
7. William C. Rempel and Douglas Frantz, "Fallout from S&L's Collapse Shadows Clinton," *Los Angeles Times,* November 7, 1993, p. A17.

8. See Monroe Freedman, "A Bum Rap for Clinton?" *Legal Times*, April 25, 1994, p. 24.
9. For more on Dan Lasater see: Micah Morrison, "Who Is Dan Lasater?" *Wall Street Journal*, August 7, 1995, p. 12; Glenn Simpson, "Whitewater Panel to Probe Clinton's Association with Ex-Bond Dealer and Convicted Drug Dealer," May 1, 1996, p. 16.

Chapter 9

1. Ellen Goodman, "Infidelity Officially Is on the Record," *Chicago Tribune*, May 10, 1987, Section 5, p. 2.
2. Meredith Oakley, *On the Make*, p. 150.
3. For more information on Susan Thomases, see Lloyd Grove, "The Clintons' Bad Cop," *Washington Post*, March 2, 1993; Jacob Weisberg, "Desperately Leaking Susan," *Vanity Fair* (June 1996).
4. Charles Babcock, "Ickes Law Firm Is Fighting Release of Investigator's Report," *Washington Post*, October 16, 1994; John Aloysius Farrell, "The President's Get-It-Done Guy," *Boston Globe*, October 15, 1995; Claude R. Marx, "White House Aide Harold Ickes," *Investor's Business Daily*, December 1, 1995; William G. McGowan, "The Mob and the Deputy Chief of Staff," *Washington Monthly* (July 1994).
5. David Maraniss, *First in His Class*, p. 441.
6. For more information on Hillary's career during this period see: John M. Broder and James Risen, "The Rose Firm Proudly Sent Four Partners to the Clinton Administration—And It's Faced Disaster Ever Since," *Los Angeles Times*, April 3, 1994; Connie Bruck, "Hillary the Pol"; L. J. Davis, "The Name of Rose: An Arkansas Thriller," *New Republic*, April 4, 1994; Audry Duff, "Is a Rose a Rose?" *American Lawyer* (July–August 1992); Maraniss, *First in His Class;* Rex Nelson, *The Hillary Factor;* Oakley, *On the Make;* Michael Putzel, "Hillary Clinton Set to Begin High-Stakes Balancing Act," *Boston Globe*, January 19, 1993; Donnie Radcliffe, *A First Lady for Our Time;* James B. Stewart, *Blood Sport*, p. 121; and Thomas G. Watts, "The Law Firm Riding Out Furor on Whitewater," *Dallas Morning News*, April 17, 1994. Interviews were conducted by the author or researcher Matt Labash.
7. For Bill's third term and the 1990 campaign, see Maraniss, *First in His Class;* Nelson, *The Hillary Factor;* Oakley, *On the Make;* Radcliffe, *Hillary Rodham Clinton: A First Lady for Our Time;* and Judith Warner, *Hillary Clinton: The Inside Story.*
8. Hillary Rodham Clinton, *It Takes a Village*, p. 43.
9. Jack Germond and Jules Witcover, *Mad As Hell: Revolt at the Ballot Box 1992* (New York: Random House, 1994), pp. 169–170.
10. Dumas, comp., *The Clintons of Arkansas*, p. 146.
11. Bruck, "Hillary the Pol," p. 91.

Chapter 10

1. In addition to interviews, general campaign material is drawn from: Connie Bruck, "Hillary the Pol"; Peter Goldman, Thomas M. DeFrank, Mark Miller, Andrew Murr, and Tom Mathews, *Quest for the Presidency 1992* (College Station, TX: Texas A&M University Press, 1994); Mary Matalin and James Carville, *All's Fair: Love, War, and Running for President* (New York: Random House, 1994); Gail Sheehy, "What Hillary Wants"; Rex Nelson, *The Hillary Factor;* Donnie Radcliffe, *Hillary Rodham Clinton: A First Lady for Our Time;* and Judith Warner, *Hillary Clinton: The Inside Story.*
2. Michael Isikoff, "Clinton Team Works to Deflect Allegations on Nominee's Private Life," *Washington Post,* July 26, 1992.
3. Michael Checchio, "Magnum Ph.D., a New Breed of Private Eyes," *California Lawyer,* February 1992, pp. 32–33.
4. Garry Wills, "Inside Hillary's Head," *Washington Post,* January 21, 1996; Garry Wills, "The Clinton Scandals," *New York Review of Books,* April 18, 1996.

Chapter 11

1. Information on the Clinton transition and the early months of the administration was compiled from published reports cited in the text, and from supplementary interviews conducted by the author.
2. Connie Bruck, "Hillary the Pol," p. 91; Elizabeth Drew, *On the Edge: The Clinton Presidency* (New York: Simon & Schuster, 1994), p. 24.
3. Sally Quinn, "Beware of Washington," *Newsweek,* December 28, 1992, p. 26.
4. Lani Guinier's book is excerpted in the *New York Times,* as "Who's Afraid of Lani Guinier," February 27, 1994, Section 6, p. 41.
5. Kathleen Parker, "UN Treaty Is a Threat to Parents," *Arizona Republic,* June 14, 1995, p. B5.

Chapter 12

1. For a general discussion of Hillary Rodham Clinton's involvement in the health reform effort see Connie Bruck, "Hillary the Pol," *The New Yorker,* May 30, 1994, p. 58; Adam Clymer, Robert Pear and Robin Toner, "What Went Wrong," *Sacramento Bee,* September 4, 1994, p. F-1; James Fallows, "A triumph of misinformation: misinformation concerning Pres. Clinton's health care reform proposal," *Atlantic Monthly,* January 1995, p. 26; Haynes Johnson and David S. Broder, *The System: The American Way of Politics Stretched to the Breaking Point* (Boston: Little, Brown and Company, 1996); Frank Marafiote, "In Sickness & in Health—Hillary Takes Charge," *Hillary Clinton Quarterly,* Spring 1993, pp. 5, 22; Helen Thomas, "Hillary Role Still Evolving," UPI, January 22, 1993; "Well-Healed: Inside Lobby-

ing for Health Care Reform," A Report by the Center for Public Integrity, Washington, DC, 1994. Interviews for this chapter were conducted by researcher Sheryl Henderson and the author.

2. For more on the specifics of the Clinton health care plan see "An Analysis of the Administration's Health Proposal," a CBO Study, Congressional Budget Office, February 1994; Thomas Bodenheimer, "The major players start dealing: the health reform game," *Nation*, March 22, 1993, p. 374; "Fighting to hold it together," *Economist*, March 20, 1993, p. 28; Robert E. Moffit, "A Guide to the Clinton Health Plan," *Heritage Talking Points*, The Heritage Foundation, November 19, 1993; Judith Randal, "Wrong prescription: why managed competition is no cure," *Progressive*, May 1993, Vol. 57, No. 5, p. 22; Anita J. Slomski, "How the Clinton plan would judge your performance," *Medical Economics*, January 24, 1994, p. 83; Robin Toner, " 'Alliance' to Buy Health Care: Bureaucrat or Public Servant?" *New York Times*, December 5, 1993, Section A, p. 1.

3. For more information on Ira Magaziner, see Jonathan Rauch, "The Idea Merchant," *National Journal*, December 12, 1992, p. 2833; Jacob Weisberg, "Dies Ira: A short history of Mr. Magaziner," *New Republic*, January 24, 1994, p. 18; Lee Bowman, "Ira Magaziner: The man behind the plan," *Dallas Morning News*, October 10, 1993, p. 14A; Steven Pearlstein, "The Many Crusades of Ira Magaziner," *Washington Post Magazine*, April 18, 1993, p. W12; Nick Ravo, "Can This Man Save Wang? America? Himself?" *Boston Business*, Vol. 5, No. 1, February 1990, p. 37; Jolie Solomon, "For Magaziner, Reform Is the Road to Paradise," *Newsweek*, September 20, 1993, p. 38.

4. Vicente Navarro's views are set forth in Sheila Collins, "Racism and class: a response to Vincente [sic] Navarro," *Monthly Review*, June 1987, Vol. 39, p. 28; David Himmelstein, Stephie Woolhandler and Vincente [sic] Navarro, "National Health Service," *Economist*, July 27, 1985, p. 6; Vicente Navarro, "Has Socialism Failed? An Analysis of Health Indicators Under Socialism," *International Journal of Health Services*, Vol. 22, No. 4, 1992; Vicente Navarro, "Swaying the health care task force: popular mobilization counts," *Nation*, September 6, 1993; Vicente Navarro, "Why Congress Did Not Enact Health Care Reform," *Journal of Health Politics, Policy and Law*, Vol. 20, No. 2 (Summer 1995), pp. 455–461; John Nichols, "Heretic in the Temples of Power," *Capital Times*, December 5, 1994, p. 1C; Walter Zelman, March 1, 1993, memo to Ira Magaziner regarding Vicente Navarro, from the Health Care Interdepartmental Working Group papers at the National Archives, Box 3305.

5. For more on Luanne Nyberg see Brigid McMenamin, "In bed with the devil," *Forbes*, September 12, 1994, p. 200; Aurelio Rojas, "Kids Come First in Minnesota Civic, Corporate Groups' Support Network," *San Francisco Chronicle*, January 5, 1995, p. A1.

6. For more on the health care task force's operations see Mary Hancock Hinds, "Is Hillary Clinton Running a Shadow White House?" *Hillary Clinton Quarterly*, Spring 1993, p. 3; John Solomon, "Health care task force enriched big-money consultants," AP in *Washington Times*, February 21, 1995; AP, "White House Disputes Republicans on Mrs. Clinton's Meetings," February 8, 1993; Byron York, "The Health-Care Paper Trail," *American Spectator*, March 1995, pp. 20–24; Clinton White House: Health Care Interdepartmental Working Group Memo from Walter Zelman to Bob Boorstin regarding "The Marketing of 'Managed Competition,' " March 10, 1993, National Archives Box 3279.

7. Information on the Robert Wood Johnson Foundation and other foundations and their involvement in the Clinton health care reform effort can be found in George Anders, "Foundation Is Accused of Playing Politics With Grants," *Wall Street Journal*, April 26, 1994, p. B1; Kristin A. Goss, "Republican Congressional Leaders Attack Johnson Fund as 'Partisan,' " *Chronicle of Philanthropy*, April 20, 1993, p. 16; John Merline, "Nonprofits Push Health Reform," *Investor's Business Daily*, August 24, 1994, p. 1; Kathleen Teltsch, "Foundations Are Finding Wealth Is a Problem, Too," *New York Times*, May 2, 1994, p. B1; "Well-Healed: Inside Lobbying for Health Care Reform," a Report by the Center for Public Integrity, Washington, DC, 1994.

8. Ethical and legal issues relating to the White House Health Care Task Force are addressed in Gregory S. Walden, *On Best Behavior: The Clinton Administration and Ethics in Government* (Indianapolis: Hudson Institute, 1996).

9. For further analysis of the ValuePartners issue, see Fred R. Bleakley, "Investment Fund for Hillary Clinton Sold Short Several Health-Care Stocks," *Wall Street Journal*, May 21, 1993, p. A14; Dan Dorfman, "Short-seller boosted first lady's portfolio," *USA Today*, June 18, 1993, p. 4B; Susan B. Garland, Dean Foust, Mark Lewyn, Greg Burns, and Wendy Zellner, "Hillary Clinton, Go-Go Getter," *Business Week*, April 18, 1994, p. 42; James K. Glassman, "The Clintons as Investors: Selling America Short?" *Washington Post*, March 18, 1994, p. G1; Frank Lalli, "How Blind Is Your Trust?" *Money*, July 1993, p. 5; Kevin McCoy and John Riley, " 'Not a Yuppie': A look at the Clintons' income through the years," *Newsday*, April 3, 1994, p. 4; S. Craig Pirrong, "Political Rhetoric and Stock Price Volatility: A Case Study" (Chicago: The Catalyst Institute, November 1993); Tony Snow, "First Lady's Investment Raises Question of Conflict," *Arizona Republic*, November 24, 1993, p. B9; and Walden, *On Best Behavior*.

Chapter 13

1. For details of the Whitewater investigation, see the Senate's Final Report of the Special Committee to Investigate Whitewater Development Cor-

poration and Related Matters, Report 104–280, 104th Congress, 2d sess., 1996. Much of the material on the travel office was first reported by this author in "The Travelgate Cover-Up," *American Spectator,* June 1994, p. 30. For more on the travel office firings, see Byron York, "The Hidden Tale of Travelgate," *Weekly Standard,* January 22, 1996, p. 18; Byron York, "Travelgate Survivors," *American Spectator,* November 1995, p. 22; Peter Boyer, "A Fever in the White House," *New Yorker,* April 15, 1996. A chronology of events prepared by the staff of the House Government Reform and Oversight Committee was also consulted.

2. Michael Kelly, "Saint Hillary," *New York Times Magazine,* May 23, 1993, sec. 6, p. 22.

3. For further information on Foster's suicide and surrounding events in the White House, see Ann Devroy and Susan Schmidt, "The Mystery in Foster's Office: Following Suicide, What Drove Associates' Actions?" *Washington Post,* December 20, 1995, p. A1; Robert B. Fiske, Jr., "Report of the Independent Counsel In Re Vincent W. Foster, Jr.," Washington DC, June 30, 1994; James B. Stewart, *Blood Sport: The President and His Adversaries* (New York: Simon & Schuster, 1996).

ACKNOWLEDGMENTS

The hard work and dedication of the researchers who worked with me on this book made it possible to meet a very demanding deadline. Sheryl Henderson, Matt Labash, John Meroney, and George Neumayr conducted interviews and did original research. Andrew Goldstein was my summer intern in 1995. Barbara Driscoll assisted in all aspects of the preparation of the manuscript, which required not only skill but patience. Tracy Robinson contributed invaluable research and fact-checking; she pulled me over the finish line.

My friends at the *American Spectator* showed extraordinary support and generosity in allowing me to take the time to research and write this book. Special thanks to Bob Tyrrell and Wlady Plesczynski, who published my previous writings on the Clintons.

The many people who were of assistance in reporting this book must remain unacknowledged: You know who you are.

As always, my agents Glen Hartley and Lynn Chu have been enthusiastic about the project from the beginning, and Lynn made several substantive contributions to the manuscript.

At Simon & Schuster and the Free Press, I owe thanks especially to Jennifer Weidman; and to Michael Jacobs, Suzanne Donahue, Theresa Horner, Ryon Fleming, Carol Mayhew, John Ekizian, and David Bernstein. Kathy Silberger did some wonderful line editing, and Kerrie Johnson helped with fact-checking. Special thanks are due Chad Conway.

My editor, Adam Bellow, who also edited *The Real Anita Hill*, continues to be a valued collaborator in going against the grain of received opinion.

The support of my parents, Raymond and Dorothea, is a constant, as is the friendship and guidance of Michael and Arianna Huffington and Ricky Silberman. Laura Ingraham's humor brightened my days. Morgan Washburn motivated me to meet my deadline.

My friends Rebecca Borders and Mark Paoletta read and commented on the entire manuscript and were a steadfast source of advice and encouragement. Becky accompanied me on several adventures to Little Rock and Fayetteville, and she also came up with the book's terrific title. Mark's editorial contributions helped make this a better book. Of course, any errors (and all opinions) contained herein are my own.

Ronald Haft is the best friend anyone could wish for. As for William Grey, I owe him much more than the dedication of this book.

INDEX